Globalisation in China, India and Russia

Published by Academic Foundation
in association with

Centre de Sciences
Humaines, New Delhi

Universite Paris III,
Sorbonne Nouvelle

Globalisation in China, India and Russia

Emergence of National Groups and Global Strategies of Firms

Editors:

Jean-François Huchet
Xavier Richet
Joël Ruet

ACADEMIC FOUNDATION
NEW DELHI

Centre de Sciences Humaines (Centre for Social Sciences and Humanities): Created in 1990, the CSH is part of the network of research centres of the French Ministry of Foreign Affairs. The Centre's research work is primarily oriented towards the study of issues concerning the contemporary dynamics of development in India and South Asia. The activities of the Centre are focused on four main areas, namely: Economic transition and sustainable development; Political dynamics and social transformations; Regional dynamics in South Asia and international relations; and Urban dynamics.

Centre de Sciences Humaines, 2 Aurangzeb Road, New Delhi 110 011, India. Tel : (91) 11 30410070; Fax: (91) 3041 0079. Email: infos@csh-delhi.com Website://www.csh-delhi.com

The Jean Monnet Chair at University Sorbonne Nouvelle aims at carrying out research on European Union enlargement and integration, on EU international economic relations, on post-socialist transformation and on new emerging market economies.

Jean Monnet Chair, Professor Xavier Richet, University Sorbonne Nouvelle, 13 rue de Santeuil, 75005 Paris, France. Tel/Fax: +33143293827. Email: xavier.Richet@univ-paris3.fr

First published in 2007 by

Academic Foundation
4772-73 / 23 Bharat Ram Road, (23 Ansari Road), Darya Ganj, New Delhi - 110 002 (India).
Tel: +91-11-23245001 / 02 / 03 / 04. Fax: +91-11-23245005. E-mail: academic@vsnl.com
www: academicfoundation.com

Published in association with:

Centre de Sciences Humaines (CSH), New Delhi and Universite Paris III, Sorbonne Nouvelle.

Cataloging in Publication Data--DK
Courtesy: D.K. Agencies (P) Ltd. <docinfo@dkagencies.com>

Globalisation in China, India and Russia : emergence of national groups and global strategies of firms / editors, Jean-François Huchet, Xavier Richet, Joël Ruet.
p. cm.
Contributed articles.
Includes bibliographical references.
Includes index.
ISBN-13: 9788171885824
ISBN-10: 8171885829

1. Globalization--Economic aspects--China. 2. Globalization--Economic aspects--India. 3. Globalization--Economic aspects--Russia (Federation). 4. China--Commercial policy. 5. India--Commercial policy. 6. Russia (Federation)--Commercial policy. 7. Business planning--China. 8. Business planning--India. 9. Business planning--Russia (Federation). I. Huchet, Jean-François. II. Richet, Xavier. III. Ruet, Joël.

DDC 381.3 22

Designed and typeset by Italics India, New Delhi.
Printed and bound in India.

Contents

Part II

Markets and Competitivity

Part III

Restructuring and Strategies of Firms

List of Tables, Figures, Boxes and Appendices

TABLES

FIGURES

BOXES

APPENDICES

Editors/Contributors

Editors:

Jean-François Huchet is Associate Professor, University of Rennes II. He has been the Head Economist of the Centre for Study of Contemporary China (CEFC), Honk Kong. He teaches at EHESS (Ecole des Hautes Etudes en Sciences Sociales, Paris). He is a specialist of industry transformation and technological catching-up in China.

Xavier Richet is Professor, University Sorbonne Nouvelle, Paris. He is a specialist of former socialist Eastern European countries, of post-socialist transition and Russian economy. In the framework of RECEP (Russian-European Center for Economic Policy), a joint EU-Russian think-tank, he has worked as an adviser to the Russian ministry of foreign trade on the economic transformation of Russia (2000-2002). His research includes technological change in several industries

Joël Ruet, an alumni from Ecole des Mines, Paris, is Fellow at the London School of Economics. He has been Head Economist and Director of Centre de Sciences Humaines in New Delhi. He taught at Jawaharlal Nehru University and currently teaches at HEC (Hautes Etudes Commerciales, France). He works on infrastructure and State-industry relation.

Contributors:

Manmohan Agarwal .... *Professor and Dean, Jawaharlal Nehru University, Delhi, has worked at the World Bank and the IMF. He is a member, Global Public Policies and Programs Team, World Bank.*

Rigas Arvanitis .... *Researcher, Institut de Recherche pour le Développement and Franco-Chinese Centre of Sociology of Industry and Technologies, Zhongshan University, Guangzhou.*

Alokesh Barua .... *Professor, Jawaharlal Nehru University, Delhi. He has been a Commonwealth*

scholar in Warwick University, and a Fulbright scholar in University of Michigan.

Eric Brunat .... *former Scientific Director at RECEP, Moscow, former Country Head, UNDP, Moscow, Minsk, Chisinau, is directing a EU-funded project in Kaliningrad and is Associate Professor at the University of Savoie.*

Prabal Roy Chowdhury .... *Professor, Indian Statistical Institute, Delhi.*

Andrei Klepach .... *Head of Macroeconomic Forecasting at the Russian Ministry of Economy and Trade, formerly Director of the Research Department in the Central Bank of Russia. He is Senior Fellow, Institute of Economic Forecasting, Russian Academy of Sciences.*

Sugata Marjit .... *Reserve Bank of India Professor of Industrial Economics, Centre for Studies in the Social Sciences, Calcutta.*

Pierre Miège .... *Researcher at EHESS, Paris and Zhongshan University, Guangzhou.*

Ajitava Raychaudhuri .... *Professor, and Head, Department of Economics, Jadavpur University, Calcutta.*

Gulshan Sachdeva .... *Professor, Jawaharlal Nehru University, Delhi and member, editorial board, International Studies (Sage).*

Hua Wang .... *Researcher and teaches at EUROMED-Ecole de Management, Marseille.*

Zhao Wei .... *Researcher, Zhongshan University, Guangzhou.*

Acknowledgements

This book has emerged out of a discussion, back in October 2001, between Jean-François Huchet, Xavier Richet and Joël Ruet, on the specifics of industrial and public policies transformations in China, India, Russia, with the understanding that each country, having developed a different 'socialism' would for this reason develop variations around a common 'post-socialist'—or at least post socialist-inspired or post command economy as far as India goes. These variations, it was felt, were to depend equally on pre-existing sectors inherited from former models, as on activation of new comparative advantages, as on trajectories that would be much more state-specific, or, rather, would be better understood under a certain specificity of state-industry relationships.

A-two-day seminar on this issue was co-organised by Centre de Sciences Humaines (CSH) and India International Centre (IIC) that took place on 19-20 December 2002, at IIC, New Delhi. The papers presented there have served as the core of this present book.

Besides the contributors, the editors wish to warmly thank the support and participation of His Excellency the Ambassador of France to India, Dominique Girad, also a Sinologist of repute, who inaugurated the seminar as his first very 'public act' after his posting to India, N. Vohra, then Director IIC, Premola Ghosh, Deputy Director IIC and Dr. Frederic Grare, then Director of CSH, restless promoter of debate, who supported this scientific endeavour along with many others.

We are thankful for their presentations, participation and useful comments to Sanjiv Ahluwalia, Joint Secretary, Ministry of Disinvestment; Claude Albagil, University Paris 12; Dr. B.B. Bhattacharya, Vice-Chancellor JNU, then Director, Institute of Economic Growth; Suman K. Bery, Director, National Council of Applied Economic Research; Dr. Horst Brezinski, Technical University of Frieberg/Saxoine, Germany;

Dr. Basudeb Chaudhari, GEMMA, University of Caen and CPNSS, London School of Economics; Dr. Subashis Gangopadhyay, Director, India Development Foundation; Prof. Amitabh Kundu, Director, Centre for the Study of Regional Dev., School of Social Sciences, JNU; Prof. Ajeet Mathur, University of Tampere, Finland and ICRIER New Delhi; Prof, Suresh Tendulkar, Delhi School of Economics, University of Delhi.

The editors also wish to thank Evelyne Thivet-Rispal for her commitment to the perfect organisation and management of this project, as well as Attreyee Roychowdhury, Rituraj, and Sanu Kapila for the prompt and efficient publishing of this book.

Foreword

"Where Do they Come from?" and "Nobody's Perfect"
The State and the Market

PIERRE-NOËL GIRAUD[1]

There are two topics that shape and keep surfacing in this book. The first is economic reforms and, in particular, privatisation in former socialist countries, namely Russia and China, as well as in countries which had and still have a large 'public sector' like India. The second topic is the globalisation of firms.

As far as economic reforms are concerned, privatisation is a central question in these countries. If one wants to privatise something, one should first look carefuly at the very nature of what one wants to privatise. Let us start with definitions. To be useful they must be simple and even simplistic. Let us define the three types of organisations: Administrations, Public firms and Private firms.

An administration always has multidimensional objectives. All its objectives cannot be measured by money. Therefore, cost calculations are not made in administrations. Or if they are made, they are not at all pivotal in decision making procedures. Political interferences in administration are not only inevitable, they are necessary, for only politics can balance the multidimensional objectives and choose the changing priorities among them.

In contrast, a firm has a single or at least a dominant and permanent objective, which can always be measured in quantitative terms. The objective of a private firm is profit maximisation or maximisation of the value of the firms for shareholders. All the

---

1. Pierre-Noël Giraud is Professor at Ecole des Mines and University Paris-Dauphine, and member of the French Academy of techiques.

objectives, like satisfying the interest of the other stakeholders, are secondary. They are met only if the management is obliged by the law to comply with, or if they are seen as actually supporting in the longer term the main objective of the firm. It is the case with the objective of being 'environmentally friendly'. It is either compulsory or a strategy to minimise risks which could harm profits, at least in the long term.

A public firm can be assigned a different objective by its shareholder, the State. But we can speak of a public firm, and not of an administration, if and only if this objective is unique, relatively stable along time and can be expressed by quantities. For example, you must provide 95 per cent of the population with electricty within 10 years, at a price affordable by the poorest households. Therefore, not only is cost calculation possible in a public firm, but it is a tool for the management; this is what makes it distinct from an administration.

Let us take the example of EDF, the French power company, which has been and still is a public firm. During the 50s and the 60s, its objective was to provide electricity to all households and to sell it at the same price across the country. During the 70s, after the first oil shock and during the 80s, its objective was energy independency through the building of efficient and safe nuclear power plants, which now account for about 80 per cent of the power produced. During the 90s the objective was cost reduction. It materialised into a contract between the State and the public firm which specified what productivity gains had to be achieved year after year. Finally, and only recently, it has been decided to privatise EDF.

When former socialist countries, like Russia and Eastern European countries or China, embarked upon economic reforms, I went there to do research on the privatisation process. It soon appeared clear to me and to some (a minority) of my colleagues[2] that the productive units in socialism were not at all public firms. These institutions: the so called 'combinates' in Russia and Europe or the so called 'Danweis' in China, had multidimensional objectives: production, indeed, but also social welfare and political control of the population.

2. See Hirschhausen, 1995.

Interestingly, the workers were not 'employees', they were 'members'. Therefore, they were administration, mere 'pieces of the State'.

It should be unquestionable that it makes no sense to 'privatise' pieces of the State. Who would buy a 'piece of State'? An intermediary step was necessary. This step was to transform first these administrations into firms, into public firms. We call this necessary step 'entreprisation'. Same conclusions came up with the study on the reform of the power sector in India. It was found that State Electricity Boards and also Water Boards were not at all public enterprises, even after 'corporatisation'. Actually, they still were administrations. They needed to be 'enterprised' before privatisation.[3] Private sector can help, but rather through management contracts than through quick and complete privatisation. These are a few examples, but each mode of enterprisation is specific: dismantling of Combinates in East Germany, Township and Village Enterprises in China—a model yet to stabilise in India.

In other words, as far as economic reforms of post-socialist (China, Russia) or post-command economies (India) are concerned, for privatisation to be used as a tool, the first step is to know what it is that the reformers are trying to privatise. If it is administration, whatever the name or the official designation, one should not insist, but rather find first the way of an 'entreprisation' process first.

Let us now deal with the respective roles of the States and markets, in particular in developing countries. There has been an impressive shift in the dominant doctrines during the last decades. During the 80s and the early 90s the dominant doctrine was the so-called 'Washington consensus'. In three words: liberalise markets, privatise almost everything, reduce the State to its minimal regalian functions. Now, 10 years later, take a look at the 2003 *World Development Report* of the World Bank. What do you read? That substainable development is driven by and made of the balanced accumulation of four types of capital: physical, human, social, and environmental. Any development of the physical capital only, at the expense of the three others ends up with the collapse of the physical capital stock itself.

3. Ruet, 2005.

And guess who is responsible for the accumulation of these four types of capital? Private initiatives and market coordination certainly do very well with the physical capital. But as far as the three others are concerned, the role of the State is paramount.

I have never read, for a long time, such an enthusiastic apology of the State. And it is the new World Bank doctrine ... free market fundamentalism now appears to be a dinosaur.

This evolution in policy issues has been strongly backed by a similar evolution in economic theory. Twenty years ago, the role of the State was seen as correcting market failures. But mainstream economists were convinced that there were actually very few true market failures: natural monopolies, a few public goods, and some environmental externalities. For the rest, free market mechanisms were seen as being by far the best way of coordinating economic activities. But then, economic theory discovered and quickly emphasised the role of incomplete and asymmetric information. Incomplete and asymmetric information generates systematic market failures. In other words, externalities are much more widespread than initially thought. There is hardly any economic activity that does not generate positive or negative externalities. Therefore, the role of the State, and more generally the role of institutions, be they public or private, made a spectacular come back.

To be honest, one must recognise that in parallel, the theory of the State has experienced a similar upturn. For a neo-classical economist, 20 years ago, the markets were almost perfect, but the State was seen as 'benevolent'. While private firms were maximising their profits, coordinated by the invisible hand of market mechanisms, the State was supposed to maximise the social welfare by correcting a few market failures. But economic theory then discovered and quickly emphasised the fact that real States, even democratic ones, may be not at all benevolent. Thus, began the reign of the so-called 'new political economy'. Using extensively cooperative and non-cooperative game theories, it models political process where politicians want nothing but to be elected or re-elected and administrators nothing but keeping or improving their position.

In conclusion, neither the markets nor the States are nowadays seen as perfect, and this book deals at many places much more with their subtle interactions or coordination, than opposition. For economists have finally been forced to recognise (like the tycoon at the end of the film: *Some Like it Hot*) that 'nobody's perfect'. Indeed, it makes it more difficult to tailor sound advices on economic policy issues, and we, economists, should be extremely modest. But it makes our discipline also much more interesting.

References

Hirschhausen (von), Christian (1995). "From Privatization to Capitalisation: Industrial Restructuring in Post-socialist Central and Eastern Europe", in E. Dittrich, G. Schmidt and R. Whitley (eds.), *Industrial Transformation in Europe: Process and Context,* London: Sage Publications.

Ruet, Joël (2005). *Privatising Power Cuts? Ownership and Organisational Reform of State Electricity Boards in India,* Academic Foundation, New Delhi, p.339.

1

Emergence of National Groups and Global Strategies of Firms

Globalisation in China, India and Russia

JEAN-FRANÇOIS HUCHET, XAVIER RICHET
and JOËL RUET

This book focuses on globalisation and aims at being not yet another book on globalisation, but at really focusing on the globalisation of firms, especially in the three major countries that have experienced post-socialist transformation, namely China, India and Russia. Before we analyse our findings and explain them in terms of the globalising strategies adopted by their firms, let us first examine why these countries made this choice. The reasons, we shall see, are not purely geographical but are deeply rooted in the diverse post-socialist transformation they have witnessed.

No study of globalisation is possible, nor is it thinkable, without referring to China, India, and Russia, that is to say, without an analysis of their firms and including them in the global network of firms. The three countries under study had socialist economies and are now going through a process of transition towards a market economy with various degrees of success and, more importantly, using different methods as far as the relationship between the state and the firms is concerned. Also, to a large extent, researchers in economics have, until now, viewed these countries in a somewhat unbalanced manner and they have seldom been the object of a comparative study from the perspective of the globalisation of their firms.

What does globalisation mean, or what should it mean, for these companies? To be clear, globalisation should not mean just exports but a global strategy on tie-ups, partnerships and outsourcing their main activities: finance, development, production and marketing. However, in all three countries, you observe difficulties and delays in various sectors, in the emergence of national groups capable of catching up with global competition. Studying this phenomenon involves studying at depth: (i) the catching-up at the national level in the field of technology and the market adjustments that globalisation simultaneously allows and requires, (ii) the ways and means available under state regulation, and (iii) how these firms develop truly international integrated strategies.

The first problem is catching up in the field of technology. National groups wanting to emerge from former planned, command or import-substitution systems must first catch up technologically and emancipate through R&D as well as by entering into technological and commercial agreements and partnerships. The important question is whether they opt for sub-contracting, producing for niche markets or directly target global competition.

In China, for example, efforts to catch up technologically were based on two different strategies that formed a part of its initial policy adopted in 1978. Firstly, all hardware purchases in state-owned enterprises (SOEs) and greenfield projects were facilitated through the development of Sino-foreign joint ventures. The first strategy encountered many bottlenecks due to lack of know-how and management expertise, fuzzy property rights, duplication of investments and inefficient corporate governance. Despite some success stories in industries like consumer electronics, the technological spin-off is essentially linked with the rapid take-off of foreign direct investment in the early 90s in the coastal region. Although, this strategy has enabled China to modernise its production capabilities, it also raises serious questions about how national firms can evolve progressively from their current position at the bottom of the sub-contracting pyramid and their dependence on foreign capital and technology without developing a national system of innovation. As for the emergence of capitalist firms, most of the planned economy apparatus has been dismantled since 1978. Bottom-up reforms have contributed to the emergence of millions of small and medium-sized companies in the collective and the private sectors, creating new competitive pressure in nearly all industrial sectors. Even after these changes, bureaucratic interference is endemic in core industrial activities and corporate governance efficiency is still very poor. Despite the privatisation process, which started in the mid-90s, national groups remain off-limits for foreign companies.

India, on the other hand, has had very few joint ventures of this type so far, most of them being joint ventures that target the emerging local Indian markets (like cars or telephone commutators/switches) with surprisingly few products for the export market. The information technology sector is the most notable exception where, from a strategy of body-shopping and outsourcing, the sector is progressively 'climbing up the value chain' and heading towards a world-integrated development of products and services. It is not clear whether the other exception, namely textiles, can fit into that framework. Indeed, it is still largely based on regular trade and hardly on the co-development of products by transnational firms or by Indian firms under transnational agreements. Indian capitalism has emerged from the State's shadow and the pursuit of patronage links. Its enterprises have diversified to a relatively large extent as compared to world trade. Today, despite the emergence of new facilities, allowances and licences, contacts within the government remain one key to success by speeding up administrative processes and rapid clearance of files under what remains of the 'licence *raj*'. Also, in their effort to seize new opportunities, Indian groups have become even more diversified and sometimes potentially vulnerable to foreign corporate raids and restructuring.

As far as Russia is concerned, in the first place, just venturing into the country is a hot issue today, largely due to problems of property rights and country risk. In Russia, capitalism has emerged from above through mass privatisation (in fact self-privatisation by insiders or 'red barons') with no transparency. The recent introduction of corporate governance measures has shown who are the owners (generally a handful of powerful shareholders). Most of the shares distributed to workers were bought by the management and what remained of the state-holding was bought by managers and bankers. Most firms have not yet been restructured and those that have been restructured have done so with great difficulty. Many firms are trying to rebuild former links of vertical dependency (tolling), thus keeping away from competition. Most industries are considered 'strategic' and the government is eager to maintain the control of Russian firms in these industries. On the other hand, the compromise amongst insiders (managers and workers) after privatisation (with productive assets going to managers and social assets to workers) has made it difficult for foreign companies to increase their stakes in such enterprises.

Finally, industrial cooperation in some segments of production (components, intermediary inputs) is favoured.

Secondly, what are the different types of state regulations and support prevalent in these three countries for the globalisation of firms? Various studies show that the state plays a supportive role at the take-off stage of national industries and services and also during their globalisation. This is done not necessarily through simple protectionist measures but also through the clarification of regulations, transfer of research material, targeted infrastructure facilitation and so on. The question that arises, from the point of view of the state, is how to redefine its role and position in globalisation?

Despite an impressive GDP growth rate since 1978, Chinese industrial groups are far from competitive in the world market. The biggest companies are still publicly owned and operate in protected sectors (petrochemical, tobacco, automobile, electricity, steel, etc.). Some sectors that were deregulated in the late 80s have witnessed the emergence of some competitive companies, but only in the national market. In this context, and as opposed to industrial development strategies in Japan or in Korea that protected national producers, China's recent adhesion to WTO will raise the competition pressure on national producers. The repercussions of the opening of the domestic market on the strategy of national industrial groups, and also on how central policy makers will formulate the technology and industrial policy, are still not clear. Economic nationalism, the desire to create big industrial groups through administrative measures, lack of sufficient funding and R&D capabilities, inefficiencies in the corporate governance system will present a serious challenge to Chinese corporate groups in their ability to cope with the opening of the internal market.

In India, it is interesting to note that the sectors and firms which were the first to globalise are those that target the Indian diaspora abroad or involve its members in their management. The information technology sector is a perfect example in this respect with new firms being set up by Indian 'transnationals' right from day one with offices in different parts of the world. In such cases, the Government's role (as seen by the Government itself and as desired by firms) seems to be confined to a simple withdrawal from regulation and licensing. Rarely does it reach the level of actual support through facilitating agencies. But there are two limitations: in practical terms, the IT sector is no less dynamic outside 'high tech cities' than inside them. Secondly, in some other sectors where the State does not disengage itself from direct regulation, as in the power sector, facilitating agencies and measures are unable to bring about any increase in partnerships.

As far as Russia is concerned, one of the shortcomings of its economy is that its main companies are not competitive in the world market (nor do they currently invest or restructure in order to be so). They simply try to maintain their supremacy in the domestic market through a variety of measures. This problem, together with the discussion on how and when to join the WTO, will soon become a crucial issue. The main problem for Russian firms, however, is upgrading their product range and adopting an integrated strategic approach to world markets. Most Russian products cannot compete in foreign markets as innovation is lacking in many sectors. Only oil and gas companies are internationalised.

Finally, how can corporate governance be brought into the public sector? The emergence of a globalised private sector will necessarily oblige governments and public administrations to question their role and scope as well as their methods of making and implementing decisions. The book will focus on firms and firm-related strategies, but it will also enlarge the scope of the debate on how compulsions imposed by the private sector could prove to be an impetus for redefining the State's role.

Since the mid-90s, according to some foreign analysts, the non-performing assets of China's biggest commercial banks have grown at an alarming rate representing between 40 to 50 per cent of China's GDP. This phenomenon is the direct result of serious inefficiencies in the corporate governance system of SOEs. Policy makers have paid a great deal of attention to this problem and China has been trying to improve the situation through various important reforms (privatisation, external control mechanism through the banking system and stock exchange). Despite these reforms, internal and external control mechanisms are still incapable of curbing rent-seeking activities, corruption and poor investment planning. Here again, China's accession to WTO is supposed to speed up the reform in this area by exposing national firms to more competition.

In India, some industries that were included in the public sector for historical or maturity reasons, are now globalising. Not only power, water and environment management but also public works, equipment manufacture and mining remain in the public sector despite reforms aimed at changing their deeply embedded administrative-style management.

In Russia, corporate governance is a secondary issue even though the Russian government is trying to bring in more transparency and regulate the behaviour of firms in the public sector. It must be clarified that by public sector we mean firms operating in the utilities sector. Most productive enterprises, that were once state property, have now been privatised although the State continues to hold a strategic stake in some of these enterprises.

These three issues, namely catching up with globalisation, public governance and private globalisation strategies, need not be addressed separately, but should really be considered together as a kind of spinal cord for the study of globalisation in these three countries today. With these questions as the focal point of our analysis, we will discuss the context of public reforms and explain what globalisation implies in a post-socialist structure (Part I of this book). We will then focus on markets and competitiveness and look at reforms in relation to extra-territorial firms and FDI (Part II). Finally, in the last part (Part III), we will analyse the restructuring of firms and their strategies from the perspective of globalisation through the creation of networks of firms and internalisation of processes in MNCs.

In Part I of the book entitled, "The Private Sector in the Context of Public Reforms: Globalisation in a Post-Socialist Structure", we present the structural inertia to which enterprises are subjected in a post-socialist or post-command economy. In order not to repeat data, and to get a direct comparative picture right from here, Table 1.1 provides figures on 'China, India, Russia at a glance'.

These figures recall that, among these three countries, pairs can be formed in a moving configuration, depending on the criteria observed. China and India obviously are the two massive, predominantly rural (though not necessarily agricultural) countries, where economic mechanisms for catching-up should be massive, at the risk of being otherwise unnoticeable. In that respect, the low level of domestic

Table 1.1

China, India and Russia at a Glance

	China	*India*	*Russia*
GDP % Annual Growth 80s	10.3	5.7	NA
GDP % Annual Growth 90s	9.7	5.8	-2.7
GDP % Annual Growth 1995-2005	8.3 (1994-2004)	6	4.4
Total Population 2005 (millions) (2002)	1,308 (1,280)	1,087 (1,049)	143.8 (144)
Rural Population 2005 (%)	60	71	26.9
GNI Per Capita USD 2005 (2002)	1280 (940)	720 (540)	4,460 (2,140)
PPP GDP 2005 (2002)	5,896 (4,580)	3,139 (2,670)	11,407 (8,230)
Domestic Credit to Private Sector as % GDP 1990	87.7	25.2	NA
Domestic Credit to Private Sector as % GDP 2002	136.5	32.6	17.6
FDI as % GDP 2002	3.9	0.6	0.9
Merchandise Trade as % GDP[1] 2005 (2002)	85.3 (49.0)	29.4 (13.3)[2]	57.5 (48.3)
Merchandise Trade as % Good GDP[3] 2002	73.8	NA	105.1
Poverty Rate, National Criteria 2005 (2002)	2.0 (6.0)	29.0 (36.0)	NA (30.9)
Population below 1 $ a day 2005	16.6	34.7	2.0 (6.1)
Population below 2 $ a day 2005	46.7	79.9	12.1 (23.8)
Gini Index 2005	44.7	32.5	39.9 (45.6)
Rank in Human Development Index 2005 (2002)	81 (94)	126 (127)	65 (57)
Gender Development Index 2005	0.765	0.591	0.795
Internet Users (per 1,000) 2005 (2002)	73.0 (46.0)	32.0 (15.9)	111 (40.9)
Life Expectancy at Birth 2005	71.9	63.1	65.4

Note: Figures in brackets are for 2002.

1. The sum of merchandise imports and exports, divided by GDP.
2. Calculated by us.
3. The sum of merchandise imports and exports, divided by GDP after substracting value added in services.

Sources: *World Development Report 2006*, *Human Development Report 2006*, *World Bank*, *International Trade Statistics 2003 & 2006* (WTO).

investment in India, the relative absence of an integrated national market (if one goes by high figures on poverty) are explanatory factors for lower growth and catching-up as of today. The importance of the rural population also shows, beyond the much advertised FDI (always localised), the need to find ways of development in the rural areas, the rightly analysed township and village enterprises of China, which India is comparatively lacking for stabilising and sustaining its economic take-off. As well, looking at domestic credit to private sector in a diachronic manner this time, one can really see that China had anyway started off much ahead of India its reforms, managing today in catching-up on average human development indexes with Russia, an otherwise long-industrialised country (not underestimating, of course, the inequalitarian aspects that China and Russia present in comparison even to India). Again, looking at things diachronically, one however finds that structurally the growth rate in India progressively rises, despite the relative 'un-integration' of its economy (both nationally and internationally), finding its own ways to stabilise the growth. Also, having a nearly 'historical' look at growth rate and what they mean in terms of the transformation of the socialist or command economy productive apparatus, figures pave the bipolar ways of transforming a post-socialist economy: on the one hand is the Russian or Eastern European way, based on a very quick reconfiguration of industrial assets by facing an initial sharp drop in the production; this could be financed by Western Europe for Eastern Europe (the German case is a case in point) or by energy resources for Russia. The alternate model (China) is of progressive construction of an economy around the planned public sector, mostly untouched or at least very gradually reformed over a period which is more of a 20 to 30 years than a few years, unlike it happened in Eastern European 'shock therapies'. Aligning a productive apparatus, that had often been designed with a political aim, to economic assets, necessitates a considerable restructuring and associated cost. Whether it is financed in a 'shock' way using a treasury that is historical (the twin Europe), of an oil rent (Russia), or rather financed through surrounding growth, a small part of which is used to progressively restructure the core of the system (China). One can wonder if India, a country that was less into socialism, but which is also a real latecomer in this process of post-socialist transformation, has really chosen its mode of reform. Not that any of the two strategies would lack supporters and advocates, but rather that, for India, inertia in reforms might be the most numerous camp...while having its own resources for instance, in an IT sector and a diaspora that now substantially contributes to external stability of the country.

Entering into the details of the post-socialist transformation, in Chapter 2, "Between Bureaucracy and Market: Chinese Industrial Groups in Search of New Forms of Corporate Governance", Jean-François Huchet and Xavier Richet discuss the diversity of public companies (some of which were first converted into joint ventures and later into private companies). They point out the differences between large state-owned enterprises run by the Central Government, small and medium-sized businesses in the state, and collective sectors set up in urban areas and run by local governments. Though the latter are officially run by local governments, in practice these fast-developing enterprises are almost part of the private sector comprising small firms in rural zones registered as collective enterprises. The authors also take note of the emergence of private firms on the fringes of the centrally planned system, especially in trade and services. They show that these groups in the state and collective sectors are leaders in the competitive sectors today, while protected firms (but how long will they remain so?) constitute the major state sector groups controlled by the centre in non-competitive sectors. They conclude that private firms may well be tomorrow's winners.

In Chapter 3, "Economic Reforms, Privatisation and Public-Private Developments in India since 1991", Joël Ruet explains that the decade that has followed 1991 symbolises economic reforms in India. With two censuses held during the period with a gap of 10 years, it is now possible to make a critical assessment of reforms, not only on the economic front but also on the social front. Going beyond a predominantly rural India, he presents the new modes of regulating the Indian economy and analyses the emergence of India as a dynamic economic power *via* its cities and services. He points out that the earlier development model, based on so-called socialist type public expenditure under a technical paradigm that, in actual practice, was not people or human resource-oriented, had reached its limits. The beginnings of a change in the development paradigm are already visible, although, its consequences for the rural world remain a major question mark for the coming decade. After more than a decade of reforms, the reality of the public sector is still full of contradictions having forward and backward movements in reforms. But the interesting fact is that the private sector in India has begun to realise the deficiencies of the earlier model, though in a much more limited manner than in China. Ruet provides clues on how public-private partnerships are likely to evolve while explaining their redistributive aspects.

In Chapter 4, titled "Productivity and Competitiveness Challenges for the Russian Economy: Room for a more Proactive Policy?", Eric Brunat and Andrei Klepach study Russia through a macroeconomic lens and look at productivity and competitiveness (*inter alia* restructuring of the industry). They suggest that even if the real exchange rate of the rouble is lowered and low labour costs are maintained, restructuring will be a *sine qua non* for the sustainable recovery of the Russian economy. They indicate a relatively regular increase in the labour productivity index. Going to the sectoral level, they identify different types of enterprises. One group brings together leading industries or sub-industries such as international competitors (aerospace, nuclear, instrument manufacture, software...) or those protected from international competition, but are strong at the national level (automobiles, tractors and agricultural machinery, specialised shipbuilding...). Another group brings together industries that are competitive but without any innovation potential (extraction industries and food processing). A third group covers the infrastructure (public monopolies), while the fourth clubs all industries undergoing a crisis (coal, small industries and some sub-industries in the machinery sector). In the case of almost all these industries, Brunat and Klepach specify the limits of the new Russian capitalism and its inability to modernise these segments.

Part II of the book, "Markets and Competitiveness: Reforms Related to Extra-territorial Firms and FDI", deals with the impact of globalisation on market structures. Chapter 5, "Impact of Liberalisation of Trade and Investment on Chinese Industrial Firms", contains Jean-François Huchet's analyses of the present stage of extreme intra-sectoral fragmentation of the Chinese economy, the lack of consolidation and heterogeneity among Chinese firms. Huchet then outlines the policies promoted by the state for reducing capacities (through mergers and bankruptcies) as well as financial restructuring. He clearly concludes that restructuring has been much more effective in coastal China, further aggravating the regional divide.

In Chapter 6, "Firm and Industry Response to Liberalisation in India: Theory and Evidence", Manmohan Agarwal and Alokesh Barua point out that a substantial increase in the levels of intra-industry trade has been observed in India since the economy was opened in 1991. This has led to increasing returns in export industries and decreasing returns in the import of competing goods. They then explore whether openness breaks domestic monopoly and forces the market to behave competitively, thereby reducing market concentration. They use a Cournot oligopoly open economy model to examine the entry of foreign firms. They show that, according to these hypotheses, with the emergence of new national firms, each firm sells less in the domestic market and more in the export market. They also show that following the entry of foreign firms, the number of firms have increased since 1991 in the machine tools, gems and jewellery, steel, electrical goods, plastic, rubber, leather, pharmaceuticals and chemicals sectors and concentration ratios in both domestic and export markets have fallen over the years. They notice, however, that the immediate and rapid increase in the number of firms after liberalisation in 1991 has been reversed since 1995, after the adoption of WTO norms. They conclude that liberalisation has increased competition in industries in India.

In Chapter 7, "The Indian Power Sector in a Command Economy: Liberal Reforms or Indian-Style Development", Joël Ruet shows how, despite the information-based technological and managerial changes that have occurred all over the world in a network industry, such as the power sector, changes in the Indian power sector have mainly occurred from within a pre-reform trajectory in a political economy that tends to favour the central government in a federal structure of this kind and with an extremely limited recourse to global companies. In sum, reforms in this highly public sector have mainly followed internal governmental logic and contexts, and have not been much in tune with globalisation, despite potential technological gains. India has generally been on the sidelines of large movements of cross-investments noticed throughout the world.

In Chapter 8, "Subcontracting in Indian Industries, Market Structure and Product Quality: Implications under Globalisation", taking the example of the garment industry in the State of West Bengal, Ajitava Raychaudhuri underlines the need to fine-tune the relationship between public governance and entrepreneurial behaviour in the context of globalisation and a fast-growing exports market. He points out that the relative under-performance of the garments industry in West Bengal, as compared to other Indian states, can be explained by a labour-public governance that, generally speaking, is not conducive to reactiveness in the case of larger contracts nor to the high output quality. This is the result of a peculiar system of contractual relationships within the subcontracting network that appears to be specific to West Bengal where a higher aversion to the risk arising from poor governance has hindered the expansion of the production base. Raychaudhuri proposes a model based on long term perceptions to improve contractual relationships between producers and subcontractors and the incentive system.

Part II ends with Chapter 9, "India-Russia Economic Relations: Gradual Shift from State-dominant Linkages to Private Initiatives", in which, through an analysis of the evolution of India-Russia economic relations, Gulshan Sachdeva examines whether relations developed under the socialist era can give rise to post-socialist trade and help both economies to modernise. His answer clearly states that these relations have 'survived' mainly in the military and defence sector. He concludes, however, by pointing out the untapped potential in industry and services, now that both countries are committed to economic reforms.

In Part III, "Restructuring and Strategies of Firms: Globalisation Viewed as Networks of Firms and Internalisation of Processes in MNCs", the book goes on to describe country-wise scenarios and the segmentation of industries. Further, it deals with the restructuring and strategies of firms and explores, in particular, strategies for the industrial organisation of firms from several sectors taken as case studies.

Chapter 10, "Foreign Direct Investment in China's Automotive Industry", by Hua Wang, uses the example of the automobile industry to illustrate the dynamics of the multiplication of firms within each sector with the correlative need for restructuring and competition to give rise to larger companies. He also shows how initial strategies favouring joint ventures mature into direct ownership by foreign owners while, simultaneously, production becomes increasingly local through the increase of local suppliers and the evident spill-over effects of FDI.

In Chapter 11, titled "On the Role of Foreign Investment in the Development of a Market Economy in China", Rigas Arvanitis, Pierre Miège, and Zhao Wei examine the operations of the economic institutions and agencies responsible for wealth creation, such as the

Chinese enterprises, public institutions, foreign investors, and organisations to promote technological development. They centre their analysis on systems of production, investigating the renewal of the oldest of the systems of production, the role of the state as promoter and regulator of economic activity, and the degrees of efficiency achieved by the systems of production which appeared with the reforms. The township and village enterprises are based on low-cost labour, but should now actively seek out foreign partners to ensure access to technology and market outlets and technology transfer, both material (in the form of products, equipment, and processes) and organisational (quality control and management skills). The second type of production, established by the second wave of investment from Taiwan and Hong Kong have some specifics of their own. Firstly, the investors not only established the enterprises, but brought with them their own networks of suppliers and customers. Secondly, they had more complex production techniques. Thirdly, these overseas Chinese involved the local power structures into the very operations of their own systems of production. The third mode is FDI, where foreign investors' objectives are no longer just to relocate the manufacturing process, to cut costs and then re-export, but to develop a market in China itself. The authors describe for all these the limits in terms of further creation of markets, need to restructure now, and difficulty in phasing out innovation and technological change. To answer whether these growth engines will continue to perform, the authors propose to go beyond the sole question of property rights. Focusing on trust and noticing that the actual rules of the game in China seem not to encourage this trust, they argue that "everything indicates that a large amount of new enterprises will emerge in a rather more difficult business environment. As the new competitive pattern will be shaped, uncertainties about the behaviour of enterprises and other economic players will become conflictual points difficult to resolve. In the end, what will make the difference between enterprises is their ability to master larger and more sophisticated markets, by mastering more complex technologies". Limits are numerous: firms avoid partnerships and external input, with the unique exception of partnerships with foreign enterprises, enterprises know their clients well enough, but they do not know the state of their market. The authors underline that firms investing in research and development (R&D), or undertaking engineering improvements are rare. Foreign investment has been instrumental in creating industrial clusters and the authors detail, how a large part of the ability of the local industrial investors to enter in these kinds of industrial systems will depend, precisely, on the ability to make dynamic clusters.

In Chapter 12, "A Theory of Buy-outs in Joint Ventures", Sugata Marjit and Prabal Roy Chowdhury propose an explanation of the empirical facts governing the establishment and, especially, termination of joint ventures. Marjit and Chowdury go beyond the argument that access to local markets and practices which, according to several authors of this book, is important in the early stages of the opening of the economy and focus on the asymmetric access to capital playing a key role in the breakup of joint ventures, particularly following a buy-out by one partner. They show that this tendency is more likely in situations where the demand is high or, in other words, when the joint venture takes off.

In Chapter 13, titled "Asset Specificity, Partnerships and Global Strategies of Information Technology and Biotechnology Firms in India", Joël Ruet compares the evolution and maturing of development and business strategies in both IT and BT sectors in India. Stylising the various business models in the two sectors, he analyses their assets and revenue models using the concept of specific assets. He shows that in India, largely due to the timeframe of its research and industrial cycles, as well as the necessary industrial scaling up, the BT sector cannot follow the same service-based revenue model as the IT sector in order to develop. Similarly, given the nature of the specific assets to be built, IT may more easily allow globalisation of the internal strategies of firms, while BT calls for more local partnerships. Ultimately, given the initial investments needed in the BT sector, Ruet underlines the initial role played by the state in the take-off of the sector through regulation, funding as well as university-firm partnerships in funding and use of research resources and equipment.

Chapter 14, "Emergence and Entry of Industrial Groups in Russia: The Case of the Car Industry" by Xavier Richet, describes the general context of a very timid policy regarding the restructuring of industry in Russia. He points out that privatisation of a few units and conglomeration have been the principal activity till now. Taking the car industry as an example, he draws attention to the fact that the entry mode of foreign companies determines the creation of spill-overs and externalities in the rest of the industry. He stresses that the joint venture is an intermediary between product exports licences or assistance on the one hand and a stronger commitment, like acquisition or greenfield investments on the other, the choice being correlated to the degree of country risk. However, neither acquisition, greenfield investments nor joint ventures have successfully managed to modernise the industry which, in terms of quality, faces direct competition from second hand imported cars. In view of the lack of investment capacity of all players, the Russian government was obliged to formulate in 2001 a 'policy for the development of the automobile industry'. This clearly implies that when the transition is incomplete, the state has a definite role to play in promoting the real involvement of foreign companies. As compared to the situation in China, we observe that Russia is lagging behind on the reform front and has been faced with an 'overcapacity problem' for some time now whereas China had stronger incentives to open up its economy in an undercapacity scenario.

Part I

The Private in Context: Public Reforms

2

Between Bureaucracy and Market

Chinese Industrial Groups in Search of New Forms of Corporate Governance

JEAN-FRANÇOIS HUCHET and XAVIER RICHET

This chapter investigates the peculiar and contradictory nature of the ongoing construction of a system of corporate governance in China. The analysis attempts to overcome the limits of traditional corporate studies that tend to focus on enterprise management, and puts the issue within the framework of the systemic and political relationships that shape economic management and state intervention in large enterprises in transitional socialist systems. The emergence of a specific managerial culture within the market, and of winners among the enterprises is related to the position still held by the state in the enterprise asset, and by the access to competitive markets available to the enterprises. State owned enterprises enjoy the protection of their status but they are more successful and adopt a more profit-oriented management culture if they operate in the internationalised and competitive markets rather than in the strategical low-profit, state-dominated sectors. Due to continuous interaction between enterprise management and external (policy or macroeconomic) factors, and the absence or underdevelopment of most of the institutions generally necessary for a sound corporate governance system (financial markets, bank independence, free press, etc.), the privatisation does not seem sufficient to engender all round market-led governance.

China's transition was, for a long time, presented as a counter-example of the transitions undergone by the countries of Eastern Europe. The virtues of Chinese-style gradualism were put forward in opposition to the pernicious effects of the 'shock therapy' applied in most Eastern European economies and in the former Soviet Union (Boone *et al.*, 1998). Nevertheless, after hesitating for a long time, the

Chinese authorities today have to go right to the heart of the matter in the transformation of post-socialist economies. More concretely, the task that lies ahead for them is to promote the emergence of a more effective system of corporate governance than that inherited first from the Maoist and then the Deng Xiaoping period. Taking as a definition of corporate governance, the set of mechanisms governing the decisions of leaders and defining their discretionary space, we can easily grasp why reforms in this area are henceforth, a priority for the future of the Chinese economy. Phenomena such as the duplication of undersized investments (Huchet, 1999), endemic corruption (He, 1998) and the stripping of state assets (Cao *et al.*, 1998; Ding, 2000), things which have all been broadly studied, show to what extent the control mechanisms operating on the decisions of those who hold the power in firms, have either been non existent or particularly ineffective in the great majority of Chinese firms. Their consequences have assumed such proportions, especially with the rapid rise of non-performing loans in the banking sector (Lardy, 1998) that, at the time of the Asian crisis, and for the first time since the start of the reform process in 1978, they have left up in the air, the possibility of a systemic type crisis similar to the one recorded in other Asian countries.

From this perspective, the Asian crisis have played a beneficial role for China by acting as an electro-shock for the Chinese leaders, who, sheltered behind a non-convertible yuan, rushed to set up a series of reforms designed to improve corporate governance more or less directly. These very ambitious reforms can be compared to those applied in the countries of Eastern Europe following the collapse of the Communist regimes in the early 1990s: the restructuring of state-owned enterprises, the privatisation of small to medium-sized state-owned and collective urban enterprises, the complete reworking of the banking and financial system, the setting up within firms of boards of directors and supervisory councils, a legal code for companies, laying out the principles of protection for minority shareholders, the rejigging of the administrative system for managing the state's assets, and finally, the completion of negotiations on China's entry into the World Trade Organization (WTO) (Broadman, 2000).

In spite of the scope of such reforms, there remain many questions on their ability to improve Chinese corporate governance. A first series of questions relate to how administrative-type reforms in the state assets management system, such as those that have been implemented since 1994 and which make only very partial modification to the power structure in the state-owned enterprises, will be able to contribute in improving the system of corporate governance in these firms? A second series of questions concerns the inter-relation between the internal control mechanisms and those that are external to firms. That is, whether privatisations (partial or total) and the measures introducing the traditional instruments of corporate governance (such as boards of directors and supervisory boards), will be enough, while a great number of basic mechanisms of external control (the financial market, the independence of banks, a free press, respect for the rights of minority shareholders) are still absent or largely deficient.

An Attempt at Categorisation of Chinese Firms

The industrial organisation of the country is particularly heterogenous, both in terms of structure and control. Such heterogeneity is due firstly to historical reasons predating the reforms, and linked to the strategy of industrial development decided by the leaders of the day and by the major political events that shook China (Great Leap Forward, Break with the Soviet Leaders, Third Front Policy, Cultural Revolution) up until 1979. This resulted, on the one hand, in the establishment of a planned system of a conventional type, managed by the central government with a functional division into sectors, but concentrated on some major state industrial firms, and, on the other, in a semi-planned, semi-free market system, geographically partitioned off and controlled by the local authorities, in which there sprang up a host of state owned or collective small businesses.

The reform period up until the end of the 1980s did not give rise to any major disruptions in the control system, apart from the marked geographic breakup of industrial structures (Huchet, 1993). Despite the progressive disappearance of the plan, the central government continued to exert its control over the major state-owned enterprises. For their part, local governments (often at the municipal and district level) became the *de facto* owners of the state and collective small businesses, after several waves of administrative decentralisation. Stimulated by a fiscal system allowing them to keep a large part of the income produced by small business, and taking advantage of a largely decentralised banking system and a promotion system for local political leaders, based on an ability to develop economic activity, the local authorities became much more entrepreneurial. Various writers have shown (Blecher and Shue, 1996; Oi, 1998) how the local authorities have sought to develop a local industry that is as complete as possible in their area, yet without taking into consideration, the waste of resources caused by the duplication of investments that are, more often than not, undersized and operating under the umbrella of local protectionist policies. Thus, in the late 1980s, we find a differentiation among firms in their control methods linked rather to property rights and to a deconcentration of the Chinese administrative system than to any principal of efficiency derived from the market:

1. Large state-owned enterprises run from the central government.
2. Small to medium-sized businesses in the state and collective sector set up in urban areas and run by local governments.
3. The rapid development of small firms in rural zones registered as collective enterprises and run by local governments.
4. The emergence of private firms on the fringe of the centrally planned system, especially in trade and services.

Since the late 1980s, there has been a second source of heterogeneity, directly linked to the effects of the rise of competition in Chinese industry, even if it has been irregular across the various spheres of activity. In some sectors, particularly those in direct contact with end consumers (light industry, food production, textiles), competition has forced firms to implement reforms to adapt to the market. Some state-owned enterprises and rural collectives (category no. 3), but equally private companies that have now reached a critical mass (category no. 6), have developed aggressive commercial strategies aimed at increasing their market share, and have been able to modernise their equipment and management practices. The big losers in the reform process, since the early 1990s, are to be found among the state-owned and collective small and medium-sized enterprises in urban areas (category no. 5). Undersized and undercapitalised, these firms are experiencing great difficulties and are only surviving, thanks to the protectionist practices of the local authorities. Finally, we are witnessing the take-off of foreign firms operating on Chinese soil, some even having a dominant share of the internal market (telecommunications with Alcatel and Motorola, or Volkswagen in the automobile industry).

Thus, since the mid-1990s, the rise of competition has led to the emergence of new categories of Chinese groups with more complex control structures:

1. The major financial holding companies in the public sector specialising in services (financial, transport, trade) dependent on the central or provincial government and with a subsidiary listed on the Hong Kong Stock Exchange, that are commonly called 'Red Chips' (CITIC, COSCO, China Resources, Beijing Enterprise).
2. The major state groups controlled by the central government and operating in protected sectors.
3. The state sector and collective groups who are leaders in the competitive fields and who have earned a greater autonomy from their overseeing administration (mainly local administrations).
4. The joint ventures, a majority of whose capital is controlled by a foreign company and the firms 100 per cent controlled by foreign multinationals.
5. Small groups in the state and collective sector controlled by local governments.
6. Private groups in the competitive sectors that increasingly operate under the control of the main owner.
7. Small private and family collective commercial firms in the service sectors in urban and rural areas.

We have left aside the categories 1, 4, and 7 that do not fit into the analytical field of this chapter. As far as collective rural firms go, it seemed to us difficult to group them together under one banner, despite there being an abundant literature that regards them as a specific feature of Chinese economic development since the 1970s. Some firms that have, since the early 1990s, become major groups such as Kelon, Chunlan, Dalian Bohai (which are now part of the country's top 100 groups), are, in fact, very close to the leading state-owned enterprises operating in the competitive sectors, and we have grouped them together in category no.3. Furthermore, an important part of collective rural enterprises is composed of smaller-sized firms and is closer, in terms of management practice, to the urban state-owned and collective small- and medium-sized companies run by local governments. On this account, we have grouped them together in category no.5. Finally, one part of the rural collective firms that is hard to assess has, since the mid-1990s, taken on the status of private enterprises. This phenomenon is particularly visible in the coastal provinces, where a considerable number of firms that had been formerly registered as collective firms, in order to benefit from the protection of the all-powerful local bureaucracy (the system of *hongmao*, literally, 'red cap'), felt that the local public institutions had sufficiently changed to provide a guarantee of protection of private property (Oi, 1998; Unger and Chan, 1999). Even if this development is far from taking place in the inland provinces, some writers (Woo, 1998) maintain that it signifies the end of the supposed anomaly of the Chinese case. The 'hybrid' property rights, which characterise the rural collective enterprises may, in fact, merely reflect a transitional stage during which the economic players were seeking to secure their rights in a particularly uncertain political and economic environment. Similar configurations have, moreover, been largely studied in other countries in transition, notably in Hungary (Stark, 1997) before the evolution of the political situation, the development of competition and financial constraints facing firms, brought about a rapid clarification of property rights (often to the benefit of the former nomenclatura).

It was relatively difficult, given the available statistical lists, to quantify the importance of the different categories of groups under discussion in our analysis. But one important aspect should be stressed. Among the 100 largest industrial groups operating in China, category no. 2 of the major state-owned enterprises operating in non-competitive sectors is by far the most important. With a very high representation of firms linked to the petrochemical industry, provincial public companies producing electricity, or working in metallurgy, and, more tangentially, in the tobacco and automobile industries.

The Protected Firms: The Major State Sector Groups Controlled by the Centre in Non-competitive Sectors

In 2000, there were 2,100 large state-owned enterprises directly run by the central government. A little over one third were in deficit, and another third were in a precarious balanced financial situation. Although, they represent only 0.4 per cent of the total number of industrial firms, they still account for nearly 16 per cent of total industrial production and 19 per cent of the entire capital of industrial firms. These firms remain in their large majority off-limits for foreign investors, with only 2 per cent of their capital being controlled by foreign companies.[1] An examination of the classification of the country's 100 largest firms in 2000 shows that a great majority of these 2,100 firms operate in areas that are still strongly regulated and largely protected from both internal and international competition. Concerning the development of property rights, the state has, on several occasions, announced that it would preserve a majority of the capital in the big state-owned enterprises. In the text adopted at the third plenary session of the XVth Congress of the CCP in September 1999, the government declared that it wished to get out of non-strategic activities, yet without clearly defining this category. Although they have an urgent need of restructuring, the groups belonging to this category should not feel the influence of property reforms, except perhaps, through a simplification of relations with the central ministries that oversee them. Furthermore, as clearly shown by E. Steinfeld in his study of the state-owned enterprises in the steel industry, the behaviour of the managers of these firms follows in the tradition of the major socialist firms (Steinfeld, 1998). Managers are still juggling with contradictory objectives, some of which are political, such as the respect of the CCP's goals. Despite closer attention being paid to financial profitability, these have frequently spilled over in recent times, into questions associated with economic nationalism, such as the defence of national industry, and the advancement of the cause of 'national technological champions' at the expense of technological and economic efficiency. Other objectives are more social in nature, like the growth in the work unit and the preservation for wage-earners, the advantages inherited from the socialist period.

1. *Zhongguo daxingqiye nianqian* (1997). *"Directory of Major Chinese Firms"*.

Finally, their career is first and foremost political, since being part of a company's management is often a springboard for moving up the hierarchy of the CCP and the state. These contradictory objectives encourage waste and other misuses of funds or deplete the state's resources, either to the benefit of wage-earners, whose increases in income (salaries and other social benefits directly underwritten by the company) remained, until quite recently, clearly above productivity increases.

From the point of view of financing, these enterprises are plainly the greatest beneficiaries of the official financial system. The large state-owned enterprises have had access to all sources of official financing, whose development has been approved by the authorities. They have benefited from their political connections to gain privileged access to the major state commercial banks and to secure all existing forms of credit (subsidised loans, short-term credits, access to foreign currency for imports of technology). Apart from the early 1990s, they have been overwhelmingly directed at the stock market. Today, they constitute almost the entire number of the 1,400 enterprises listed on the two domestic stock markets, in Shanghai and Shenzhen, as well as those listed in Hong Kong (type 'H' shares) or New York (type 'N' shares). The interviews that we conducted, indicate that the impact of the financial market on their corporate governance has been limited. The state has locked in the capital of these firms in which it maintains an average participation close to 60 per cent,[2] thereby discouraging private or foreign shareholders from taking over. When it is realised that a non-negligable part of A and B type shares are also held by public institutions (state-owned enterprises, banks, firms controlled by local administrations), it becomes all the more clear, to what extent the capital of companies listed on the stock exchange is still very largely controlled by the State. Private investors have put up money for purely speculative reasons, taking little interest in the management of the company. A recent three year long study of the Shanghai Stock Exchange and firms listed on it denounced, in unambiguous terms, the various types of interference practised by the relevant overseeing administrative bodies. Moreover, the domestic stock markets are forever being rocked by scandals associated with the

2. *Zhongguo zhengquan qihuo tonji nianjian*(*Chinese Bureau of Statistics Directory on Securities and Futures*), 1997, 1998, 1999.

spread of confidential information prior to IPO, and with the lack of transparency in the account-keeping practices of companies. The same study concluded saying that there is no direct relationship between the evolution of share prices and the efficiency of the companies listed on the stock exchange. Finally, the way in which the laws are applied does not allow minority shareholders (even if they were to obtain strategic information about the company) to defend their rights before the courts. In this context, the control mechanisms derived from the financial market are severally limited.

These major state-owned enterprises have also benefited from the central government's policy of industrial group creation, that has authorised them to set up financial companies (subsidiaries) (*caiwu gongsi*) enabling them to raise funds for the group and manage its internal flow of financial resources. At the present time, 65 out of the list of 156 groups authorised by the State Council have been given the go-ahead to set up financial subsidiaries of this kind. In other terms, this type of enterprise should continue to siphon off a significant portion of bank credits, particularly due to the important needs of technological modernisation.

Such firms have also been the sole beneficiaries of the recapitalisation programme of the state banks. This programme allows the debts of the state-owned enterprises to be converted into assets for the state banks. The bank wipes from its balance sheet the amount of the non-profitable loan and the corresponding asset of the state-owned enterprise is taken over by liquidating companies created for the purpose (based on the American model of the late 1980s at the time of the savings cooperative banks crisis), which become responsible for selling it off. The difference between the initial value of the debt and the amount recovered through the asset sale should be financed by state bonds. The programme has cancelled nearly 1,500 billion yuans in debts deriving solely from this category of the major groups in the state sector. However, from the point of view of an improvement in the system of corporate governance, the programme does not go to the root of the problem. These new liquidating companies, like the banks which are entering into the board rooms of these major state-owned enterprises, are unable to play their role as 'active' stakeholder, namely to control the actions of managers and even less to censure them, and that for a variety of reasons: an asymmetry in information on the firm, that is knowingly controlled by the managers of state-owned companies, their lack of human resources and skills in terms of corporate governance, the high number of companies affected by the programme (nearly 1000) which multiplies the problems of competence, and finally, the statutes given to such companies, which do not bestow them with any absolute and real shareholder power, but rather a power that is subject to negotiation with the bureaucracies of the central ministries in charge of big state firms.

Concerning financing, the establishment of formal corporate governance institution within the firm should not eradicate the culture of free and plentiful financing, in which such companies have lived since their creation, something also pointed out by the OECD in its report on the reform of Chinese firms (OECD, 2000). Only a hardening of the budgetary constraint due to external factors (bankruptcy, reformed banking system, opening up to foreign capital, competition) will bring about a greater financial rigour in these groups.

Finally, the last factor, one that is more difficult to appraise, and which works against any major changes to the system of corporate governance in this category of groups, lies in the fact that they constitute an important link in the chain of financing and patronage by the CCP. In spite of the greater importance having been given to economic efficiency by the CCP over the past 20 years, such firms remain subject to the objectives and strategies of the political leadership that very markedly go beyond those of a company in a developed economy, as A. Hussain and J. Chen recall in their study of Chinese groups (Hussain and Chen, 1999). According to one of the few studies published in China, carried out by the Shanghai Stock Exchange and devoted to the decision making processes of firms listed there, 99 per cent of the important investment decisions or those relating to the appointments of the top executive staff and their salary packages are taken by the firm's CCP committee in conjunction with the CCP's local authorities.[3] Furthermore, even if very few analyses have been published on the subject in China, given the secrecy surrounding this phenomenon, the experiences of single-party political

3. Quoted by *The Financial Times*, November 5, 2000.

regimes elsewhere are sufficiently well-documented (see, for instance, Blasi *et al.*, 1997; Haggard and Kaufman, 1995; Maxfield and Schneider, 1997), for us to think that such a problem is very widespread in companies of this kind. In this context, the development of specific and intentional mechanisms for corporate governance such as board of directors, supervisory board have little chance of really being effective for this category of company. There is certainly more to be expected from the competition policy (particularly the opening up of the internal market to imports and foreign firms operating on Chinese soil), as well as from a vast reform of the banking sector, in order to improve their control and performance. From this point of view, China's entry into the WTO has in some still-protected sectors, such as the automobile and steel industries, machine tools, or even telecommunications, imposed a greater discipline on such firms, and speeded up regroupings to reach a critical mass in order to face the competition battle coming from foreign multinationals for whom China represents a major market to be conquered. However, in the protocol signed by China for its accession into WTO, there remain a lot of restrictions to the opening up of the sectors that are today protected (such as telecommunications or the automobile industry, where foreign capital has a ceiling of 49 per cent) as well as grey areas which enable such firms to continue to enjoy protection in the national market. In parallel, the agreement on the WTO has given renewed impetus to the debate on economic nationalism. In spite of high levels of indebtedness, these groups are regarded by the Chinese government as the flagship of Chinese industry. That should enable them to continue to have access to virtually free finance in the name of defence of national industry, thus perpetuating the lack of control over the use of investment resources. China's entry into the WTO could therefore have contradictory consequences for this category of firm.

Also, to the extent that the State remains the principal stake-holder, the more it will be able to put in place and have a respected system of objectives (exports, profitability, technological innovation) and sanctions (an end to financing and assistance packages, disciplinary action for managers, privatisations, bankruptcies) that are clearly defined with respect to this type of group, the better corporate governance will be, as is shown by the experience in Korea and in other developing countries (Amsden, 1989; Fields, 1995).

The Winners: The Groups in the State and Collective Sector that are Leaders in the Competitive Sectors

In areas such as retail electronics, household appliances, some parts of the food industry, textiles and clothing, which have been marked by price liberalisation—a lowering of the entry barriers for producers, and the development of unbridled competition—the past 10 years have witnessed the advent of new types of corporate groups (including in the collective sector) in which the State has a majority stakehold. Such firms, leaders in their respective market, like Haier, Huabao, Kelong (household appliances), Konka, TCL and Changhong (television sets), Lenovo (computers), have forged their reputations based on strategies which are in no way different from the major companies in capitalist economies. It is interesting to observe, that such firms were far from figuring among the most well known ones in China at the end of the 1980s. Groups like Changcheng (Great Wall) in the computer industry, Mudan in Peking, or Panda in the province of Jiangsu, or again Shanghai Number One Television company, were all much more important firms receiving massive support from their parent authorities during the 1980s. The case studies that we have carried out on such leading conglomerates like Changhong and Konka, or the one produced by S. Kennedy on Stone (Kennedy, 1997) in the computer industry, show that whilst these firms have not been deliberately discriminated against, in the industrial policy of the central or local state, they are far from having been supported, either financially or logistically, to any equivalent degree to that of the major state-owned enterprises which dominated their sector during the 1980s. The fate of a firm like Huaiyou, in the province of Hebei, in the city of Shijiazhuang, is an interesting one in this respect. Considered as one of the largest conglomerates in the television manufacturing industry, the state gave it very broad access to bank finance in the 1980s, to import production lines from abroad, and to develop its distribution network nationally, well before all other domestic firms in the sector. However, right from the start of the 1990s, after serious errors of strategy in terms of diversification, difficulties in controlling its costs and a faulty assimilation of foreign technologies, the Huaiyou group quickly lost its position in the face of competition from more dynamic firms like Changhong. Huaiyou had to file for bankruptcy in 1993. As for Changhong, not having privileged access to the major sources of state finance, it used as best as it could, the human and technological skills, left over from the Maoist period when it used to make military hardware, in order to assimilate foreign technologies. It was to aim small at the start, by favouring the province of Sichuan with its some (nonetheless) 100 million inhabitants, seeking to develop a distribution and after-sales service network that would make its reputation, at the same time as taking advantage of the low labour costs in the small city where it was set up (Mianyang), compared to those of its competitors (domestic and foreign) operating in the coastal provinces. Changhong launched a price war from the start of the 1990s, enabling it to benefit from economies of scale and to break into the national market as a whole, at the same time as maintaining a quality expectation for its products, making it very quickly the leading producer of television sets in the domestic market.

These firms also rather easily won their management autonomy, in so far as the State did not regard them as priority companies, which allowed them to reduce, quite considerably, the deleterious influence of bureaucratic interference in their decision-making. Most of these cutting edge firms are situated in medium-sized townships and not in large industrial cities. Due to their success, they have become important enough for the parent municipalities to have henceforth, little leverage on them. Changhong had in the year 2000 an annual turnover of more than US $ 2 billion, mainly from its Mianyang factories, that is more than the city's income from taxation, or than the total combined turnover of the other companies operating in Mianyang municipality. The management of these companies has also gained a relative independence from their parent authority. The very strong personalities of their executive heads and the results achieved have led to a *de facto* privatisation of the management of these companies. The case studies that we have carried out show that the executives now have a free hand in virtually all the company's management decisions, with the exception of the sale or purchase of assets with respect to which the administrative authorities maintain a certain degree of control (Huchet, 1999).

Their independence is also derived from their finance strategy. Not having benefited from the State's largesse in the 1980s, the first bank finances were put to good use, and the ensuing profits were reinvested in relatively well-planned new investments, thereby avoiding an over-dependence on the State's banking sector. All these firms have in common, the fact that they have a relatively low level of debt, not exceeding 50 per cent in the majority of cases (when debts are taken as a ratio of the firm's capital). The development of the Shanghai and Shenzhen stock exchanges, or the possibility of being listed on the Hong Kong Stock Market, have been widely used by such firms which have been able to achieve a quick listing, in view of their reputation and performance. Given the still inadequate operation of the domestic stock exchanges (see above category no. 2), which remain still largely incapable of influencing corporate governance, and even less of censuring the CEOs, managers of these companies saw the possibility of raising funds without any excessive counter-measure on the degree of control over their decisions, and of avoiding at the same time, any recourse to bank credit that is synonymous with State control. Over a period of time, this phenomenon could turn out to be prejudicial for such firms which, too sure of themselves, could launch into badly planned investments, without receiving any signs from the stock exchange are likely to reorient their decisions. Nevertheless, the fact remains that at the present level of development of the Chinese economy, and paradoxically, this inadequate operation of the stock markets has allowed the leaders of such firms to not see their decisions as being dictated by the short-term profitability demands of financial investors.

Overall, the strong competition in their market combined with a privatisation of their management have considerably improved the system of corporate governance of such firms, even if institutions like the boards of directors and supervisory board that exist in these firms are far from operating in an efficient manner.

China's entry into the WTO had an overall positive effect on their system of corporate governance. Competitive pressures have increased, yet without being a shock like that of the liberalisation policies put in place in the former socialist countries of Eastern Europe in the early 1990s. Indeed, these firms were already familiar with strong competition in their domestic market and had already incorporated a strong capacity for adaptation and reaction to the market into their management. Furthermore, they have massively invested over the past 10 years in after-sales service networks focused on quality, which gives them a certain edge over foreign producers possibly tempted to invest heavily in China. However, in the short to medium term, such leading firms are going to have to increase their portion of external finances, to allow a diversification and an increase in the quality of their products through R&D, but also because they will have to consolidate their position in their main market by developing a vast distribution network and by buying up firms in other provinces.

From this viewpoint, both stock markets and domestic and foreign banks should constitute more important sources of finance and contribute to diversifying the control structures that, for the time being, rest solely on the competitiveness and personality of the present bosses. Since they have become market leaders, the State is more inclined to help them, particularly *via* the banking sector.

Beyond the often strong and upright personality of their current bosses, they will also have to institute effective instruments of corporate governance (outside experts on their board of directors, recourse to the expertise of foreign investors). Beyond the nationalist rhetoric of the central government, one can be reasonably confident in these firms which have already a considerable experience in cooperating with foreign companies behind them (notably in terms of technology transfer and management methods), and in their ability to combine an intelligent strategy of cooperation/conflict with foreign companies in China as abroad. Such cooperation, indeed even the opening up of capital to foreign companies, should equally lead to a better functioning of the formal institutions of corporate governance in these firms, thus broadening the internal control mechanisms which are largely lacking today.

Overall, China's entry into the WTO has been beneficial for the system of corporate governance of these category of corporate groups, by significantly increasing the opportunities for cooperation with foreign groups both in the industrial and financial fields, at the same time as strengthening competition in the domestic market.

'Sink or Swim': Small Groups in the State and Collective Sector

These firms correspond to the bulk of state and collective small- and medium-sized enterprises. In industry and for the state sector alone, they represented nearly three-fourth, of some 110,000 state-owned enterprises in 1996. For the most part, such firms are experiencing significant financial difficulties (OECD, 2005). The figures vary according to the province. In the hinterland or in the North-east, where the state sector has the lion's share of the local economy, it is estimated that nearly three-fourths of the state-owned small-and medium-sized enterprises have either a deficit or precariously balanced books. Conversely, in the coastal provinces, the situation is less of a concern with, depending on the estimate, 30 to 40 per cent of companies in the red or with a precarious balance sheet. Their influence is also less important in the local economy, where foreign investment and private enterprises represent an increasing part of activities (Boillot and Michelon, 2000).

This category of enterprise suffers from a system of corporate governance that is especially inefficient. Here are to be found, with only slight variations, the same problems as for the major groups in the state sector in category no. 2. There is, however, one (significant) difference, which is the inability of the local parent authorities to keep the manna of bank credit wide open to finance their existence, as they do for the large state-owned enterprises. The poor functioning of the internal control mechanisms (massive interference of the local bureaucracy in decision-making processes, inefficient management, the absence of any board of directors or supervisory board) has come on top of an inefficiency in the external control mechanisms (local anti-competitive protectionism, huge subsidies dressed up as bank credits, an absence of bankruptcies until recent years). It is not surprising therefore, that the firms in this category which have not managed to respond to the challenge of competition under the guidance of a capable and honest CEO (in fact, the few ones which have succeeded have moved into category no. 3), woke up in the mid-1990s to a difficult financial situation. The rise of competition in the wake of an overproduction capacity throughout Chinese industry, and the willingness to reduce subsidies disguised as bank credits in order to reform the state banks, sounded the death knell for such enterprises. It was in this context that the central state introduced in the mid-1990s a policy of drastic reform, summarised by the slogan "sink or swim", targeting such firms.

In parallel to the mergers and the leasing of management to a private individual, privatisation constituted the major axis of the restructuring of these enterprises. According to various statistics nearly 60 per cent of small state-owned firms managed by municipalities have been privatised. Whether it be complete privatisation with the sale of capital to outside investors, partial privatisation with the sale of a part of the capital to third-party companies, or privatisation with sale of capital to employees under the guise of cooperative stockholding (*gufenhezuozhi*), all these models have been tried to varying degrees by local governments.

We are, thus, headed towards a stakeholding system of varying configurations among local players: the directors and employees of companies, the local governments represented by local state asset management companies, and, finally, either other state-owned enterprises, collective or private, or institutions linked to the local bureaucracy. In a general way, the local bureaucrats have not wished to see the most profitable firms get away from them. Personal rewards, CCP local financing, the continuation of a system of local patronage, all these factors explain to varying degrees this willingness to keep control over the most profitable enterprises. As we were able to note in our enquiries, confirmed moreover by other fieldwork studies (Sargeson and Zhang, 1999), the local political leaders control the whole privatisation process of asset evaluation, including allocation procedures all the way through to price fixing of the assets. We also accordingly find all the possible situations, from total privatisation to the maintenance of majority control *via* the (local) state assets management companies. In the cases of total privatisation, particularly in medium-sized cities, the local leaders also often become the official new owners of the enterprises, through the use of figureheads, or by integrating the privatised enterprise into a group structure controlled by them (Ding, 2000). From this perspective, privatisation allows them to make all the subsidiaries that they have created or helped to create outside the state sector official, most often based on an abuse of state assets, and to set the whole up in a group structure of a financial-holding type which has the (totally or partially) privatised state-owned enterprise at its core. When it is the company directors who assume control, they nonetheless need the cooperation of the local bureaucracies. The reform of ownership also allows the negotiation of a contract with the bureaucrats in exchange for a part of the privatised firm's capital (Sargeson and Zhang, 1999).

The selling off cheaply of profitable state assets for the benefit of the local cadres or company directors was widespread enough to produce a critical backlash on the part of the central government at the end of 1998, putting a brake for a short while on such practices by local governments.

In the cases of partial privatisation, local governments have maintained majority control *via* the state asset management companies who act, in fact, like former industrial bureaux of the municipalities. Thus, despite the privatisation, we are far from observing any serious break with the mode of control of these enterprises, the bureaucracy remaining an inescapable player and one that often has a decision-making power for the most profitable companies.

The loss-making firms, on the other hand, have been either sold off to the employees or put on the market and sold off in asset exchange centres that have opened up shops in all of China's major cities (*guoyou zichanjiaoyi zhongxin*). With regard to the number of enterprises put on the market, very few foreign investors have risked taking up such firms, on account of the high transaction costs in this kind of operation and the rather unattractive nature of the assets of such firms (the level of indebtedness, obsolete technology, inefficient management, decreasing market share). We are not aware of any statistics published at the national level on the number of state-owned and collective small-and-medium-sized businesses taken up by foreign investors, but during our research in the provinces of Liaoning, Hubei, Shaanxi and Jilin, those in charge of privatisation and sale of state assets confirmed to us that this concerned only one or two companies, sometimes not even any at all, as in Wuhan. The failure of the sale, for even one symbolic yuan, of state-owned enterprises in the city of Shenyang, during a European tour in 1998 of the political leaders from Liaoning province, bears witness to such difficulties. On the other hand, the cases of buy-back by Chinese investors have been much greater in number. There again, statistics are lacking. Nonetheless, during our case studies on the leading state-owned and private enterprises (categories 3 and 6), we have been able to observe that such firms had embarked on a path of external growth by buying up state-owned small businesses in other provinces. Since 1993, the private Chinese food industry group New Hope (whose head office is in Chengdu, in Sichuan province) had bought up 13 state-owned enterprises in various provinces. Between 1994 and 1998, the Haier group, no. 1 in household appliances in China, had already taken over around 15 state-owned enterprises in trouble in various provinces. The enterprises placed in the state assets exchange centres have not, however, all found buyers, far from it. The CEO of the Haier group, Zhang Huimin, has stated that the central administration, but also various local governments, regularly put pressure on the group for it to take over moribund enterprises in the sector. However, he added that he did not take on just any business in trouble, choosing rather those that had a good product, a market and good technology, but bad management. This meant that he was in a position of strength to negotiate take-overs in advantageous conditions, particularly in terms of debt reduction for the firm. The enterprises that have not been taken over by outside investors have either been merged with other enterprises in the region by administrative decision, sold off to employees, or, in a limited number of cases, have filed for bankruptcy.

The sale of the capital (in the form of shares) to the employees has, in fact, been the preferred method for reforming the urban state-owned and collective small-and medium-sized enterprises in difficulty. Various provincial studies carried out in the inland provinces, that we have cross-checked with our own interviews in Hubei, Shaanxi and Liaoning provinces, indicate that this method has been used in nearly 30 per cent of the urban state-owned and collective small businesses affected by the reforms. The first large-scale experiment, and one that received a lot of media coverage, took place in Zhucheng in 1994, in a small city in Shandong province, where 210 state-owned and collective enterprises (out of a total of 288) were privatised (Dong, 1999). This type of shareholding, called 'cooperative', was extended to all of China's cities in the wake of the CCP's XVth Congress in the autumn of 1997.

What can be said about the influence of privatisation on the system of corporate governance of this category of firm? The most positive results have been recorded by enterprises bought up by outside investors (foreign or national). Such enterprises have not only been freed of bureaucratic shackles, but have also benefited from a new, more dynamic style of management, a brand name that is recognised by consumers and new outlets guaranteed by the new purchaser, as well as an easing of their debts with banks negotiated by the buyer with the local authorities. All these improvements have radically changed the system of corporate governance by strengthening the internal and external control mechanisms guaranteed by the buyer and no longer just by the local bureaucrats. In fact, such restructuring method, has amply proved its efficiency already in capitalist economies, as well as in former socialist countries of Eastern Europe, and broadly confirms the positions of certain economists, advocates of the 'agency theory,' who think that the taking over of control by active investors in order to restructure an enterprise is clearly more efficient than the development of new internal control mechanisms within the firm (Jensen, 1997).

As far as firms whose capital has been sold off to its employees are concerned, the results seem rather negative. Once again, it is difficult to get a proper idea nationally, as no serious impact study has been published (or even perhaps carried out) by the central authorities. By comparing the enquiries we conducted in the inland and northeast provinces with provincial studies in the Chinese economic literature, two chief types of problems emerge, which have also been widely documented in other countries in transition, particularly in Russia.

On the one hand, the capital injected from the sales of employee shares is too limited to eradicate the debts and provide a response to the needs of the restructuring of this category of firms that require a drastic modernisation of the whole production process. The enterprises in the city of Zhucheng, which were the first in 1994 to benefit on such a large scale from this type of privatisation, by 1997 had need of a new increase in capital to the tune of 750 million yuans (that is three times more than the first release of shares). The contribution of employees (which was the major part in 1994) amounted to only 180 million yuans (that is 24 per cent of the total), the rest of the finance having been provided by the banks and outside investors who entered into the capital of the enterprises (Dong, 1999). The intervention of the local state banks has been widely analysed as a bail-out package and a partial renationalisation of the city's firms. The banks also lent massively to company directors at the time of the initial purchases of shares, as well as when they tried to buy back the shares of workers to secure a majority control of the firms. In short, after three years experience, the state has massively reentered into the capital of firms *via* the banks which, with limited capabilities and above all responding to the orders of the local authorities, risk having just as weak a grip over the firms as in the past.

On the other hand, the power structure and the incentive system that emerges from this type of privatisation are often incapable of generating any real reforming impulse within the enterprise. Admittedly, certain CEOs have an undeniable managerial know-how and may benefit from their new found autonomy with respect to the administration in order to put in train audacious reforms, as is shown by some of the success stories made much of in the Chinese economic press. However, the impact on control is generally limited, and for two main reasons. Firstly, the CEOs of the enterprises are still appointed by the local political leaders. They are still regarded as local functionaries. Their membership of the CCP also remains a determining factor for their career. This factor does not allow a break with the political allegiances that are sometimes contrary to the company's interests, but above all, it encourages the pursuit of rent seeking strategies (which most often lead to corruption), the company CEOs consider themselves to be both poorly rewarded and not responsible for the firm's fate (even if they control a majority share of the capital which cannot be sold outside the company). Secondly, despite privatisation, there appears to be no countervailing power within the company, even when the employees have a majority holding in it. During the first few years following the initial sale of shares to employees, company directors sought to buy back the workers in order to become the majority shareholders. The workers unloaded their shares all the more quickly—in exchange for a few benefits—in so far as they sought to recover, as fast as possible, their savings that they had invested in the non-negotiable shares outside the company. In larger cities, such as Wuhan or Chengdu, informal markets (*guitai jiaoyi zhongxin*) sprang up, enabling the workers to negotiate their shares with people outside the company. However, after repeated scandals in 1997 and 1998, these informal markets were banned by order of the central authorities. But it is especially the absence of free trade unions, the rise in unemployment and the end of jobs for life that have finally taken away from employees, all organised and official means of pressure regarding their future and that of the company. In this context, similar to what happened in

Russia, none of the new institutions which have emerged from the privatisation process, such as boards of directors and supervisory board are in any position to exert any internal control over the actions or decisions of the companies' CEOs who, in most cases, assume the position of chairman of both the board of directors and the supervisory board, as well as being managing-director of the company and party secretary. These institutions still have little existence other than to rubber stamp decisions taken by the CEOs in consultation with the local bureaucrats. Finally, as regards the incentive system for workers, it was supposed to have been transformed by their new status as owners of the company. This influence, when it existed at all, operated only very briefly, just long enough for the workers to sell off their shares, and to realise that they had not won any real decision-making power or any real control in the company through privatisation. In fact, the above-mentioned factors, such as the threat of unemployment and the end of jobs-for-life, have proved to be much more powerful elements than the holding of shares in modifying the attitude of workers in their workplace.

Thus, this type of privatisation is far from constituting a sufficient condition for success in the restructuring process of this category of firm. In fact, improvement in the governance of such companies depends especially on an improvement in the external control system (the depoliticisation of banks so as to increase the budgetary constraint of firms, the deregulation or suppression of local protectionist measures so as to expose such firms to competition) and on the establishment of a system of social protection enabling preparation for the social costs associated with bankruptcies that should become more marked for this category of company. With an improvement in external control, the internal disciplinary mechanisms will have a greater chance also of improving, as in this category of firms the only companies that will survive will be those who succeed in reforming their management practices, and in limiting, as far as possible, the waste of resources stemming from the search for returns. There is nothing surprising in the fact that a greater proportion of these firms are experiencing better results in terms of restructuring in the coastal provinces, where local protectionism is not as strong as it was, where competition is stiffest, where the banks have better means of discriminating between firms in relation to their credit risk, and where the social security systems work well enough to enable the exit from the market of the most inefficient firms. (Lu, 1999).

It is, however, for this category of firms that China's entry into the WTO is providing the rudest awakening. During the transitional phase of its entry into the WTO (2002-2007), we have seen a pursuit of the reform of the banking sector in order to prepare the Chinese commercial banks for competition with foreign banks, as well as the lowering of tariffs and a greater opening up to direct foreign investment in hitherto protected areas. For these enterprises, this has resulted in a tighter budgetary constraint imposed by their principal creditor, namely the state banks, as well as by an upsurge in competition in the domestic market. The state-owned and collective urban small businesses, in spite of the wave of reforms, were the least prepared for taking on this twin challenge. Given their importance in terms of jobs in the inland and northeast provinces (60 per cent of the urban wage-earners live in these areas[4]), we have seen the local leaders, with the assent of the central authorities, to put up non-tariff barriers and ask the state banks to keep on subsidising the state-owned small businesses, and those recently privatised, so as to avoid the risks of social instability. Nevertheless, the choice of the Chinese authorities to join the WTO represents a clearly displayed willingness to put Chinese consumers first, who will be able to choose goods independently of the manufacturer's nationality (contrary to the development strategies being pursued by Japan, South Korea and Taiwan, who have given special treatment to national producers). We can therefore expect, over the next few years, a radical restructuring in which only a minority of these firms will continue to exist. The others will be either bought up (best case scenario), merged, or simply go into bankruptcy if China is capable of generating adequate growth and of redistributing it to those provinces most affected by the restructuring process.

Tomorrow's Winners? Private Groups in the Competitive Sectors

Finally, the last category brings together the private enterprises that have succeeded in reaching a critical mass in competitive sectors of

4. Zhongguo tongji nianjian (1999). *China Statistical Yearbook*.

the market. Private firms have experienced rapid development since the end of the 1980s. According to the OECD private enterprises (not including foreign funded firms) could represent 30 per cent of industrial output.[5] In the vast majority of cases, however, the private companies are small in size and mainly operate around the family unit in the service sector, particularly in the restaurant business, or small commercial activities in urban areas (category no. 7). But a study of their situation goes beyond the object of the present chapter.

The companies that are of interest to us here are only a handful, and are precisely those that have managed to get beyond the frame of the small family business. The country's first private enterprise, New Hope (*Xinxiwang*), whose headquarters are in Sichuan province, is a leader in the animal food industry, with a turnover of nearly 2 billion yuans (US $ 240 million) in 1998. Only three private companies (New Hope, Sichuan Tongwei, and Beijing Changning), had a turnover greater than a billion yuans.[6] By way of comparison, the 1997 turnover of the top five Chinese groups (all state-owned enterprises) was 35 times greater than that of the five biggest private enterprises.

Their control structure has remained relatively simple, since these companies have been set up by an individual, sometimes a family, who directly runs the operation. Their performance is all the more remarkable in relation to the leading state-owned enterprises in category no. 3, in so far as they have been very largely discriminated against in terms of access to finance and raw materials. This discrimination has been especially acute in the hinterland and northeast regions, where the state-owned enterprises remain dominant in the local economy and the bureaucracy carries on a predatory stance with regard to private capital. In Wuhan, short-term loans granted to private enterprises in 1996 represented only one per cent of the total amount of short-term loans provided by the banking sector. Even in Guangdong province, where private enterprises are highest in number, the credits granted by the four major state commercial banks (which still monopolise the field of credit extended to companies), did not exceed one per cent of the overall amount of

5. OECD (2005). *China Economic Survey*, Paris.

6. *Zhongguo shehuikexueyuan gongyejingji yanjiusuo, Zhongguo gongye fazhan baogao* (1997). *"Report on Industrial Development in China"*, 1997, Beijing, Jingji guanli chubanshi.

Table 2.1

Diversity and Development in Corporate Governance of Chinese Groups

	Evolution of Property Rights	*Behaviour of the Board of Directors*	*Behaviour of Managers*	*Finance Strategy and Budgetary Constraint*	*Role of the Party*
Major State Groups in the Non-competitive Sectors	Privatisation very unlikely.	No decision-making role. Strong interventionist role of the central ministries *via* financial holding companies.	Political	Soft budget constraint. Continues to benefit from the extravagance of the domestic banking and financial system.	Very strong.
The State-owned and Collective Groups that are Leaders in the Competitive Sectors	The State remains the principal stakeholder, but there is *de facto* privatisation in favour of managers.	Weak decision-making role. Internal control through chief executives. Local governments maintain an influence in the management of assets even if the power of managers tends to increase.	Increasingly profit seeking oriented	Hard budget constraint. Based on capacity for self-financing and the stock market. Non-official finance Low debt level.	Remains present but in decline. Possible conflicts over time with firm. strategy.
Small Groups in the State and Collective Sector	Policy of 'sink or swim'. Move towards privatisation.	Weak decision-making role. Internal control through chief executives or local state assets management companies.	Trying to survive	Soft budget constraint. Heavily indebted system of cross participation between local firms.	Decline.
Private Groups in the Competitive Sector	Strengthening of the protection of private property rights.	Importance of family control.	Profit seeking oriented	Hard budget constraint. Self-financing and unofficial financing. Willingness to self-finance on the stock market and through foreign banks.	Limited, but need to be sure of the CCP's protection.

contd. ...

contd. ...

	Salary Growth, Fringe Benefits Bargaining Power of Workers	*Expected Results of the Reforms to the System of Corporate Governance*	*Impact of Entry into the WTO*
Major State Groups in the Non-competitive Sector	Stable bargaining power Continues to benefit from fringe benefits. Rise in salaries likely to continue to be above growth in productivity.	Weak influence. Remain under the inefficient control of the central bureaucracy.	Little impact, are going to seek government support to protect themselves against competition and to continue to have access to finance from state banks
State and Collective Groups, Leaders in the Competitive Sector	Negotiating power declining with the increase of unemployment. Growth rate of salaries below that of productivity, but possibility for compensation through share allocations. New management interested in developing the pool of technological skills.	Could take advantage of the reforms. More autonomy, better access to different forms of finance, in particular on the stock and bank markets. Stronger pressure of financial markets if the banking reform is implemented. Withdrawal of the Party/State from restructuring and group creation activities.	Potential winners. Second phase in their development: difficult strategic decisions, have to position themselves with higher value added goods. Possible reform of management through cooperation with foreign companies entering the firm's decision-making bodies. Will have to avoid the risks linked with the policy of defending national industry.
Small Groups in the State and Collective Sector	Negotiating power on the wane with the growth of unemployment.	Weak influence. Risk of insiders control as in Russia.	The big losers. High transaction costs for foreign investors. Bankruptcies, mergers, and privatisation.
Private Groups in the Competitive Sector	Negotiating power declining on account of the increase in unemployment. Growth rate of salaries below that of productivity, but possibility for compensation through share allocations. New management interested in developing a pool of technological skills.	Could take advantage of the reforms. More autonomy, better access to different forms of finance, in particular on the stock markets and through foreign banks.	Potential winners. May win if the Party/State keeps its promises to grant the private sector greater access to finance and gives them greatest representation nationally with less interference at the micro level.

Source: Huchet, Jean-François Xavier et Richet (2005). *Gouvernance, coopération et stratégie des firmes chinoises*, Paris: L'Harmattan, p.212.

credit handed out to companies. Despite central government directives, the banks remain very cautious with loans, considering in particular that private enterprises are unable to provide good quality collateral when they take out credit. It is, therefore, not surprising that institutions like IFC (International Finance Corporation, a subsidiary of the World Bank specialising in loans to the private sector in developing countries) have until recently had great difficulty in China in financing projects that are solely in the private sector. In its 12 years in the Chinese market, IFC had (by late 1997) financed only 40 projects for a total of US $1.5 billion, and only two projects had been concluded with fully private enterprises—the other projects concerned Sino-foreign firms. The only sources of finance available for private firms have been of the self-funding type, informal channels of finance—for the most part regarded as illicit—and similarly, albeit more tangentially, rural and urban credit cooperatives. It is difficult to find figures nationally concerning the importance of such recourse to informal channels of financing, but one study dealing with rural collective enterprises indicates that what is grouped together under the Chinese name of *minjian jiedai shichang* (popular credit market, including tontines, loans from private individuals, as well as assistance and loans from the family) might account for between a quarter and a third of the total amount of their finances. The small-to-medium-sized businesses in Taiwan and Korea were, until the 1980s, facing a similar situation with financial markets that remained under tight political control and were mainly intended to serve the major firms close to the Nationalist Party in power in Taiwan, or the *chaebols* in South Korea (Fields, 1995). Paradoxically, in the initial phase of development of Chinese private firms, such rationing of finance constituted an effective external control, to the extent that those in charge were forced to avoid wasting resources and to reinvest a large part of their profits to ensure growth.

Such companies could, in the near future, be the big winners on the internal industrial scene. The political discrimination by the regime against the private sector is not anymore explicit as it used to be in the 1980s. The National People's Congress voted a constitutional amendment in 1999 recognising the place of the private sector alongside the state sector in the nation's economic development, and the State Planning Commission has just announced that the Chinese government is going to lift all forms of restriction and discrimination against the private sector. A few private enterprises have won legal proceedings against local administrations, something that was unimaginable at the beginning of the 1990s. The private firm New Hope (*Xinxiwang*) became, in 1998, the largest shareholder in the Minsheng Bank—the sole private commercial bank to exist in China—with 9.9 per cent of the bank's capital. Moreover, the bank has invited the principal managers of the major private enterprises onto its board of directors. By the same token, in January 1999, 41 private firms obtained permission to trade abroad, and more private firms should be authorised to join the Shanghai and Shenzhen stock exchanges. Discrimination regarding private firms should ease off as the regime knows that it has a problem, linked to population growth, that is difficult to solve without the help of the private sector. The Chinese economy created 287 million new jobs between 1978 and 1996, but this pace has considerably slowed since 1990. Between 1978 and 1990, 238 million new jobs were created, that is at an average rate of nearly 20 million new jobs per annum. Between 1990 and 1996, only 49 million new jobs were created, that is at an average annual rate of about 8 million. But several structural reasons indicate that the employment situation should not pick up in the coming years. Despite the fall in the birthrate since the late 1970s, on average 15 million people will arrive on the labour market every year till 2010. Furthermore, the rural collective enterprises that absorbed a good part of the oversupply from the countryside during the 1980s, are now creating fewer and fewer jobs. From 1978 to 1988, employment in such firms grew on average at the rate of 7 per cent per annum, whereas it was only 5 per cent between 1988 and 1996.[7] Productivity gains, concentration and other sectorial restructuring plans to deal with the present overcapacities in industry, mean that this category of firms will not be in a position to create as many jobs as in the 1980s. As to the state sector, it contributed to half of the jobs created between 1978 and 1995 in urban areas, but it has now entered a phase of job elimination that will be more or less accelerated depending on the political and financial demands. Despite rapid growth in job creation in Sino-foreign firms, with nearly 30 million employees, this category of firm will be unable to absorb alone all of

7. *Zhongguo tongji nianjian* (1996). *China Statistical Yearbook.*

the new job seekers coming onto the labour market, in addition to the unemployed.

Thus, the rise in unemployment and the development of a political ideology with regard to the private sector, could result in a noticeable improvement in access to official financing and in respect of property rights. The factors likely to promote the development of the private sector go well beyond the mere context of economic policy. The willingness of the present political rulers to accept the appearance of really independent private economic powers, along the lines of the nationalists' transition in Taiwan in the mid-1980s (yet so decried in China), will be decisive in enabling the emergence of major private groups. The amount of room for manoeuvre that such firms have *vis-à-vis* the local and central bureaucracies remains after all quite limited, with the administration having no qualms in closing down private firms that threaten local monopolies or throwing into prison bosses of private companies seeking a free rein from the CCP. Liu Yonghao, the managing director of New Hope, readily confesses in interviews to not being a member of the CCP, but he is nonetheless fairly well coopted by the regime into taking his place on the National Consultative Conference of the Chinese People. Without fail, Chinese private businessmen bear witness to the need to have the CCP on their side for their business dealings (Becker, 2000). Private businessmen are represented by two associations, one for individual workers (*geti laodongzhe xiehui*, concerning small private businesses) and the other for private firms (*siying qiye xiehui*), which only operate at a local level, under the watchful eye of the local organs of the CCP. Both these associations are represented nationally by the very official Federation of Industry and Commerce which is, again, very largely controlled by the CCP.

China's entry into the WTO has been beneficial for the corporate governance of private groups, just as it was for the leading state-owned enterprises in category no. 3. Such groups have, like foreign companies, benefited from progressive deregulation in certain still protected activities. Furthermore, the possibility for self-financing through foreign banks (which will be possible after 1 January, 2007) is eagerly awaited by such firms who are mistrustful of the state banks, which, in their eyes, are tantamount to state interference in their management. The directors of New Hope have clearly indicated to us that they were seeking to establish relations with foreign financial institutions. This would enable them to ease domestic political constraints in terms of finance, at the same time as strengthening the outside control of their investment decisions. Future reform of the financial system should, moreover, speed up the merger on the stock exchange between the market in 'A' stocks (reserved for nationals only) and the one in 'B' stocks (open to foreign investors), thereby opening up the possibility of a participation by foreign groups in the capital of the major private companies listed in Shanghai or Shenzhen, or even a taking over of control, which would tighten the disciplinary mechanisms derived from the financial markets.

Conclusion

This review of the state and possible developments in the corporate governance of various categories of Chinese groups allows us to measure, to what extent the emergence of competitive forces in Chinese industry have constituted the most effective factor in controlling the actions of company executives. Given the poor effectiveness of the mechanisms outside the firm (application of laws, labour market, political system), which are supposed to support the functioning of traditional mechanisms (board of directors, supervisory board, remuneration of senior executives) that China is seeking to introduce, competition in the goods and services market should, for several years yet, remain the most effective mechanism for regulating the behaviour of executives. Against this background, China's entry into the WTO have allowed an increase in competition in still protected areas, and thereby push businesses to restructure even more quickly.

Nevertheless, competition alone seems very far from being able to contribute to the emergence of systems of efficient corporate governance. Indeed, it acts *a posteriori*, once the investment decisions have been taken, the market then chooses the most effective units. It is not by chance that China has, since the mid-1990s, been paying the price for investments made in the 1980s and early 1990s, that were badly planned, undersized and ill-adapted to the market. This price to pay is far from being negligible, if we think in terms of the recapitalisation needs of the banking system, which, at the end of the cycle, reflects the quality of investment decisions. A more efficient approach to corporate governance would precisely enable company decision-makers, before taking their decisions, to get some indication of likely success of their investments. Overall, it would allow a better use to be made of national savings (whatever their importance, as in the case of China).

As to the administrative reforms of the state assets management system, we have seen that they are primarily about an internal reorganisation of the bureaucracy's prerogatives, without really changing in any way the efficiency of the mechanisms for controlling companies.

The Chinese government, therefore, needs to work on several fronts at once, not only to respond to the distinct needs arising from the various categories of company, but also to improve the functioning of other disciplinary mechanisms that will come to reinforce the effects of competition. This concerns the pursuit of reforms in the banking and financial sector—and doing so much more fundamentally than hitherto—the fight against regional protectionist measures, an improvement in the labour market, particularly regarding company managers, and the further development of the rule of law and a freer press.

Such reforms go well beyond the mere economic sphere, making them at once more complex and difficult to implement, as they mean forcing change on institutions affecting economic or political interests but that are difficult to budge, all the more so in present political circumstances. This also explains why the economic reforms have now entered a different phase, and one that is more difficult than that of the 1980s, during which time what mattered was to bring reform at the periphery of the economic system, without going to the very core of its organisation (property rights, system of financing, judicial environment, social protection and so on).

In this connection, the future will tell whether a political system, which is systematically holding back the emergence of counter-balancing powers in companies, as it is in civil society, thereby restricting the production of mechanisms for controlling those who wield power in the companies, will be in a position to respond to such challenges.

References

Amsden, A. (1989). *Asia's Next Giant: South Korea and Late Industrialization*, Oxford: Oxford University Press.

Becker, Jasper (2000). *The Chinese*, London, John Murray, p.464.

Blasi, Joseph R., Kroumova Maya and Kruse Douglas (1997). *Kremlin Capitalism: Privatising the Russian Economy*, Ithaca: Cornell University Press, p.249.

Blecher, Marc and Shue Vivienne (1996). *Tethered Deer, Government & Economy in a Chinese County*, Standford: Standford University Press, p.267.

Boillot, Jean-Joseph and Michelon Nicolas (2000). "La Nouvelle géographie économique du monde chinois" ("The New Economic Geography of the Chinese World"), in *Perspectives Chinoises*, No. 59, pp.14-37.

Boone, P., S. Gomulka and R. Layard (ed.) (1998). *Emerging from Communism: Lessons from Russia, China and Eastern Europe*, Cambridge: The MIT Press.

Broadman, Harry (2000). "China's Membership in the WTO and Enterprise Reform: The Challenge for Accession and Beyond", *Discussion Paper*, The World Bank, pp. 21.

Cao, Yanzheng, Qian Yingyi and Barry R. Weingast (1998). "The Sale Goes on: Transforming Small Enterprises in China", in *Transition*, February, pp.5-7.

Ding, X.L. (2000). "The Illicit Asset Stripping of Chinese State Firms", in *The China Journal*, No. 43, January, pp.1-28.

Dong, Ying (1999). "Shandong Zhucheng gufen hezuozhi qiye yanshi fenxi" ("An Analysis of the System of Cooperative Stockholding in the City of Zhucheng in Shandong Province"), in *Gongye Jingji yanjiu*, No. 11, pp.5-11.

Evans, Peter (1995). *Embedded Autonomy. States & Industrial Transformation*, Princeton: Princeton University Press, p.323.

Fields, Karl J. (1995). *Enterprise and the State in Korea and Taiwan*, Cornell: Cornell University Press, p.269.

Granick, David (1990). *Chinese State Enterprises*, Chicago: University of Chicago Press.

Haggard, Stephan and Robert R. Kaufman (1995). *The Political Economy of Democratic Transitions*, Princeton: Princeton University Press, p.391.

He, Qinglian (1998). *Zhongguo de xianjing (China's Pitfall)*, Hong Kong: Mingjing Chubanshe, p.410.

Hirschman, Alfred O. (1970). *Exit, Voice and Loyalty*, Cambridge Mass.: Harvard University Press, p.162.

Huchet, Jean-François (1997). "The 15th Congress and the Reform of Ownership. A Decisive Stage for Chinese State Enterprises", in *China Perspectives*, No. 14, November-December, pp.14-25.

———. (1999). "Concentration and Emergence of Corporate Groups in Chinese Industry", in *China Perspectives*, No. 23, May-June.

———. (1993). "Transferts internationaux de technologie et industrialisation tardive: le cas de l'industrie électronique en République Populaire de Chine", Ph.D., ("International Technology Transfers and Late Industrialisation: The Case of the Electronics Industry in the People's Republic of China") Universite de Rennes I, p.635.

Hussain, Athar and Chen Jian (1999). "Political Economy of Chinese Corporate Groups", paper presented at the international conference, *The Emergence and the Structuring of Corporate Groups in P.R. of China: An International Perspective*, Hong Kong, November 04-05.

Jensen, Michael C. (1997). "The Modern Industrial Revolution, Exit, and the Failure of Internal Control Systems", in D.H. Chew (ed.), *Studies in International Corporate Finance and Governance Systems: A Comparision of the US, Japan and Europe*, Oxford: Oxford University Press, pp.18-37.

Kennedy, Scott (1997). "The Stone Group: State Client or Market Pathbreaker?", in *The China Quarterly*, No. 152, December, pp.746-77.

Lardy, Nicholas R. (1998). *China's Unfinished Economic Revolution*, Washington DC.: Brookings Institution Press, p.304.

Lu, Zhongyuan (1999). "Ruhe fangzhi guoyou zichan yingyun jigou biancheng fanpai gongsi. Shanghai, Wuhan, Shenzhen de shixian ji qishi (How to prevent institutions in charge of State assets from becoming buraucratised companies)", in *Zhongguo gongye jingji*, no. 7, pp.18-20.

Maxfield, Sylvia and Ben Ross Schneider (1997). *Business and the State in Developing Countries*, Ithaca: Cornell University Press, p.348.

McNally, Cristopher (1997). "Shanghai's Way Forward. A Prelude to China's Next Stage of Enterprise Reforms", in *China Perspectives*, No. 14, November-December, pp.33-39.

O'Brien, K.J. (1992). "Bargaining Sucess of Chinese Factories", in *The China Quarterly*, No.132, December, pp. 1086-100.

OECD (2005). *Reforming China's Enterprises*, Paris: OECD p.130.

Oi, Jean (1998). "The Evolution of Local State Corporatism", in Walder A. (ed.), *Zouping in Transition*, Cambridge Mass.: Harvard University Press, pp.35-61.

Rawski, Thomas G. (1995). "Implications of China's Reform Experience", in *The China Quarterly*, No. 144, December, China's Transitional Economy, pp.1150-73.

Sargeson, Sally and Jian Zhang (1999). "Reassessing the Role of the Local State: A Case Study of Local Goverment Interventions in Property Rights Reform in a Hangzhou District", in *The China Journal*, No. 42, July, pp.77-99.

Shirk, Susan L. (1993). *The Political Logic of Economic Reform in China*, Berkeley: University of California Press, p.399.

Stark, David (1997). "Recombinant Property in East European Capitalism", in Grabher G. and D. Stark (ed.), *Restructuring Networks in Post-Socialism*, Oxford: Oxford University Press, pp.36-69.

Steinfeld, Edward S. (1998). *Forging Reform in China. The Fate of State-Owned Industry*, Cambridge: Cambridge University Press, p.300.

Unger, Jonathan and A. Chan (1999). "Inheritors of the Boom: Private Enterprise and the Role of Local Government in a Rural South China Township", in *The China Journal*, No. 42, July, pp.45-74.

Weitzman, M.L. and Xu Chenggang (1993). *Chinese Township Village Enterprises as Vaguely Defined Co-operatives*, London: Development Economics Research Programme, London School of Economics.

White, Gordon, Jude Howel and Shang Xiaoyuan (1996). *In Search of Civil Society: Market Reform and Social Change in Contemporary China*, Oxford: Clarendon Press Oxford University Press, p.241.

Woo, Wing T. (1998). "Why China Grew?", in P. Boone, S. Gomulka and R. Layard (ed.), *Emerging from Communism. Lessons from Russia, China and Eastern Europe*, Cambridge: The MIT Press.

3

Economic Reforms, Privatisations and Public-Private Developments in India since 1991

JOËL RUET

There has been, since 1991, more than a decade of economic reforms in India, following their rhythm, gradually, beyond political changes. This distance provides the opportunity for a critical assessment. Since 1991, two population censuses have been conducted, thus also allowing a focus on the social front. Despite India's population that is still predominantly rural in nature, we, however, here aim at characterising the structural modes of regulation of the Indian economy, its cities-based economics and the evolution of its firms. We will further lay a wager, moreover, on the dynamic emergence of India as an economic power, *via* its cities and services. In other words, this chapter will concentrate on 'India' seen as urban India, more than on 'Bharat' (India, in Hindi), the rural and traditional India. The earlier development model, based on public expenditures under a technical, ultimately not so people-oriented paradigm, had reached its limits. The beginnings of a change in the paradigm of development are already visible, while the consequences on the rural world remains a major question mark for the coming decade. Looking beyond a rapid survey of the macroeconomic figures (section 1), what is the reality of the public sector, that still importantly shapes the economy (section 2)?, and how does the private sector start articulating upon the deficiencies of the earlier model (section 3)? Finally, what are the wagers of reallocation in the India of tomorrow, which the emergence of the private sector gives rise to or strengthens (section 4)? If 'India' is changing, how deep has 'Bharat', started getting integrated in the consuming society patterns?

Looking at Macroeconomic Facts Alone

'Facts', or a Classic Interpretation which Creates its Own Meaning

After the first 10 years of reforms, in 2001-02, the per capita GDP in India was $ 480. The total GDP of the country was about half that of China. India therefore remains, on an average, a poor country, and moreover overwhelmingly rural (70 per cent of the population). But this should not mask certain disparities which sometimes throw a veil over what are some veritable trump cards specific to urban India. The successive central governments since 1991 have pursued more or less an active policy of reforms. This policy was officially launched following a foreign exchange crisis during the first part of 1991. Before 1991, India's economy had been, by and large, a closed economy with a policy based on import substitution. The banking sector, including private banks, was very largely controlled in order to finance, at subsidised rates, public investments in what were called the priority sectors, leading to a large 'ousting effect', that is, a siphoning of investment for them, at the expense of other sectors, which suffered from investment penury. This analysis, expressed in terms of investment availability for the private sector, has structured the reforms, from 1991 onwards, through policies of opening up of imports, reduction of taxes, and incentives to private investment, both foreign and Indian. What has been their result?

The reforms were initiated subsequent to the foreign reserves crisis, and India has indeed succeeded in controlling the problem of its debt, whose ratio to the GDP has crossed from 37.7 per cent in 1992 to 21.4 per cent in 2001. Inflation, which was of the order of 15 per cent in 1991-92, seems to have been contained, and has remained since 1997 at 4 per cent, although it did shoot up suddenly in 1998-1999 to 13.1 per cent! The public deficit of the government of the Indian Union ('the Centre') was to the extent of 8.3 per cent of the GNP in 1991-92. This came down to 5.9 per cent of the GNP in 1995-1996 (World Bank, 1996), but has stabilised since then, to remain at this level. Moreover, the combined public deficit of the federal government and of the governments of the states within the federation is higher and has structurally stabilised at 10 per cent of the GNP (and, if we add to it the deficit of the public sector enterprises, it is structurally even higher at 11 per cent). And this is so without taking into account the total deficit of the public enterprises, only a part of which is covered by subsidies budgeted within both the central budget and the state government budgets. But above all, we are witnessing a very marginal growth in exports, and the expected foreign direct investment (FDI) has not materialised,[1] partly due to the complexity of the administrative system and partly to the absence of any clear rules on the matter.[2] The FDI, initially very small, at $ 150 million in 1991, crossed over to $ 2 billion in 1995-1996 (World Bank, 1996) but has remained at just $ 2.3 billion in 2000-2001. But this continues to be structurally small. Thus, while it has soared upwards in countries such as China, it has stagnated in absolute terms as regards India, and has hence, by comparison, fallen, relatively speaking.[3] Generally speaking, after a few good recovery years, there has only been a 5.5 per cent growth on an average since 1998 and it will be comparable for the financial year 2002-03. Hence, despite the reforms, we are not very far from the '*Hindu* rate of growth' (around 4 per cent) of the earlier period.

Thus, on the macroeconomic level, the reforms, undertaken following a liquidity crisis arising out of the fiscal situation, have been reduced largely to the management of the obverse side of taxation, through a distinct reduction of transfers from the Centre to the states, but without a real change in the fiscal or financial paradigm (with a reduction of almost 25 per cent of transfers between 1990-91 and 1996-1997, which have stabilised since then). The states were not able to generate new revenues through tax reforms, and constitutionally they have little latitude in external financing, while not disposed to structurally lower the subsidies they distribute. This constraint has thus been translated for a large part in a reduction of investments in favour of short term expenditures. Thus, the investments of the states went down from 2.5 per cent of the GDP in 1990-91, to 2 per cent in 1997-1998, and have remained stable since then, for a total level of expenses

1. Domestic investment also is declining, as is demonstrated in the recession noted in the industrial production of capital goods for the last year.
2. For example, in the electrical sector which is considered as a priority sector, Parikh (1999) points out that in the course of a few years the institutional pattern has passed through the stages of memorandums with the states, to open tender invitations, to tenders guaranteed by the states or the Centre, finally to the study of government to government bilateral cooperations, in its last form.
3. This being moreover a regional phenomenon: in 1991, South Asia's share represented 60 per cent of the total foreign direct investments in Asia, but came down to no more than 20 per cent in 1999 (RIS, 2001).

remaining stable at around 16 per cent of the GDP (MEF, 1998; RBI, 1998). Thus, India is macro economically stable, but the establishment of the financial and fiscal conditions required for a rapid and sustainable development has not yet been initiated. The care devoted to some macroeconomic indicators has ended up by creating its own space of coherence and justification ('India has stabilised its inflation', 'India has reduced its deficit and restructured its debt'), without this discourse being related to sectoral evolutions (which are discussed in sections 2 and 3 of this chapter, and which are, more than the financial and tax systems) the real determinants of change in the economic organisation of the country and its system of accumulation. Let us demonstrate how the sole macroeconomic interpretation leads to a cloaking of the developmental paradigm initiated in India.

An Interpretation which Ignores More Complex Realities

While they were triggered by the financial crisis, the reforms were actually long overdue, and Manmohan Singh, the then Finance Minister who formulated them, acknowledged subsequently that it was the crisis that had served as a catalyst. For, while the earlier system of accumulation had enabled, over a period of 40 years, the setting up and the integration of a national economy, a relative industrialisation, and had, more than anything else, put an end structurally to the problem of food security, it had been very largely based on a controlled economy. We are not referring so much to the influence of the planned nature of Indian development, which has been vastly overstated, as to the working of its economy. Indeed, it was and remains largely coordinated by discretionary interventions conducted by the state at different levels (Ruet, 1999 and 2001b). It had reached its limits in several key sectors (cf. Ruet 2001c, 2001d, as regards electricity, Ruet and Zérah, 2001, for water). Thus, in the early 1980s, the members of the Parliament, for instance, had a discretionary budget for the allocation of cement, steel, even watches, with waiting lists and the consequent building up of a constituency. It was this system which Bibek Debroy has called, "Indian socialism or Soviets without electricity". But, more structurally, Indian development has been characterised conceptually by the administered control over budgeted expenditures, more than by a real management of public investments. Indeed, the study of the strategies of decision-making in several 'utilities' and public enterprises shows that the projects revolve around expenses, and that no effort is made, either on the level of the project evaluation, on the level of its maintenance, or on the level of its operation, to arrive at a convergence between the expenses allocated and the returns achieved. In other words, no costs and benefits ratio is established, and hence there is no investment as such (cf. Ruet 2001e).[4] This functioning is moreover administered in the sense that it is totally subjected to centralised procedures and in fine subject to the discretion of the state, which moreover does not possess structurally any information system integrating costs and benefits, nor physical quantities of public goods or services and financial amounts. This has an immediate practical implication, in the sense that preference is systematically given to expenses on new infrastructure as compared to a management/maintenance of the existing one. Thus, there exists in the overall fields managed by the State, considerable scope for creation of internal resources, which are often politically neutral in terms of implementation (cf. for instance Planning Commission, 2000; Ruet, 2000; Ruet and Zérah, 2001).

The public sector is structured on a model of expenditure. Its crisis is therefore always analysed in terms of absence of resources. Given the poor informational framework available in the public sector, never based on costs, the development of internal resources is structurally neglected. To sum up, we have a paradoxical situation. On the one hand, a macroeconomic policy of reduction of expenditures and of recourse to private investment is not capable by itself to bring out the structural deficiencies of the earlier development model. However, on the other hand, such a policy is mechanically supported because of the expenditure-centred functioning of the public system. The reporting, the way the decision-making process is organised, converge in underlining the need for funds at the expense of any other line of explanation for the public sector's failures. The structure itself of the public sector, through these reports, produces a set of the very 'narratives' sustaining the idea that funds only are required, and that a macroeconomic policy may be enough. However, what this account does not reveal is why the private sector should participate in the

4. During a conversation, an executive in charge of water management in the public system in Kolkata, asked me in reply to one of my questions on the investment policy of the city: "But what exactly do you mean by 'investment'?"

public sector (section 2), nor what the private sector is doing in the meantime (section 3).

Changing the Paradigm for the Public Sector

The earlier section has already given an idea of the obstacles inherent in a controlled organisation of the public sector. Let us re-examine for a moment the classic narration.

An Impossible Privatisation

There are 210 public enterprises, or more precisely 'public sector undertakings',[5] which are dependent on the central government, and 1020 which are dependent on the states. During the last five years of the supposedly 'pro-privatisation' BJP government at the Centre, six firms under the Union Government have been privatised, and in another 46, the shares held by the state have been reduced while still remaining the majority shareholder. Privatisation at the level of the states has been negligible. The 2001-02 Budget had fixed an ambitious objective in the matter of privatisation, since disinvestments were to be of the order of Rs. 120 billion (around $ 2.5 billion), of which Rs. 70 billion were to be used for reforms in the remaining public enterprises, and Rs. 50 billion for the social sector and for the infrastructure. By the middle of the financial year, hardly 2 per cent of this objective had been achieved and some severe setbacks had been experienced, among these being Air India which found no takers, or the exit of the American firm, AES, from a regional distribution company in the state of Orissa, privatised two years earlier in incredible circumstances. [6] By the end of the year, the achieved result was of 47 per cent only of the target. This marked the

5. Indeed, independent of their legal status, their very nature as enterprises is debatable, if we consider that, limited rationality apart, the concept around which decision making is structured in an enterprise is primarily the cost, whereas these organisations are based on political arbitrages between heterogeneous objectives. This is the definition of an administration, cf. Banfield (1976) and this is so in the case of India (cf. Ruet, 2001, 2001b).

6. A first round of bidding had shown the interest of few companies, which finally retracted. Then a second round of negotiations began, to know if AES, already present in generation, could bid. Further, AES negotiated the securitisation of financial supporting schemes from the government of Orissa. After the privatisation, it again renegotiated the timing of these disbursements with the government, to finally resign from the activity. An *ex post* analysis shows that, in any case, the guarantees given by the government were neither sufficient nor credible enough given the information which finally emerged after the take-over.

end of the privatisation policy. In the field of energy, the opening up of the sector was badly conducted, as everybody acknowledges today. From 1950 to 1996, the electrical sector had represented from 17 to 20 per cent of the total five-year plans expenditures (Das *et al.*, 2000). The reform in this sector has been restricted nevertheless to opening up production to the private sector, without restructuring the distribution of electricity. In 1998, after seven years of reforms and opening up to investment, a production capacity of 1.4 GW only had come from private projects (out of a total installed capacity of 89 GW), as mentioned by Das *et al.* (2000).

Standing Back to Look at the Problems of the Public Sector

The Indian public has the impression today that its enterprises are being 'sold for a song', as well as the more justified impression that the few buyers are not really ready to invest. The overall rationality of the process of privatisation hence needs to be restated. Keeping in mind their present controlled working, it is practically impossible for investors to valorise many PSUs; their value is therefore a matter perfectly impossible to base on the 'fundamentals' of economics (cf. Ruet, 2001d). As Bibek Debroy (2000) has said, "Disinvestment has been driven by the tactical compulsion of financing the fiscal deficit. This is perhaps why the word privatisation has not been used until recently, the word disinvestment tending to imply a soft choice". Debroy rightly mentions that improved efficiency, competition, as well as the opening up and development of a capital market should be the other determinants for disinvestment. In this truncated context, potential investors have simply not found the disinvestment policies to be credible. With just a few exceptions discussed in the next section, the Indian State has not been able to establish a comfortable relationship with investors.[7] It has not been able to make an impact in the public sector either, since the income from the few sales has not been reinvested in the concerned sectors.

In this context, a reappraisal needs to be made of the relationship between the public and the private sector. After all, it is not so much private investment that the state needs, but rather a change in its

7. We can regularly read in the press, for instance, assertions on the subject 'of the private sector not having fulfilled its commitments', demonstrating a misreading of its working. It is not because the Government or the Planning Commission desires that investment is made; this only works with a controlled expenditure...

methods of management, more likely to bring about a change of paradigm in the management of resources. Indeed, in the Indian public sector, it is not the decision-makers who are a problem, but rather the processes of decision-making. For instance, 40 per cent of the executives in the private sector Reliance Group, have come from the public sector where, according to Mukesh Ambani, CEO of the Reliance Group, "they were not allowed the freedom to manage and to lead." It is not an issue of proposing the private sector as a solution *per se*, but simply of taking note of the fact that the public sector is no longer providing its services or its products in satisfactory conditions, that its users and clients have to devise strategies to confront the very expensive shortages and have to turn, in fact, towards the private sector or the illegal appropriation of public resources (corruption), and finally, that the indiscriminate state subsidies are actually regressive in the sense that they benefit largely those sections of society which have the means to deploy their own techniques of supply from the state. A plethora of studies have been made on these points (cf. among others, TERI, 1999; Ruet and Zérah, 2001). In this context, though far from being ideologically-inclined towards privatisation, we should not rule out either the forms of decentralisation of the decision-making power (Mishra, 2002; Ranganathan, 2002), or the forms of contractual partnership in management (Ruet 2001e and 2002a).

The challenge to be met is therefore that of management. All the more so, as the Indian public enterprises are called upon either to evolve global strategies to be able to compete with globalised enterprises, or to sustain the economic take-off of India. The good news is that now, after a decade of limited reforms having met with failure, the economic analysis of the Indian public sector has made some progress. There is a greater awareness of its complexity and of the impact of the various solutions; a learning process has taken place.

The Private Sector as an Aid or Driving Force of 'Development'?

Let us discuss the way the private sector has evolved during the past decade as well as its linkage with the public sector. Let us bring out the difference between the communications and information technologies (IT) sector on the one hand, and the sectors of industry and the conventional services on the other hand.

Two Sociologies of Indian Enterprises

In the last 10 years, certain sectors of production or services have indeed witnessed a good deal of development; automobiles and the hotel industry being the most visible ones. But the perspective for the overall economy remains one of moderate development. While a market has developed in the big cities, it has been very largely catered to by imports (from China among others), and outside of the largest cities, there is no trace of the much talked about 'middle class' supposedly consisting of 100 to 200 million inhabitants.[8] With the measures permitting Indian enterprises to invest abroad remaining limited and still in the process of formulation, the financial structures remaining largely covered by banks which maintain links with the State, Indian capitalism conserves to a great extent its structure of: (i) family, (ii) political power base, (iii) relatively centralised and hierarchised conglomerates, steeped in a sea of microenterprises (Dorin, *et al.*, 2000). These enterprises support the setting up of some reforms such as the removal of controls over enterprises, and an end to the 'licence *raj*', i.e. control through licences delivered by the administration. This part of the reforms has moreover been advocated and urged since long by Indian employers who saw the opportunity opening up to them in 1991 to tread this path. However, employers remain *in fine* satisfied with a slow opening up of the country, as it gives them time to launch into a restructuring of their finances and of their activities, pre-empting the too great exposure to external fusion-acquisitions that too rapid an opening up would render probable. Conglomerate groups, which have evolved this way because of the policies for restriction on monopolies, and which continue to be a peculiar trait of Indian capitalism, have not yet been restructured. Their present incompatibility with the forms of capitalism worldwide, necessitates a transition period for them. The possibility of developing a real banking industry is something that industrialists and bankers are still hoping and praying for.

The telecommunications sector, for its part, has undergone a complete transformation. The opening up of telecommunications has

---

8. Which is hardly surprising, when we consider that these are found in the 50 odd cities in India claiming to have 'millionaires' in their population, and that in all these cities the rate of urban poverty is of the order of 30 per cent, and that in the remaining 70 per cent, everyone does not belong, not by a long shot, to the 'middle class'.

been slow, lively debates have accompanied the working of the regulatory authority, and the original telecommunications services remained for a long time associated with the regulatory and licence delivering authority. But today, this sector has become truly competitive, prices have been considerably reduced, and the mobile phone has made an important entry, in relative terms.[9] This has been made possible thanks to the technological revolution of the last 10 years, which has led to a considerable lowering of the costs of infrastructure and has put an end, the world over, to the dynamics and the character of natural monopoly that this activity had taken on. It is in the process of recomposition, and the industrial strategies relating to the local loop and connection to long distance communications or to local internet are in the process of being formulated (Bomsel and Ruet, 2001).

Within a few years, *via* software followed by services, the information technology sector has truly emerged as an export sector and has spectacularly 'climbed up the value-chain'. Since 1994, the growth of this sector has varied between 40 to 50 per cent per year. It had a turnover of $ 8.7 billion in 2000-01 and is expected to reach $ 12 billion in 2001-02 (around 2 per cent of the GDP). NASSCOM (National Association of Software and Services Companies) has set for itself, the objective of achieving $ 90 billion in 2008. While this sector initially undertook semi-skilled sub-contracting, the quality of services and consultancy it offers today are at par with the world level. Certain 'start-ups' adopt right from their creation an absolutely world-wide strategy and thus contribute to the emergence of a perfectly innovative model of growth of the enterprise. Thus, they start off right from the beginning with a contribution from venture capitalists who are American (or of Indian origin who have grown wealthy in the USA), and contracts with large American software, telecommunications and consultancy firms. Their internal organisation and decision-making also follow a model that is new to India: a flat hierarchical structure, organised in a modular fashion, project-wise. The IT sector has not only acquired an undeniable maturity and world class but has, by itself, led to a chain effect on services, housing, the hotel industry and telecommunications, as is demonstrated, for

9. In absolute terms, let us not forget that we are talking of a country in which just three per cent of the homes possess a private telephone.

instance, in the booming development of cities such as Bangalore, Hyderabad, or even Gurgaon, in the suburbs of Delhi (Bomsel and Ruet, 2001).

Bureaucrats and Entrepreneurs

The IT companies avail of state support for their development. Conversely, this sector in turn can promote some of the state policies. Indeed, the Indian government has set up the Software Technology Parks of India (STPI) so as to help the development of the sector, along with the grant of some tax exemptions. This is an important tool in urban development, since 18 zones have already been identified for setting up an STPI. Conversely, the governments of some states which have demonstrated a political will, have been able to reap dividends: an interesting example is that of the southern state of Andhra Pradesh, whose capital, Hyderabad, has rediscovered its economic dynamism. The model adopted by this state is a very attractive one: indeed, the government of Andhra Pradesh has invested only 20 per cent in the construction of 'Cyberabad'—the STPI of Hyderabad—the rest having been financed by private enterprises. Moreover, it can be estimated that for every job created in the IT sector, four or five others follow in the conventional sectors.[10] Thus, the new economy is basically financed by the development of the networks, and not through a model of planned expenses. Can this be transposed on to other sectors? And, can it constitute a new model of development?

Let us examine the possible involvement of the IT sector in the management of municipal services, as well as the general issue of the overhaul of the public service in association with the private sector. The wagers of reallocation allied to this are discussed in the following section. On these matters India and its cities can be considered, along with other countries or cities (Johannesburg, for example), as a laboratory in which interesting experiments are being conducted and in which some innovative models of co-operation between the public and the private sectors will evolve. The first issue at stake can be illustrated by the experience of the Bangalore Agenda Task Force (BATF), based in the capital of the southern state of Karnataka, which

10. Conversation, STPI, Hyderabad.

is moreover an absolutely first rate IT district (cf. Bomsel and Ruet, 2001). The BATF is an initiative set up by the largest IT firms of the district with the objective, in coordination with the government of Karnataka, to help the Bangalore municipality in determining the specifications, the formulation, and the production of a master plan for the development of the city. This help takes on a multiplicity of forms: it ranges from the regular (biannual) organisation of public meetings with representatives of the civil society and of the public services to give priority to short term measures and to define long term objectives, to the financial participation in certain projects, along with making manpower available for conducting certain studies. Launched in end 2000, the BATF is still by and large at an experimental stage, but its promoters are already toying with the idea of revamping the municipal services in Johannesburg, and are planning to serve as models for the other cities of India. According to one of those in charge of the BATF, over and above the institutional and financial support, one of the major assets of this experiment is the possibility for private enterprises, to develop a much more flexible management than the one conducted by any administration. For example, when a specific expertise is required for a project, this framework allows for a flexibility of recruitment and decision-making which the strictly public framework does not provide. Thus, while waiting for the necessary internal reforms of the administration and the necessary change in the paradigm of development, such experiments can *a minima* ensure a smooth transition. Another example of the back-up role played by the IT sector, and which is common to all the Indian megalopolises, is the setting up of new models of training institutes dependent on private structures. Training enterprises are being created, with a growth model varying from a traditional teaching but imparted through computerised aids, or distance learning, to the management of training institutes meant to ensure a prerecruitment, or again agreements entered into with existing universities. At the end of it all, it is the IT enterprises which provide a growing part of the production of higher education required to satisfy the demand (Bomsel and Ruet, 2001). Thus, on the basis of a more flexible internal organisation, the IT sector participates effectively in the necessary reforms of the public sector, by giving it an impetus as much as by temporarily marching ahead of it.

But the small-scale private sector also can have a role to play. Let us examine for instance, some organisational and institutional innovations which have come into place during the last two years with regard to the distribution and purification of water in Chennai (formerly Madras), in a situation of extreme water shortage. They hinge around: (i) the delegation of power, internally, (ii) in interface with the private sector, the delegation of the operation of some pumping stations, and agreements entered into with private water sellers, and (iii) outside the public sphere, a real segmentation of the distribution of water in an independent manner, with the creation of a private market for water. Several of these measures have led to a greater availability of water for the inhabitants as well as the economies for the local municipal 'authorities' in charge of water distribution.[11] While in detail, the structural linkage of these measures may be somewhat restricted (Ruet and Zérah, 2001), this experiment proves here again that under certain specific conditions (here again, let us not be dogmatic[12]), the private sector can play a role in the matter of reforms in the public sector.

To what extent these measures are propagated, or on the other hand neglected in favour of more 'conventional' ventures, will determine the form of the private/public linkages in India, and will determine, in a sense, the effectiveness of the reforms undertaken by the state. The speed and intensity with which the 'new sociology of the Indian private sector' will spread to the rest of society will also constitute the wagers of reallocations.

The Wagers of Reallocation: India, the 'Urban Poor', and 'Bharat'

Let us return to the broad indicators. In 10 years, from 1991 to 2001, the literacy rate has crossed over from 52 to 65 per cent. The poverty rate has, at the same time, decreased from 36 to 24 per cent. Yashwant Sinha, when he was Finance Minister, had given the pledge that a sustained growth of 7 per cent over the next 10 years will bring

---

11. Administratively: a 'Board'.
12. In particular, and on this precise example, one can praise the involvement of local enterprise, but express reservations on certain modalities of contract management with international firms. This is incorrect in other cases; in short, pragmatism, based on a solid institutional analysis, is a must.

the poverty rate down to below the 5 per cent threshold. The Tenth Five Year Plan is, however, less optimistic, as it plans to reduce poverty rate from 26 per cent in 2002 down to 21 per cent in 2007 (and this, by considering a non-credible economic growth of 8 per cent). Over and above the blinked view of growth, what is certain is that in those places where it is seen today, that is to say in the richer sections of the cities of 'India', it has shifted conceptually from expenses to investments, from the rural areas to the cities, from a certain balance between states to a growing imbalance.

Indians of the Cities and Indians of the Fields: India versus Bharat?

As already mentioned, India has a predominantly rural population. Farmers account for 67 per cent of the working population, but produce only 30 per cent of the wealth (Landy, 1993), in a situation in which the green revolution had already engendered a 'social and regional polarisation' (Landy, 1996). Indeed, the green revolution has brought benefits to the irrigable areas, and within these, to those peasants who had the means to invest in irrigation and in the new techniques. Ten years of reforms not centred around the rural world have not remedied this situation. For the Indian state, the problem of the rural areas is simple; it is financial and fiscal. For instance, the annual deficit of the electrical sector alone may represent twice the budget on health and education (this is so in Andhra Pradesh). When, moreover, its teachers no longer take their classes, or its hospitals practically no longer have an operational budget, the states have the choice between undertaking cosmetic measures (which they generally do), or radically innovative ones whose results will be known a few years hence. Thus, Andhra Pradesh is giving a push forward to 'e-governance', whose effects are taking time to penetrate the countryside, and Madhya Pradesh (Central India) has launched its Education Guarantee Scheme. The latter consists in recruiting and giving on the spot training to some of the villagers who then impart primary education on a minimum salary.

Whatever be the success of such measures, and even if the state governments were to search for some sponsors (the Centre, the World Bank), it seems that implicitly the political choice has been made: the budget allocations for the rural areas will remain minimal as long as additional resources are not found. Will they be forthcoming from the cities (the tax collection mechanisms are quite poor)? And will it be possible to convince the cities to agree to a reallocation? At present, it seems that the only economic chain effects are confined to local limits: while the large megalopolises are visibly changing, the rural areas remain as they are. And, while the population of the cities is growing rapidly, there is no massive rural exodus, and the population of the countryside is also growing (Landy, 1996). However, even if 67 per cent of the population lives in rural areas, one has to notice that only 30 per cent derives its revenues from the agricultural sector, the remainder being involved in the small scale industries. For this sector, there is not necessarily a 'trickle-down' effect from liberalisation or globalisation (they are rather becoming more exposed to non-tariff competition), but they, in reverse, do contribute to the industrial and equipment demand, providing a multiplicator factor at the macroeconomic level. Indeed, the rather exceptional growth of the year 2003-04 (8 per cent) is largely explained by the good monsoon, not only directly through the agricultural sector but also indirectly through the rural demand. Finally, rural areas start constituting markets for the national economy, as the NCAER (2003) survey shows.

The Core of the Cities

Simultaneously, while the cities in India account for only 28 per cent of the population, they produce 50 per cent of the wealth, although they shelter 100 million of the urban poor. Sheltering the largest amount of wealth along with the largest amount of poverty, the cities thus constitute the wager of the social contract of the nation. Delhi, for instance, witnesses an annual influx of 5,00,000 additional inhabitants. Delhi attempts its redevelopment through the creation of satellite towns (Dupont, 2001), but while doing so neglects to keep intact, in tandem, the social fabric of the present Delhi (Tarlo, 2000; Soni, 2000). True, the model adopted in the 1960s of small industry on the scale of the home, drawing its inspiration from Japan's experience, has reached its limits. It is in the process of being submerged by the arrival of manufactured goods arising out of globalisation. Nevertheless, this model of development has generated a very large geographic intermingling between social classes, and has given rise to the appearance of economic services in the chinks created by the deficiencies of the public machinery. The legitimate policy of reorienting this model, is actually being done today, in accordance with a process of social dualisation and of eviction of the poor towards the peripheral areas, which revives the now outmoded principle of the 1930s, i.e., the garden cities in the English manner. That is to say a city devoid of a socio-economic fabric, and hence, *in fine* devoid of an economic fabric. Over and above matters of policy, the management of Indian cities is moreover hindered, also by the poor coordination of a bureaucratic machinery with its unnecessary multiplicity of administrative levels. Thus, Delhi, for instance is jointly administered by three municipalities or organisations (one of which shelters an army base), the Delhi state government and the Union government. To be illustrative on the impact, in order to simply set up a bus stop on an existing line, the Delhi state government is obliged to refer the matter to four Union ministries, then coordinate with the municipalities.[13] Thus, in the Indian cities and their satellites, a new class of the well-to-do is emerging, with probably a new identity (Ruet, 2002b), but the social bond is becoming weaker and *a minima* is forming anew.

From One State to the Next

How does the matter stand, on the countrywide scale, between the various states in India? The decrease in the transfer of allocations from the centre leads one to question the economic convergence of the different states. Indeed, Cachin and Sahay (1996) have shown that these transfers have enabled in the long term (1960-1995) to reduce the differences in the per capita income between states, despite the divergence in the per capita gross domestic product. Today, the historic situations are evolving imperceptibly. While Maharashtra (capital, Mumbai) remains industrially active, Tamil Nadu (capital, Chennai) has overtaken it in terms of investment. Bangalore, as also Hyderabad, are able to attract large investments. Apart from any hazardous prospective assessment of these end evolutions, we note over the last 10 years a correlation between composite growth and the per capita GDP. Thus the richest states continue to get richer more rapidly. Nevertheless, certain states are going about the process of

13. For a study of the impact of administrative red tape on water management in Calcutta, see Ruet and Zérah, 2001.

'catching-up', like West Bengal (capital, Calcutta) or Kerala (capital, Thiruvananthapuram), which, with an initial per capita GDP level twice smaller, have witnessed a composite growth over 10 years equivalent to that of Maharashtra, while Punjab (capital, Chandigarh) which was the richest, demonstrates a growth half that of these states (MEF, 1998). Since then, slowdown in Maharashtra's industrial growth has been confirmed. The Indian states have begun to compete with each other.

Conclusion

The impression of economic and social change given by the Indian megalopolises is, therefore, both qualitatively true and corresponds to a radical change in some of the elements of Indian society, and at the same time quantitatively overestimated on the scale of the country. That is how the macroeconomy ('the scale of the country') is overshadowing the microeconomy.

In terms of balanced distribution, and in an India whose cohesion is secured politically only through the power of an idea which today evolves due to centrifugal forces (Khilnani, 1997), the mediation of the bond between the economic and the social has been affected by a ratio of production based on the massive integration of a manpower producing small goods and carrying out small services. The dimension of geographic, near intermingling with the middle classes marked their social acceptance of what was then nothing other than labour. In an urban India which wants to ignore the workers in its shanty towns, and in which new ideas are being formulated (Ruet 2002a; 2002c), the persistence of this social bond requires to be reassessed.

References

Banfield, E.C. (1976). "Corruption as a Feature of Governmental Organization", *Journal of Law & Economics*, December.

Bomsel, Olivier and Joël Ruet (2001). "Digital India: Report on the Indian IT Industry", CFCE Study Report, CERNA, Paris & CSH, New Delhi, pp.170.

Boyer, Robert and Yves Saillard (1995). Un précis de la régulation, Chapter 5, pp.58-68, in *Théorie de la régulation, l'état des savoirs*, Boyer and Saillard (ed.), La Découverte, Paris, pp.568.

Cachin, Paul and Ratna Sahay (1996). "Regional Economic Growth and Convergence in India", *Finance & Development Journal*, IMF, March.

Das, Anjana; Jyoti Parikh and Kirit S. Parikh (2000). "Power, the Critical Infrastructure", in Kirit S. Parikh (ed.), *India Development Report*, New Delhi: Oxford University Press, pp.113-124.

Debroy, Bibek (2000). "Privatisation in India, Issue on Privatisation in South Asia", *Journal Liberal Times*, Vol. VII(2), New Delhi, pp.9-16.

Dorin, Flamant, Lachaier and Vaugier-Chatterjee (2000). *Le patronat en Inde: contours sociologiques des acteurs et des pratiques*, June, New Delhi: CSHi.

Dupont, Véronique (2001). "Noida: nouveau pôle industriel ou ville satellite de Delhi? Le projet des planificateurs, ses failles et son devenir", *Revue Tiers Monde*, No.165, December, pp.189-212.

Giraud, Pierre-Noël (1996). L'inégalité du monde, Gallimard, Folio essays, Paris.

———. (1998). *Economie: le Grand Satan?*, Paris: Editions Textuel.

Khilnani, Sunil (1997). *The Idea of India*, UK: Penguin.

Landy, Frédéric (1993). "Campagnes et villes de l'Inde: deux cultures antagonistes", *Cahiers des Sciences Humaines*, Vol. 29 (2-3), Paris, pp.313-332.

———. (1996). "Réforme agraire et révolution verte: l'impossible synthèse indienne", *Cahiers Agriculture*, Vol. 5, Paris, pp.271-81.

Lazarus, Sylvain (1996). "Anthropologie du nom", *Collection 'Des travaux'*, Paris: Le Seuil, p.249.

MEF (1998). "Les Etats indiens: finances publiques et développement", Note of the Economic and Financial Mission, French Embassy in India, New Delhi, October, p.32.

Mishra, R.K. (2002). "Internal Audit as a Reform Technique in Power Sector in India", in Joel Ruet (ed.), *Organisational Restructuration of SEBs in India: Decentralisation, Information Building, Profit Centre and Management Contracts*, New Delhi: Manohar Publishing (to be published in), p.15.

Morris, Sebastian (2002). "Restructuring Gujarat Electricity Board: Outline of a Strategy and Proposal for Action, in Joel Ruet (ed.), *Organisational Restructuration of SEBs in India: Decentralisation, Information Building, Profit Centre and Management Contracts*, New Delhi: Manohar Publishing (to be published in), p.21.

Parikh, K. (1999). *India Development Report 1999-2000*, New Delhi: Oxford University Press, India, xiv+pp.300.

Planning Commission (2000). *Annual Report on the Working of State Electricity Boards for the Year 1999-2000*, Government of India.

Ranganathan, V. (2002). "Profit Centres as Instruments of Performance Enhancement of SEBs", in Joel Ruet (ed.), *Organisational Restructuration of SEBs in India: Decentralisation, Information Building, Profit Centre and Management Contracts*, New Delhi: Manohar Publishing (to be published in), p.8.

Reserve Bank of India (RBI) (1998). "Finance of State Governments", *RBI Bulletin*, February, New Delhi.

RIS (2001). "Foreign Direct Investment, Regional Economic Integration and Introduction of Restructuring in Asia: Trends, Patterns, and Prospects", by Nagesh Kumar, *Occasional Paper No.* 62, New Delhi: Research & Information System for the Non-aligned and Other Developing Countries, p. 51.

Ruet, Joël (1999). *Administrations for Sale: The State Electricity Boards; Private vs. Public "Entreprisation*, Paris: Cahiers du CERNA.

———. (2000). "Investment Needs and Possible Incomes in Indian Power Sector to Bridge the Energy Gap", Working Paper, *Indian Economic Journal* (to be published), New Delhi.

———. (2001a). "Winners and Losers of the Reform of SEBs", An Organisational Study, *Occasional Paper*, New Delhi: CSH, p.85.

———. (2001b). "The Future of State Owned Companies: Is Privatisation the Answer?", paper presented at the *IIPA-CSH Conference on Administrative Reforms*, January, New Delhi.

———. (2001c). La mondialisation limitée du secteur électrique: de la prééminence des etats au retour relatif du centre, in Chaudhuri (ed.), *Questions d'échelle: du mondial au local*, Paris: Basudeb and Frédéric Landy, Collection Sciences Sociales, CNRS.

———. (2001d). Le secteur électrique en Inde: réforme libérale ou persistance d'une forme de développement à l'indienne?, *Revue Tiers-Monde* No.165, December, Paris.

———. (2001e). La réforme du secteur électrique de l'Inde: administrations à vendre; Transformer les State Electricity Boards en entreprises, Doctorate Thesis CERNA, Ecole des Mines, Paris, p.349.

———. (2001f). "A New Paradigm for the Indian Power Sector: Going Beyond the 'Silver Bullet' Privatisation", paper presented at the International Conference *Indo-French Perspectives on Privatisation*, Hyderabad, March 2000.

———. (2002a). "Information Technologies and Development: Clusters as Economic Policy Tools for India", article presented at the International Conference on *Communication for Development*, 6-8 February, Madras University, p.17.

———. (2002b). "Delegation of Power in SEBs Under Management Contracts",in Joel Ruet (ed.), *Organisational Restructuration of SEBs in India: Decentralisation, Information Building, Profit Centre and Management Contracts*, New Delhi: Manohar Publishing (to be published in), p. 23.

———. (2002c). "A Trans-regional Network of E-Identity; Information Technology Clusters in New India", to be published in 2002 in the proceedings of the conference on *Material Vitality and Imagined Authenticities*, 14-15 December, Jadavpur University, Kolkata.

Ruet, Joël and Zérah, Marie-Hélène (2001). "Water Supply and Sanitation in Indian Metros: Bombay, Kolkata, Madras", Research Report for Ondeo Services, New Delhi: CSH, p. 71.

Soni, Anita (2000). "Urban Conquest of the Outer Delhi: Beneficiaries, Intermediaries and Victims, the Case of the Mehrauli Countryside", Chapter 4, in Dupont, Tarlo and Vidal (eds.), *Delhi, Urban Space and Human Destinies*, New Delhi: Manohar Publishing, pp.75:96.

Tarlo, Emma (2000). "Welcome to History: A Resettlement Colony in the Making," in Dupont, Tarlo and Vidal (eds.), *Delhi, Urban Space and Human Destinies*, New Delhi: Manohar Publishing, p.261.

TERI (1999). *A Study on Willingness to Pay for Electricity in Orissa*, Report of the Tata Energy Research Institute, New Delhi.

World Bank (1996). "India Country Economic Memorandum: Five Years of Stabilization and Reforms: The Challenges Ahead", August, *Report No.* 15882-IN, New Delhi, p.215.

4

Productivity and Competitiveness Challenges for the Russian Economy

Room for a More Proactive Policy?[1]

ERIC BRUNAT and ANDREI KLEPACH

In the years of recovery following the financial crisis and default, the Russian economy has shown not only high rates of growth but a dramatic increase in efficiency and competitiveness. Industrial output has grown by 34 per cent over three years (1999-2002), and productivity by 35 per cent. At the same time, the generally low level of competitiveness inevitably causes concern for the Russian authorities and business, especially in the face of Russia's forthcoming accession to the WTO and further integration of Russia into the world economy. According to the estimate of the International Management Institute, Russia has moved from 47th (2000) to 43rd (2002) place in the rankings of national competitiveness, which is only a return to the level of 1998, 1.5-2 times lower than the rankings of such countries as Hungary and Estonia. With further real appreciation of the rouble and dwindling of price advantages secured by the 1998 devaluation, the issue of competitiveness of the Russian economy acquires new importance. Advanced increase of import is strengthening acuteness of the problem and affects the reduction of the economy growth rates.

It can be asserted that the Russian economy is at a crossroad. One road leads to sustaining competitiveness by lowering the real

1. The draft of this article was issued in summer of 2002. The statistical database was updated in September 2003. A Russian version of this paper is published by the Academy of National Economy of the Russian Federation. The first version of this paper was funded by the EU (EuropeAid-Tacis) RECEP IV. The views contended in this paper are those of authors and do not necessarily represent the position of UNDP.

exchange rate of the rouble again and maintaining low labour costs and energy prices on the domestic market. The other takes to improvement of non-price competitiveness and production efficiency, modernisation of production facilities and creation of incentives for innovation. Real life suggests a combination of both, since on the one hand, the Russian economy still has considerable idle capacities, but, on the other hand, the need for modernisation is already coming to the forefront and substantial growth of national competitiveness is impossible without it.

What is Happening to the Competitiveness of Russian Goods, to What Extent is Rouble Appreciation Responsible for its Decline?

It is general knowledge that there is no absolute criterion of competitiveness of products and firms themselves, and a variety of individual indicators (market share, price-quality ratio, etc.) reflect only individual aspects of market rivalry. To use a popular adage, competitiveness is like health, "no one knows what it is but everyone feels it when it is lost". In order to appraise change in competitiveness of Russian goods and intensity of market competition, we shall use the data of surveys of enterprise managers. Subjective as managers' appraisals are by themselves, the overall picture that emerges from them is not fragmentary but consistent and quite realistic.

First of all, all the surveys show fairly high intensity of competition in the main markets (3.6 points on the scale from 1 to 5 points, the data of the Russian Economic Barometer, REB), with competition being strongest among Russian producers on Russian markets.[2] The 1998 crisis resulted in an increase in the competitiveness of Russian goods, both in general and in foreign (non-CIS) markets, by 17-19 per cent, with intensity of competition dropping by 7-10 per cent. Data of the surveys suggest that after a peak of 1999 competitiveness of Russian goods started to decline both in domestic and foreign markets, while intensity of competition started to rise. According to estimates of Russian industrial producers, the competitive edge shrank to 10 per cent over the pre-crisis level, while the 'price umbrella' based on the rate of real appreciation of the rouble is larger—about 25-44 per cent (Table 4.1).

2. For details of appraisal of competition using business surveys, see papers by S. Tsukhlo (IET) and S. Aukutsionek (Russian Economic Barometer, REB).

In relation to consumer prices, the real exchange rate was under the pre-crisis level (July 1998) by the year 2002 and had declined by 25 per cent (by mid-2003 the break was equal to 14 per cent), while relative to producer prices it had dropped by 44 per cent (31 per cent by mid-2003).[3]

Thus, the real exchange rate for consumers, indicating price competitiveness of Russian goods on the consumer market, shows twice as low competitive advantage as that offered by the real exchange rate for producers. At the same time, as regards price competition with imports, domestic producers have an even smaller competitive edge of about 20-40 per cent, which was caused by a decline in import prices in the previous years (this trend has been reversed only recently).

In general, the ratio of the exchange rate to the purchasing power parity (PPP) and price efficiency of exports are so far fairly favourable for Russian goods, exceeding the pre-crisis (1997) figures by 1.5-1.2 times (Table 4.1). At the same time, in the last two years the decline in competitiveness has been clearly due to appreciation of the rouble and increasing unit costs of production (especially labour costs) (Figure 4.2). Nevertheless, we think that important as they are, the ratio of import prices to prices of domestic goods and the rate of real rouble appreciation, are currently not the major factors affecting changes in competitiveness of Russian goods, let alone intensity of competition on domestic markets. A new real depreciation of the rouble would not address problems central to competitiveness of Russian goods, for they are not related to prices. The key issues are whether factors of production and management are used efficiently, how good is the quality of the products and how new they are, and to what extent they meet modern international requirements.

What immediately catches the eye is that labour productivity growth falls behind the rate of real rouble appreciation and the pace of increase in unit labour costs, which undoubtedly lowers the competitiveness of Russian goods. The increase in labour productivity in 1999-2000 compensated for 36-50 per cent of the rise in the real

---

3. The cost stock in relation to the real exchange rate (regarding to euro, YPI , YPI to dollar deflated by producer price index) was equal to 24 per cent by the end of 2002 and reached 20 per cent by mid-2003.

Table 4.1

Dynamics of Competitiveness

	1995	1996	1997	1998	1999	2000	2001	2002***
Competition								
Intensity of Competition (REB)	3.1	3.45	3.4	3.6	3.35	3.5	3.6	3.6
With Foreign Producers	2.4	2.65	2.85	2.95	2.65	2.7	2.7	2.6
Competitiveness (CEK)	2.92		2.87	3.07	3.29	3.35	3.28	3.16
On Foreign Markets	2.22		2.27	2.41	2.68	2.70	2.63	2.49
Exchange Rate								
RER, $/R, Deflated by Producer Price Index (93=100)*	41.1	37.7	38.4	58.3	84.8	72.7	65.4	62.7
Ex. Rate/PPP (final demand deflator**)	290.5	231.0	226.5	319.5	468.5	423.7	366.0	337.2
Export Efficiency	228.2	103.9	98.8	138.7	264.5	280.2	199.9	194.3
RER Elasticity of Productivity	0.03	0.43	-4.85	0.04	-0.42	0.53	0.36	1.41
Competition, Per Cent								
Intensity of Competition (REB)	91	101	100	106	99	103	106	106
With Foreign Producers	84	93	100	104	93	95	95	91
Competitiveness (CEK)	102		100	107	115	117	114	110
On Foreign Markets	98		100	106	118	119	116	109
Exchange Rate, Per Cent								
$/R deflated by producer price index*	107	98	100	152	221	189	170	163
Ex. Rate/PPP (final demand deflator)**	128	102	100	141	207	187	162	149
Export Efficiency	231	105	100	140	268	283	202	197

Note : * Average annual real exchange rate deflated by the PPI; the sharpest depreciation occurred in 1999 due to the effect of the average annual figure;
** The ratio of the exchange rate to the purchasing power parity, with extrapolation of PPP by investment and household expenditures;
*** first half of the year.

Source : Development Centre, Goskomstat.

Figure 4.1

Movements of the Real Exchange Rate

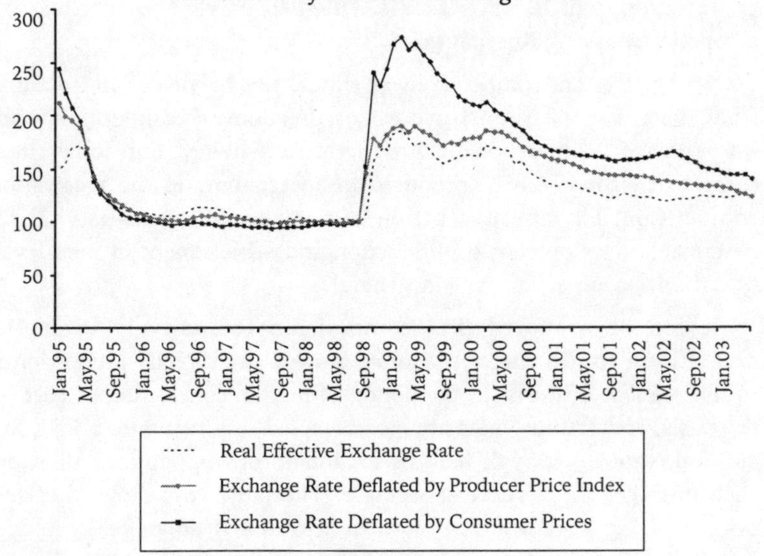

Source: Development Centre, Central Bank of Russia.

Figure 4.2

Factors Affecting Competitiveness

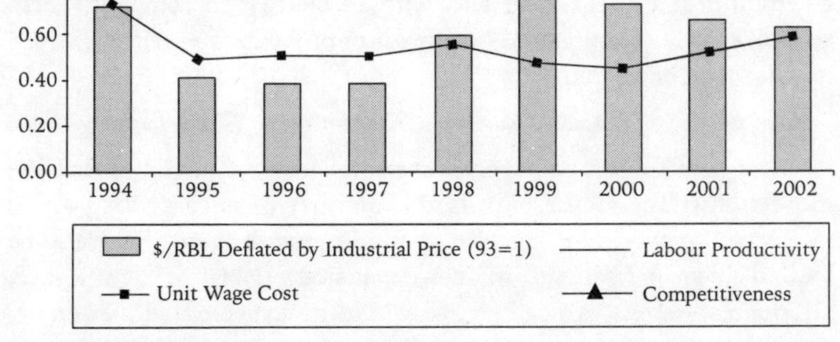

Source: Development Centre.

exchange rate of the rouble (deflated by the producer price index) and only in the current year, productivity outran the pace of rouble appreciation, which, nevertheless, failed to prevent further loss of competitiveness by Russian goods.

We believe that competitiveness should not be viewed in isolation from the action of competitive forces, freedom of competition, and influence of competition on production efficiency. For some time competitive goods can be produced in an economy in the absence of competition, but effective action of competitive forces is vital to sustainable development of production and achievement of high level of national competitiveness in general.

It can be assumed that competition intensity is inversely proportional to the rate of economic growth and directly proportional to the number of firms. In the period of market contraction as part of the crisis, competition intensity increases and may turn into a fight for survival, whereas growth reduces toughness of competition, allowing each business more space to operate. The larger the table, the less people eating at it interfere with each other. If an increase in the number of competitors intensifies competition, then a rise in production concentration is likely to reduce competition intensity, although it may also cause such competition to turn into a fight to death. Real appreciation of the rouble promotes imports and lowers competitiveness of Russian goods, but its influence on competition intensity is not so obvious. Decline of the exchange rate in real terms, reducing prices, may ease the pressure exerted by competitors, but it may also lower buyers' income and cause the market to collapse, which in turn would intensify competition (as was the case in 1998, Table 4.1). *Au contraire*, appreciation of the national currency may to a certain degree occur in parallel with an increase in competitiveness as long as it is compensated by growth of production efficiency, which is what happened in 2000.

$$\textit{Competition} = \textit{Output}^{-}, \textit{Number}^{+}, \textit{Concentration}^{-}, \textit{Real Exchange Rate}^{-}$$

Testing of the above hypotheses using survey data shows that the most significant factor here is the number of enterprises, which intensifies competition. The rate of output growth (which may also be viewed as an indicator of market expansion) is of low significance, although its effect is negative, as would be expected (Equation 1).

Both the real exchange rate and the level of production concentration are insignificant. At the same time, the level of competition with foreign companies is the stronger, the higher the share of exports in production and the lower the real exchange rate of the rouble (Equation 2). It seems, real depreciation of the rouble helps Russian companies to get rid of competition from foreign producers, or it crowds-out foreigners from the Russian market, thus improving competitiveness of Russian goods (Equation 3).

1) $CI = 3.16 - 1.42\ Q + 0.01\ N$, $R2 = .77$, $F=5.7$

(3.46) (-1.4) (3.25)

2) $CFI = -1.4 + 18.7\ EX/Q - 0.76\ RER$, $R2 = .90$, $F=14.4$

(-1.1) (4.47) (-4.7)

3) $CF = 2.02 + 0.49\ EX + 0.73\ RER - 1.02\ WR/Productivity$,
$R2 = .96$, $F=15.3$ (6.1) (2.1) (3.75) (-1.87),

where

CI is competition intensity based on REB data;

CFI is intensity of competition with foreign producers;

CF is the level of competitiveness on foreign (non-CIS) markets (Centre for Economic Analysis, (CEA));

Q is the rate of industrial output growth (Goskomstat);

N is the number of industrial enterprises (Goskomstat);

EX is growth of exports in physical terms;

EX/Q is the share of exports in industrial output at comparable prices;

RER is the rouble exchange rate deflated by producer prices (R/$, 1993=1);

WR/Productivity is change in unit wage cost in real terms.

Estimation period is 1995-2002.

Empirical calculations are consistent with the results of business surveys conducted to find out factors intensifying competition. Demand is the most significant factor (demand growth reduces competition), the second most significant factor is emergence of new Russian competitors holding back the price-rise (Table 4.2). Note an increase in 2002 of the relative weight of such factors as competition from new (for this market) Russian enterprises increases plus an increase in imports and its superior quality. In 2000-2002 the competition situation was radically different from that in 1996-1998. First, the weight of the lack of demand factor has declined dramatically, which suggests a movement from competition for survival to competition for development. Second, the effect of low import prices does not play such a role as it did earlier, whereas the weight of the factor of superior quality is rising substantially. At the same time, the contribution of import growth has started increasing rapidly, although it has not returned to its pre-crisis peak yet. This is consistent with a decrease in import prices. The value of imports will come to 84 per cent of the pre-crisis maximum (1997) in 2002, while in physical terms imports will exceed this maximum by more than a third. Third, competition among Russian companies for penetrating new markets increasingly plays the role of the main driving force of competition. The recent decline in competitiveness of Russian goods in foreign and domestic markets is probably due to a change in the very nature of competition—it is becoming more oriented to non-price factors and emergence of new players and markets. It may be assumed that the post-crisis model of growth, based largely on the undervalued exchange rate and utilisation of idle capacities, has run its course, as has the model of competition corresponding to it. Russian companies are to face a new toughening of competition due to deceleration of growth and an increase in initial production costs, as well as to rising technological and quality standards of foreign, and, more importantly, domestic competitors.

Despite dramatic deceleration of investment growth in industry caused by structural factors (overaccumulation of capital in the exporting, primarily oil sector), investment and innovation activity of Russian companies is beginning to rise, although at a slower pace than required by competition. Based on the survey of enterprise managers conducted by the Institute of Economic Forecasting of the Russian Academy of Sciences, while only about 19.6 per cent of enterprises undertook modernisation of their fixed assets in 1992-1997, this figure rose to 34.3 per cent in 1999-2001. The share of enterprises carrying out innovation projects rose to 79 per cent in

Table 4.2

*Frequency of Reference to Factors Intensifying Competition on Markets of Russian Industrial Enterprises, Per Cent**

	1996	*1997*	*1998*	*1999*	*2000*	*2001*	*2002*	*2002/01*	*2002/97*
Drop in Domestic Demand	40.5	41.1	37.4	37.9	27.1	29.1	25.6	-3.5	-15.5
Import Growth	15.5	11.7	13.8	4.7	5.1	7.7	11.1	3.4	-0.6
Better Quality of Imports	3.5	4.6	5.4	4.1	7.9	5.5	8.7	3.2	4.1
Low Prices for Imports	8.5	7.1	8.9	3.0	5.1	6.6	5.8	-0.8	-1.3
Ability of Enterprises to Advertise their Products	2.0	1.0	2.0	1.8	3.4	2.2	2.4	0.2	1.4
Price Rises are Held Back by Russian Competitors	7.0	7.6	7.4	11.8	13.0	12.6	12.6	-0.1	4.9
Penetration of Markets by Russian Producers	9.0	12.7	12.3	15.4	19.2	19.8	21.3	1.5	8.6
Measures by Ministry and the Government for Anti-Monopoly Policy	4.0	4.6	2.0	3.6	1.7	2.7	2.9	0.2	-1.7
Agents' Operations	4.5	6.6	7.9	14.2	12.4	9.9	7.2	-2.6	0.6
Other	5.5	3.0	3.0	3.6	5.1	3.8	2.4	-1.4	-0.6

Note : * A total of all answers = 100 per cent.

Source : Tsukhlo, S. (2002). *Rossiiskii byulleten kon'yunkturnyk oprosov promyshlennosti*, 124 *opros*, September.

2002 from 59 per cent in 1999.[4] Intensification of competition with foreign (non-CIS) producers, reported by 44.3 per cent of respondents at the beginning of 2002, has become one of the incentives for modernisation and innovations. In this context, it is important to note that, according to estimates of enterprise managers, the quality gap between foreign and Russian machinery has widened in favour of imported machines (43.2 per cent of respondents *versus* 15.2 per cent of those who indicated its narrowing in favour of Russian products). The loss of competition for quality and innovation cannot be remedied without increasing investment in human and fixed capital dramatically, without boosting investment in R&D and raising the level of management. Therefore, despite relatively high rate of economic growth in the current year, stagnation of investment (investment is expected to grow by 3-3.5 per cent over the whole of 2002, while industry might see a fall or stagnation of investment) suggests that there is something seriously wrong in Russian business. Against the background of growing export industries benefiting from high world prices, the machinery industry and industries producing consumer goods are experiencing stagnation, which cannot be explained by too rapid a pace of rouble appreciation, since it has deeper structural causes.

Production Efficiency, from the Effect of Demand to Real Increase in Factor Productivity

- Productivity growth began before the 1998 crisis, from 1996 it was based on faster pace of employment reduction than on output decline. Productivity growth did not result in better competitiveness of Russian products, since this growth was largely not due to its modernisation;
- A new type of productivity growth emerged in 1999-2002. It was based on output growth and an increase in the rate of capacity and labour utilisation (Table 4.3).
- Productivity growth (since 2000) has most of all benefited employees of enterprises, whose wages have also returned to the pre-crisis level (in real term). Now the potential for further productivity growth at a faster rate than other factors is petering out, which first of all applies to manufacturing

4. Kuvalin, D. (2000). *Rossiiskiye predpriyatiya v nachale 2002 g.: problemy modernizatsii* (Russian enterprises at the beginning of 2002: issues of modernisation), INP RAN.

Table 4.3

Indicators of Industrial Efficiency

1993=1	*1994*	*1995*	*1996*	*1997*	*1998*	*1999*	*2000*	*2001*	*2002*	*2002/97*
Output Growth*	0.79	0.766	0.732	0.746	0.708	0.785	0.879	0.922	0.956	1.28
Employment*	0.836	0.791	0.728	0.685	0.658	0.645	0.664	0.669	0.644	0.94
Capital**	0.870	0.836	0.813	0.793	0.780	0.770	0.765	0.766	0.77	0.97
Adjust. for Moral Depreciation	0.622	0.613	0.651	0.664	0.618	0.608	0.639	0.642	0.675	1.02
Capacity Utilisation Rate***	0.61	0.6	0.54	0.54	0.55	0.62	0.66	0.69	0.68	1.26
Labour Productivity	0.95	0.97	1.01	1.09	1.08	1.22	1.32	1.38	1.46	1.36
Wage Cost, PPI Deflàted****	0.69	0.48	0.51	0.54	0.59	0.57	0.59	0.72	0.82	1.51
Unit Wage Cost****	0.73	0.50	0.51	0.50	0.55	0.47	0.44	0.52	0.55	1.11
Investment****	0.63	0.59	0.49	0.49	0.43	0.49	0.55	0.61	0.60	1.24

Note : *: Goskomstat data; **: Estimations of the Development Center; ***: REB data; ****: Goskomstat and Development Center data.

Figure 4.3

Productivity Growth

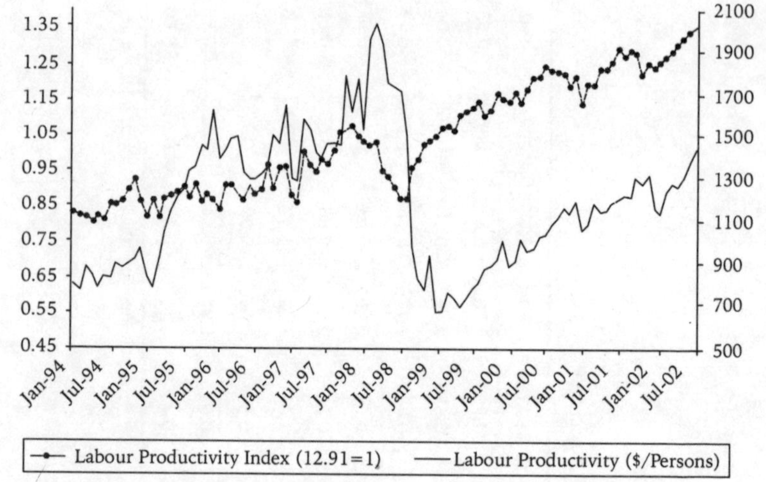

Source: Development Centre.

Figure 4.4

Productivity Growth and Wage Gains

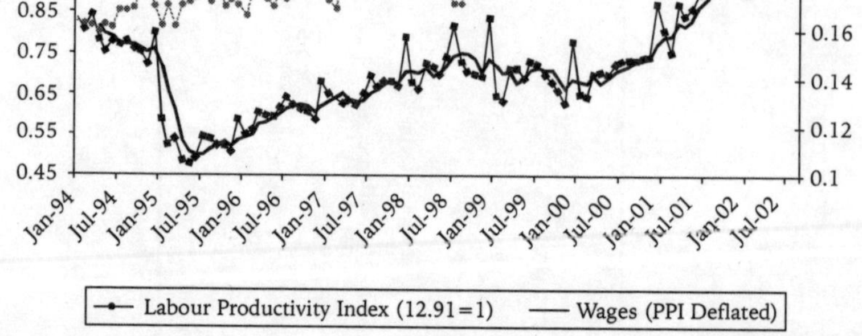

Source: Development Centre.

industries facing especially tough foreign competition. The manufacturing sector showed the highest rate of wage growth, although from a very low initial level (Table 4.5).

- There should be more capital intensive growth of output and competitiveness with considerable capacity utilisation reserves still in place. Utilisation of these reserves is to be brought about by growth of demand and financing.

Under the conditions of considerable capacity under-utilisation and surplus labour, a straightforward use of production function would yield a distorted picture of factor productivity. Instead of showing real factor productivity, estimates indicate change in the level of utilisation of factors of production reflecting change in demand. In the period of recovery, the rate of capacity and labour utilisation has grown considerably: according to REB data, capacity utilisation rate has risen by 26 per cent, labour utilisation rate by 14 per cent, but the problem remains acute. We estimate the potential reserve of unutilised resources at 15 per cent—20 per cent, i.e. 4-5 years of almost 5 per cent growth given sufficient demand and financing.

Models of Industrial Policy or Competitiveness and Productivity Enhancement Policy

The challenge of modernising the economy and the public sector as well as sustainable fast growth cannot be met with existing institutions and policies pursued. We share the view of experts and politicians who believe that liberalisation of the economy (i.e minimisation of red tape, tax cuts, liberalisation of foreign currency and capital flow controls), WTO accession, reform of the banking sector and the judicial system, should be complemented by active industrial policy aimed at development of competitive medium and high-tech production facilities.

Different sectors of the Russian economy have different levels of competitiveness and different prospects for improvement. Due to the large technology gap and low non-price competitiveness the (civilian) machinery, building materials and light industries depend the most heavily on the low exchange rate. Judging by the surveys of enterprise managers, these industries are distinguished by the lowest competitiveness and sizable losses suffered in recent years due to real appreciation of the rouble (Table 4.4).

Table 4.4

Competitiveness of Individual Industries (CEA)

	1997	*1998*	*1999*	*2000*	*2001*	*2002 (1h)*	*2002/ 97*	*2002/ 00*
Industry as a Whole*	2.87	3.07	3.29	3.35	3.28	3.16	1.10	0.941
Fuel	2.85	3.35	3.53	3.72	3.84	3.45	1.21	0.927
Ferrous Metals	3.51	3.67	3.72	3.82	3.73	3.70	1.06	0.970
Non-ferrous Metals	3.89	3.86	4.44	4.64	4.09	4.06	1.04	0.875
Chemicals and Petrochemicals	3.31	3.50	3.84	3.80	3.78	3.76	1.14	0.991
Machinery and Metal-working	2.96	3.16	3.47	3.49	3.47	3.25	1.10	0.931
Timber, Wood and Paper	2.31	2.72	2.95	3.01	3.08	2.82	1.22	0.938
Building Materials	2.25	2.30	2.30	2.38	2.23	2.20	0.98	0.924
Light Industry	2.46	2.68	2.93	2.79	2.63	2.45	0.99	0.877
Food-Processing Industry	2.26	2.35	2.44	2.56	2.63	2.74	1.21	1.071

Note : * Weighted average.

Sources : Development Centre, Goskomstat.

Competitiveness of the export-oriented fuel and metal industries exceeds the average level substantially, and changes in their competitiveness bear little relation to the pace of real appreciation of the rouble (although after the 1998 devaluation, exporters' competitiveness also surged). According to the data of the surveys, the food processing industry shows the steadiest growth of competitiveness. This sector not only benefited from devaluation and expansion of the market but could also modernise equipments and management substantially, relying, among other things, on capital and expertise of foreign companies.

After the crisis, the largest increase in comparative labour costs occurred in the power industry, reflecting both its ability to raise tariffs as a monopolist and stagnation of labour productivity in the industry. The food-processing industry, showing relatively stable competitiveness, also has stable unit wage costs, which are still 36 per cent than in 1994 (with the average of 4 per cent for industry as a whole). The food industry and the pulp and paper industry are the only industries where unit wage costs are still lower than before the

Table 4.5

Changes in Unit Wage Costs (Industry as a Whole = 100)

	1994	*1995*	*1996*	*1997*	*1998*	*1999*	*2000*	*2001*	*2002 (1h)*
Industry*	0.749	0.521	0.548	0.554	0.613	0.565	0.537	0.643	0.720
Export-Oriented Industries	96.8	92.3	95.9	95.7	93.7	83.8	81.5	87.3	88
Fuel	95.1	94.5	88.4	88.9	86.6	85.9	69.6	77.1	80
Ferrous Metals	88.7	78.7	88.1	90.8	90.8	85.7	83.1	87.7	90
Non-Ferrous Metals	109.7	108.4	125.2	123.6	117.3	74.5	91.7	107.9	98
Chemicals and Petrochemicals	95.2	88.6	92.7	91.5	95.0	86.7	82.9	74.5	75
Timber, Wood and Paper	98.6	91.9	97.0	88.9	78.0	65.5	66.7	63.3	63
Industries Oriented to Domestic Market	103.0	107.1	102.9	103.1	105.1	113.6	116.6	107.4	106
excluding Power Industry	109.1	111.0	105.4	103.4	98.8	92.2	92.7	86.8	88
Power Industry	75.8	83.6	82.8	86.5	98.7	141.6	156.2	134.5	122
Machinery and Metal-Working	108.8	107.5	97.3	95.8	94.5	92.7	92.3	88.5	91
Building Materials	91.5	111.1	99.7	93.5	86.2	95.3	94.0	83.4	86
Light Industry	136.1	142.2	155.4	147.9	137.4	113.2	115.1	110.5	116
Food-Processing Industry	102.8	102.3	103.1	102.3	93.8	77.8	79.5	72.5	71

Note : * Rate of growth for industry as a whole, 1993=1.

Source : Calculations by the authors based on Goskomstat data.

crisis, whereas the machinery industry exceeded the pre-crisis level by 23 per cent, the export industries—by 19 per cent. Industries suffering intensely from foreign competition (machinery, the light industry) have, thus, increased their labour costs almost as much as exporters, who experience much less severe competitiveness problems.

The effect of wage (or, rather, wage growth rate) equalisation among industries showing different performance as regards competitiveness, has worsened the relative positions of manufacturing industries in which the largest idle capacities, and, thus, the largest growth potential, are concentrated. In fact, high wages, and excessive costs in general, are not the main barriers to growth in these industries. The major factor hampering growth is still, lack of demand and finance (including long-term finance). While in industry as a whole capacity utilisation was estimated at 52 per cent in the middle of the year 2002 (according to CEA data), it was 43 per cent in the machinery industry and 45-48 per cent in the light and food-processing industries. However, this potential is not easy to realise even if demand is sufficiently high. Manufacturing industries showing low capacity utilisation rates also have the largest proportions of worn-out and obsolete capacities. This is evidenced by a large gap between the level of actual utilisation (based on CEA estimates) and 'economic' utilisation rate, i.e. relative to what the respondent regarded as 'normal' (REB data): in the machinery industry this is 32 per cent (economic utilisation rate is 75 per cent), whereas the average for industry as a whole is 21 per cent. Based on economic capacity utilisation, manufacturing industries do not have superior growth potential compared to extractive industries, while the problem of equipment modernisation seems to be more vital to them.

Identification of potential, the 'nuclei of growth' is impossible on the basis of only macro and mesoeconomic data on productivity changes and ratios of production costs. There should be evaluation of the long-term growth potential associated with the ability to use the existing and potential innovations and not only current but also future demand. Industrial policy is impossible without outlining priorities at the level of industries, technologies, projects and firms. From the perspective of dynamic, long-term rather than current competitiveness we could identify first, groups of leading industries (sub-industries), such as:

- industries with limited current competitiveness in the domestic market and a certain export potential, which is capable of producing a considerable macroeconomic effect (automotive industry, tractors and agricultural machinery, specialised shipbuilding); and
- industries competitive worldwide and capable of acting as nuclei of the post-industrial economy (aerospace industry, nuclear power and production of isotopes, instrument-making, software); at the same time large output and export volumes are unlikely to be achieved in these areas (with the exception of the aerospace industry and nuclear power) in the coming years.

Second, conventional industries could be pointed out (extractive industries, to a certain extent the food-processing industry), showing relatively high competitiveness and making important contribution to overall economic growth but lacking serious innovation potential. This does not imply their modernisation needs, which are, on the contrary, vital but which also means that they have a limited ability to absorb high technologies and to contribute to science-intensive growth of the Russian economy.

Third, industries related to infrastructure, with a very substantial monopolist element in them, whose restructuring implies considerable direct intervention by the government and the need for long-term capital intensive projects.

Fourth, industries in crisis, which require considerable restructuring, employment and capacity reduction, as well as reduction of their contribution to economic growth (the coal and light industries as well some sub-industries of the machinery industry).

Of course, industrial policy is not based on such aggregate identification of priorities, but we are not seeking to pose specific problems for the government to address, or to propose mechanisms for this. We mean to identify broader areas where the efforts of the government could secure the greatest economic effect in the long term, hence the industry-specific level of industrial policy does matter.

Different groups of industries probably require specific types of industrial policy, although the liberal model of government regulation does not accept identification of priorities and differentiation of terms and conditions of regulation. What would the institutional choice of the Russian business and authorities in the area of industrial policy be, if this path were to be taken? What kind of industrial policy model is capable of kick-starting modernisation processes in the Russian economy and raising its competitiveness dramatically. The following models of industrial policy are usually considered:

- Dirigiste policy (pursued by France and Japan in the 50s till beginning of the 70s, in South Korea prior to the 1987 crisis), relying on active direct intervention by the state in shaping industrial development priorities; implementation of national strategic projects with government participation (for example, the programme of development of the nuclear power industry and telecommunications in France, European aircraft programmes), financing investment in priority industries and fundamental science as well as innovative R&D, fostering 'national champions' competitive in world markets.
- Oligarchic (chaebolisation) industrial policy is implemented by large corporations using, in large part, government funds or funds of government controlled banks and financial institutions. This model is in fact another version of the above dirigiste model. Although the Russian business, which has started to diversify assets and move from the extractive to the manufacturing sector, is often labelled as chaebolised, this is hardly justified. Large Russian companies do not rely on significant government fundings in their industrial strategy, the projects themselves do not go beyond the commercial strategy of diversification and have very little in common with strategic venture projects. It would be more appropriate to speak of the 'transnational' version of industrial policy, where market penetration by multinational companies (as shown by Ford and GM) brings not only capital but also new technologies, new projects and new management culture. It is primarily large multinational companies in alliance with Russian companies that are playing the main role in shaping and implementing industrial policy.
- Market-oriented competitive industrial policy, which does not imply direct involvement of the government in determining and financing development priorities, seeking instead to

establish institutions and rules encouraging innovations. Although the Russian government may be tempted to regard its policy as a version of the above market-oriented industrial policy, it looks more like the lack of any systematic industrial policy combined with *ad hoc* decisions to support individual projects and companies.

A consistently deregistered industrial policy can hardly be pursued in Russia now. Not because it is not needed. Just the opposite, recovery of high-tech industries and facilities (for example, the civil aircraft industry) is now unlikely only on the basis of private capital, both independent and as part of financial-industrial groups. However, the Russian government, although discussing a string of programmes for specific industries, seems so far incapable of taking real financial or managerial responsibility (at least partial) for development of these industries or implementation of some national civilian projects (for example a medium range commercial aircraft). The only exception is the federal programme 'Electronic Russia', but it is oriented more to an education and information breakthrough than to development of the telecommunications and information technologies (both hardware and software). However, private business lacking support from the government and an opportunity to share risks with domestic financial institutions is at best shifting onto foreign partners. It seems that if development 'takes its natural course', degradation of Russian high-tech and competitiveness potential in the manufacturing sector can be reversed not so much by a free play of competitive forces as Russian business involvement in the processes of cooperation with foreign capital or the 'transnational' model of industrial policy. However, the roles that Russians would play in the framework of such policy may vary. While in the projects currently implemented with Western partners (Boeing, Airbus, Ford and others), the Russian side acts as a supplier of parts and components. Russia's fragmentary engineering approaches, partnership with companies and government institutions of new industrial countries (India, Egypt, China, etc.) would secure a niche for jointly manufactured products in the world markets.

Certainly, each industrial policy can be considered as deemed to collapse due to ineffective management and threat of corruption. Such challenge exists in every private corporation. If the private corporations have the right to follow the market or even to guide the process, implementing the strategic planning, then the state also has the same rights. Such governmental activism is very important due to the following reasons: necessity to liquidate 'market collapses', to support the private entrepreneurship in risky spheres of business and facilitation of coordination of the private interests with the interests of the society. It doesn't mean that Russia has to use Korean or any other governmental policy as the model to support the competitiveness. The new approaches to this problem have to be developed and it has to be an integral policy aimed at increasing of national competitiveness and formation of the new development centres outside the oil and gas sector.

The issue of industrial policy is more difficult than the mere issues of tax reduction policy. The corruption and inefficient bureaucratic administration could be considered as the realistic barriers for effective vital activity of the society and from our point of view, the main reason is the inability of the private business and the governmental institutions not only to solve the current and private challenges, but to resolve strategic and system-formatted interests of the Russian society. It invokes pity that Russian capitalism is unable to modernise the economy according to the worlds' demands without the government support, but such is the situation by the end of the 20th century and at the beginning of the 21st century. It is obvious, that the top-down governmental model of modernisation is untimely in a period of globalisation. New Russian modernisation is the inevitable process, and has to have the open character and be based on active participation of foreign capital (the same situation occurred at the beginning of the 20th century), but the partnership collaboration and influence of the Russian business will depend on the efficiency of the governmental support.

The progressive structural transformations and fundamental technological and managerial modernisation, and not just steady stabilisation policies, are able to support the activities of the future generations of the Russian people. This can provide a well deserved position to the Russian Federation in tune with the requirements of the 21st century. There is little time left, if any, in front of the United Europe, American leadership and rapidly developing Asian countries.

Part II

Markets and Competitivity

5

Impact of Liberalisation of Trade and Investment on Chinese Industrial Firms

JEAN-FRANÇOIS HUCHET

Introduction

China's accession to the World Trade Organization (WTO) constitutes a landmark decision for China's economic reform, comparable, to some extent, to the 'open door policy' launched in December 1978. The agreements signed by the Chinese government with its main trading partners for its accession to the WTO did promote a broad Liberalisation of Trade and Investment (LTI).

China is better prepared to cope with the negative short-term adjustments of a broad LTI than were the countries of Eastern Europe and the former USSR, which implemented a 'shock therapy' at the beginning of the 1990s. First, the different agreements that China has signed with its different trading partners leave some room for a progressive adjustment. Second and more important, Chinese enterprises have benefited from two decades of uninterrupted reforms. The large part of the apparatus of China's planned economy has been progressively dismantled (prices, procurements and quantitative plans). Chinese enterprises, even in the state sector, have enjoyed a relatively high degree of autonomy in day-to-day management decision-making. Finally, the level of competition in the domestic market has grown very rapidly since the beginning of the 1990s in the majority of industrial sectors: Township and Village Enterprises in rural areas (T&VE), private companies and foreign-funded enterprises (FFE), were non-existent till 1978, while today they represent more than half of the industrial production.

Nevertheless, China's accession to the WTO brought some substantial changes in terms of tariffs, industry regulations, competition through imports and FDI, rules governing the attribution of public market, and opening up of services and domestic trade, which had till then been heavily protected. Domestic firms and regions indeed responded in very different ways to such changes.

The industrial corporate landscape has changed dramatically in the 20 years of reforms. Some sectors, such as consumer electronics, textiles, garments, food-processing and steel, already enjoyed a high degree of competition. Domestic leaders in these sectors, which have established well-known brand names (e.g. Konka, Haier, Changhong, etc.) were already familiar with strong competition in their domestic market and had already developed a strong capacity of adaptation and reaction to the market in their management. Furthermore, they have massively invested over the past 15 years in after-sales service networks, focusing on quality, which gives them an edge over foreign producers possibly tempted to invest heavily in China. This type of company did not suffer too much from a LTI. However, a majority of small and medium enterprises (SME) in the state and urban collective sector are suffering from structural problems such as undercapitalisation, low profitability, a lack of economies of scale and technological capability, poor management skills, and heavy control by the local bureaucracy in their decision-making processes. These companies are surviving under the umbrella of local protectionism and help from the banking system, which is funding their working capital. Their chances of survival under such conditions after China's accession to the WTO are very low. Special programmes to help such companies restructure their activities should, therefore, be a priority in the Chinese government's economic policy agenda, but many are now laying off workers.

A LTI also affects regional economic growth, in addition to the disparities among regions which, by world standards, are already very high. The cost of the transition from a planned to a market economy differs greatly from one region to another. Moreover, the benefits of 20 years of reforms and an opening to FDI have been mostly concentrated in the coastal regions. In such a context, the impact of a LTI following China's accession to the WTO is extremely different: Guangdong province, for example, where the share of the state sector in terms of the total industrial production is only 28 per cent, which has received 27 per cent of the total FDI, and where most private and collective companies are well integrated into the international division of labour, is benefiting from its comparative advantage in the international and the domestic market. The provinces of the hinterland such as Jilin, Inner Mongolia, Hebei, Shaanxi, Shanxi, Anhui, Jiangxi, Hunan, Sichuan, Chongqing, Guangxi and Guizhou, without even considering the situation of remote western provinces like Ningxia, Gansu, Tibet, Xinjiang or Qinghai, face a different situation. The share of the state sector of total industrial production is in excess of 60 per cent; their private sector is undersized and they have received little FDI; furthermore, except for a few cases, companies originating from these provinces have not been able to maintain a competitive edge in the domestic market nor have they been able to integrate themselves efficiently into the international division of labour. It is these in provinces that we find the highest concentration of SMEs in the state and urban collective sector that are suffering from structural problems. In this context, the LTI requires the implementation of urgent policies to help these provinces to cope with their restructuring needs.

More generally, in the area of industrial restructuring, the WTO accession confronts the Chinese government with some specific problems that are linked with the legacy of the industrialisation during Mao's period and with the way reforms were implemented between 1978 and the mid-1990s. The first problem lies in the fact that Chinese industry has witnessed a proliferation of inefficient enterprises. This dynamic birth rate of enterprises is, without any doubt, directly related to the impressive growth rate of the Chinese economy. Part of this phenomenon, however, is also the result of an inefficient governance structure both at the enterprise and the government level. There are still more than 100 producers of cars, most of them producing just a few thousand cars a year. In the cement industry, 8,000 enterprises are competing in the domestic market. The LTI will force policy makers in China to restructure these inefficient producers and to attack the roots of this problem, mainly by reforming the corporate governance and banking systems to guarantee a more efficient use of investment resources. The second problem, which is directly related to the first one, concerns the necessity to budget for the hidden debt of the restructuring process composed of unfunded social protection liabilities (pensions, unemployment compensations, employee retraining fees and unpaid salaries of laid-off workers) and non-performing loans (NPL) owned by the banking system in state-owned (SOE) and collective enterprises. The Chinese government needs to address this problem in order to reduce the short-term adjustment costs of the LTI and to speed up the industrial restructuring process.

CHALLENGES

The Transformation of the Industrial Landscape

In contrast with the situation in 1978 on the eve of the reforms, industrial firms now operate within a very different environment. Two decades of reforms and continuous restructuring have brought about some tremendously positive results in China's industry leaving China in a very different position in comparison with other former socialist countries in the wake of a broad LTI.

One of the most important changes to have occurred lies in the increase in competition within China's industry, especially in sectors close to end-consumption (electrical appliances, garments, textiles and foodstuffs). These are the result of several converging factors:

- The dismantling of the planning mechanism, with the deregulation of prices, supply and distribution (Naughton, 1995). Over 90 per cent of retail prices in industry and over 80 per cent of agricultural prices are set by the market. Plan obligations for procurement or subsidised inputs have also been abolished.
- The appearance of T&VEs, i.e. collective ownership in rural areas, whose property rights status is unclear, and the tolerating of private activities carried out by different categories of actors in the countryside and urban zones (Weitzman and Xu, 1993). By 1999 already, the non-state sector was estimated at nearly 77 per cent of total industrial production (Figure 5.1).
- The opening up of the internal market to FDI. Joint venture companies with mixed capital have been instrumental in boosting competition in the domestic market. FFEs had

become the dominant producers in four industrial sectors (instruments, electronics and telecommunications, sports goods, and leather, furs and related products) and had surpassed SOE production in 13 other sectors competing directly with collective and private companies already before WTO accession (Lemoine, 2000).

- Finally, from the mid-1990s on, the duplication and poor planning of investments in most industrial sectors, together with a levelling-off in household demand due to an increase in insecurity linked to a rise in unemployment following the various implemented restructurings of the state sector and the effects of the privatisation of education, housing and social welfare, have created a huge overcapacity in virtually the entire industrial sector. Companies thus found themselves in markets now dominated by supply (a phenomenon hitherto unknown in a reformed socialist economic system), exacerbating all the more the competitive pressures and elements of concentration around the most efficient ones (Huchet, 1999).

Figure 5.1

Share of Industrial Output by Ownership (Pre-WTO Accession)

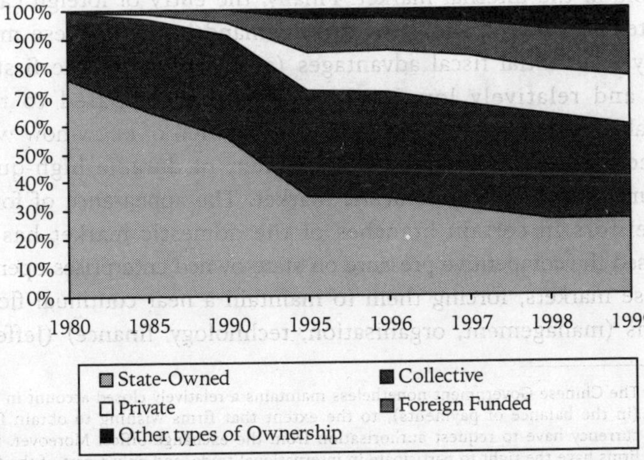

Source: Huchet, 1999.

Since 1994, the monetary policy of the central government has led to a noticeable tightening of budgets, affecting SOEs, which are by far the main consumers of credit allocated to the economy, with 60 per cent of total credit provided to industry by the banking system. Restrictions on credit and subsidies to SOEs (the latter, according to World Bank estimates, reportedly dropped from 7.5 per cent of GDP in 1992 to 2.3 per cent in 1994, then to less than 1 per cent after 1995) have been imposed so as to limit the inflation caused by the overheating of the economy following Deng Xiaoping's trip to southern China in 1992. These steps were followed by a series of reforms in the banking system. The most significant of these was a reduction in the number of provincial subsidiaries of the People's Bank of China (PBOC) (which plays the role of a central bank) and the creation of supra-regional branches in order to limit the power of local cadres in the allocation of credit to companies. The 'sink or swim' economic policy applied to state-owned small businesses since 1994 seems to have considerably increased the pressure to make them modify their behaviour.

The opening up of the Chinese economy and its world market niche have contributed to an encouraging of exports, especially from companies in the non-socialist sector. The possibility for a growing number of firms[1] of gaining access to the foreign currency market, has facilitated the acquisition of foreign technologies superior to those available in the internal market. Finally, the entry of foreign capital, attracted by prospects for growth in demand in the Chinese market and by substantial fiscal advantages (a tax rebate for the first few years and relatively low levels of taxation compared to those applicable for SOEs), has enabled the acquisition of know-how within the receiving firms and the development of durable high-quality consumer goods in the domestic market. The appearance of foreign competitors in certain branches of the domestic market has also increased the competitive pressure on state-owned enterprises operating in these markets, forcing them to maintain a near continual flow of reforms (management, organisation, technology, finance) (Jefferson

---

1. The Chinese Government nonetheless maintains a relatively closed account in capital (in the balance of payments), to the extent that firms wishing to obtain foreign currency have to request authorisation from the exchange office. Moreover, not all firms have the right to participate in international trade, and only a part of the foreign currency earned by exports may be retained by such firms.

et al., 1994). China's accession to the WTO could allow these kinds of pressures to be extended to sectors that were till then protected.

At the microeconomic level, reforms have brought a greater management autonomy and separation from public administration. The transfer of decision-making power from the bureaucracy to the management of enterprises has been the main tool that Chinese policy makers have used to reform the management of SOEs. From the time when the 'contract responsibility system' was generalised in Chinese SOEs, management autonomy has increased significantly (Byrd, 1992; Lu and Child, 1996; Warner, 1995).

Compared with the old centralised and planned system before the reforms, the transfer of decision-making power has created many new incentives for SOEs to invest in new production and to respond to the needs of the market.

Unbalanced Industrial Structure

Despite these broad transformations, the legacy of the industrialisation strategy followed during the Maoist period and the way in which reforms were implemented during the Deng Xiaoping era have created an unbalanced industrial structure.

China holds some unenviable world records when it comes to fragmentation of its industrial structure. Thousands of undersized producers, manufacturing the same products, are spread all over the country: in the automobile industry, for example, even though the 13 biggest companies by 1998 represented 90 per cent of total production (1.5 million cars at the end of 1998, or about 19 times less than the annual production of the five biggest world manufacturers at that time!), there are still officially 123 independent automobile producers in 2006. The building materials industry is also interesting from this point of view. Despite declining demand since 1993, local protectionism and the lowering of the barriers to entry in certain production sectors such as cement and steel produced by electric furnaces, have led to a rapid growth in the number of companies operating in this sector.

Another example is the cement industry where there are still some 8,000 independent companies operating, against only 1,500 at world level (110 in the United States, 51 in Russia, 58 in Brazil and 106 in India). The leading Chinese company in the sector has only 0.6 per cent of the national market.[2] Table 5.1 shows that there was no concentration between 1990 and 1997, despite a fierce price war between the various producers. The cement industry is a good illustration of the differences that exist between China and other countries where industrial organisation is concerned, and it is still a long way from achieving the market share of some of the leading companies in other countries, which easily achieve 30 per cent of the national market, as in India, or 60 per cent in the case of Thailand.[3]

Table 5.1

Evolution of the Number of Companies in the Building Materials Sector

Sectors	*1990*	*1994*	*1997*
Producers of Ferrous Metals			
Local Companies*	3,391	6,400	6,109
SMEs	201	175	159
Glass Producers			
Local Companies*	2,816	2,697	2,689
SMEs	287	259	265
Cement Producers			
Local Companies*	5,383	5,956	6,403
SMEs	128	127	712

Note : *: Includes only companies registered above district administrative level.

Source : Bureau of Chinese Statistics/State Statistical Bureau, quoted by China Research Team, "China: Price War and Price Control" in *Warburg Dillon Read*, Dec. 1998, p.14.

Chinese industry faces a double problem, which lies in the slow pace of consolidation in the different sectors and a slow exit from the market of inefficient producers. In 1994, the 500 leading Chinese groups accounted for only 16 per cent of GDP, considerably less than that in the industrialised countries where the 500 leading companies generally account for at least 30 per cent of GDP. China's biggest company, Daqing Petroleum, had sales of US$ 3.6 billion in 1996, about half of that of the company at the bottom of the Fortune 500 list of the world's biggest companies. The sales of Baogang, China's

2. China Research Team, "China: Price War and Price Control", in *Warburg Dillon Read*, December 1998.

3. *ibid.*

leading steelworks (before the recent mergers in November 1998) amounted to a mere 10 per cent of those of the Japanese giant Nippon Steel.[4] An analysis of the levels of concentration reveals different developments according to the industrial sector concerned. In the 25 main industrial sectors, the market share of the eight leading companies have increased only very slightly, if one refers to the overall average of the industries, rising from 11.7 per cent to 12.2 per cent. However, these figures are too highly aggregated. It would have been necessary to go down to a more precise level in the statistical nomenclature in order to show the variety of situations, and to analyse the evolutions not by sector, but rather at product level. Certain markets, such as consumer electronics, shown in Figure 5.2, or processed food or consumer chemical products, have been the scene of a process of rapid consolidation. Nevertheless, despite this consolidation, inefficient producers are very slow to exit the market as they still operate independently under the umbrella of local protectionism and with the help of subsidies (disguised in the form of loans) provided by the banking system.

Figure 5.2

Market Share in Consumer Electronics Sector in 1999

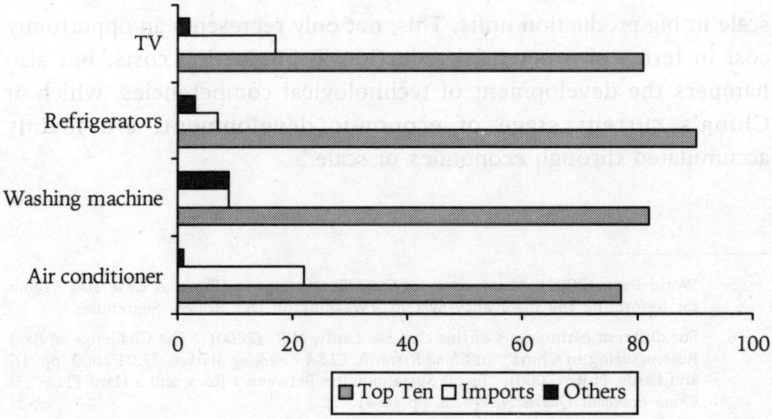

Source : *China Light Industry Yearbook*, 2000 (Zhonguo qinggongye nianjian).

4. *Dongfang qiye yanjiuhui, "Woguo xuyao yipi shejieji da gongsi"* (China needs world size companies) in *Qiye wenhua*, No. 5, 1997, pp.25-27.

The phenomenon of unbalanced industrial structures has created several negative consequences for the Chinese industry. First, it is responsible for a tremendous waste of investment resources and a misallocation of the country's savings. It has contributed to the rapid growth in Non-Performing Loans (NPLs) in the books of the main domestic state commercial banks, which the government has been trying to recapitalise since 1998. Given the total NPLs, which varies according to different estimations from 25 per cent to 50 per cent of total loans, and the current low recovery rates by creditors in SOE bankruptcies (between 3 per cent and 10 per cent[5]), the macroeconomic cost of this phenomenon will probably be very high.[6] The second negative consequence lies in the creation of huge overcapacities in nearly all industrial sectors. A survey conducted by the State Statistical Bureau revealed that the ratio of production to capacities, including equipment, for close to half of 900-odd major industrial products has dropped to below 60 per cent.[7] This is, in turn affecting returns on capital and profitability for all industries especially in sectors where there is no brand name awareness and where inefficient producers can produce and sell at a loss (steel, cement, construction materials, and other intermediary goods). Finally, in a more subtle way, though very important for the future of industry, the slow consolidation rate prevents the development of economies of scale in big production units. This, not only represents an opportunity cost in terms of a potential reduction in production costs, but also hampers the development of technological competencies, which at China's current stage of economic development, are mainly accumulated through economies of scale.[8]

---

5. World Bank (2000). "Bankruptcy of State Enterprises in China. A Case and Agenda for Reforming the Insolvency System", Washington DC, Roneo, September.
6. For different estimations of this cost see Lardy, N.R. (2000). "The Challenge of Bank Restructuring in China", in *China Research, CLSA Emerging Market*, 27.04.2000, pp. 16; and Lardy, N.R. (2000). "Fiscal Sustainability: Between a Rock and a Hard Place", in *China Economic Quarterly*, No. 2, pp.36-41.
7. *China Daily*, January 27, 1999.
8. Teitel, S. (1984). "Technology Creation in Semi-industrial Economies", in *Journal of Development Economics*, No. 16, pp.39-61; Lall, S. (1990). *Promouvoir la compétitivité industrielle dans les pays en développement*, Paris: OCDE; Dalhman, C.J., B. Ross-Larson and L.E. Westphal (1987). "Managing Technological Development: Lessons from the Newly Industrialising Countries", in *World Development*, Vol. 15 (6), pp.759-777.

Regional Discrepancies

Regional discrepancies in terms of economic development have greatly expanded during these two decades of reforms. A recent study on regional development stated "that despite its relatively low per capita GDP (...) regional differences among China's 30 provinces are so large that they resemble the gap between the advanced industrial countries and the poorest countries in the world" (Wang and Hu, 1999). The cost of the transition towards a market economy and the extent of the restructuring vary greatly among provinces. In this context, we see big differences in the capacity to adjust and meet LTI challenges among provinces.

The cost of the transition towards a market economy is proportional to the importance of heavy industry and to the share of the state and urban collective sector in the local economy. One of the most outstanding factors of discrepancies in economic development among provinces has been the level of growth of non-state companies; either foreign-funded enterprises, T&VEs or private companies, which have progressively overcome the state sector. This phenomenon has allowed a reduction of the impact and the cost of the restructuring process in the local economy, providing new job creation and economic activities, and more fiscal revenues. Figure 5.3 shows that the share of the state sector in industrial production is below 50 per cent in all coastal provinces and is well over 60 per cent in northeastern, western, and central provinces. Coastal provinces in all have received 88 per cent of FDI, with 30 per cent for Guangdong province alone. Concurrently, Zhejiang, Jiangsu and Shandong have the greatest concentration of T&VEs. The share of heavy industry in total output is also a good indicator of the extent of restructuring that each province has to face. All provinces in the northeast, central and western regions as shown in Figure 5.4 have not been able to eliminate the distortion in favour of heavy industry, a product of the legacy of the socialist industrialisation and industrial policy of Mao's period that saw the channelling of massive investment into traditional heavy industry.

Thus, in the context of the WTO accession, which speeds up industrial restructuring in the northeast, central and western provinces, the problem of fiscal transfer between provinces should be addressed urgently by the central government in order to help these provinces in their restructuring efforts and to avoid a further increase in economic development discrepancies between regions.

So far, the coastal regions have also managed to set up a more efficient social security system than provinces in the hinterland and that has made them progress more rapidly with the restructuring of their companies. In China, the social security system is mainly organised at the municipality level, which means that only the economically dynamic cities have been gradually able to in the last few years finance an unemployment, retirement or health insurance fund. On the other hand, regions of the northeast and of the interiors, which have to restructure the largest number of inefficient companies and have the most need for an effective social security system, are encountering difficulties in funding such a programme, particularly given the difficult financial situation of the SOEs and urban collective companies there, and the lack of contributions from an underdeveloped private, rural collective, and foreign investment sector.

Without adequate policies the LTI might accentuate these discrepancies among China's provinces.

POLICIES

The central government has launched a series of policies to accelerate industrial restructuring since 1994. These were deepened, first in 1997 after the 15th Party Congress, and once again in 1998 at the height of the Asian financial crisis and in preparation for China's accession to the WTO. These policies have three main directions: 1. government programmes to reduce capacity in several sectors, mainly in promoting mergers and in allowing more companies to go bankrupt; 2. several measures such as the promotion of debt-for-equity swaps for big SOEs, the launching of IPOs on foreign stock exchanges, and the reform of credit policies in the banking system, which have tackled the financial restructuring of industrial companies; and 3. disengagement, by government decision, of the state from the running of SMEs in the state and urban collective sector, mainly by allowing local governments to privatise this category of enterprise. These policies have already produced encouraging results in solving a portion of the problems in the industrial structure and in promoting an improved business environment for domestic companies.

Figure 5.3

Property Rights Distribution by Provinces in 1999

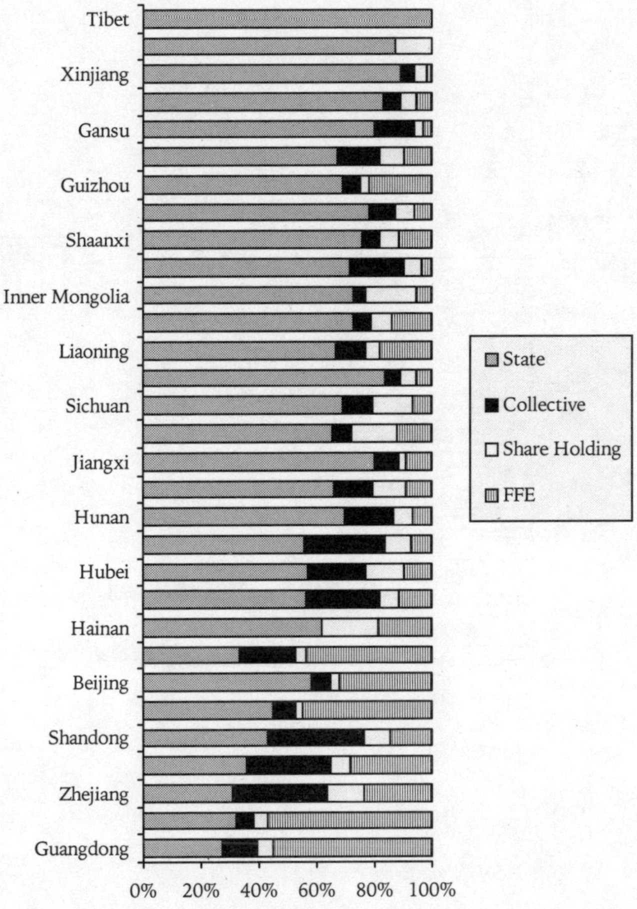

Source : *China Statistical Yearbook*, 2000.

Nevertheless, these policies are encountering several problems in their implementation, and a reorientation of these policies as well as new measures were needed right from the transitory period, before China fully implemented the different agreements it had signed with its main trading partners for its accession to the WTO.

Figure 5.4

Distribution of Heavy and Light Industry by Provinces in 1999

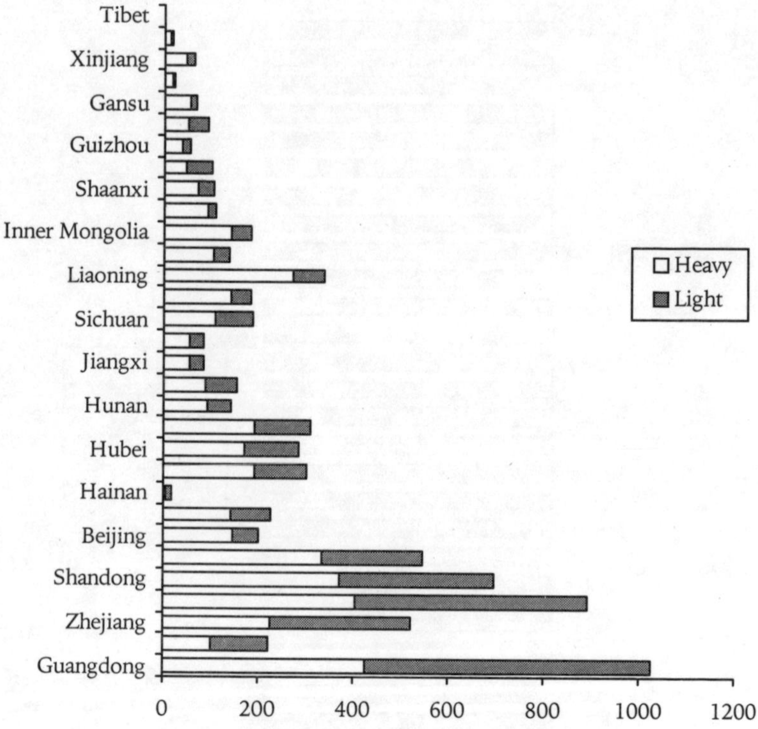

Source : *China Statistical Yearbook*, 2000.

Reduction of Capacities

Efficiency of the New Measures

Since the mid-1990s the central government has launched a series of restructuring plans in several industries in order to reduce production capacity as well as to push for further consolidation. The content of these capacity reduction programmes involve a number of measures:

- The formation of 156 big groups mainly in industry. This measure affects only the biggest SOEs and has the objective of creating 'national champions' in their respective industries, and pushing some of them into the Fortune 500 classification of the world's largest groups. This policy involves mergers or take-overs of huge proportions by the biggest SOEs in each sector and contributes to the reduction of production capabilities.

- The streamlining of unproductive assets, mainly all the social welfare units of companies not directly related to the main activity of the SOEs or urban collective enterprises.
- Despite price control measures in 12 sectors,[9] government enforcement has been weak, and price competition in some industries such as consumer durables has further increased the degree of consolidation in several sectors and pushed inefficient producers out of the market.
- The promotion of mergers for SMEs in the state and collective sector by local governments.
- More bankruptcies and closure of inefficient companies in the state and collective sector.

These different measures have clearly brought about some improvements in the structural problems affecting the domestic industry. The financial performance of the state sector has greatly improved. Industrial profits, losses and inventories are all showing improvement since 1999. Part of this positive trend is related to the change in the price of oil, to a lower interest rate, which had a positive impact on SOE interest on debt, and also to the debt for equity swaps scheme for big SOEs that has enabled these companies to substantially reduce their debt. Accounting irregularities might also have some influence in artificially boosting SOEs' financial results, given the alarming reports on accounting practices of SOEs published by the Auditing Bureau of the State Council. Nevertheless, there are some clear indications that the reduction of capacities have also brought about some positive results on financial improvement in several industries.

First, there has been a stabilisation of prices in most of the industries where a drastic plan to reduce capacity has been

9. Glass, tractors, steel, sugar, passenger cars, fibreglass, colour TVs, caustic soda, urea, cement, aviation, see *Warburg Dillon Read* (1998). "China: Price War and Price Control", December, Hong Kong, p.15.

implemented; such as in coal, steel, textiles, construction materials and sugar. In industries where prices have continued to drop, such as in consumer electronics (refrigerators, air-conditioners, TVs), 'price wars' have been orchestrated by big industrial groups at a national level and have contributed to the pushing of inefficient firms out of the market or to them being subject to take-overs by the leaders. For example, in the refrigerator market, the number of domestic producers had shrunk already before WTO accession: from 40 in 1993 to 11 at the end of 1999.[10]

For the first time since 1978, there has been a drastic decline in the number of state and collective urban companies (Figure 5.5.a and Figure 5.5.b) as well as in their employees (Figure 5.6), despite a further increase in the number of private and shareholding companies and FFEs. Since the peak year of 1996, the number of SOEs has decreased from 1,26,000 to 61,300. Nevertheless, this reduction is not synonymous with a closure of nearly 50 per cent of all SOEs. Part of this reduction is due to mergers, privatisations, especially in the case SMEs, and the transfer of some SOEs into the statistical category of shareholding companies. In the most extensive study done on the bankruptcy situation in China, a recent report of the World Bank shows a clear acceleration of bankruptcy cases after 1995 (Figure 5.7).

For a long time, as in former socialist countries, mergers in China have been the most privileged tool for the restructuring of companies, being used as an administrative way to escape from bankruptcy. Enterprises had little to say on the overall process of merger and had to comply with decisions made by the bureaucracy, giving very inefficient results in terms of restructuring. Yet, case studies conducted at the beginning of the last wave of mergers in 1996 (Huchet, 1999), show that in competitive sectors, leading companies still had to respond to government wishes concerning mergers but could act with much more autonomy and were able to resist pressure from the tutelary authorities that sought to oblige them to acquire loss-making state companies. In this context, mergers have been creating more efficient results than in past and in fiercely competitive industries and with many candidates for take-over, leading companies have been able to get good deals with which to expand their operations around China (debt reduction prospects, good technology).

10. *China Light Industry Yearbook, 2000.*

Figure 5.5.a and Figure 5.5.b

Evolution of Number of Industrial Enterprises by Ownership

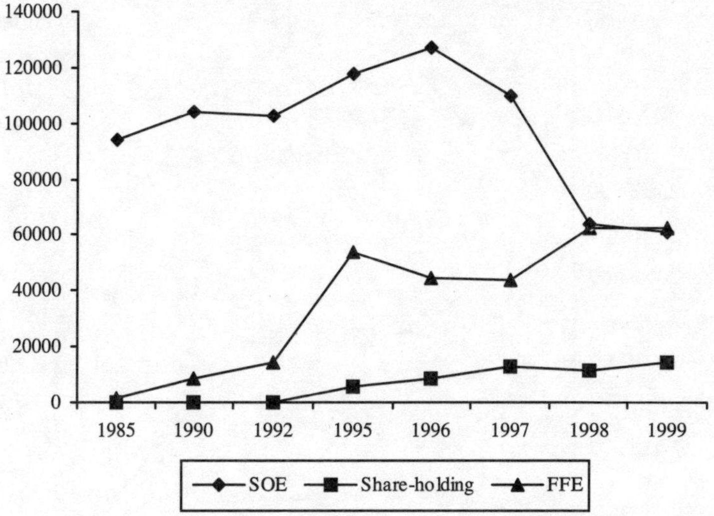

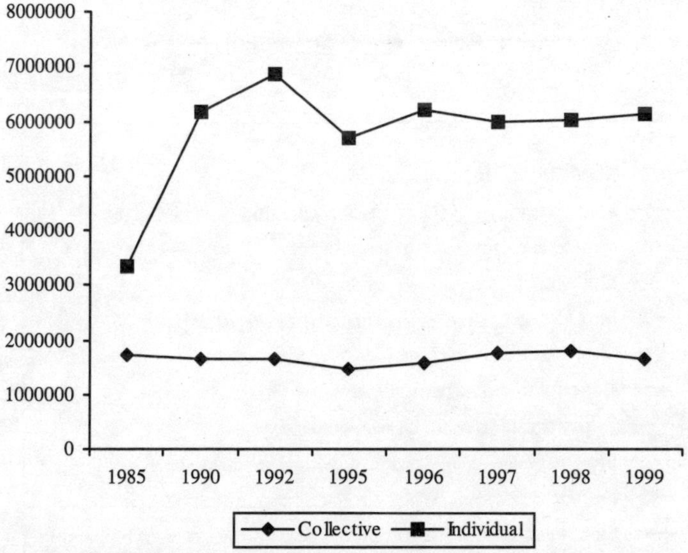

Source: *China Statistical Yearbook*, 2000.

Figure 5.6

Evolution of Staff and Workers by Sector and by Ownership

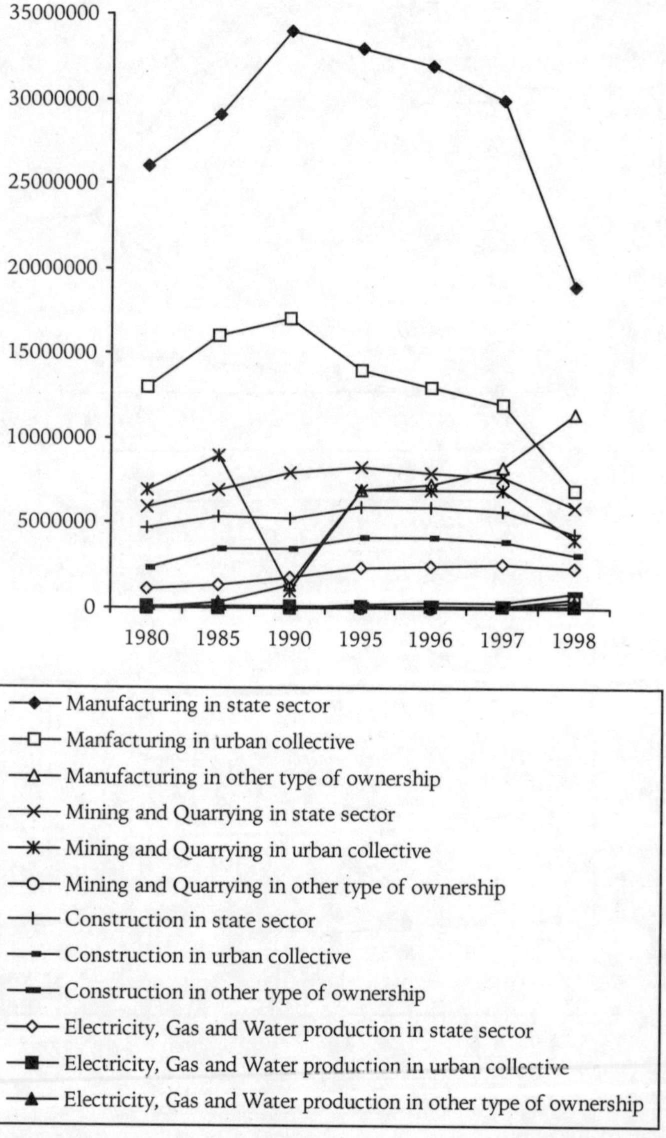

Source : *China Labour Statistical Yearbook*, 1999.

Figure 5.7

Evolution of Bankruptcies and Mergers under the Capital Structure Optimisation Programme of 1994-1999 (Number of Cases Implemented)

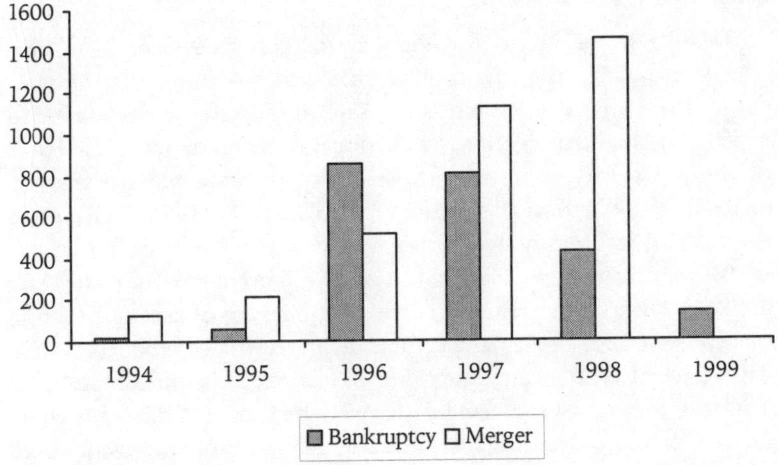

Source: World Bank, 2000.

More generally, two variables have been decisive in the evolution of restructuring. On the one hand, there are the sectors that are close to the end user where consumer choice and competition have led to the existence of a selection of companies and to a process of rapid concentration. In these sectors, the domestic industry has entered a new phase: following a demultiplication of units in the 1980s, we expect to see a rapid process of consolidation, after which only a few domestic players will compete in the domestic market along with the global players. For example, there were at that time more than 200 home electronics brand names, but in 2000 the figure had dropped to about 20 and a recent survey by the Association of Light Industry predicted that after China's accession to the WTO only two or three domestic brand-name manufacturers would remain active in the market.[11] The other decisive variable has been the geographic concentration of industries and the number of bureaucratic entities involved in this sector. The more an industry is concentrated in a relatively small area and the less bureaucratic entities there are involved

11. *China Online*, August 24, 2000.

in the restructuring process, the easier it is to reform and to achieve economies of scale by the promotion of a concerted concentration not only by the market, but also by the administrative authorities.

Limits and Bottlenecks

Despite some progress in the way mergers have been used, this restructuring tool remains controversial and has shown its limits in the context of Chinese industry. The authorities have preferred superficial band-aid solutions in the form of mergers under the cover of the policy of promoting groups in order to avoid bankruptcy procedures, which still remain very difficult to follow given the conflicts of interest between creditors and the inefficiencies of the social security system. Mergers constitute more a way of concealing problems than a sane solution to the phenomenon of excess industrial capacity. Even for the leading companies in consumer products, which have enjoyed greater autonomy on this matter, it is difficult to know if all these groups have acted as they wished, or if, feeling the wind turn, they sought to anticipate the merger movement, which would allow them to negotiate company take-overs in favourable conditions (payment of debt, maintenance of the workforce, etc.). Outside these sectors many examples show that the state continues to intervene in an authoritarian manner in promoting groups. Furthermore, the smaller the size of the companies, and the lower the level of the tutelary administration, the more the mergers are carried out in an authoritarian fashion by the local authorities, who are not excessively preoccupied with the strategy of companies, or the possibility of creating synergy in production, technology, financing, or the merging of distribution networks. The Chinese economic press is full of examples of this phenomenon since the launching of the reform decided at the 15th Party Congress. Case studies on the activities of the local state asset management companies, of the big municipalities (Zhongyuan, 1999; Huchet 1999; Yingquan, *et al.* 1999; Rengui, 1999; Qing, 1999; Wu, 1999), which are directly in charge of carrying out these mergers on behalf of the municipal governments, show that except for a few cases in Shanghai and coastal cities (Cheng, 1999; Wang, 2000; Shanghaishi, 1999), the formation of these groups was more a product of makeshift financial repairs aimed at avoiding bankruptcies and concealing company losses, than a real job of restructuring, that respected the interests of the companies concerned. Furthermore, in the restructuring process, political patronage remains the key point, with fierce interdepartmental rivalry over allocation of state assets inside the local bureaucracy. It is not surprising in this context to see, after the danger of the Asian financial crisis, that the central authorities have shifted their policy in 2000 from mergers to bankruptcies, and further deregulation to promote competition in their industrial restructuring efforts (see Box 5.1 for the automobile industry).

Box 5.1

Still Too Many Players in the Automobile Industry

At the end of 1997, the central administration approved the umpteenth plan to rationalise the industry. The 13 biggest manufacturers were supposed to take over the smallest producers in order to transform them into subcontractors, which would, according to the government plan, make it possible to develop economies of scale. The objective was to set up four big automobile groups, each with a minimum production capacity of 4,00,000 cars. The government project also provided for greater control by the central administration in the approval of new joint venture projects in the industry with foreign companies. The project also emphasised that mergers should be carried out, not administratively as in the past, but according to the market and the strategic interests of the company taking over. The various case studies carried out on the industry (Wang, *et al.*, 2001) indicate that, since the middle of the 1980s, the central administration has met with multiple obstacles connected with local protectionism. The nature of the demand, which is still almost 90 per cent dominated by administrations and companies, as well as the large number of central and provincial bureaucracies with interests in the industry, prevent the market mechanisms from playing their role fully. The local governments have preferred, until recently, to subsidise companies that produce only a few thousand vehicles annually, rather than to give up the idea of having an automobile industry on their territory. It is also interesting to note that the local authorities have gone so far as to challenge the major projects to develop the automobile industry set up at the national level, which, at the beginning of the 1990s, provided for the limiting of the number of Chinese and foreign joint ventures to three major centres: Shanghai (Volkswagen), Wuhan (Citroën) and Changchun (Audi-Volkswagen). Since then Shanghai has welcomed Ford and General Motors; Tianjin has increased its cooperation with Daihatsu and Toyota; Honda has replaced Peugeot in Canton and Renault is said to be on the point of negotiating a joint production project, by itself or through Nissan.

Efforts to streamline non-core assets in SOEs and in the urban collective sector (in-house social services, upward or downward activities not directly related to core activities such as transportation and electricity production) have been curbed by the slowness and the inefficiencies of the social security system reforms. In coastal areas, where the funding of the social security system has not been too problematic, big companies have been able to sell or transfer their social in-house assets to their respective city governments and to sell or lease their non-core activities. SMEs in these areas were also able to dismantle these activities more easily as the city governments provided better medical care systems for employees and retraining programmes for laid-off workers. However, while cities in the north-east, central and western regions have been struggling to fund their social security systems, they have been unable to take over social assets of big companies, which still have to provide most of the traditional social care services of the socialist firm. The steel industry is a good example. If we take production per employee as an indicator of the degree of the downsizing of non-core assets, Baogang Steel in Shanghai (before the wave of mergers in 1998), provides a striking example of success. After various agreements with the Shanghai city government, Baogang, leader in the steel industry, had in 1998 only 32,095 employees, each of them producing 307 tonnes of steel per year (Table 5.2). In comparison, other major steel producers in the northeast or the hinterland provinces, e.g. Shougang in Peking, Angang and Bengang in Liaoning province or Wugang in Hubei, or Taigang in Shaanxi, are all still struggling with over-employment in their non-core assets.[12]

Table 5.2

Employment and Non-core Asset Weight on Productivity

Tonnes	*Production in Million tonnes*	*Employees*	*Production Per Employee in tonnes*
Shanghai Baogang	9,8	32,095	307
Beijing Shougang	8	177,355	45
Angang	8,45	163,746	51
Wugang	6	109,457	55
Taiyuan Gangjie	2,4	71,727	34
Benxi Gangjie	2,9	86,126	33

Source: China Steel Industry Yearbook, 1999.

12. *China Steel Industry Yearbook*, 1999.

Financial Restructuring

Debt for Equity Swaps

In 1998, the central government launched a programme of recapitalisation for the four biggest state commercial banks that have helped the biggest SOEs to reduce their debt. This programme has allowed banks to wipe from their balance sheet some of the NPLs made to SOEs. The corresponding assets of the SOEs, allowed to benefit from the programme, have been taken over by four liquidating companies created for the purpose (China Cinda, China Huarong, China Great Wall Asset and China Oriental) based on the American model of the late 1980s at the time of the savings cooperative banks crisis. After taking over the assets, these asset management companies (AMC) become responsible for selling them off. The difference between the initial value of the asset and the amount recovered through the asset sale should be financed by state bonds.

Since the beginning of 2000, this programme has contributed in reducing substantially the huge piles of debt of the largest SOEs and boosting the profitability of the public sector. It also represents a first step in resolving the structural problem that links the investment performance of SOEs and the evolution of state commercial bank lending practices. AMCs are normally not supposed to take over new NPLs (after 1996) nor to concentrate on old loans that are difficult to recover. It is supposed to will further help the state commercial banks concentrate their efforts in reforming their credit-lending practices on the new loans made since the mid-1990s as well as to clean their portfolio. On this basis, the governor of the PBOC declared in his annual speech in January 2000 that the cancellation of debts anticipated by this programme would constitute the last 'free lunch' to which the major state-owned enterprises would be entitled. Furthermore, AMCs have a clear mandate to focus on debt resolution and should play a more active role than the banking system in pushing SOEs to restructure their activities. They are entitled to exchange between them some assets in order to become larger creditors and concentrate their efforts on a more limited number of enterprises.

However, from the point of view of an improvement in the system of corporate governance, the programme does not go to the root of the problem. But, for the following reasons, the AMCs, which are entering into the boardrooms of these major SOEs, are unable to play their role as 'active' stakeholder, namely to control the actions of managers and even less to censure them:

- An asymmetry in information on the firm. Given the lack of transparency in the accountancy system and the poor functioning of the board of directors, managers of the SOEs still control access to strategic information in the firm.
- Their lack of qualified human resources and skills to play a strategic role in SOE governance.
- The high number of companies affected by the programme, nearly 1,000 big SOEs, which multiplies the problems of competence. For Huarong alone, its 407 billion yuan of assets involves about 71,000 debtor companies.[13]
- Finally, the statutes given to such companies do not bestow them with any absolute and real shareholder power, but rather a power that is subject to negotiation with the central and the local bureaucracies in charge of big SOEs. In several cases, AMCs have been unable to drastically restructure companies in a hopeless situation despite becoming, after asset disposal, the main shareholder of these companies, nor has it been able to combat the manipulation of the bankruptcy proceedings by local authorities.

Credit Policy in the Banking System

Some important reforms in lending practices have also been implemented in the state commercial bank sector, which dominates the credit market for industrial enterprises. After the first reforms, in the beginning of 1980s, most lending was channelled through the state commercial banks which received money from the PBOC. Banks were under control of the local bureaucracy and lent money to SOEs without questioning the profitability of investments. This phenomenon greatly contributed to the proliferation of undersized investments in all sectors and the lack of concentration in the industry. After 1993, the government realised that NPLs were growing at an alarming rate and that this policy was not sustainable. The PBOC reacted by significantly reducing both its subsidies to the SOEs

---

13. *South China Morning Post*, February 19, 2001.

and its loans to the commercial banks; subsidies to SOEs were reduced, according to the World Bank, from 7.5 per cent of GDP in 1992 to 2.3 per cent in 1994, then to less than 1 per cent after 1995. From 1994 to 1998 loans from the PBOC to state commercial banks grew at an average annual rate of 6 per cent instead of 20 per cent before 1994. Loren Brandt and Zhu Xiaodong have calculated that, between 1996 and 1998, the stock of PBOC loans to the banks actually declined from 142 billion yuan to 121 billion yuan.[14] In such a scenario, decision to turn the big four state banks into commercial banks and to clean their balance sheet made the banks more conservative knowing that bad loans were now less likely to be financed by new loans from the PBOC. These steps were followed by a series of reforms of the banking system. The most significant of these were a reduction in the number of provincial subsidiaries of the PBOC (from 31 to 12); and the creation of supra-regional branches in order to limit the power of local cadres in the allocation of credit to companies. By the same token, those in charge of the Central Bank's supra-regional subsidiaries, as well as the four major commercial state banks, were no longer appointed by the local authorities, but by their head offices in Peking. The four state commercial banks were also required to increase their profits and to 'clean up their balance sheets' by restricting bad debt. They were thus seeking, even if insufficiently, to develop competence in risk analysis. In this context, they were increasingly unwilling to lend money to companies that are already heavily in debt. Companies, for their part, had been required, since 1996, to deal with only one bank (the principal bank system, called *zhuban yinghang*) and to close their accounts in the other banks.[15] They were also subject to an evaluation of their financial situation by auditing firms, or to ranking agencies, copied (even if somewhat clumsily) on the American model. During the course of 1997, after the implementation of this measure, some 2,000 large- and medium-sized Shanghai state companies were audited and ranked according to their financial situation. Moreover, they were issued a 'loan certificate' summarising their credit track record, a document they are supposed to present to their bank for any new credit request.

14. *Asian Wall Street Journal*, April 7, 2000.

15. Zhongguo jinrong xuehui (Chinese Society for Financial Studies), *Zhongguo jinrong nianjian* (Chinese Financial Annual), Peking, Zhongguo jinrong nianjian bianji bu, 1997, p.339.

Thousands of inefficient SMEs in the state and collective sectors that were not able to sustain their development on their own profits were progressively starving of funds. In tandem with a market dominated by demand, it is now more difficult for the local authorities not only to embark on industrial projects where demand is already saturated or dominated by efficient producers in other provinces, but also to sustain local companies which have not succeeded in modernising and adapting themselves to the competition. State commercial banks certainly continue to subsidise, in the form of credit, unprofitable companies, but they do so on the orders of the central authorities to ensure social stability.

Nevertheless, the situation is less obvious for the biggest SOEs. Since the beginning of the Asian financial crisis when it was evident that exports and domestic consumption were not going to sustain a high growth rate, the central government turned to an expansionary fiscal policy. In macroeconomic terms, this constitutes a wise decision but in terms of resource allocation, foreign investment banks[16] and other observers[17] are all arguing that most of the money is directly channelled to big SOEs, which also partly explains the spectacular reversal in their financial indicators. If we leave aside the problem of resource allocation efficiency that Loren Brandt and Zhu Xiaodong are raising, (mainly that the non-state sector has proved to be more efficient in allocating resources than have SOEs), in terms of corporate governance, this policy does not help to change the large SOEs' culture of easy money nor does it help to use the banking system as an efficient external control mechanism for their investment decisions.

Privatisation of SMEs

The disengagement of the state in SMEs in the state and the collective sector has happened in various ways. After having established the principle 'grasp the big and release the small', the central government has let local governments use a number of ways in which to reform state and collective SMEs. For example, in the Guangxi autonomous region, between 1993 and 1998, 1,205 state

16. BNP Parisbas Peregrine, "Inside China", March 2001; Credit LyonnaisSecurities, "Emerging Markets", 1st Quarter 2001; S G Economic Research "Quarterly Economic Review, Fundamental Asia", July 2000.

17. Brandt, Loren and Zhu Xiaodong (2000). *Asian Wall Street Journal*, April 7.

SMEs (about 15 per cent of the total number of SMEs in Guangxi) were reformed in various ways: 93 were made into joint stock companies in which the state remained the major stakeholder; 222 were made into joint stock companies and sold to their workforce in the framework of the so called cooperative shareholding system (*gufen hezuo zhi*); 29 were sold to a Chinese investor (without it being specified whether it was the director of the company, a local investor or one from another province); 44 were merged with another company in the region; 469 were leased; 30 went into liquidation; and 318 were reformed using other unspecified means (Wu, 1999). Another example, this time in a more highly developed coastal city, the municipality of Shunde in Guangdong province, has since 1992 implemented an ambitious programme to reform its 1,001 state companies. Only 94 remained under the direct ownership of the municipality; in infrastructure, certain high technology industries, or those considered to be strategic at the national level. The government maintained a minority interest in another 70 by 1998.[18] All the other companies had been sold or leased.

Privatisation has been an important means of restructuring. Among the various methods of privatisation, certain general principles have been accepted by the central authorities. They have chosen to favour the sale of state shares rather than the free distribution of shares, whether inside the company as in Russia, or outside (to the population as a whole) as in former Czechoslovakia. The sale of capital to employees (in the form of shares) has in fact been the most widely used method to reform state and collective urban SMEs in difficulty. The various monographs produced in the provinces of the interior[19] indicate that this method may have been applied in almost a third of state and collective urban SMEs affected by the reforms (which amounts to much less if one refers to the total number of state and collective companies). Although less frequently used than co-

18. *China Daily*, January 18-24, 1998, Business Weekly.

19. Yingquan, Lei, Huang Xingguo, Hu Yuqing and Ren Zhiqin (1999). "Dui Sichuansheng qiye guoyou zichan linke guanli youguan qingkuang de yanjiubaogao" (Research report on the situation of the management and ownership of state assets in the companies in Sichuan province), *Guoyou Zichan Guanli*, No. 4, pp.50-51; Rengui, Ma (1999). "Guozi guanli tizhi gaige de youyi tansuo. Nanning shi zujianguozi jingying gongsi qingkuang de diaocha" (Exploration of the advantages of the reform of the state assets management system. Enquiry on the situation of state asset management companies established by the city of Nanning), *Guoyou Zichan Guanli*, No. 3, pp.63-64; Xu, Qing, *op. cit.*

operative shareholding, another method has been put to use consisting of totally privatising the capital of companies by auctioning it off in the centres for sale and exchange of state assets (*guoyou zichan jiaoyi zhongxin*), which have been set up in all large municipalities. Total privatisation, accompanied by sale of the capital to investors outside the company, has mostly involved companies with heavy debts. Finally, the last method used by local governments, has been based on partial privatisation with the maintenance of majority or minority ownership by the state. This method has been widely favoured by local authorities in companies in good financial condition as it has made it possible to combine the continuing state ownership with financial deals that are attractive to local cadres and company managers who have acquired part of the capital of these companies.

If one refers to the numerical data published by the municipalities in an effort to work out how many state and collective SMEs have been privatised, one could conclude that a widespread move to privatisation has taken place in China. But faced with the lack of precise statistics made public on a national level, it is extremely difficult to evaluate the extent of the privatisation of state and collective SMEs. One of the first pitfalls lies in confusing the selling of state assets with the privatisation of companies. Not only have local authorities kept 100 per cent ownership of a relatively large number of urban state and collective SMEs, but they have also resorted to the leasing of companies, which does not alter the property structure in any way. In cases of partial privatisation, the local authorities have maintained their control over the businesses through state AMCs set up in all China's large municipalities. While these companies have made possible a simplification of the organisation chart of the administrative apparatus of municipalities responsible for the management of state and collective SMEs, case studies made on these companies found that they tend to behave as did the old municipal industrial offices (Huchet and Richet, 2000). Moreover, even when all or part of the capital has been sold, this does not necessarily mean that it has been acquired by a private investor, whether Chinese or foreign. On the contrary, a part of the transactions in the assets of state and collective SMEs—which is difficult to estimate given the lack of statistics at the national level on property reform, but probably considerable if one goes by the monographs at local level—has taken place within the state and collective sector. Similarly, mergers have, in most cases, been organised by the local administrative authorities who have simply transferred all or part of the capital of a company to another state company organised as a group or holding company.

Where foreign private investors are concerned, there have been one-off transactions at knockdown prices of production equipment belonging to state and collective SMEs which have gone out of production.[20] But in general, given the considerable number of companies put on the market, very few foreign investors have ventured to take them over because of the high transaction costs of such operations and the unattractive nature of their assets. On the other hand, take-overs by Chinese private investors have been much more numerous. Case studies made on Chinese private corporate groups (Huchet, 2000) have shown many examples of aggressive external growth by the taking over of state SMEs in difficulty in other provinces. The Xin Xiwang (New Hope) group in Sichuan, for example, China's biggest private group, the leader in the animal foodstuffs sector, has taken over 13 state SMEs in various provinces since 1993.[21]

In general, the figures for sales and exchanges of state assets available to us in the monographs produced by the municipalities are a poor indicator for determining the extent of the privatisation of urban state and collective SMEs. The *China Statistical Yearbook 2000* shows a sizeable decrease in the number of state companies in industry; these have fallen from 1,27,000 in 1996 to 61,300 in 1999. However, this figure includes all state companies regardless of size, and does not tell us if this drastic reduction is due to the closing of state companies, to the merging of public sector companies, or to the transfer to the heading of 'joint stock companies' (*gufenzhi jingji*) of some of the state companies that have in fact been transformed into joint stock companies. After approximations of these three factors, one would arrive at a figure of between 23,000 and 30,000 state companies privatised in the industrial sector, or between 18 per cent and 23 per cent of public sector companies in relation to the peak in

20. Yanzheng, Cao, Qian Yingyi and Barry R. Weingast (1998). "The Sale Goes On: Transforming Small Enterprises in China", *Transition*, February, pp.5-7.

21. Interview, New Hope, Chengdu, April 20, 1998.

1996. It is a sizeable figure which, if confirmed by studies at the national level, would signal profound changes in the Chinese economy.

If we consider the effectiveness of restructuring, the most positive outcomes have been achieved by companies acquired by outside investors, Chinese and foreign. These companies have not only been freed from the stranglehold of the local bureaucracy, they have also benefited from new, more dynamic management, from a brand name with high consumer notoriety and new markets provided by the new owner as well as a reduction of their debt load by the banks, negotiated by the new owner with the local authorities. The case studies on the private group *Xin Xiwang* New Hope have shown that two key players, the company director and the financial manager, were immediately replaced by senior managers from Xin Xiwang, with a view to inculcating rapidly financial discipline and new methods of personnel and production management in the acquired SME. In fact, this process of 'subsidiarisation' with the arrival of an active investor able to bring know-how and with the power to reform the company, has already proved its effectiveness in the capitalist economies, as well as in the restructuring of companies in the former socialist countries of Eastern Europe.

As for those companies whose capital has been sold to the workforce, the results so far seem pretty negative. Once again, it is difficult to get an idea at the national level as no serious impact study has been published (or perhaps even carried out) by the central authorities. When we compare the results of different studies carried out on the reform of SMEs (Wu, 1999; Xu, 1999; Huchet, 2000; Dong, 1999; Zong, 2000), two major kinds of problem emerge, which have, moreover, been widely documented in other countries in transition, particularly in Russia (Blasi, 1997). On the one hand, the injection of capital from the acquisition of shares by employees is insufficient to wipe out the debts and meet the need for restructuring, which includes a drastic modernisation of the production system. And on the other, the power structure and the incentive system that emerge from this kind of privatisation are often unable to generate any real reforming impulse in a company. There are some company directors with undeniable managerial know-how who can take advantage of their new autonomy *vis-à-vis* the administration to spark daring reforms, as is shown in some of the success stories highlighted in the Chinese economic press. However, the impact on control is generally limited, for two main reasons. Firstly, managers are still appointed by local political leaders and are still considered to be local government officials. Their membership of the Party is also still crucial for their careers. This factor makes it impossible to break with relations of political allegiance that are sometimes contrary to the interests of the company, but above all it encourages rent-seeking strategies, since company managers consider themselves to be both underpaid and not responsible for the destiny of the company (even if they are majority shareholders). Secondly, in spite of privatisation, no alternative power emerges within the company, even where the employees are the majority shareholders. The lack of independent unions, the growth of unemployment and the end of jobs for life, have permanently deprived employees of any means of bringing organised and official pressure to bear on their future or on that of the company (Leung, 1998). In a context similar to what has happened in Russia, none of the new institutions arising from privatisation such as boards of directors and supervising committees are able to exercise internal control over the behaviour and decisions of company bosses who, in most cases, concurrently hold the positions of chairman of the board of directors and supervisor, company chairman and Party Secretary. Lastly, the workers' incentive system was supposed to have been improved by their new status as owners of the company. In places where this influence existed, it was exercised only briefly, long enough for the workers to resell their shares, and to realise that they had not gained any decision-making power. In reality, factors such as the danger of unemployment and the end of jobs for life, have proved to be much more powerful factors in modifying the attitude of workers on the job than has the holding of a few shares (Zhao and Nichols, 1996; Lee, 1999).

Whatever the methods used, the effectiveness of restructuring has nonetheless varied very widely from one region to another. According to the monographs and the information collected in different case studies, there is a fairly clear-cut difference between the coastal regions and those of the northeast and the interior. In the Guangxi autonomous region, after five years of reforms, almost 70 per cent of companies had not recorded any improvement in their profits, while 25 per cent had registered a decline in profitability (Wu, 1999).

Coastal cities such as Dalian, Shanghai and Canton, and provinces such as Shandong, Jiangsu, Zhejiang and Fujian, are apparently doing much better. The profitability and debt ratios of state companies in 1999 by provinces show, in Table 5.3, that with some exceptions (Yunnan where high profits come from the tobacco industry, which is entirely state-owned, Tibet where value is too low to be significant, and Heilongjiang, which has surprising profitability given the size of its state sector), the coastal provinces are much better off than those of the northeast and of the interior where the state sector share remains above the national average. This difference lies in the fact that restructuring in the coastal provinces has benefited from a much more propitious environment in the coastal cities with a more dynamic and transparent market for take-over of these companies, with more competent managers with experience of competition. Also, a higher price of the land in coastal cities has given more opportunities for these companies to sell their land use rights to restructure their activities or even to go into bankruptcy (World Bank, 2000).

Thus, this kind of privatisation is far from being a sufficient condition of success in the restructuring of this category of company. In fact, any improvement in the performance of these companies depends, above all, on an improvement in the system of external control (depoliticisation of the banks that would make it possible to increase the budgetary constraints on companies, deregulation or abolition of local protectionism in order to expose these companies to competition) and the establishment of a social insurance system, that would allows them to deal with the social costs linked to bankruptcies, which are likely to increase in this category of company.

Concluding Remarks

Despite some positive results following the implementation of a large programme of enterprise restructuring since the mid-1990s, we have shown various limits and bottlenecks in this reform process. China's accession to the WTO will bring some substantial changes in the business environment of domestic firms, and will more than ever confront the Chinese government with some specific problems that are linked with the legacy of industrialisation during Mao's period and with the way reforms were implemented between 1978 and the mid-1990s.

Table 5.3

Profits and Debt by Provinces in the State Sector

	Profits/ Production Costs	*Assets/Debt (Per Cent)*	*Share of the State Sector in Industrial Production (Per Cent)*
National Average	2,89	61,98	48,6
Heilongjiang	15,43	64,88	83
Tibet	14,42	35,6	78
Yunnan	8,80	52,81	81
Fujian	6,36	60,62	33
Guangdong	5,80	57,22	28
Shanghai	5,57	50,95	51
Zhejiang	5,25	52,24	21
Peking	3,63	60,16	73
Shandong	3,24	62,87	40
Hebei	3,20	59,92	55
Jiangsu	2,61	60,3	31
Hubei	1,94	65,03	60
Jilin	1,55	66,78	84
Henan	1,12	65,56	51
Anhui	0,83	61,31	64
Liaoning	0,76	59,96	66
Shanxi	0,59	65,54	67
Sichuan	0,57	63,66	66
Guizhou	0,36	69,02	81
Hunan	0,12	70,21	66
Guangxi	-0,02	69,81	69
Xinjiang	-0,16	63,35	88
Hainan	-0,63	73,73	72
Inner Mongolia	-0,65	61,54	84
Qinghai	-0,75	66,48	87
Ningxia	-0,90	67,78	78
Shaanxi	-0,95	69,77	77
Jiangxi	-1,09	70,34	81
Tianjin	-1,60	65,92	31,8
Gansu	-1,85	69,83	78
Chongqing	-2,36	67,5	71

Note : * Only firms with accountancy autonomy are considered here (that excludes firms with a turnover below five million yuan).

Source : *Zhongguo tongji nianjian*, (2000), p. 433 (*China Statistical Yearbook*).

Policymakers should tackle these limits and bottlenecks in a rather short period of time if they want to limit the social and financial costs of China's accession to the WTO. If the Chinese government does not address these problems, several negative consequences could reduce the positive gains of China's accession to the WTO:

- Firstly, a real risk exists to see domestic enterprises not sufficiently prepared to cope with the new competition, especially the category of SME in the state and the collective sector.
- Secondly, without some adequate policies, inequalities among regions which are already very large, will continue to grow and will bring some serious consequences for the social stability of the country.
- Finally, international experiences show that industrial and financial restructuring should be swift and decisive in order to limit its costs. In this respect, if the data are accurate and reliable, Chinese policy makers have a window of opportunity to accelerate industrial restructuring, given the current level of their financial resources. Delaying reforms in this area would certainly further deteriorate the fiscal situation and make the reform even more difficult in the future.

References

Amsden, A. (1989). *Asia's Next Giant: South Korea and Late Industrialization*, Oxford: Oxford University Press.

Blasi, J. (1997). "Corporate Ownership and Corporate Governance in the Russian Federation", Ira W. Lieberman, Stilpon S. Nestor and Raj M. Desai in *Between State and Market. Mass Privatization in Transition Economies*, Washington D.C.: The World Bank & OECD, pp. 162-170.

Byrd, W.A. (1992). *Chinese Industrial Firms Under Reform*, p. 438, Oxford: Oxford University Press.

Chenhong, Xujing (1999). "Guanyu Xiamenshi guoqi gaige de diaocha", (Research into the Reform of State Companies in the city of Xiamen), *Guoyou zichan guanli*, No. 4, pp.52-54.

Cheng, Enfu (1999). "Shanghai Guoyou Zichan Yunxing Fenxi" (Analysis of the workings of State Assets in Shanghai), *Guoyou Zichan Guanli*, No. 3, pp.44-49.

China Research Team (1998). "China: Price War and Price Control" in *Warburg Dillon Read*, December.

Ding, X.L. (2000). "The Illicit Asset Stripping of Chinese State Firms", in *The China Journal*, No. 43, January, pp.1-28.

Dong, Ying (1999). "Shandong Zhucheng Gufen Hezuozhi Qiye Yanshi Fenxi" (Analysis of the Co-Operative shareholding system of the City of Zhucheng in Shandong Province), *Gongye Jingji yanjiu*, No. 11, pp.5-11.

Evans, P. (1995). *Embedded Autonomy. States & Industrial Transformation*, Princeton: Princeton University Press, p.323.

Fields, K.J. (1995). *Enterprise and the State in Korea and Taiwan*, Cornell, Cornell University Press, p. 269.

Huchet, J.-F. (2000). "The Hidden Aspect of Public Sector Reforms in China; State and Collective SMEs in Urban Areas", in *China Perspectives*, No. 32, November-December, pp.37-48.

———. (1999). "Concentration and Emergence of Corporate Groups in Chinese Industry", in *China Perspectives*, No. 23, May-June.

Huchet, J.-F. and Richet, X. (2000). *Between Bureaucracy and Market: Chinese Industrial Groups in Search of New Forms of Corporate Governance*, Working Paper, Centre d'Etudes Français sur la Chine Contemporaine, October.

Jefferson, G.H. (1993). *Are China's Rural Enterprises Outperforming State-Owned Enterprises?*, Symposium on Economic Transition in China, July, Haikou, China.

Jefferson, G.H., Rawski, T.G. and Zheng Yuxin (1994). *Institutional Change and Industrial Innovation in Transitional Economies*, Research Paper Series, Washington D.C.: World Bank, p.25.

Lardy, N.R. (2000). "The Challenge of Bank Restructuring in China", in *China Research, CLSA Emerging Market*, April 27, p.16.

Lardy, N.R. (2000). "Fiscal Sustainability: between a Rock and a hard Place", in *China Economic Quarterly*, No. 2, pp.36-41.

Lee Ching-Kwan (1999). "From Organised Dependence to Disorganised Despotism: Changing Labour Regimes in Chinese Factories", *The China Quarterly*, No. 157, March, pp.44-71.

Lei, Yingquan, Huang Xingguo, Hu Yuqing and Ren Zhiqin (1999). "Dui Sichuansheng Qiye Guoyou Zichan Linke Guanli Youguan Qingkuang de Yanjiu Baogao" (Research report on the situation of the Management and Ownership of State Assets in the Companies in Sichuan province), *Guoyou Zichan Guanli*, No. 4, pp.50-51.

Lemoine, F. (2000). *FDI and the Opening Up of China's Economy*, Paris: CEPII, Document de travail, Working Paper, p.88.

Leung, Trini W.Y. (1998). "S'organiser Pour Défendre Ses Droits; Contestations Ouvrières en Chine dans les années in *Perspectives Chinoises*, No. 48, juillet-août, pp.6-23.

Lu, Zhongyuan (1999). "Ruhe Fangzhi Guoyou Zichan Yingyun Jigou Biancheng Fanpai Gongsi", Shanghai, Wuhan, Shenzhen de shixian ji qishi" (How to Prevent Institutions in charge of State Assets from Becoming Bureaucratised Companies), *Zhongguo gongye jingji*, No. 7, pp.18-20.

Lu, Yuan and Child, J. (1996). "Decentralisation of Decision Making in China's State Enterprises" in *Management Issues in China; Vol. I Domestic Enterprises*, David H. Brown and Robin Porter (eds.), London: Routledge, p.268.

Ma, Rengui (1999). "Guozi Guanli Tizhi Gaige de Youyi Tansuo. Nanning shi Zujianguozi Jingying Gongsi Qingkuang de Diaocha" (Exploration of the Advantages of the Reform of the State Assets Management system. Enquiry on the situation of state asset management companies established by the city of Nanning), *Guoyou Zichan guanli*, No. 3, pp.63-64.

Maxfield, S. and Schneider, B.R. (ed.) (1997). *Business and the State in Developing Countries*, Ithaca: Cornell University Press, p348.

Naughton, B. (1995). *Growing Out of the Plan Chinese Economic Reform 1978-1993*, Cambridge: Cambridge University Press, p.379.

Nee, V. (1992). "Organisational Dynamics of Market Transition: Hybrid Forms, Property Rights and Mixed Economy in China", in *Administrative Science Quarterly*, No. 37, pp.1-27.

OECD (2000). *Reforming China's Enterprises*, Paris: OECD, p.130.

Oi, J.C. (1995). "The Role of the Local State in China's Transitional Economy", *The China Quarterly*, December, No. 144, pp.1132-49.

Putterman, L. (1995). "The Role of Ownership and Property Rights in China's Economic Transition", *The China Quarterly*, December, No. 144, pp. 1047-64.

Rawski, T.G. (1995). "Implications of China's Reform Experience", *The China Quarterly*, December, No. 144, pp.1150-73.

Shanghaishi guoyouzichan guanli moshi yanjiu kejizu (1999). "Shanghai Shi Guoyou Zichanguanli Moshi Zhong de Lingkong Xitong", *Zhongguo Gongye Jingji*, No. 3, pp.19-24.

Shen, Zhiyu (1999). *New Developments of Enterprise Groups in China*, Paper prepared for the International Conference on "The Emergence and the Structuring of Corporate Groups in the P.R. of China", University of Hong Kong, November4-5.

Stark, D. (1997). "Recombinant Property in East European Capitalism", in G. Grabher and D. Stark (eds.), *Restructuring Networks in Post-Socialism*, Oxford, Oxford University Press, pp.36-69.

Wade, R. (1990). *Governing the Market. Economic Theory and the Role of Government in East Asian Industrialisation*, Princeton: Princeton University Press, p.438.

Wang, Shaoguang and Hu Angang (1999). *The Political Economy of Uneven Development. The Case of China*, Armonk: M.E. Sharp.

Wang, Hong (2000). "Shunde Qiye Chanquan Gaige de Diaocha" (Enquiry Into the Reform of the Property of Companies in Shunde), *Gaige*, No. 1, pp.43-46.

Wang Hua, Richet, X., Wang Wei (2001). "Foreign Direct Investment in the Chinese Automotive Industry: Country of Origin Effects", unpublished, Paris.

Warner, M. (1995). *The Management of Human Resources in Chinese Industry*, London: Macmillan.

Weitzman, M.L. and Xu Chenggang (1993). *Chinese Township Village Enterprises as Vaguely Defined Cooperatives*, London: Development Economics Research Programme, London School of Economics.

Wong, Christine P.W. (ed.) (1997). *Financing Local Government in the People's Republic of China*, New York: Oxford University Press, p.377.

Wong, Christine P.W. (2000). "La Nouvelle Donne Entre Gouvernement Central et les Collectivités Locales. La Gestion des Finances Publiques et la Réforme Fiscale de 1994", in *Perspectives Chinoises*, juillet-août, pp.56-67

World Bank (2000). "China: Overcoming Rural Poverty", *Report no. 21105*, Washington D.C.

Wu, Pinggui (1999). "Dui Shenhua Guoyou Zhongxiaoxing Qiye Gaige de Sikao" (Reflections On The Deepening of the Reform of State SMEs), *Guoyou zichan guanli*, No. 4, pp.35-37.

Xu, Qing (1999). "Dangqian Zhiyue Ningxia Guoyou Zhongxiao Qiye Gaizhi Nandian Wenti Youxi" (Analysis of the problems in the Reform of the State SME System in the Province du Ningxia), *Ningxia Shehuikexue*, No. 3, pp.47-52.

Zhao, Minghua and Nichols, T. (1996). "Management Control of Labour in State-Owned Enterprises: Cases from the Textile Industry", *The China Journal*, No. 36, July, pp.1-24.

Zong, Han (2000). "Gufen Hezuozhi de Fazhan ji qi Jiaojian" (Development of Co-Operative Shareholding), *Zhongguo Gongye Jingji*, No. 2, pp.9-12.

6

Firm and Industry Response to Liberalisation in India

Theory and Evidence

MANMOHAN AGARWAL and ALOKESH BARUA

INTRODUCTION

The process of closer integration of a national economy with the world economy is through reduction of both tariff and non-tariff barriers to trade as well as barriers to the establishment of foreign firms. Usually such economic reforms at the external level or globalisation are accompanied by internal reforms also. Economic reforms in India since 1991 have resulted in removal of many entry restrictions for production domestically including entry of foreign firms. External liberalisation has meant reduction of tariffs and removal of quantitative restrictions. In this chapter, we examine the effects of internal liberalisation on firm behaviour in the Indian manufacturing sector.

For any analysis of the possible effects of globalisation on an economy we first of all require a framework for analysis. Economists following the standard HOS model generally view globalisation or increased openness in terms of expansion of trade and foreign investment with the desirable consequences of increased efficiency and welfare. The increase in efficiency is seen in terms of industrial adjustments through specialisation in industries in which the country has a comparative advantage. Such specialisation is usually associated with gains from trade. The basic mechanism that brings such changes in the economy is the change in the relative prices of goods and services. For the developed countries, however, the price effects of reducing tariffs may be insignificant as these countries have already lowered their tariff rates substantially (Rodrik, 1999). So Rodrik argues that increased openness in these countries affects the elasticity of (labour demand in his case) demand due to increased competition from the cheap labour intensive products of the developing countries. However, Adrian Wood (1999) argues that price changes may be substantial for developing countries as these countries begin the process of lowering their tariffs from very high existing tariff rates. In India, as far as we know, no attempt has so far been made to examine the price effects due to liberalisation but casual empiricism confirms that for many industrial products there has been a substantial fall in prices.

Openness however has costs, which can be measured in terms of industrial adjustments and movements in relative factor-returns. The adverse movement in factor-returns against the scare factor makes the acceptability of the liberalisation drive a difficult political proposition, if the scare factor has dominant lobbying power in the political decisionmaking process. Further, in a federal state if the fruits of liberalisation are not shared among the states on some egalitarian basis, a problem of making liberalisation politically acceptable created. Das and Barua (1996), have observed significant increase in inter-state inequalities in India since 1991. How trade liberalisation contributes to such increasing inequalities has not been carefully studied so far. Finally, an important point to be noted is that the distinction between the firm and the industry becomes blurred under the assumption of perfect competition.

On the other hand, increased openness, under the assumption of market imperfections and scale economies, is expected to lead to an increase in scale efficiency through intra-industry specialisation and improvement in welfare *via* the effects of increased varieties on consumer demand. A substantial increase in the levels of intra-industry trade has been observed in India since 1991 (Chakraborty, 2002). The real benefits from increasing returns are, however, not unambiguous as scale advantage from increased production in export goods must be balanced against the diseconomies from the decline in the production of import competing goods (Rodrik, 1988). Chakraborty (2002), provides some evidence of increasing returns in export industries and decreasing returns in import competing goods. The cost of adjustments may be minimal if the industrial structures in import and export goods are similar and this would limit the adverse implications on income distribution due to increased openness.

Openness also plays an important disciplining role in the market. It breaks domestic monopoly and forces the market to behave competitively. Thus, one would observe reduction in market concentration due to globalisation.

We however cannot decide *a priori* which particular framework will be the appropriate one to examine the possible implications of globalisation on Indian industries and firms? While economists are often tempted to draw *ad hoc* conclusions based on certain presuppositions, it may be misleading to draw such conclusions if the presuppositions are incorrect. For instance, the existence of market imperfection does not necessarily preclude the relevance of the HOS framework to analyse the effects of globalisation. The relative price effect may play a far more dominating role than the standard conclusions based on market imperfection. The issue is therefore open to empirical verification.

Preliminary investigations of the effects of globalisation on the direction of changes in trade and production structure for the Indian industries for the period of 1987-88 to 1995-96 (Barua, 2003) reveal the following:

1. For 166 ASI 3-digit industries, the estimated capital: labour ratio has been significantly increasing over time.
2. The estimated K/L ratios are negative and skilled/unskilled wage rates are positive and significantly related to net trade, suggesting that India is poor in capital but abundant in skilled labour.
3. Net trade deflated by output shows a significant negative relationship with the net value-added thereby implying a negative relationship between industry size and export.

While the first two results are in tune with the standard conclusions based on the HOS model, the third result is new. It echoes the well-known result based on firm level studies that there is a negative relationship between firm size and export intensities.

The above results strongly suggest that the HOS framework explains well the economy wide responses to globalisation.

The Role of Market Imperfection

Casual empiricism reveals the existence of various forms of market imperfections in Indian industries. One obvious example is high market concentration in many sectors (Leff, 1979). We also know that Indian industries had been subject to many types of entry restrictions such as the licensing system before 1991. The removal of entry restrictions is expected to increase the level of market competition both amongst domestic firms as well as foreign firms. It is, therefore, important to examine also the effects of market imperfections on firm behaviour and of globalisation on market imperfection.

THE EFFECTS OF ENTRY

We use a Cournot oligopoly open-economy model, elaborated in Agarwal and Barua (1993; 1994), to look at the effect of entry on export behaviour of firms and industries. We describe the basic model in the Technical Appendix A-6.1 of this chapter. The main objective of the model is to examine how entry liberalisation for domestic firms affects firm behaviour in respects of exports and domestic sales, and what are its effects on industry concentration. Entry may also affect profits, an important indicator, as profit expectations govern investment and growth which is an important objective of liberalisation. We then see how liberalisation of entry of foreign firms has affected the behaviour of firms in the Indian economy.

The model assumes that all the firms in the industry produce a homogenous good. The country under consideration is a small country in the world market and hence the firms face an infinitely elastic foreign demand curve. However, the country protects the industry from import competition by ascribing a sufficiently high tariff or quota so that the industry's imports are zero. The domestic market is characterised by an oligopoly where all the firms face an inverse demand function and employ a Cournot strategy.

Each firm maximises profits which are defined for a representative firm as

$$\Pi = f(Q_d)q_d + p_r q_r - C(x) \qquad (1)$$

Under the Cournot assumption, an interior, profit maximisation gives the first-order conditions from which the following important results follow:

Result 1:

In equilibrium the firm equates the domestic marginal revenue (defined in terms of domestic sales) and the given foreign price (foreign marginal revenue) with the marginal cost (defined for the total output).

Result 2:

In equilibrium the firm produces on the rising segment of the marginal cost function depicting that it exhausts all internal economies of scale.

Result 3:

Provided all firms face identical cost function, in equilibrium each firm will produce the same output, sell same amounts in the domestic and foreign markets. The aggregate output and sales in each market then will be a multiple of the individual firm output and sales in each market.

Since all firms face the same marginal costs and foreign price, the output at which the firm's marginal cost will equal the marginal revenue from foreign sales will be the same for each firm so that each firm produces the same output. Because of the symmetry of the Cournot assumption, the domestic sales of each firm will be the same; since output of each firm is the same, exports are the same for all firms.

Result 4:

For non-identical cost function, the most efficient firm (firm facing the least cost function among the cost functions of all firms) will export the maximum amount, although all firms will sell identical amounts in the domestic market.

This is an interesting result at variance with many empirical observations, that small firms export a proportionately larger share of their output.

The more efficient firm will produce more, and since all firms because of symmetry, sell the same amount in the domestic market, the more efficient firm will export a larger output.

A diagrammatic exposition of the equilibrium situation for a typical firm is provided in Figure 6.1. AC is the firm's average cost curve and the point C indicates the point at which the average cost is the minimum. P_f is the foreign price. F (Q_d) is the domestic demand curve (shown as linear) and MR is the marginal revenue curve. We have drawn the figure in such a way that production for the domestic market alone is not viable since the average cost curve lies uniformly above the demand curve. However, with the possibilities for trade the firm may produce at C where the foreign price is tangent to AC and export the entire amount. But it is very unlikely that a firm would decide to produce for the export market only. So we assume that there exists a domestic market for the good. Under protection the firm may be able to discriminate between the domestic and the foreign market and will charge a higher price, $P_{d,}$ in the domestic market. The firm will still produce at C but it will export only an amount BC and sell the remaining amount P_f B in the domestic market. However, the world price may lie below P_f. If P_{f*} is the foreign price then the firm may produce either at M or P. But P is not a stable equilibrium. At the point M that satisfies the conditions, (2)-(3) of the appendix unit cost exceeds the marginal cost by an amount of TM. The firm, however, is making a profit in the domestic market per unit of sale equal to the amount NQ, though making a loss on foreign sale as unit cost is higher than foreign price. The firm will only produce and export when the profits in the domestic market exceed the loss on exports. Possibilities of exports may lead to positive production even though no production would take place if there were only domestic sales, e.g. when foreign price is P_f ; but possibility of export need not necessarily lead to production, e.g. when foreign price is P_f^*.

Now the effects of entry can be examined in the model by increasing the number of firms. In doing this exercise we assume for simplicity that all firms are identical and further that all firms export. As firm output in our model is determined by the international price, which is independent of the number of firms, output of an individual firm is not affected by entry. Two results follow from this.

Result 5:

Firm output is independent of the entry of new firms. Therefore, aggregate output increases monotonically with the increase in the number of firms in the industry.

As the number of firms in the industry increases, the domestic sales of each individual firm decline. Since output of the firm is fixed, the exports of each firm would increase. Thus,

Figure 6.1

Equilibrium for a Typical Firm

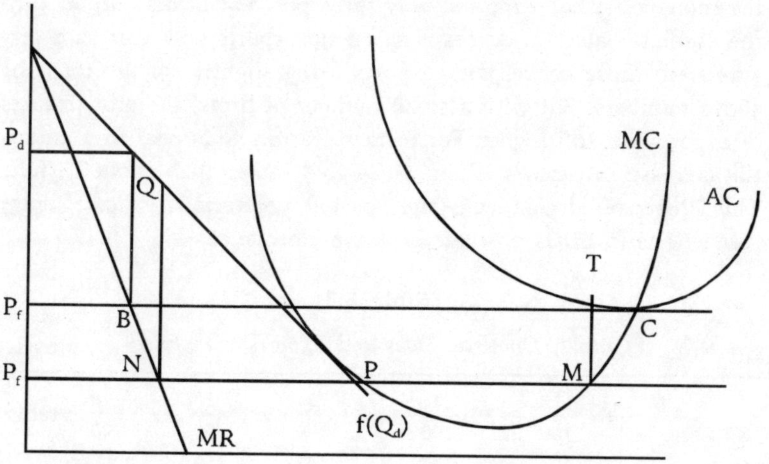

Result 6:

With entry each firm sells less in the domestic market and sells more in the export market.

Table 6.1 below shows the level of output, domestic sales and exports for a few values of N.[1] It is based on the assumptions that domestic demand is characterised by a linear demand curve and that in the initial situation of a monopoly, 5 per cent of the firm's output was exported. So if we assume that output is 100, then exports would be 5. In this case the constant of integration C would be 190.

It is obvious from Table 6.1, how rapidly exports increase as entry occurs. If the monopolist was exporting only 5 units then entry of one additional firm leads to an almost 15 fold increase in exports. If the number of firms in the industry increases to 5, exports are almost 70 fold higher compared to the monopoly situation. In the limiting case, output would be infinite and since domestic sales would be only twice that as under the monopolist, namely 190, the rest of the output

1. The numbers are generated by assuming a parameterised linear demand function and initial monopoly equilibrium where the monopolist exports 5 per cent of its outputs. Then we allow entry with firm output remaining unaffected due to infinitely elastic foreign demand curve. We can thus easily calibrate the exports of each firm and the domestic sales of each firm from which we derive the aggregate exports and domestic sales and outputs.

would be exported. Of course, one would expect that once the industry becomes large, its domestic cost conditions would change. If the monopolist had exported only three per cent of his output, then the absolute values of domestic sales and exports with entry are very similar to those above, with exports being slightly smaller than the above numbers. But with a small number of firms, the growth rates of exports are still higher. For instance, as an additional firm enters, the increase in exports is almost 24 fold rather than about 15 fold. This illustrates dramatically the possible deleterious effect of entry restrictions in LDCs on their export performance.

Table 6.1

Output, Domestic Sales and Exports with Entry

N	*1*	2	3	5	*10*
X	100	200	300	500	1000
Q_d	95	127	143	159	173
Q_f	5	73	157	341	827

Since domestic sales increase with entry, domestic price will decrease. Consequently, total revenue decreases. Since costs remain the same, as output is the same, firm profit declines unambiguously.

The Entry of Foreign Firms

The entry of foreign firms can be considered in two different situations. In one, the foreign firm is losing competitiveness in its home base of production. It then closes its home base and shifts to the foreign country. In that case, the firm behaves just as a domestic firm and its behaviour would be described by the propositions noted above. If the foreign firm is more efficient than domestic firms it will produce a larger output, sell the same amount as other firms in the domestic market and export a larger part of its output.

The other possibility is that the foreign firms can drive out domestic firms, if foreign firms are more productive and can go on producing at the constant foreign price and can duplicate this technology in India. Then they will keep producing at the fixed foreign price and Indian firms will be driven out of production in the long run if the average cost curve lies above the foreign price. In the short run the Indian firms would be able to meet their variable costs and continue to produce. But in the long run they would earn less than normal profits and so go out of production. So, the danger to domestic firms is there only if their average cost curve is completely above the foreign price and currently losses from exports are being covered by profits from domestic sales.

Empirical Results

We now attempt to verify a few propositions, regarding domestic sales, exports and firm size, and the effects of increasing the number of firms on these domestic sales and exports, mentioned above. The balance sheets of firms belonging to nine different industries provide information on most variables we require for our empirical verification. The nine industries were chosen on the basis of: (i) their relative share in India's exports, and (ii) the availability of data in the ITD archives. However, we first discuss a few important points about the data. First, the data are related to the firms in the organised industries whereas much of the expansion in exports has presumably taken place in the unorganised industrial sector where firms are relatively smaller. Second, the number of firms reported in a given year may not be all-inclusive as many firms may fail to report their balance sheets on time. Thirdly, entry of new firms or exit of firms is not always reported immediately after their entry or exit. Thus, the firms in our sample are only a subset of the whole family of firms that exist in a given industry at a given point in time. Keeping these factors in mind we propose to verify some of the propositions of our model for the following industries, *viz.* machine tools, gem and jewellery, steel, electrical goods, plastic, rubber, leather, pharmaceuticals and chemicals. Our sample firm data covers the period of 1991 to 1998. We analysed the standard four firm concentration ratio for both domestic as well as export sales for each of the nine industries. Further, on the basis of the panel data on domestic and export concentrations we have examined the link between domestic sales concentrations with export concentration in a fixed or random effect model. We report our results in Appendix A-6.1–A-6.6.

Appendix A-6.1 and A-6.2 give estimates of the four firm concentration ratios for the period 1991 to 1998 for domestic sales and export sales respectively. We draw two main observations, first, the number of firms has increased since 1991 and second, concentration ratios in both domestic and export markets have fallen over the years. However, it is interesting to note that the immediate rapid increase in the number of firms after liberalisation in 1991, has been reversed since 1995 after adoption of WTO norms.

These observations confirm that liberalisation has increased competition in industries, and perhaps they have become more efficient too. But we could not examine the efficiency issue more systematically. Also, we could not verify whether concentration resulted in lower price-cost margin propositions and prices so that consumer welfare increased.

Concentration ratios in domestic as well as in export sales show a significant decline in many cases (Appendix A-6.4a and A-6.5a). For domestic sales in plastic, pharmaceuticals and machine tools industries the linear trend has the expected sign but is not significant whereas for the electrical industry the sign shows increasing concentration though not significant. We examine whether non-linearities are the cause of the very low R^2 in many cases. We do find some evidence of non-linearities (Appendix A-6.4b and A-6.5b). In these tables, the sign of the time coefficient has the expected sign in all the cases and the adjusted R^2 usually shows a substantial increase.

Finally, we did a time-series cross-section panel estimation of the relationship between domestic sales concentration and export concentration (Appendix A-6.6). We are interested in this relationship because most empirical analysis of India's export performance shows a negative relationship between firm size and export intensities, though our model predicts a positive relation.

We tried both the fixed effect model and the random effect model for the panel estimation. The Hausman specification test confirms that the fixed effect model cannot be rejected. The coefficient of the regression of export concentration on sales concentration shows a very significant positive relationship confirming our theoretical result that firm size and export performance should be positively related. The adjusted R ^ 2 also shows a good fit of the model.

---

2. Even in the case of non-identical cost functions we get a symmetrical solution for the domestic market provided all firms export (see Agarwal and Barua, 1994).

Conclusion

We have developed a multimarket Cournot model to study the effect of entry on the structure of domestic industry. The model shows that with entry, concentration in domestic sales and in exports decreases. The model also shows that the larger firms export more. Our empirical analysis of firms in nine industries shows that with liberalisation of entry after 1991, concentration both in the domestic market and in exports has declined. We also find that there is a positive relation between domestic sales concentration and export concentration; the larger firms export a proportionately larger part of their output. This result is interesting because it is in variance with the standard empirical results on firm size and export performance in India.

References

Agarwal, M. and A. Barua (1993). "Trade Policy and Welfare in Segmented Markets", *Keio Economic Studies*, Vol. 30(2), pp. 95-108.

———. (1994). "Effects of Entry in a Model of Oligopoly with International Trade", *Journal of International Trade & Economic Development*, Vol. 3(1), pp.1-13.

Barua, Alokesh (2003). "Some Preliminary Results of Testing the Heckscher-Ohlin Model in India's Manufacturing Trade", Unpublished Draft paper, International Trade and Development Division, SIS, JNU.

Ben-Zvi, Shmuel and Elhanan Helpman (1992). "Oligopoly in Segmented Market", in Gene M. Grossman (ed.), *Imperfect Competition And International Trade*, Cambridge, Massachusetts: The MIT Press, pp.31-53.

Brander, J. (1981). "Intra-industry Trade in Identical Products", *Journal of International Economics*, Vol. 11, pp.1-14.

Bulow, J.I., J.D. Geanakoplos and P.D. Klemperer (1985). "Multimarket Oligopoly: Strategic Substitutes and Complements", *Journal of Political Economy*, Vol. 93, pp.488-511.

Chakraborty, Debashis (2002). "India's Intra-industry Trade: An Analysis of the Re-reform and Post-reform Trends", unpublished M. Phil dissertation, International Trade and Development Division, SIS, JNU.

Das, S. and A. Barua (1996). "Regional Inequalities, Economic Growth and Liberalisation: A Study of the Indian Economy", *Journal of Development Studies*, Vol. 32, pp.364-90.

Dixit, A.K. (1984). "International Trade Policy for Oligopolistic Industries", *Economic Journal Conference Papers*, Vol. 94, pp.1-16.

Eaton, J., and G.M. Grossman (1986). "Optimal Trade and Industrial Policy under Oligopoly", *Quarterly Journal of Economics*, Vol. 101, pp.383-406.

Frank, C.R. (1965). "Entry in a Cournot Market", *Review of Economic Studies*, Vol. 32, pp.245-50.

Friedman, James (1987). *Oligopoly Theory*, Cambridge Surveys of Economic Literature, Cambridge University Press.

Hahn, F.H. (1962). "The Stability of the Cournot Oligopoly Solution", *Review of Economic Studies*, Vol. 29, pp.329-31.

Horstmann, Ignatius J., and James R. Markusen (1986). "Up the Average Cost Curve: Inefficient Entry and the New Protectionism", *Journal of International Economics*, Vol. 20, pp.225-247.

Krugman, Paul R. (1980). "Scale Economies, Product Differentiation, and International Trade", *American Economic Review*, Vol. 70, pp.950-959.

Lancaster, Kelvin (1980). "Intra-industry Trade under Perfect Monopolistic Competition", *Journal of International Economics*, Vol. 10, pp.151-175.

Leff, N.H. (1979). "Monopoly Capitalism and Public Policy in Developing Countries", *Kyklos*, Vol. 32, pp.718-38.

Markusen, James R. and Anthony J. Venables (1988). "Trade Policy with Increasing Returns and Imperfect Competition: Contradictory Results from Competing Assumptions", *Journal of International Economics*, Vol. 24, pp.299-316.

Novshek, William (1980). "Cournot Equilibrium with Free Entry", *Review of Economic Studies*, Vol. 11(7), pp.473-86.

Novshek, W. (1985). "On the Existence of Cournot Equilibrium", *Review of Economic Studies*, pp.85-98.

Okuguchi, Koji (1973). "Quasi-competitiveness and Cournot Oligopoly", *Review of Economic Studies*, Vol. 40, pp.145-148.

Rodrik, Dany (1988). "Imperfect Competition, Scale Economies, and Trade Policy in Developing Countries", in R.E. Baldwin (ed.), *Trade Policy Issues and Empirical Analysis*, NBER.

———. (1999). "Globalisation and Labour, or: If Globalisation is a Bowl of Cherries, Why are there So Many Glum Faces Around the Table?" in R.E. Baldwin *et al.*, (eds.), *Market Integration, Regionalism and the Global Economy*, CEPR.

Ruffin, R.J. (1971). "Cournot Oligopoly and Competitive Behaviour", *Review of Economic Studies*, Vol. 38, pp.493-502.

Seade, Jesus (1980). "On the Effects of Entry", *Econometrica*, Vol. 48(2), pp.479-89.

Tirole, Jean (1990). *The Theory of Industrial Organization*, The MIT Press.

Wood, Adrian (1999), "Openness and Wage Inequality in Developing Countries: The Latin American Challenge to East Asian Conventional Wisdom", in R.E. Baldwin *et al.*, (eds.), *Market Integration, Regionalism and the Global Economy*, CEPR.

Appendix A-6.1

The Model

We assume that all the firms in the industry produce a homogenous good. The country under consideration is a small country in the world market and hence the firms face an infinitely elastic foreign demand curve. However, the country protects the industry from import competition by a sufficiently high tariff or quota so that the country's imports are zero. The domestic market is characterised by an oligopoly where all the firms face an inverse demand function, $f(Q_d)$, and employ a Cournot strategy. We define the following: x^i is the output of the ith firm, N is the number of active firms (exogenous), X is the industry output, i.e., $X = \Sigma x^i$, i = 1,....N, q_d^i is the domestic sales of the ith firm, $q_f^{\ i}$ is the exports of the ith firm, Q_d is the total domestic sales, i.e., $Q_d = \Sigma q_d^{\ i}$, i =1,..... N, P_f is the international price (constant), Q_f is the aggregate exports of the country, i.e., $Q_f = \Sigma q_f^i$, i= 1,.......N, and Q_τ is Σq_d^j for j = 1, 2 ... τ-1, τ+1,...N and, τ ≠ j, namely the sales of all the firms except the tth firm.

We also assume that the inverse demand function $f(Q_d)$ is twice continuously differentiable (f ¢ (Q_d) is negative), that the cost function of the ith firm C $(x^{\ i})$ is twice continuously differentiable and C(0) = 0 implying that the firm can freely exit from the market and that the average cost, AC, is strictly U-shaped with the minimum attained at an x > 0. All firms are assumed to have identical cost functions, i.e., $C(x^i) = C(x)$ for ∀ i. Since the cost functions are identical, either all firms will export or no firm will export. We assume the former case.

The profit function for a representative firm is defined as:

$$\Pi = f(Q_d)q_d + P_r q_r - C(x) \tag{1}$$

Each firm maximises (1) on the assumption that Q_τ is fixed. Under the Cournot assumption, an interior, profit maximisation gives the following first-order conditions,

$$\delta\Pi / \delta q_d = q_d f'(Q_d) + f(Q_d) - C'(x) = 0 \tag{2}$$

$$\delta\Pi / \delta qr = P_f - C'(x) = 0 \tag{3}$$

Any solution to equations (2) and (3) is a Cournot equilibrium. Since firms are identical, it can be seen that there exists a symmetrical equilibrium in which all the q's are equal.[2] From (3) it is also clear that each firm produces the identical level of output, x.

The fundamental result of the model from (2) and (3) can be stated as:

$$q_d f'(Q_d) \pm f(Q_d) - C'(x) = P_f \tag{4}$$

This implies that the firm equates marginal cost with the marginal revenue in the domestic market and the foreign price. The firm exports will be zero if $P_f < C'(x)$. With non-identical cost functions it may be possible to have a set of firms for which exports are zero.

The Symmetric Case:

Equations (2) and (3) together imply that $q_d^i = q_d^j = q_d$ for any pair of firms i,j for which $q_f^k > 0$ where k = i and j. The assumption of identical cost implies that all the firms produce the same output, $x^i = x^j$ for all i. Since MR in the domestic market is the same for all firms, each firm sells the same quantity of output in the domestic market, and, as all the firms produce the same output, each firm will export the same quantity, $q_f^i = q_f^j$ for all i. We can, therefore, write the aggregate output, domestic demand and exports as:

$$X = N\,x \tag{5}$$

$$Q_d = N\,q_d \tag{6}$$

$$Qr = N\,q_r \tag{7}$$

Looking at the second-order condition of profit maximisation by differentiating (2) and (3) we can write the conditions following Agarwal and Barua (1994) as:

$$E + N + Nk > 0 \tag{8}$$

$$E + 2N > 0 \tag{9}$$

where $E = Q_d\{f'(Q_d)/f(Q_d)\}$ is the elasticity of the slope of the demand curve $f(Q_d)$ and $k = \{1 - C''(x)/f(Q_d)\}$. Since $C''(x) > 0$ and $f'(Q_d) < 0$, k > 1, so that E+N+NK> E+2N. The condition (8)

2. Even in the case of non-identical cost functions we get a symmetrical solution for the domestic market provided all firms export (see Agarwal and Barua, 1994).

includes (9) as a special case.[3]

With non-identical cost curves, it is clear that the more efficient firm will reach the same level of MC as the less efficient firm at a higher level of output and so will produce more. But under the Cournot assumptions each firm will face the same MR curve in the domestic market so that domestic sales of each firm will still be the same. Since the more efficient firm produces more this implies that it will export more.

The Effect of Entry

We now examine the effect of an increase in N. We have assumed that all firms export. As firm output in our model is determined by the international price which is independent of the number of firms, so output of an individual firm is not affected by entry.

(i) Firm Output

From (3) we know that the marginal cost, $C'(x)$, is constant[4] so long as the world price P_f is given. Since we are considering only the partial equilibrium case, the rental rates for factors of production do not change with entry of new firms and the cost curve of any individual firm is not affected as the number of firms increase. Therefore, the output of a firm is fixed at the point where the international price intersects the firm's marginal cost curve.

(ii) Domestic Sales of Firm and Industry

Totally differentiating (5) we get

$$dX = Ndx + x\,dN \tag{10}$$

As we have argued above that an individual firm's output is determined at the point where its MC equals the world price, P, and this does not change with entry.

---

3. In the Cournot case k > 0 (see Seade, 1980), which also implies Hahn's stability condition f-C" < 0. In our open-economy model we do not need to assume it as it is always satisfied.
4. The assumption of the constancy of the cost function while letting the number of firms to tend to infinity is quite in consonance with the standard approach to examine the limiting behaviour of the oligopoly model (see Tirole, 1990: 220). Further, this is a much weaker assumption than the standard assumption of infinite supply elasticity in deriving the Marshall-Lerner condition for exchange stability in trade theory.

Thus, dx = 0 and 10 becomes

$$dX = x\,dN \tag{11}$$

Differentiating (2) with respect to N we get:

$$q_d f'(Q_d)(dQ_d / dN) + 2f'(Q_d)(dQ_d / dN) - C''(sx / dN) = 0 \tag{12}$$

Or using (8) we may write (12) as:

$$(dq_d / dN) = -[(E+N) / E+N+1)](q_d / N) \tag{13}$$

Therefore, $dq_d /dN < 0$ if $E+N > 0$ and $E+N > 0$ is the Ruffin condition for quasi-competitive outcome. Therefore, as the number of firms in the industry increase, the domestic sales of each individual firm decline. Since output of the firm is fixed, the exports of each firm would increase.

Equation (13) can be rewritten as:

$$\mathbf{dq_d /q_d = - [(E+N)/(E+N+1)](dN/N)} \tag{14}$$

Integrating (14) assuming that E is constant we get:

$$\ln q_d = -[1/(E+1)] \ln (E+N+1) - [E/(E+1)] \ln N + \ln C$$

$$\text{or } q_d = C[(E+N+1)N^E]^{-1/(E+1)} \tag{15}$$

Since $Q = Nq_d$, the equation for Q_d can be written as:

$$Q_d = C[N/(E+N+1)]^{1/(E+1)} \tag{16}$$

which in the limiting case implies that:

$$N \rightarrow \alpha, Q_d = C \tag{17}$$

Namely, as the number of firms increases to infinity, total industry domestic sales converge to a constant value, C. The rest of the industry output is exported. Differentiation of the above equation also shows that while the domestic sales of each firm decline the domestic sales of the industry increase. Under the conditions described, the total output of a firm is independent of the number of firms in the industry. Domestic sales of a firm decline with the increase in the number of firms. However, total domestic sales of the industry increase with an increase in the number of firms.

(iii) Exports

By definition, we know that:

$$q_f = x - q_d \tag{18}$$

Using (18) we can write:

$$N \rightarrow \alpha, Q_f = x \qquad (19)$$

that is, the firm in the limiting case exports its entire output. The total exports also become infinity, that is,

$$N \rightarrow \alpha, Q_f = X - Q_d = \alpha \qquad (20)$$

Thus, as the number of firms increase, exports by each firm and the industry increase.

(iv) Profits

Since entry does not affect x and therefore does not affect C(x), the change in the profits of a firm depend on the change in its revenues. The revenue of a firm is given by:

$$R = p_d q_d + p_f q_f = q_d \{p_d - p_f\} + p_f x \qquad (21)$$

Then,

$$dR/dN = \{p_d - p_f\}(dq_d/dN) + q_d f' ¢(Q_d) dQ_d/dN \qquad (22)$$

or, substituting for dq_d/dN and dQ_d/dN, we get

$$dR/dN = -(q_d/(E+N+1))\{(p_d - p_f)/N\}(E+N) - f'(Q)\} \qquad (23)$$

Since $(P_d - P_f) > 0$ from (2) and (3), therefore, as long as the Ruffin condition is satisfied, $dR/dN < 0$, namely, the revenue of existing firms declines with entry. So profit declines with entry.

Appendix A-6.2

Sales Concentration Ratio, 1991-1998

Year	Chemical	Electrical	Steel	Rubber	Plastic	Pharma	Machine	Leather	Gem
1991	0.32 (67)	0.66 (56)	0.67 (112)	0.91 (8)	0.63 (21)	0.33 (71)	0.42 (118)	0.80 (16)	0.85 (10)
1992	0.31 (85)	0.33 (70)	0.66 (139)	0.86 (11)	0.53 (31)	0.27 (108)	0.36 (142)	0.74 (21)	0.84 (14)
1993	0.39 (117)	0.57 (87)	0.64 (174)	0.79 (16)	0.44 (49)	0.24 (154)	0.37 (179)	0.67 (42)	0.82 (21)
1994	0.33 (150)	0.55 (104)	0.60 (23)	0.67 (23)	0.38 (75)	0.25 (210)	0.32 (216)	0.64 (53)	0.68 (29)
1995	0.32 (166)	0.53 (118)	0.57 (241)	0.63 (30)	0.34 (98)	0.22 (236)	0.28 (256)	0.58 (54)	0.64 (36)
1996	0.22 (119)	0.52 (119)	0.53 (34)	0.61 (34)	0.36 (98)	0.19 (242)	0.28 (253)	0.54 (48)	0.34 (39)
1997	0.20 (148)	0.55 (105)	0.52 (205)	0.61 (35)	0.41 (91)	0.21 (211)	0.33 (219)	0.55 (51)	0.64 (38)
1998	0.27 (86)	0.68 (66)	0.56 (124)	0.73 (17)	0.50 (45)	0.28 (127)	0.38 (132)	0.63 (19)	0.69 (24)

Note: Number in the parentheses indicates the number of firms in a particular industry in a particular year.

Appendix A-6.3

Export Concentration Ratio, 1991-1998

Year	*Chemical*	*Electrical*	*Steel*	*Rubber*	*Plastic*	*Pharma*	*Machine*	*Leather*	*Gem*
1991	0.650305 (67)	0.677293 (56)	0.919314 (112)	0.988067 (8)	0.955428 (21)	0.51603 (71)	0.574133 (118)	0.693768 (16)	0.893039 (10)
1992	0.492849 (85)	0.431198 (70)	0.873907 (139)	0.991639 (11)	0.84398 (31)	0.347447 (108)	0.418347 (142)	0.617208 (21)	0.894987 (14)
1993	0.52287 (117)	0.638506 (87)	0.833859 (174)	0.87415 (16)	0.78103 (49)	0.399982 (154)	0.442796 (179)	0.555188 (42)	0.8614 (21)
1994	0.470174 (150)	0.65423 (104)	0.820095 (220)	0.847235 (23)	0.812613 (75)	0.370743 (210)	0.394068 (216)	0.590077 (53)	0.749076 (29)
1995	0.463677 (166)	0.475082 (118)	0.706646 (241)	0.647511 (30)	0.620232 (98)	0.343448 (236)	0.352674 (256)	0.449863 (54)	0.745868 (36)
1996	0.363501 (157)	0.417169 (119)	0.512879 (235)	0.635985 (34)	0.621588 (98)	0.342382 (242)	0.336272 (253)	0.525717 (48)	0.38051 (39)
1997	0.328212 (148)	0.494162 (105)	0.554245 (205)	0.851203 (35)	0.774308 (91)	0.381025 (211)	0.390351 (219)	0.397859 (51)	0.684191 (38)
1998	0.400083 (86)	0.571531 (66)	0.631205 (124)	0.893002 (17)	0.818224 (45)	0.438191 (127)	0.386711 (132)	0.662873 (19)	0.774771 (24)

Note: Number in the parentheses indicates the number of firms in a particular industry in a particular year.

Appendix A-6.4a

Linear Time Trend of Sales Concentration

Name of the Industry	*No.of Obs.*	*Constant*	*Coeff. of t*	*AdjustedR-sq.*	*F-statistic*
Steel	8	42.47572 (-5.80)	-.0209993 (5.88)	0.8234	33.64
Chemical	8	33.61262 (2.13)	-.0167046 (-2.11)	0.3307	4.46
Gem	8	86.35596 (2.05)	-.0429523 (-2.03)	0.3082	4.12
Electrical	8	-25.23602 (-0.74)	.012929 (0.76)	-0.0640	0.58
Rubber	8	74.2904 (3.02)	-.0368827 (-2.99)	0.5310	8.93
Plastic	8	43.12598 (1.55)	-.0213977 (-1.54)	0.1634	2.37
Pharmaceuticals	8	18.58457 (1.47)	-.0091933 (-1.45)	0.1360	2.10
Machine	8	17.52087 (1.18)	-.0086136 (-1.15)	0.0452	1.33
Leather	8	60.30651 (3.50)	-.0299135 (-3.46)	0.6107	11.98

Appendix A-6.4b

Non-Linear Time Trend of Sales Concentration

Name of the Industry	*No.of Obs.*	*Constant*	*Coeff. of t*	*Coeff. Of t^2*	*Adjusted R-sq.*	*F-statistic*
Steel	8	.724488 (24.43945)	-.04346 (-2.87542)	.002495 (1.522258)	0.855191	21.66975
Chemical	8	0.332559 (4.396236)	.006000 (6.15557)	-.002523 (-0.603055)	0.251346	2.175056
Gem	8	1.069729 (5.836673)	-0.15622 (-1.67187)	.012586 (1.241778)	0.365481	3.015989
Electrical	8	.633332 (4.215070)	-.071460 (-.932824)	.009377 (1.128470)	-0.017629	0.939367
Rubber	8	1.096234 (19.87)	-.1583078 (-5.36)	.0134917 (4.42)	0.8854	28.03
Plastic	8	0.7987307 (58.5)	-.1739338 (-24.99)	.0169485 (22.45)	0.9901	352.34
Pharmaceuticals	8	0.3891834 (11.86)	-.0688036 (–4.11)	.0066234 (3.65)	0.7171	9.87
Machine	8	.5013299 (14.60)	-.0814841 (-4.65)	.0080967 (4.25)	0.7528	11.66
Leather	8	.920148 (23.71004)	-0.11481 (-5.80257)	0.009433 (4.395401)	0.903965	3.015989

Appendix A-6.5a

Linear Time Trend of Export Concentration

Name of the Industry	*No.of Obs.*	*Constant*	*Coeff. of t*	*Adjusted R-sq.*	*F-statistic*
Steel	8	112.1258 (4.93)	-.0558507 (-4.90)	0.7666	23.99
Chemical	8	73.10268 (4.61)	-.0364208 (-4.58)	0.7409	21.02
Gem	8	79.76185 (1.76)	-.0396159 (-1.75)	0.2270	3.06
Electrical	8	30.66856 (0.95)	-.0151034 (-0.93)	-0.0189	0.87
Rubber	8	55.02145 (1.41)	-.0271649 (-1.39)	0.1164	1.92
Plastic	8	47.77957 (1.50)	-.0235654 (-1.47)	0.1425	2.16
Pharmaceuticals	8	14.09463 (0.74)	-.00687 (-0.72)	-0.0740	0.52
Machine	8	43.45737 (2.55)	-.0215821 (-2.53)	0.4346	6.38
Leather	8	37.1664	-.0183529 (1.23)	0.0618 (-1.21)	1.46

Appendix A-6.5b

Non-Linear Time Trend of Export Concentration

Name of the Industry	*No.of Obs.*	*Constant*	*Coeff. of t*	*Coeff of t ^ 2*	*Adjusted R-sq.*	*F-statistic*
Steel	8	1.037121 (9.508409)	-0.08842 (-1.5899)	0.003618 (0.59864)	0.738745	10.8969
Chemical	8	0.700835 (10.40601)	-0.081711 (-2.37964)	.005032 (1.351138)	.7722228	12.86622
Gem	8	1.109591 (5.505936)	-0.14962 (-1.45617)	0.012223 (1.096725)	0.25228	2.180894
Electrical	8	0.689071 (4.445189)	-0.060829 (-.769661)	.005081 (0.592673)	-.142427	0.563654
Rubber	8	1.231751 (9.53)	-.1882109 (-2.85)	.017894 (2.50)	0.5293	4.94
Plastic	8	1.122128 (11.98)	-.1661604 (-3.48)	.0158439 (3.06)	0.6417	7.27
Pharmaceuticals	8	.5670685 (10.46)	-.0931184 (-3.37)	.0095832 (3.20)	0.5767	5.77
Machine	8	0.6397252 (13.65)	-.0999943 (-4.18)	.0087125 (3.36)	0.7918	14.31
Leather	8	0.828902 (7.355539)	-0.1292 (-2.24873)	0.012316 (1.976358)	0.367905	3.037145

Appendix A-6.6

Panel Regression of Sales Concentration Ratio on Export Concentration Ratio

No .of Obs	Obs per gr (avg)	A	B	R^2 overall	F-statistic	Corr(u_i,Xb)	Sigma_u	Sigma_e	rho
Fixed Effects Regression; Group Variable (i) : Industry Code									
72	8	.0953584 (2.63)	.6722036 (11.46)	0.6165	131.35	0.1724	0.1141512	0.05430645	0.8154413
Random Effects GLS Regression; Group Variable (i): Industry Code									
No.of Obs	*Obs per gr (avg)*	*A*	*B*	*R^2 overall*	*Wald chi-sq*	*Corr(u_i,Xb)*	*Sigma_u*	*Sigma_e*	*rho*
72	8	0.0908572 (1.73)	0.6796079 (11.97)	0.6165	143.17	0 (assumed)	0.1177916	0.05430645	0.82470394

Note: In case of fixed effect model the numbers in the parentheses indicates the t value but in case of random effect model it is the z value.

Hausman Specification Test

—— Coefficients ——

ecr	Fixed Effects	Random Effects	Difference
scr	.6722036	.6796079	- .0074043

Test: Ho: difference in coefficients not systematic.

chi²(1) = (b-B)'[S^(-1)](b-B), S = (S_fe-S_re)

= 0.26

Prob>chi² = 0.6128

7

The Indian Power Sector in a Command Economy

Liberal Reforms or Indian-style Development?

JOËL RUET

This chapter attempts to assess the impact and the singularity of the post-1991 reforms in the power sector of India. For this sector vests a very symbolic role in the model of command economy, given the redistributive aspects it conveys, it brings an exemplary picture of what remains today, after more than a decade of reforms—the state sector at its very heart. The power sector is at the heart of debates for this reason, and, while Lenin used to say that, "socialism is Soviets plus electricity", Bibek Debroy once commented that, "Indian socialism, is the soviets without electricity." At the governmental level, reforms are based more on the need to attract substantial private funds than on a genuine industrial plus social analysis of the issues at stake. The chapter puts things into perspective, stressing the need for managerial reforms in the organisations governing power distribution and consumption, that today need to be effectively delivering both services and targeted social help (Section I). Section II demonstrates that the reforms have mostly been a 'hit and try' (often a hit and miss) process, due to over-emphasis on quantitative factors at the expense of qualitative and organisational factors. It shows the limited impact of reforms on both aspects. Lastly, Section III analyses the political economy of Centre-State relationship in reforms, and highlights the fact that in the power sector, 1991 was only a step in the ongoing process of influence-building by the Centre, rather than an ideological point of rupture due to the new liberalisation policy, which in fact had already been initiated in the 80s.

Critical Analysis of the Indian Power-Question

If one looks at the role of energy in the Indian economy, the end consumption of the various energy sources is as follows: 47 per cent for petroleum products, 29 per cent for coal, 17 per cent for electricity and 7 per cent for natural gas.[1] Several possible growth scenarios of the demand for power and the national production capacity[2] were forecasted by the Planning Commission, a Government of India body (Table 7.1).

Table 7.1

Demand for Energy Forecasted by the Planning Commission, 1998

	1996-97	*2009-10*	*2019-20*
Electricity (TWh) (Final Consumption)	327	868	1656
Coal (MMT)	296	724	1392
Petroleum (MTEP)	79	192	420

Source: Planning Commission (1998). *Business As Usual.*

Playing as a planning agency, the Planning Commission was a bit on the alarmist side, indicating capital requirements that could increase for 15 years to US$ 384 billion for the energy sector as a whole, i.e. more than US$ 25 billion per year, of which 50 to 60 per cent is for power. In particular, the Planning Commission estimates that from 1990 to 2020, electricity demand will increase 6.5 times and the installed capacity 5 times.[3]

Table 7.2 indicates the amount of investment needed in the principal energy sectors. It is the magnitude of the investment requirements that has officially justified the opening of the Indian power sector to outside investment, in order to enhance production capacity to the required levels.

1. Electricity production of course increases the share of coal and gas among the primary energies, as 71 per cent of the total consumption of coal and 30 per cent of natural gas are used for generating electricity.
2. Cooperation in the nuclear field is for the moment limited to security with most of the countries—except Russia—India not being a signatory to the Non-Proliferation Treaty. India has developed renewable energy research programmes, but this energy remains an expensive source.
3. Taking as basis for the year 1996-97, a generation of 394.5 TWh and a capacity of 86.2 GW. Generation is of 515 TWh and installed of 105 GW in 2001-02. The trend set by the Commission has not been followed.

Table 7.2

Investment Requirements of the Energy Sector in Billions of Dollars

	Ninth Plan (1997-2002)	*Tenth Plan (2002-2007)*	*Eleventh Plan (2007-2012)*
Electricity	54	71	74
Coal	5	11	15
Petroleum	91	125	149

Note : Based on the 1996-97 cost and dollar index.

Source : Planning Commission (1998). *Business As Usual.*

Lastly, macroeconomically, power in India remains an important player in economic activity, the ratio of the elasticity of growth of the GDP to that of electricity consumption being 1.59. Also, it should not be forgotten that the power sector is a powerful vehicle of social redistribution and rural development. So, cross-subsidisation between types of consumption is important, as agricultural consumers pay on an average 14 per cent of the cost of electricity, whereas industrialists pay 166 per cent of the average cost (Planning Commission, 1999).

Present structure and importance of the power sector is the outcome of a historical series of adjustments. Until 2003, within the framework of the 1948 Electricity Act, the Indian power sector rests on a structure almost completely articulated by the public sector and is highly centralised. The two levels of government—State and Centre—are both vested with regulatory powers, with the Centre taking precedence over the State in case of dispute. At the level of each state, a State Electricity Board (SEB) is in charge of the means of production, and the transmission and distribution networks. The Central Electricity Authority is responsible for dealing with national level problems and inter-state issues. After 1975, the means of production pertaining to the country as a whole were developed. This depended on public bodies specialising in a particular mode of production (National Thermal Power Corporation and National Hydropower Corporation). The new framework of the Electricity Act (2003) is now trying to implement generalised private participation, unbundling and competition, though in a structurally non-credible manner, given the tariff structures, information systems and regulations inherited from the command economy system (Ruet, 2005).

The current composition of the units in stock is 30 per cent owned by the Union Government, 59 per cent by the states as a whole, that is, still an 89 per cent by the public, and limited to 11 per cent by private companies. The nuclear development programme comes directly under the Government of India (limited to 2 to 3 per cent of the generation). Except for some private firms, mainly in Calcutta, Bombay, Orissa and Delhi (in the latter two states, distribution was privatised in 1999 and 2002 respectively), the SEBs have a *de facto* monopoly on electricity distribution.

Table 7.3

Ownership of Power Stations

Ownership of the Means of Production:	
- States	59%
- Union Government	30%
- Private	11%

Source: Planning Commission (2003).

Table 7.4 gives a breakdown of the total Indian electricity production.

Table 7.4

Classification of (Electricity) Production in India

Gross Production at Power Stations:	515 TWh
Breakdown by Category of Production:	
- Thermal	71%
- Hydraulic	25%
- Nuclear	3%
- Renewable	1%
Energy Deficit[4] in Relation to Demand	11%
Peak Demand Deficit	24%

Source: Planning Commission (1999).

4. This concerns unserved energy in relation to the demand currently electrified.

The earlier estimates of investment requirements are partly based on conservative plant load factors.[5] As a matter of fact, the load factor is approximately 60 per cent in the states and 71 per cent in the corporations attached to the Union Government and in private companies. The share falling to the SEBs is characterised by significant regional variations (North 64.7, West 70.2, East 42.2, Northeast 27.1).

Thus, a more efficient working of existing power stations, but also more ambitious hypotheses with regard to the running of new power stations as well as favouring transmission capacities, should enable a reduction of the total investment requirements. Besides this, official data on transmission losses is erroneous. In fact, if the official loss amounts to 22 per cent[6] (Ministry of Power), the real figure in all likelihood is around 40-50 per cent,[7] constituted mainly by electricity thefts or unmetered electricity consumption. Taking into account more realistic estimates and integrating existing progress margins in loss reduction, enables significant reduction in the volume of investment requirements.[8]

Taking just the annual variable costs—including the valorisation of the cost of capital—the power sector, according to the tariff regulations in force, must recover $ 19.5 billion annually. But actual tariffs allow recovering of only 76 per cent of this amount, that is an annual turnover of $ 14.8 billion (Planning Commission, 1999). In the year 2001-02, the total deficit of all SEBs reached $ 7.3 billion (1.5 per cent of GDP). Debts have more than doubled in four years.

---

5. Ratio of mean power to capacity, which corresponds to the fraction of time equivalent to a full power operation. Hundred per cent is never achieved, but, by way of comparison, the load factor of French nuclear plants is approximately 80 per cent.

6. In Table 7.4, 'consumption' is deducted from production by taking into account the percentage of official loss. This is not in contradiction with the fact that the percentage of unofficial loss is much higher, in fact, 'non-technical losses' —electricity thefts—are well and truly consumed but not billed. This is explained by the inherent flaws in the metering and information systems. The internal coherence of the statistical system is visibly not ensured.

7. These figures can be verified at the Indian level or in some of the more progressive states, hence more transparent, from the following sources: World Bank (1996), World Bank (1997), Gridco (1998), Quraishi (1998) and APSEB (1998).

8. See, for details, Ruet (2002; 2005; 2006a). Improving the load factor, along with reducing technical losses would provide the same result at a cost much lower than in the 'Planning Commission' type strategy.

The above critique—incorrect figures, pricing and management problems arising from electricity thefts—shows that the level of investments being assessed by the Planning Commission greatly depends on supporting data. Therefore, the official figures need to be revised. More than anything else, this suggests that the important issues are to be found downstream, at the power station and network level, including commercial policy. For this let us describe how SEBs, a key element in the system, function.

The management of a SEB, to be understood, is to be set in the perspective of the Indian administered economy. A two-year investigative study (Ruet, 2001) shows that the internal organisation is characterised by:

- The non-existence of budget allocations to the various operating units forming the SEBs.
- Non-existence of real hierarchic delegation of power in the sanctioning of projects and also in relation to human resources (career management).
- Non-integration of the commercial and technical aspects with regard to reports submitted for overseeing internal management.

In the SEBs, the decision-making process is diluted between several hierarchic levels. The process has to pass through two successive stages: the first examines and approves the technical pertinence of the decision proposed, the second guarantees the respect for internal administrative regulations, whatever the extent of the expenditure. Not less than three levels are involved, including the initiating decision level. Once the decision is doubly approved, the head office has still to decide to release the necessary resources. In reality, each unit's 'budget' is not, despite its name, a real budget in the sense that it is not allocated once and for all. Rather, it represents a *pro-forma* framework, which the units do not respect, and to which no allusion is made when a decision is being examined. As each demand is submitted to the head office for approval, there is no decentralisation of the budgetary power or of the power to arbitrate locally within a given budget. Hence, there is no proper budget. Similarly, there is no allocation of power with regard to human resource management. Each decision, to assign a particular post or task, is subjected to the same multi-stage process and is left at the discretion of the head office. Thus, there is no allocation of hierarchic power either. Lastly, the information system can be described as non-integrated for two reasons. Firstly, the system of internal reporting does not compare the technical data with the financial data (for example collections compared to billing compared to energy consumed). Secondly, the accounting system itself is non-integrated in the sense that often data is based on formal statements and statistics and not accounting entries.

The logical consequence of these three characteristics is the practical impossibility of making cost-benefit comparisons and then using them to make decisions. The latter are taken collectively, without any hierarchical level taking precedence. Over and above the final sanction, the decision will not really be applied unless other implementation procedures are completed, also collectively, by other departments. Practical implementation in fact, largely depends on procedural rationality. That is, in the absence of objective or stable (predictable) norms, the system functions on the avowed respect for procedures. Hence, officials take decisions in conformity with existing procedures and not in relation to the situation encountered. This results in structural inefficiency, which is not linked to the current situation, a point constantly brought up by reformers.

Moreover, the end profitability of SEBs depends on *ex post* administrative decisions (amount of subsidies allocated, negotiations as to their mode of payment, effective payment) taken by the state. The SEBs thus have no incentive to act in a 'classic' manner and introduce a business-type management. Although, they are economically ineffective, they operate in a completely rational manner in accordance with the system in which they function: over and above the management of the technical aspect, the SEBs are the meeting ground for productive, financial, social, electoral,[9] and criminal logic (problem of corruption and more so of misappropriation of funds in slums).

9. In a more systemic manner, some suboptimal investments are explained by the creation of jobs locally and by financial misappropriation in the electoral fiefs of the state leaders. Similarly, rural electrification respects priorities of time and place faithfully, dictated by electoral schedules and monitored in the day to day context by the custodians of the said fiefs. On the employment front also, Rajiv Gandhi, the Indian Prime Minister, called the SEBs the 'State Employment Boards'. Individual careers too depend on postings and transfers decided politically at the state level.

SEBs are Not Enterprises, By Nature they are Not Looking for Productive Efficiency but they are Still an Important Tool of the Command Economy

The internal organisation of the SEBs has been inherited from the administered structure of the Indian economy. Within this framework, the SEBs operate not as enterprises, but like administrations, which by nature (cf. Simon, 1947; Banfield, 1975) simultaneously pursue several inherently different objectives (economic, but also distributive, social, political). It is impossible to arbitrate between these objectives on the basis of an objective criterion. In particular, the decisional criteria applied to firms—cost and productive efficiency—is not adapted to this framework, hence we arrive at this particular type of internal organisation. This type of organisation is consubstantial with a vision of the power sector in terms of quantitative and mono-technical growth (there is a mono-input—planned expenditure, and a mono-output—the installed MW) directly inherited from input-output macroeconomic models. This vision was suitable in a country whose electrification was to be accomplished from scratch, using new equipment. However, it is no longer adapted to today's India, which has diversified its electrical use, the services that are required, a country in which very varied technical problems exist, such as the maintenance of the existing networks or the supply of services to an extremely diversified industry with very specific requirements. The decisions taken on the basis of complex procedures in an administrative setup inspired by a mono-technical vision, thus, have no reason to lead to effective decisions from the point of view of diverse modes of productive efficiency. In other words, this system is not adapted to a mature industry that needs to carry out regular, decentralised cost-benefit comparisons in order to improve its efficiency.

In consequence, there is no reason to expect, even if there is no shortage of means, that SEBs would be more efficient, because, structurally, efficiency is not a parameter that can be taken into consideration in their decision-making. The organisational reform of the SEBs is thus a limiting factor in the same way, if not more, as the lack of resources. The global effects of this inefficiency are very clear: in 1997-98, for example, the subsidies given by the Andhra Pradesh Government to its SEB—hailed by experts as one of the least inefficient—to balance its accounts, represented 1.6 per cent of the GDP of the State, and accounted for 46 per cent of its public deficit (World Bank, 1999). If not mostly for thirst for efficiency, reforms have to be explained differently.

Uncertain Reforms...Uncertain Effects

'The reform of the power sector' can, in reality, be divided into several successive phases and multiple readjustments of a policy that is feeling its way. Exemplary of hesitations of the Indian Government in reforming the economy, we can distinguish three phases from 1991 onwards.

Phase 1: 1991-1996

In 1991, the Indian government opened the development and use of new means of production to foreign investment. This liberalisation was limited to production and applied only to key projects. The principal modalities were:

- Share of foreign investment up to 100 per cent.
- Promoter's share to be at least 11 per cent.
- At least 60 per cent of the investment must be financed from sources other than Indian financial institutions.
- Import of equipment authorised.
- Sixteen per cent profit margin for a load factor of 68.5 per cent proposed on the basis of retail tariffs to networks, but not guaranteed downstream by the selling price to consumers.
- Tax holiday for five years and a 30 per cent tax rebate for the next five years.

However, during this period the administrative and financial difficulties increased manifold. In particular, obtaining the numerous administrative authorisations, getting payment guarantees, drawing up contracts between private producers and SEBs (the Power Purchase Agreements) turned out to be a long and arduous task. The singular example of this reform is the ENRON case. ENRON wanted to set up a production unit without taking a local partner. It had to contend with administrative red tape because of an absence of clear definitions as to the roles of the central and local governments. At the same time, it became the target of a media campaign. During this phase, various secondary policies were grafted to the initial body of the reform (assuring counter-guarantees by the states and the union government, and setting up of investment cells in the ministries of some SEBs, as well as the launching of 'fast-track projects'). However, projects continued to lag behind and investment was nowhere near the expected level. From 1996 onwards, it became increasingly clear to industrialists that the success of the reform would depend on revising the tariff structure and reorganising the SEBs from scratch. After that, in 1998-99 mega-projects made their appearance, whose sustainability was rather uncertain.

Phase 2: 1996-1998-2001

In view of the considerable production and financial deficit, the Centre reacted. In 1993, a conference had been organised in Jaipur,[10] in which representatives of the Government of India and the Chief Ministers of the states got together. The outcome was that those states that so desired were authorised to open the transmission and distribution sectors to private investment. The principle of the creation of a Central Electricity Regulation Commission (CERC) and a State Electricity Regulatory Commission (SERC) in each state, which would be independent of the governments, was also adopted. This agreement did not specify the modalities of setting up the commissions or the scope of their powers. Some momentum was actually given after the 1996 and 1998 elections. A law ultimately ratified these commissions only in 1998, the Electricity Regulatory Commissions Act of 1998.

At the same time, with the creation of the CERCs and the possibility of creating the SERCs, this law framework authorised several types of reforms, ranging from simple 'corporatisation' (see below) of the SEBs to a very largely deintegrated and competitive model. The scope of these reforms and the manner of their implementation were left to the states, aided by development agencies. Five models were proposed:

- The SEB remains vertically integrated, but is 'corporatised'

10. cf. Ministry of Power (1993).

(i.e. it is legally transformed into a company whose initial capital is with the state, instead of a public autonomous agency).

- The SEB becomes a transmission network company but has to face competition in the production and distribution fields (this raises questions about the definition and regulation of purchase tariffs and payment of electricity transmission; the implementation of such reforms presupposes considerable regulatory competence).
- The SEB retains existing transport and production activities; the new production units are independent and distribution is privatised (the SEB is allowed to retain some shares; the question that now arises concerns purchase tariffs and regulations governing access to the network in order to ensure equal treatment to producers).
- The SEB ceases to exist; it becomes a simple transmission company, having to face competition on the production front and undergo horizontal deintegration of distribution; the old SEB is excluded from this competition and cannot participate in production or distribution activities.
- A transmission company and Zonal Electricity Boards are created in which independent producers can participate; the SEB becomes a holding company (problems of participation and attractiveness to independent producers arise).

What we call now 'structural reforms' of the SEBs, include their corporatisation, their vertical deintegration (and horizontal in the case of distribution) and the effective creation of a regulatory commission at the state level. The first set of structural reforms—corporatisation and deintegration—is meant to give the SEBs the control of their technical, management and financial activities.[11] The objective underlying the creation of regulatory commissions is to establish viable tariffs for the SEBs.

The reform scenario varies greatly from one state to another, the

11. It should be noted that in practice the deintegration proposed is not intended by its promoters to increase competition, unlike the reforms undertaken in developed countries. In India the promoters perceived it as a means of isolating the various elements, as some were easier to reform than others and therefore would need a different treatment.

most advanced being Orissa, which adopted the fourth model and privatised the network in 1999; Haryana, until a ruling put a stop to its privatisation policy in 2000; and Andhra Pradesh. At the commencement of 2000, only 12 commissions out of 25 states[12] were set up. Only four had issued 'Tariff orders'. Similarly, only Gujarat, Haryana, Karnataka, Orissa and Uttar Pradesh had formally established separate distribution zones (Powerline, 2000a; 2000b; 2000c). It took till 2004 to generalise in nearly all the states, though with unenthusiastic assessment on their functioning by experts (Rao, 2004).

In a continuation of this phase of the reforms, the high tension segment has also been opened to private and foreign participation since 1998-99. But here too no particular project has made any notable headway.

A Third Phase of Reforms?

The reform of both distribution and transmission was initiated once the liberalisation policies of the power sector had been declared to be ineffective. But the second phase did not succeed in imposing, (or only very marginally), these changes on the states. On the tariff reform front especially, it was powerless. As a result, from 1996 to 1998, the Centre tried to impose a restrictive framework on the states. In particular, it intended to make SERCs mandatory; the SERCs would thereafter have the same status as courts of law; they would decide tariffs on the basis of the performance of the SEBs, or of the companies having obtained a licence. It also envisaged a minimum tariff for farmers, fixed at Rs. 0.5 per kWh.[13] The Indian Parliament discussed a new project, entitled: "Power Policy 2000",[14] which would integrate these elements in a restrictive manner. It got finally passed as the 'Electricity Act, 2003', that is...after three years of parliamentary debate.

---

12. Not counting the three newly created states of Uttaranchal, Jharkhand and Chhattisgarh, which now make it 12 out of 28.

13. At this time, calculations were based on an average supply price of Rs. 2.07 per kWh in 1997, or a subsidy 'limited' to 75 per cent instead of the current 86 per cent. Electricity is practically free for farmers:
    - including the big farmers, and
    - in some states, or completely free as in Punjab.

14. cf. Ministry of Power (2000).

However, the whole set of measures has had little or no effect, neither on investment, nor on the working of the SEBs. Both have been 'waiting for Godot'. In terms of level of investment, if we examine the production capacity, for example, the figures presented in Table 7.5 speak for themselves.

Table 7.5

Estimated and Completed Generation Addition

Eighth Plan (1992-1997), Total Construction Estimates	38 GW
Public sector completed addition	18 GW
Private sector completed addition (1993-97)	1.8 GW
Gap	18.2 GW (42%)
Ninth Plan (1997-2002)	40 GW
Central public completed addition	4.5 GW
State public sector completed addition	13.6 GW
Private sector completed addition	0.9 GW
Gap	21 GW (52%)
Tenth Plan (2002-2007)	45 GW
Central public completed addition (2002-04)	4.2 GW
State public sector completed addition (2002-04)	1.9 GW
Private sector completed addition (2002-04)	0.6 GW
Gap (linear extrapolation)	63%

Source: Planning Commission (1998; 2003) and Ministry of Power (2004).

In 2003-04, financially moribund SEBs did not have enough credibility for investors. Thus, financial guarantees are necessary: financial 'counter-guarantees' by the Centre in the case of default on payment by the states, and regulations guaranteeing 16 per cent returns to independent producers, instead of the earlier 3 per cent. Despite this, out of the 20 GW expected from the private sector by the Planning Commission in the Eighth Plan (1992-1997), only 1.8 GW were achieved. Private addition does not even total 4 GW in 12 years. The opening up policy proved a failure, as investor response was poor, despite the high publicity that some investments received. Among those who had invested, some acknowledged during interviews that the investment they had made was too high.

Similarly, if we examine the one example of the privatisation of distribution in Orissa in 1999, out of the four companies on sale, initially there was no offer from a foreign investor, and one company received no offer. The latter was ultimately bought after direct negotiations between the investor and the state of Orissa. The Indian buyer of this zone had already exhausted the credit payment facility margin within the first year of operation, which it had been agreed was to cover three financial years. The Indian buyers of three out of four zones expected to make a loss of two billion rupees in 2000 (source: interviews). In this context, most investors did not hide their lack of enthusiasm for subsequent privatisation.

They have Changed the Name, but the Shop Remains the Same

With regard to the working of the SEBs, a detailed investigation (Ruet, 2005) has shown that the structural reforms ('corporatisation', 'deintegration' and setting up of regulatory commissions) have not affected their actual working nor their internal organisation. Their organisational nature remains that of an administration. Let us examine this in detail.

Corporatisation signifies a change in legal status, which does not in itself affect the organisational nature of the SEBs (their current status of Board already guarantees them an independence *de jure* that they do not exercise *de facto*. More interesting are the measures accompanying the reforms supported by the World Bank (until now: Orissa, Andhra Pradesh, Haryana). These reforms are characterised by a more broad-based conception of corporatisation, which views it as a process, incorporating training and assistance (on the operational side), maintenance, accounting, commercial activities, as well as an overhaul of the information system. Corporatisation in this sense resolves one of the SEBs' problems, the non-integration of information. But the characteristic absence of discretionary power and recourse to procedures, instead of using the cost-benefit analysis remains. In this context, the information system remains a potential tool, but one which is not really utilised.

Deintegration is an interesting process independent of reasons, which have a quasi-theoretical basis, that motivate it. Indeed, by compartmentalising the diverse activities, it is permitted to think that deintegration introduces property rights—right of control, financial rights, at least in budget ownership. However, it should be noted that even in the present case, this mechanism does not necessarily introduce discretionary power *vis-à-vis* the state, nor *a fortiori* discretionary power at the unit level. But over and above this, in practice deintegration has not been implemented. A study of the officially deintegrated structures shows, in terms of control, that budgetary power has still not been allocated. Also, the financial flows between structures are not decided according to the objective rules of ownership. The only rule that really exists is that all the ascending flows continue to be transferred directly to the former head office and the descending flows continue to be managed discretionally. A distribution entity, for example, is only able to carry out 'its' decisions if the parent entity not only sanctions them but also physically supplies stocks to the distribution entity. There is no greater allocation of budgetary power than in an erstwhile SEB. The regulatory commissions (SERC), bodies that are outside the state-SEB province, do not confer discretionary power to the SEBs, do not influence their internal organisation, etc. In practice, they place them in a financial situation, which is just as difficult as before, if not more, by creating an environment that they are not structurally capable of integrating into their functioning. In reality, the structural reforms do not confer discretionary power on the financial side, neither to the units of the former SEBs, nor to the old SEBs in relation to the state. The system of pseudo budget remains, no unit has sufficient discretionary power to decide and implement measures by which, for example, technical losses and theft can be reduced, measures that are demanded by the SERCs.

An official from a SEB whose structural reform phase was officially claimed to have been completed, stated in an interview, "they have changed its name, but the shop remains the same."

Reforms that Do Not Change the SEBs' Administrative Manner of Functioning

Thus, the power sector reform is still searching for a foothold. Which industrial segment should one open up: production, transport, or distribution? According to what modalities: investment alone, management, or privatisation? On the basis of what arrangements: financial guarantees, administrative or regulatory restrictions? In this sense there has never been a general, stable policy, nor a long term overall vision, a fact that is emphasised in interviews but also in the press, even on 'prime time' television, by all the investors. As a result, successive policies—one is tempted to call them measures— have only had one goal in mind: how to attract investors? As and when difficulties cropped up and admissions of failure kept totting up, corrective measures were introduced, giving the impression of a process not so much progressive as chaotic. On this account, however, one has to be fair and stress that the introduction of reforms is the result of several compromises: between forces obstructing them, but also, on the other side, those promoting them. The latter used failures as arguments to bring about more fundamental changes. This is analysed in the last section, but on the basis of statistics we are forced to conclude that the reform has not achieved the goals that had been set. The argument given in explanation in the next section is that in reality, 1991 did not constitute a break from previous practices.

1991—A Continuation of the Earlier Measures for the Public Sector

As specified in the Indian Constitution, the development of the power sector is part of the Concurrent List, i.e., the domain of co-responsibility of the Centre and the States. The 1948 Act on the organisation of the power sector defines the practical modalities. It entrusts the Centre, *via* the Planning Commission, the Central Electricity Authority (CEA) and the Ministry of Power, with the definition of the sectoral policy. Its implementation is left to the states. However, the Planning Commission does not control *ex post* the expenses incurred by the SEBs, any more than the CEA or the Ministry. The principal role of the Ministry is administrative coordination. In this context reports are produced that 'are intended purely for government use' (Gridco), e.g. presenting results for the purpose of obtaining subsidies. In this context, the Centre is constantly enhancing and consolidating its direct power. The reforms are in keeping with this, and their procrastination corresponds to the growing weight of the Centre in its power struggle with the states.

In view of the *de facto* dominance of the states, the Centre attempted to regain control in the 1980s. In order to satisfy the increasing power requirements of the country, the Centre created public sector companies, placed directly under its authority, for the production and transmission of electricity. With regard to the provisions of the 1948 Act, it founded its legitimacy on the inter-state character of the projects developed. For example, a large capacity power station was built for the purpose of supplying electricity to several states. When redistributing and apportioning electricity production to the states, the Centre is in its natural element of intervention. The principal companies are the National Thermal Power Corporation (NTPC), a company producing thermal electricity, and the National Hydra Power Corporation (NHPC), a company producing hydroelectricity. NTPC, created in 1984, also installs and manages the high-tension lines carrying electricity from the power stations to the state networks. In 1992, this activity was transferred to Powergrid, a newly created company under the aegis of the Centre, whose task was to develop interconnections between the states and establish a national network sourcing electricity from five major electricity producing regions.

The Centre's comeback was highly successful as it now controls 32 per cent of the production. In actual fact, this restored the supremacy of the Ministry of Power, which is responsible for monitoring relations between the entities and the SEBs in relation to project development and for settlement of disputes. In particular, from the mid-90s financial mechanisms were introduced for the payment of arrears of the SEBs to the NTPC and the NHPC, i.e., accounts credited by the SEBs' principal clients are blocked, thus enabling the two corporations to recover their dues in case of a default in payment on the part of the SEBs. By this mechanism, the Centre regained control over a portion of the financial flows and thus enhanced its negotiating power at the policy implementation level. This mechanism was at its height in 1997 with the takeover by the NTPC of the Thalcher thermal power station, which came under the SEB of the State of Orissa, by way of unpaid dues. By the same logic, the Centre took advantage of its position and authorised itself to deduct up to 15 per cent of the Plan Funds allocated by the Planning Commission, in settlement of arrears. This amount was returned directly to the Corporations.

From an institutional perspective, the Centre flexed its muscles again with the creation of the Power Finance Corporation (PFC), a public organisation responsible for financing projects for the SEBs over and above the usual public investment system. PFC support can thus vary in its format. In particular, from 1989 onwards, the PFC began to determine the conditions of loans, based more on Operational and Financial Action Plans. Since 1997, PFC introduced a system of conditionalities based on the objectives underlying institutional reforms, and a corresponding monitoring mechanism to oversee implementation. In 1985, the Centre also made new accounting rules. The effect of this was to bring out more clearly the inefficiencies of the SEBs.

By extending to all the producers—and therefore to itself—the possibility of establishing bulk tariffs on the principle of 16 per cent returns on assets, the Centre put its company, the NTPC, known for its technical capabilities, in an advantageous position. As a result of this, the pressure by the Centre on the states to introduce reforms became greater.

The indecision and the corrective measures, characteristic of the power policy, also correspond to the Centre's enduring power. In 1985, it could only reform the accounting system and create institutions that had to stand on their own feet. In 1991, it could only, in conformity with the Constitution, open up production. From 1996 to 1998, it became strong enough to change this state of affairs and make the Regulatory Commissions Act constitutional. From 2000 onwards, fortified by the backing of some states and public opinion, it engaged in a power struggle to render the provisions mandatory and far-reaching. This little game, however, started way back in the 1980s, at a time when the need for reforms was really felt. This is seen, for example, in the debate on the introduction of plan contracts (cf. Trivedi, 1990; 1992).

All in all, the 1991 turn has not been a U-turn as far as the administered sector is concerned. For the power sector, it has merely, and in phases, signified a gradual shift of emphasis from a capacity addition logic to pragmatism. We have seen that what underlies each new phase of the power policy is the admission of failure with regard to the capacity to attract private financing. From this point of view the reform does not question the quantitative growth mono-input and mono-product model adopted by India after Independence. This model remains a development model for an industry financed by external funds, and not a management model for a now mature industry.[15] This

15. Which could perfectly incorporate the targeted subsidies, it is not antithetical.

type of analysis is thus quantitative, which is thought to be pragmatic when confronted with the shortage of public funds, but does not try to generate resources either through tariffs or through internal resources (better management, optimisation, maintenance, etc.). Analytically, the model remains the same. Here too, 1991, but also 1996-1998, is a continuation of past practices. Indeed, the choices present in 1991, and in 1996-1998, result from an analysis still marked by development practices and the policies implemented since Independence. We have retained a quantitative vision of the power sector in terms of expenditure levels and development of production, at the expense of a vision which systematically questioned the modes of management of the SEBs, and also at the expense of a choice between investment and maintenance, which although less costly gives an identical result. In 1996, the issue of broadening the scope of investments was raised, but the financial and quantitative aspects continued to be given precedence over the organisational problem. In other more telling words, we are always ready to put more water in the pipes without plugging the leaks. We continue to ask investors to pay but not to manage better.

A last *avatar*, that might end up turning into a caesura in the analysis, started being apparent—but not dominant—in the public debate from 1997. Some experts have been manifesting their desire to address this vital reform from a different angle and with different priorities. Some of the studies (IMI, 1999; Ranganathan, 1997; Ruet, 2001) have criticised the dominant vision and highlighted the need to change the internal organisation of the SEBs and to go beyond the 'industrial mecano' of corporatisation and deintegration, which has no reach and no effect. The solutions proposed are diverse (broadly speaking, they are: IMI wants monitoring on the basis of cost centres, Ranganathan advocates profit centres, and Ruet proposes decentralisation and allocation of budgetary power). According to diverse principles and modalities, all these studies propose the introduction of autonomisation mechanisms in the operational units, at which level the principal decisions affecting the SEBs' productive efficacy and profitability should be directly taken. It is proposed to allow the units room to manoeuvre with regard to budget and decision-making, to decentralise the supply circuits as well as stocks and to permit these units to keep and manage a portion of the revenue receipts. This would apply to maintenance, current investments, billing and collection sectors. Mechanisms of answerability and evaluation *ex post* are proposed. In relation to the reforms in place, including those supported by the World Bank, these measures have the advantage of regulating the day to day functioning of the organisation. They are more than the mere cosmetic restructuring of the activities. This also applies to the privatisation credo, a privatisation in which the investors do not want to participate given the current management conditions prevailing in the SEBs. The administered functioning of the SEBs till date (that is controlled by the Centre), does not enable investors to assess the latitude they would have once the organisations are privatised.

Conclusion: The Role of the Power Sector in Modern India

In 15 years, official liberalisation has not resulted in a quantitatively significant influx of investments and private players into the Indian power sector. Neither has it resulted in a qualitative modification of the functioning of the public sector. Seen from the 50-year perspective of development policies, in other words, the quantitative construction of the electricity infrastructure, there has been no break. This development policy was a success in itself, i.e. taking its own quantitative criteria as a gauge. The SEBs provided electricity to the Indian subcontinent, making its industrialisation and its agricultural revolutions possible. The SEBs have erected a cathedral.

However, today this success has been transformed into a relative failure: of economic efficiency, of growth, but also of social redistribution in a system where proportional tariff subsidies benefit in fine the well-off segments of the population. This system not only makes production difficult but also makes living difficult. At the turn of the millennium, metropolitan cities still see several houses with a day of power cuts in some of their colonies, while several middle-size towns see a few hours of power availability. It is really a strange hardship, for studies have shown that many users are ready to pay for a reliable electricity[16] service. The cathedral is there, but no one wants to pay for its upkeep.

16. Interviews and TERI (1999).

India has become industrialised, and some of its sectors claim regional, and even international competitiveness; the urban phenomenon is growing. Agricultural India has turned to commercial production, rural India must also take up the challenge of the small industries. This modern India needs a reliable and efficient power sector. We have seen that the modernisation of the power sector does not necessarily entail privatisation in which investors do not have faith, but rather modernisation of the way existing organisations function. It is, thus, on a paradigmatic shift, on the role of the state in a post-socialist environment that the new reforms must focus.

We should not, in any case, look for it in the hypothetical and changing '1991 policy'. If there are recent signs that suggest this evolution, they are limited to the economists' domain and are not transcribed in the reforms. All in all, in the long duration of the modes of representation and categories of thinking, the model of the electricity sector has barely evolved. It is, in fact, structured as if India still needed to be electrified, and remains in fine a post-colonial model.

On the social front, the TERI report (1999) brings out the immense willingness and capacity—more than the majority—to pay for electricity, in a state that is actually the poorest in India, Orissa. Similarly (cf. Ruet, 2006), on the basis of current cross-subsidies, the adjustment of tariffs to costs still leaves considerable elbow-room with regard to socially targeted subsidies. India has to make a choice. And it is possible to take full responsibility for it without distancing itself from a country still predominantly rural or underprivileged.

References

Banfield, E.C. (1975). "Corruption as a Feature of Governmental Organization", *Journal of Law & Economics*, December.

Gridco (1998). *Reform in Gridco—Revenue Improvement Action Program*, a Gridco Information Cell Document, Bhubaneshwar, Orissa.

IMI (1999). "A Study on Financial Management of the State Electricity Boards", a three volume report for the Finance Wing of the Ministry of Power, International Management Institute, New Delhi, pp.3 x 250.

Ministry of Power, Government of India (1993). *Proceedings of the Conference on Power Sector Reforms in India*, co-sponsored by the Government of India and the World Bank, held in Jaipur on October 29-31, New Delhi, p.243.

———. (1997). *Annual Report 1996-97*, New Delhi.

———. (2000). *Conference of the Power Ministers*, February 26, Agenda Notes, New Delhi, pp.41.

Powerline (2000a). *Powerline*, Vol. 4(12), September, New Delhi.

———. (2000b). *Powerline*, Vol. 5(2), November, New Delhi.

———. (2000). *Powerline*, Vol. 5(3), December, New Delhi.

Planning Commission (1998). "Prospects on the Demand for Energy in India", presented by M.R. Srinivasan, Planning Commission, at the Symposium on *L'énergie en Inde*, Janvier, CGEMP, Université Paris-Dauphine.

———. (1999). *Annual Report on the Working of SEBs*, New Delhi.

Quraishi, S.Y. (1998). "Power Sector Regulation and Restructuring: Haryana's Experience", paper presented at the International Forum on *Power Sector and Restructuring*, New Delhi.

Ranganathan, V. (1997). "Commercialisation of Nepal Electricity Authority", report for the Nepal Administrative Staff College, Indian Institute of Management, Bangalore, pp.50.

Rao, S.L. (2004). *Governing Power: A New Institution of Governance: The Experience with Independent Regulation of Electricity*, TERI Press, XV, New Delhi, p.484.

Ruet, J. (2001). "Winners and Losers of the SEB Reforms: An Organisational Analysis", *Occasional Paper* CSH No.2001-1, New Delhi, pp.85.

———. (2002). "A New Paradigm for the Indian Power Sector: Going Beyond the 'Silver Bullet' Privatisation", in Mishra & De Bernis (eds.), *Privatisation of Public Enterprises, Indo-French Perspectives and Global Relevance*, Delhi: Manak Publishers, pp. 220-262.

———. (2005). *Privatising Power Cuts? Ownership and Reform of State Electricity Boards in India*, New Delhi: Academic Foundation, p.339.

———. (2006). *Cost Effectiveness of Alternative Investment Strategies for the Power Sector in India: A Retrospective Account of the Period 1997-2002*, June, Utilities Policy.

Simon, Herbert (1947). "Administration et processus de décision", Paris, Economica 1983, translated from *Administrative Behavior; A Study of Decision-making Processes in Administrative Organisations*, New York: Free Press, Macmillan.

TERI (1999). *A Report on Willingness to Pay for Electricity in Orissa*, New Delhi: Tata Energy Research Institute.

Trivedi, Prajapati (1990). *A Critique of Public Enterprise Policy*, New Delhi: International Management Publishers, p.475.

——— (ed.) (1992). *Memorandum of Understanding, an Approach for Improving Public Enterprise Performance*, New Delhi: International Management Publishers, p.896.

World Bank (1996). *Staff Appraisal Report*, Orissa Power Sector Restructuring Project, Report No. 14298-IN.

———. (1997). *Project Appraisal Document*, Haryana Power Sector Restructuring Project, Report No. 17234-IN.

———. (1999). *Staff Appraisal Document*, Andhra Pradesh Sector Restructuring Project.

8

Subcontracting in Indian Industries, Market Structure and Product Quality

Implications under Globalisation

AJITAVA RAYCHAUDHURI

Introduction

The developing countries are facing new challenges in the present era of economic liberalisation and globalisation. The major consequence of the drive for liberalisation has given rise to drastic reduction in tariff rates all across developing countries and India is no exception to that. Once the price distortions are largely done away with, the competition for global market share increasingly moves into the domain of non-price competition (Marjit and Raychaudhuri, 1997). The major non-price factor seems to be quality of the product that includes marketing and after-sales servicing. In the coming age of strict standards quality competition will be a key to success for most of the developing countries, which are liberalising of late. India, which is effectively opening up its economy from mid-80s faces such a daunting prospect.

In this context one may highlight the changed notion of industrialisation that has been underscored by some of the newly industrialising countries (NICs). As originally shown by Japan and later replicated in Taiwan, Thailand, etc. vertically integrated giant firms may have alternatives in big firms having a large network of subcontractors. The subcontracting activities really divide a vertically integrated process into different stages. As Nagraj (1984) mentions, different forms of subcontracting exist in Indian economy, "Activity subcontracting divides the production process in different stages whereby the parent firm could get one or more activities undertaken by subcontracting and then sell the final product under its own brand names. Assembly subcontracting is a type where the firms farm out most of their assembly work to subcontractors. The third type may be product subcontracting where subcontractors produce the complete product and the parent firm undertakes the marketing functions."

This process of subcontracting is labelled as flexibilisation by Lauridsen (1995). The advantage of subcontracting lies in huge reduction of overhead costs and advantage of using cheap labour from unorganised labour markets. Thus, the parent firms can adjust the scale of production to market signals without major frictions. The large firms shift the burden and losses of market fluctuations to the ancillary firms (subcontractors) given the low bargaining strength of the latter (Patibandla, 1988). This leads to low quality of the products because in most cases the subcontracted units are unable to install state of the art machines for productions. Lauridsen (1995) calls it, "A low wage, low technology and low quality strategy, which becomes easily trapped in low profit competition."

The present chapter highlights a case of negative impact of subcontracting on product quality, such that the product quality is severely compromised, leading to a loss of competitive edge of the producers. The chapter suggests the causes of such phenomenon, the effect thereof and a possible remedy using the industrial organisation literature.

Garments Industry in West Bengal, India and the Perceived Risk Dominance

Readymade garments, in the last two decades, have become a major export-earning item. From a mere share of 2 per cent in the total export earnings of India in 1970-71, it occupied values around 13 per cent for the better part of the 1990s (Chatterjee and Raychaudhuri, 1996). So, when it was flourishing in the rest of India, did West Bengal follow suit, given its long history of production of readymade garments? Unfortunately, among the major garments producers and exporters in India, one does not find producers from West Bengal.

According to Anjali Kumar (1988), one may distinguish two important phases in the evolution of garments industry in India. In the 60s and early 70s, integrated large units attached to textile mills produced the readymade garments. These units got the fabrics from the textile mills and used power driven sewing machines together with complementary specialised equipments. From mid-70s onwards the export markets saw a switch from woven fabrics to handloom fabrics, from standardised garments to women's garments and seasonal wears. Along with this the demand volatility, mainly due to changing tastes and fluctuating income, gave rise to a regime change from integrated large factories to smaller units engaged in subcontracting their production in various stages. This also led to an increased use of workers employed mainly on the piece-rate basis. The subcontracting system provided the flexibility to parent firms of adjusting to demand fluctuations without too much friction. However, this affected the productivity per person, which was compensated by low labour costs mainly because of the subcontracting system.

Chatterjee and Mohan (1993) characterised the garments industry as composed of small-scale job working units, which worked under the aegis of a few parent firms. The subcontracted job working units actually belong to the informal sector having very flexible or no labour contracts as well as flexible contracts with the parent garment-producing firms. Although, the whole of India had more or less the same characteristic, West Bengal could not put its mark in the garments market, both domestic and exports. West Bengal has a very large number of small-scale garments manufacturer who are also multi-product in nature. The common characteristic of these small enterprises is that most of the activities are carried out with the help of subcontracted job working units, which are paid on piece-rate basis. Whatever manufacturing activity the parent units undertake, they mainly finish the product with the help of workers who are also paid on piece rate. In many cases, the subcontracted units even get raw materials and machines from the parent units and thus, the parent firms avoid either large overhead costs or maintenance of a permanent labour force. However, there are plenty of varieties available in the market, which are locally branded and have only local clienteles. Thus, as mentioned in Chatterjee and Raychaudhuri (1996), the readymade garments market in West Bengal largely reflect a monopolistic competition variety.

An old survey, whose essence has remained largely unchanged, conducted in 1994-95 reports the following typology of garments producers in West Bengal (Chatterjee and Raychaudhuri, 1996):

(1) Hundred per cent job done from outside by the parent firm.

(2) Own production unit, but piece-rate payment to non-permanent contractual labour.

(3) Composite mill, whose workers are paid fixed monthly wages and are substitutable among different types of jobs.

The above survey revealed that most of the units belonged to either (1) or (2). In fact, case (1) is the overwhelmingly predominant form. The survey concentrated on gents' shirts, jeans and knitted T-shirts. So ladies wear and woollen garments were excluded, which would have required a different kind of survey. Surprisingly, despite variety in production as well as almost no dearth of working capital and skilled or unskilled workers, the producers were found to be extremely reluctant to either venture into the national or international markets. They were happy to operate in the local market. In fact, the more enterprising ones invested their capital outside the state, like in Tirupur garments complex in Tamil Nadu.

As one tries to investigate into the causes of this lack of initiative of garments producers in the state of West Bengal, one may identify the perceived attitude towards risk as the main reason for this. The producers are found to be risk-averse in nature. This is not unusual once one looks into the background factors, as viewed by the producers, which helped them to form such attitudes. One may summarise them as follows:

(a) Unproductive nature of labour force—In view of the producers, labour by nature has an unproductive attitude. The manifestation is that whenever any big order is obtained or any expansion is contemplated, the workforce under the direct control of the producers starts a planned work stoppage or resort to 'go slow' for overtime or increased wages or bonus. This, according to producers, is an absolute hindrance towards expansion of production since any big scale of production to aim at national or international market requires some direct production at the finishing stages to ensure quality control or timely delivery.

(b) Absence or high cost of monitoring of subcontracted job-working units—The prevalence of job-working units is a nationwide phenomenon in garments sector in India and

West Bengal is no exception. However, the producers in West Bengal have a common complaint that there are problems of moral hazards among subcontracted units and monitoring is either costly or simply absent. This is rather tricky since such problems in all probability exist in other successful states also, but the producers there must have minimised such hazards successfully. So this may be taken as lack of entrepreneurial talents in West Bengal.

(c) Poor credibility of promise of good governance—Poor governance is not uncommon in states where garments production flourished. Tirupur, one of the success stories for garments production suffers from water shortage, power outages and bad infrastructure. But despite this, a network of producers and subcontractors emerged successfully and it has become one of the major export centres in India. A similar story could have been possible in the state of West Bengal also but it is not to be. The producers are not only unhappy at the existing problems of infrastructure and government promises but the credibility of government commitments appears to be very low. So the question of expansion does not get that prominence due to a lack of credible commitment of good governance.

Going through the above list, one may clearly differentiate between two types of factors behind formation of the risk perception in the minds of the producers towards more expansion of the existing scale of production. They may be classified as follows:

1. Factors beyond the control of the producers—Some of the factors mentioned above like the question of good governance and credible commitments towards better infrastructure and a good working environment lie in the domain of state government and the political process. The government has to come out with transparent policies and achievable time limited goals. The ruling political party has to inculcate more responsible collective bargaining attitudes in the labour force (Raychaudhuri and Chatterjee, 1998). These factors are beyond the control of any individual producer and have to be solved with state intervention.

2. Factors within the control of individual producers—Some of the factors outlined above are very much matters of good entrepreneurial practices. A common example is innovating right sets of contract on the part of producers with subcontractors on one hand and direct workforce on the other. It is not sufficient to complain that monitoring and enforcing better quality cannot be done with the subcontractors. It has to be innovated through better incentive schemes, which encourages the outside job-working units to produce their best. Also, an expansion of scale with an enlarged direct workforce is entirely possible with sufficient incentives for the workers to increase their productivity.

An earlier paper (Chatterjee and Raychaudhuri, 1996) by the author explored the question of risk-dominance of a larger scale of production over a smaller one in the perception of the producer. The above paper explained the West Bengal scenario in terms of second order stochastic dominance of a 100 per cent job-working unit over a vertically integrated firm under uncertainty. The paper proved the following proposition:

Proposition—Output will decline if a production unit switches from 100 per cent job-working from outside to vertically integrated form of production.

The moral of the story is quite clear—garment producers in West Bengal are not only risk-averse but also are extremely unwilling to have any direct production base under them. They believe the uncertainty will increase much more in case of the latter and will lead to lowering of output, which is already, much smaller than the potential. As a result, the garment producers though having a historically strong base in West Bengal, face a negative effect of subcontracting on their production potentials. Thus, even if the new phase of globalisation opens up new avenues for exports, producers in West Bengal's readymade garments sector are not prepared to take this advantage. The factors, which are beyond their control, have to be tackled by the state, like provision of good infrastructure and credible promise of good governance. However, a simultaneous change of attitude must dawn upon the producers who must innovate new varieties of contracts, which could give proper incentive to, say, subcontractors so that they provide the best quality output. One should not forget that Japan, Taiwan or Thailand flourished exceptionally well within the frame of subcontracting. So removal of one set of hindrances by government's proactive policy is a necessary condition for a better production environment. But this must be complemented by better management policies. The model which follows addresses this issue in greater detail.

A Model of Subcontracting Along with High Quality

The following is a model applicable to search good under new product monopoly. Although some modifications are needed to fit it in the monopolistic competition models outlined above the essence of the story does not change. This model was originally proposed in Chatterjee and Raychaudhuri (2000).

The Model

In this model we assume that a monopolist is bringing a new product in the market. It is further assumed that the product is a non-durable commodity. The production process is subdivided into two stages. Subcontractors undertake the first stage of production process. In the second stage, the monopolist finishes the product and supplies it to the market. The quality level of final product is determined by quality of unfinished product supplied by the subcontractors to the monopolist. The monopolist only finishes the product and supplies it to the market. The contractor can supply high or low quality product. In the present case, we assume that the monopolist cannot observe the quality of the product supplied by the contractor, that is, the monopolist has no information about the quality of the product that he is receiving from the contractor. For this reason the quality of the final product is also unknown to him.

Here we consider a two period scenario. The consumers can infer about the quality of the product at the end of first period. In the second period the product quality is a common knowledge. The product becomes obsolete at the end of second period. We assume that in the first period consumers form an expectation about the quality of the product supplied by the monopolist and this expectation is formed exogenously (Metrick and Zeckhauser, 1996). Given these assumptions we try to find the incentives scheme, which will induce agent firms to produce high quality product, whereby the monopolist can exist in the market in the second period.

Monopolist with No Information about Quality, Facing Large Number of Agents

We assume that a monopolist is facing a continuum of consumers with index of willingness to pay, defined by the variable q where q has equal probability of occurrence over an interval $\lfloor \underline{\theta}, \overline{\theta} \rfloor$. Assume q is the quality level of the final product which can assume two different values q_h and q_l where $q_h > q_l$.

Consumers are assumed to have an average idea about the product quality independent of firm's decisions. They assume the product will be of high quality with the probability Ω.

It is assumed that consumers will infer about the quality perfectly at the end of first period, and they will again purchase the product if quality is high, that is, $q=q_h$. It is assumed that the product becomes obsolete at the end of second period. The utility function of an individual is defined as

u= θq-p. If he purchases one unit of product with quality q and price p

= 0 otherwise.

In other words, the consumers get Σq amount of utility per unit of consumption while paying p. Thus, his net gain is θq-p.

Assume p_1 and p_2 as prices charged by the monopolist in period 1 and 2 respectively and x_1 and x_2 are the corresponding demands. Construction x_1 is based on the perception of average quality while x_2 is based on the perception of high quality of the consumer. Thus $X_1 = \overline{\theta} - \frac{p_1}{q}$ and $X_2 = \overline{\theta} - \frac{p_2}{q_h}$ for $q=q_h$ in previous and current period and $x_2=0$ otherwise.

In this case, the subcontractor undertakes the first stage of production of each unit of output and quality level is determined at this stage of production. However, the monopolist cannot observe the quality level supplied by the subcontractor. In the second stage of production, the monopolist finishes the product and supplies it to the market. Let 'c' be the monopolist's per unit finishing cost of the product. It is assumed that c is constant and independent of level of output and quality level of the product. It is assumed that there are a large number of identical competitive contractors and each can produce one unit of output in a particular period. Each subcontractor maximises present value of his two periods' income. Let $\bar{\pi}$ be the income that a contractor in each period gets from his alternative source of employment. If he works under the monopolist he earns income r_1 per unit of output in the first period. If he produces high quality goods his unit cost of production is c_h and if he produces low quality product his unit cost of production is c_l where $c_h > c_l$. If the subcontractor produces high quality product in the first period then only the monopolist gives the contract in the second period and pays r_2 per unit of output produced by the subcontractor. It is further assumed that subcontractors make their quality decision in the first period only.[1] The subcontractor will accept the offer of the monopolist and produce high quality product if and only if present value of his two periods' income is at least as great as the present value of his income from alternative source of employment, that is, if:

$$(r_1 - c_h) + \delta(r_2 - c_h) \geq \pi(1 + \delta) \tag{1}$$

This is the individual rationality or reservation constraint (IR) of a subcontractor. Here δ is the discount factor. A subcontractor will actually produce high quality if and only if:

$$(r_1 - c_h) + \delta(r_2 - c_h) \geq (r_1 - c_l) + \delta\bar{\pi}$$

$$\left[r_2 \geq \left\{ (\bar{\pi} + c_h) + \frac{c_h - c_l}{\delta} \right\} \right] \tag{2}$$

This is the incentive compatibility constraint (IC). This gives a lower limit to the price paid by the monopolist to the subcontractor. It is assumed that the monopolist first announces r_1 and r_2. If contractors accept the offer, they supply the product to the firm. Given the demand function, and r_1, in the first period the monopolist maximises his profit to determine his price p_1. If the final product is a high quality one, in the second period the monopolist will give the contract to the subcontractor again. The subcontractor will supply the product and receive r_2 in period 2. In the second period, quality is

1. If a contractor firm takes quality decision in each period then in the last period, that is, in period 2 he will obviously cheat as there is no future.

common knowledge. Given r_2 and p_1, the monopolist determines p_2 and p_2 is equal to full information monopoly price.

However, if quality supplied at the initial period is low, the monopolist faces zero demand in period 2. Thus, the profit of the monopolist when high quality is supplied in period 1 is given as:

$$\pi = (p_1 - c - r_1)\left(\bar{\theta} - \frac{p_1}{\bar{q}}\right) + \delta(p_2 - c - r_2)\left(\bar{\theta} - \frac{p_2}{q_h}\right) \qquad (3)$$

In this case, the monopolist is facing large number of identical agents. It is a two-period model. So he cannot employ new agents in period 2 because the new agent will supply low quality product. There are two reasons for this situation—firstly, there is no future and secondly, the monopolist cannot observe the quality level served by the contracting firms. For this reason the monopolist faces a sales constraint in period 2. The size of demand in period 2 must be equal to the size of demand in period 1 as in this case where the size of demand is equal to the number of agents employed. Thus, while determining the prices of the product, the monopolist faces an additional constraint, that size of demand in both periods must be equal.

So, the maximisation problem becomes

$$\max\,(p_1 - c - r_1)\left(\bar{\theta} - \frac{p_1}{\bar{q}}\right) + \delta(p_2 - c - r_2)\left(\bar{\theta} - \frac{p_2}{q_h}\right)$$
$$\text{subject to}\left(\bar{\theta} - \frac{p_1}{\bar{q}}\right) = \left(\bar{\theta} - \frac{p_2}{q_h}\right) \qquad (4)$$

Maximising this we get the equilibrium price p_1.

$$p_1 = \frac{\left[\bar{\theta}(\bar{q} + \delta q_h) + c(1+\delta) + (r_1 + \delta r_2)\right]\bar{q}}{2(\bar{q} + \delta q_h)} \qquad (5)$$

So, the price of first period depends on both r_1 and r_2. Basically, p_1 depends on the present value of total payment made by the monopolist (i.e. r_1+dr_2) to the subcontractor.

Lemma 1

The reservation constraint of an agent is always binding.

This is because in a principal agent framework with large number of competitive agents a profit maximising monopolist will always keep an agent on the reservation level. This leads us to the following proposition (proof is in Chatterjee and Raychaudhuri, 2000).

Proposition 1

Under this principal agent framework, the monopolist who does not observe product quality cannot separately determine r_1 and r_2, but the composite present value $(r_1+\delta r_2)$, which shows that incentive compatibility constraint is non-binding.

Thus, reservation constraint is always binding and incentive compatibility constraint is non-binding. Given the sales constraint, the monopolist is actually concerned with $(r_1+\delta r_2)$. Thus, from the profit maximisation condition, value of $(r_1+\delta r_2)$ is determined.

$$r_1 + \delta r_2 = (\bar{\pi} + c_h)(1+\delta)$$

The important point to note is that in this case incentive compatibility constraint is not binding. The implication can be explained as follows—in this two-period framework due to imperfect information, the monopolist will employ same set of agents in both periods. So, to induce them to produce high quality for both periods, the monopolist has to offer an excessively high value of r_2, which is more than enough to induce agent firms to produce high quality product. So we have:

$$r_2 > \left\{(\bar{\pi} + c_h) + \frac{c_h - c_l}{\delta}\right\}$$

Given this restriction on r_2, any combinations of (r_1, r_2) can be chosen by the monopolist, which will satisfy reservation constraint as equality. Due to the imperfect information with large number of agents the monopolist would be facing a sales constraint in period 2 and that is really the root cause behind an excessive payment in period 2.

Hence, we conclude that when future profit of the monopolist depends on the level of quality served in the initial period, the monopolist should find an incentive scheme for which an agent will actually supply the high quality product. The major implication is that, second period's price per unit of product supplied by the agent should be announced higher than the minimum required to induce the agents to supply high quality product.

Thus, models described above show that high quality can be provided even with subcontracting. The basic underlying assumption is that in a dynamic framework consumers will purchase the product in the second period if the quality of the final product is high in the first period. With this assumption it is found that the monopolist can determine the returns to the contractors in such a way that high quality is actually supplied in that market, when the monopolist has no information about the quality of the product supplied by the subcontractor. In the first possible case, the monopolist faces a large number of identical agents with capacity constraint. In this case, due to moral hazard problems, the monopolist faces a sales constraint in period 2 as he has to employ same set of agents in both periods. For this reason the monopolist makes an excessively high payment in period 2. In the second case, the monopolist does not face any sales constraint as he is employs a single agent with unlimited capacity and payment to the agent need not be excessively high.

Conclusion

The empirical studies show that under subcontracting the quality variability of the final product may be high [Raychaudhuri and Chatterjee (1998)]. In this case, we have shown that under monopoly structure with subcontracting, quality variability will arise, when a monopolist is concerned about the current period only. In this case he is not interested in building up reputation for the future. However, we have also shown that if the quality level of the final product affects future sales of the monopolist the incentive scheme will be such that only high quality will be sold in the market.

Thus, the chapter shows that the parent firm will invest for provision of high quality product if it maximises its profit. The system of subcontracting may not be the reason of quality variability in the final product. Much depends on the long-run outlook of the monopolist firm. A single-period monopolist will not ensure quality while a two-period monopolist will do just the opposite. Subcontracting will not cause any damage to high quality production provided that the monopolist innovates the right schemes and incorporates this in his profit maximisation. In a recent work on a similar theme, Raychaudhuri (2004) has explored the possibility of using the imperfect contract in a world of asymmetric information which would allow inclusion of clauses in the contract to ensure such a performance on the part of the subcontractors.

The overall story then sums up as follows—Subcontracting is quite a common form of production organisation in case of garments industry all over India. Some states have utilised the arrangement to their best possible advantage and have occupied important ranks in the garments exports from India. West Bengal, in spite of her long history of industrialisation and skilled workforce, could not utilise its subcontracting framework to aggressively capture the garments market nationwide, let alone internationally. The chapter attributes this to the perception of risks in the mind of the producers, which prevent them from expanding the production base. The chapter also emphasises the fact that, although the State cannot escape its own responsibilities to minimise this perception, the producers are also to blame in not being innovative enough and not having long-term goals. In this connection, with the help of a set of models, it is shown that it is not difficult to negotiate contracts with the subcontractors to ensure high quality of products, thus helping the producers to capture larger market shares. This is one of the ways in which the garments producers in West Bengal can exploit their historical advantage to reap some benefit consequent upon liberalisation of the economy.

References

Chatterjee, B. and Ajitava Raychaudhuri (1996). "Some Aspects of Production Organisation and Cost Behaviour of Garments in West Bengal", in Ajitava Raychaudhuri and Debjani Sarkar (eds.), *Economy of West Bengal: Problems and Prospects*, New Delhi: Allied Publishers.

———. (1998). "Pattern of Industrial Growth in West Bengal During Last Two Decades—Some Policy Suggestions", *Economic and Political Weekly*, Vol. XXXIII, pp.3061-3065.

Chatterjee, S. and R. Mohan (1993). "India's Garment Exports", in *Economic and Political Weekly*, August 28.

Chatterjee, Tanmoyee and A. Raychaudhuri (2000). "Subcontracting and Product Quality", DSA Centre for Regional Economic Studies, *Working Paper* Series 2000-01, #3, Department of Economics, Jadavpur University, Calcutta.

Fudenberg, D. and J. Tirole (1992). *Game Theory*, Cambridge: The MIT Press.

Hirschliefer, J. and J. Riley (1992). *The Analysis of Uncertainty and Information*, New York: Cambridge University Press.

Hirshmeier, J. and T. Yui (1981). *The Development of Japanese Business 1960-1980*, (Second Edition), London: George Allen & Unwin.

Kumar, A. (1988). *India's Manufactured Exports, 1957-1980*, New Delhi: Oxford University Press.

Lauridsen, L.S. (1995). "New Technologies, Flexibilisation, and Changing Capital Labour Relations: the East Asian NICs", With Special Reference to Taiwan and South Korea.

in A. Bagchi (ed.), *New Technology and Workers' Response: Microelectronics, Labour and Society*, New Delhi: Sage.

Marjit, S. and A. Raychaudhuri. (1997). *India's Exports: An Analytical Study*, New Delhi: Oxford University Press.

Mas-Colel, Whinston, A.M.D., J.R. Green (1995). *Micro Economic Theory*, New York: Oxford University Press.

Metric, A. and R. Zeckhauser (1996). "Price versus Quality: Market Clearing Mechanism when Sellers Differ in Quality", *Discussion Paper* No. 1775, Cambridge: Harvard Institute of Economic Research, Harvard University.

Mussa, M. and S. Rosen (1978). "Monopoly and Product Quality", *Journal of Economic Theory* 18, pp. 301-317.

Nagraj, R. (1984). "Subcontracting in Indian Manufacturing Industries—Analysis, Evidence and Issues", *Economic and Political Weekly*. Vol. XIX, pp.1435-1452.

Patibandla, M. (1988). "Role of Large and Small Firms in India's Engineering Exports", *Economic and Political Weekly*, May 28, pp.M53-M66.

Ramaswamy, K.V. (1999). "The Search For Flexibility in Indian Manufacturing—New Evidence on Outstanding Activities", *Economic and Political Weekly*, Vol. 34(6), pp.363-368.

Raychaudhuri, A. (2004). "Subcontracting and Economic Reforms in India with Special Reference to Agro-based Industries in India", *Working Paper*, Kolkata: The West Bengal National University of Juridical Sciences.

Tirole, J. (1988). *The Theory of Industrial Organisation*, Cambridge: MIT Press.

Watanabe, S. (1983). "Intersectoral Linkages in Japanese Industries: A Historical Perspective", in Sammu Watanabe (ed.), *Technology, Marketing and Industrialisation: Linkages Between Large and Small Enterprises*, Macmillan.

Appendix A-8.1

Assume that there is an undifferentiated product q_0 and a differentiated product having 'n' number of varieties (e.g., varieties of gent's shirts) denoted as q_i. All prices are expressed in terms of the undifferentiated product. Using a standard symmetric model of monopolistic competition under certainty, one can derive (Tirole 1988) the demand and supply of the differentiated product. On the demand side, suppose the consumers have Dixit-Stiglitz utility function of the type: $U = U(q_0, \{\pi\, q_I{}^r\}^{1/r}), r \leq 1$. Each consumer faces a budget constraint given by: $q_0 + \pi\, p_I\, q_I \leq I$, where, I = income. On the supply side, the producers have a common marginal cost 'c' and fixed cost of production 'f''.

Equilibrium Under Certainty

The first order condition of utility maximisation is given by: $q_I = kp_I^{-(1/1-r)}$, $k > 0$.

Let us define: $\boldsymbol{\varepsilon}_I = \mathbf{1/1\text{-}r}$ = Elasticity of substitution, assuming 'n' is large.

Under symmetry, we assume: $q_I = q$, $p_I = p$, $\varepsilon_I = \varepsilon$

Equilibrium output under uncertainty and zero profit condition is given by: $q^* = fr\,\varepsilon/c$.

Equilibrium Under Uncertainty

However, this model of certainty changes once one brings in the possibilities of production uncertainties due to either labour non-cooperation or bad governance or subcontracting. The nature of uncertainty differs between these cases. These are subdivided into two stereotypes—one is called 100 per cent job-working from outside and the other is labelled as vertically integrated firm. There may be combinations of the two varieties and can be accommodated without much difficulty. One can state the perception of risk of the producers as follows: The Job-working units may have uncertainty associated with them, but full vertical integration puts all the uncertainties attached with hazards related to labour or infrastructure or bad governance on the original producers. Thus, the job-working units stochastically dominate vertically integrated units. In technical terms, marginal cost 'c' becomes state dependent.

Suppose, producers wish to maximise a utility function $U(q) = E(v(\pi))$, where $v(\pi)$ is a preference scaling function on the profit of the producers denoted as p. In case I of 100 per cent job-working from outside, if $c \in (\alpha, \beta)$, then it has a distribution given by F_1 (c). In case II of vertically integrated firms, let the same 'c' has a distribution F_2 (c). By the argument stated above, F_2 (c) is a Mean Preserving Spread (MSP) of F_1 (c), but F_1 (c) second-order stochastically dominates F_2 (c). Thus, $E_{F1}(v(\pi(q,c))) > E_{F2}(v(\pi(q,c)))$.

Following the above analysis one comes up with the following proposition:

Proposition—For a risk-averse producer, output will decline if a production unit switches from 100 per cent job-working from outside to vertically integrated form of production. Three sufficient conditions, which produce this result, are:

(a) Relative risk aversion is an increasing function of profit p

(b) Elasticity of p with respect to quantity q is less than 1 and

(c) Relative risk aversion is less than 1.

9

India-Russia Economic Relations

Gradual Shift from State Dominant Linkages to Private Initiatives

GULSHAN SACHDEVA

In this chapter, an attempt has been made to understand present realities of Indo-Russian trade and other economic relations. It is argued that economic changes in both the countries had adverse impact on bilateral economic ties. Economic relations are still surviving mainly because of defence purchases, protection to exporters and some public sector investments by India. 'Special relationship' is limited only to arms trade and defence technology. Private commercial initiatives are very slow to take advantage from Russian economic transformation. Due to heavy defence purchases, from Indian point of view the relationship becomes 'strategic', but for Russians, it is pure economics.

Background

Despite having solid economic and trade relations in the past, a large part of the 1990s was a period of difficult adjustments, both for Indian as well as Russian businesses. One important point of old Indo-Soviet friendship was a special bilateral trade and economic relationship. Although, this arrangement had many usual weaknesses like corruption, patronage transactions in low quality products, it helped many small and medium size private Indian companies to become exporters. After the disintegration of the Soviet Union, this relationship has been badly damaged. Economic transformation in Russia from a centrally planned economy to a market economy in 1992 coincided with the policies of economic liberalisation in India. These developments changed the nature and character of foreign economic relations in both the countries.

One of the most striking characteristics of the Soviet centrally planned economy was that it had created a system of exchange in non-convertible currencies with many of its trading partners. This trade behaviour existed not only with the CMEA member countries, but also with some other friendly countries like India. Similar to 'convertible rouble' the value of exchange between the Rouble and Indian currency Rupee was arrived through periodic bureaucratic negotiations.

Most of the ideologically motivated scholars in India regarded this arrangement as Soviet version of bilateral aid. The 'mainstream' academia in India also declared that India had, "derived substantial benefits from its trade with the socialist world." In the late 70s and early 80s a few scholars in India had already warned that despite short term gains, this type of arrangement would harm long term requirements of efficiency and growth. After initial industrialisation, India had problems of importing further machinery either for joint production for third countries or for exclusive production for the socialist bloc. India did not want Soviet participation in those areas where it could get markets of its own. It also did not want 'captive units' whose production could not be exported anywhere else but to the Soviet bloc and could give Soviets a possibility of dictating terms. Except for a few works, the academia in India by and large did not bother to critically examine this pattern, as the whole arrangement reflected political imperatives rather than economic rationality. This is evident from the views of a scholar who wrote, "The rupee-rouble rate is notional in the sense that it is an artificial rate of exchange between two inconvertible currencies. All kind of sophisticated arguments theoretical or otherwise, are applied while negotiating the rate, and since both currencies have a notional relationship with the basket of western currencies, we feel that the rate is equally unfavourable or favourable to both sides." Some others, however, argued that even in a system of bilateral trade with a non convertible medium of exchange, the exchange rate does affect trade performance, particularly when the trading partners are both not centrally planned economies. New policy elite in Russia also found these 'irrational' arrangements with developing countries unaffordable. The haste with which bilateral payment arrangements were scrapped in favour of payments in convertible currencies indicate that Russian and Indian policy makers considered such bilateral arrangements undesirable under new economic policy regimes in both the countries.

The decade of 1990s was a very difficult period for Russian business. It was not only that Russia was transforming its economic system, but this transformation was also taking place in a period, when Russian economy faced one crisis after another. As a result, the Russian economy was already reduced to half of what it was in 1990, when another financial and economic crisis hit the economy in August, 1998. Its GDP now ranks only 19th in the world, with social indicators close to those of medium-income developing countries. In contrast, the Indian economy in the 1990s grew fast, compared to any other time in the recent past. The average annual growth rate between 1990 and 2000 was negative 4.8 per cent for Russia and about positive 6 per cent for India. As a result of these developments, relative economic positions of both the countries also changed. So Indo-Russian economic relations also have to be looked within this context. After the collapse of the markets in former Soviet Union along with other eastern European countries, a major structural change has taken place in Indian merchandise trade. Exports to former Soviet Union declined from 16 per cent in 1990-91 to about 3 per cent in 1995-96. Last year, it amounted to less than 1 per cent only. India, however, has been able to diversify its exports to the United States and the East Asian countries. In 2002-03, India's biggest trading partner was European Union with more than 21 per cent of total trade. USA was also very important trading partner with more than 13 per cent trade.

Bilateral Trade

Since 1953, when the first trade agreement took place, seven long-term agreements were signed between the two countries up to the collapse of the USSR. This bilateral trade as discussed earlier, was conducted through a specific system of trade and payment, called Rupee Trade System based on annual plans. Important point of the system was payments in non-convertible currency. The trade turnover between the two countries increased from less than Rs. 2 crores in 1953 to about Rs. 8,000 crores in 1990-91. In 1990-91 more than 16 per cent of Indian exports went to USSR and about 6 per cent imports came from it.

Table 9.1

Indo-USSR Trade Relations from 1960-61 to 1990-91 (in Rs. Crores)

Year	*Exports*	*% Share in Total Export*	*Imports*	*% Share in Total Imports*
1960-61	29	4.5	16	1.4
1970-71	210	13.7	106	6.5
1980-81	1226	18.3	1014	8.1
1990-91	5255	16.1	2528	5.9

Source: Economic Survey, Government of India.

After the collapse of the Soviet Union, Indian and Russian governments renegotiated the entire trade regime. The 1993 agreement terminated the traditional Rupee trade arrangement and mandated all bilateral trade transactions to be conducted on hard currency basis. But with this agreement, the issue of repayment of civilian and military loans taken by India from the former USSR also came up. Finally, after prolonged negotiations, the Rouble credit was denominated in Rupees and repayment schedule was drawn up. The agreement provided for an annual repayment of about US$ 1 billion equivalent in Rupees to Russia over a period of 12 years starting from 1994, with smaller amounts for a further period of 33 years. The rupee debt funds were to be used by the Russian side for import of goods and trade related services from India. The rupee debt funds are maintained in a central account with the Reserve Bank of India. Under a three year perspective plan, which came to an end in 1997, a part of the rupee debt funds was allocated for import of tea, tobacco, soyameal and pharmaceuticals to designated Russian agencies. The balance was either auctioned or allocated to various states or importing organisations in Russia. In January 1998, this mechanism was replaced with a weekly auction of rupee debt funds conducted by the Vnesheconombank (The Bank for Foreign Economic Affairs). During 1999, allocations made for import of pharmaceuticals and medical equipment from India were utilised by several Ministries of the Russian Federation. Since 2000, the utilisation of rupee funds has continued through the auctions.

As a result of these changes, now the trade is based on payments in freely convertible currencies. All Russian exports to India follow the new system. But only about 20 per cent Indian exports follow the new route. The rest of Indian exports are financed through the renegotiated rupee-debt repayment mechanism. As a result of all these economic policy changes, traditional actors in Indo-Russian trade and other economic relations like the public sector units and state trading corporations are no longer as relevant as they used to be in the Soviet era. Sections of Indian private sector, which used to get away with selling many products of questionable quality under the bilateral system, also found it difficult to adjust to radically changed economic and commercial environment in Russia, driven by market forces.

There is an argument that things would have been much more transparent if majority of Indian exports to Russia were not financed through rupee-debt repayment mechanism. This could have forced Indian companies to compete in Russian markets without looking for repayment mechanism protection. Compared to Russia, there was no protection available to Indian exporting firms in Central and Eastern Europe. However, in these markets also trade has declined significantly. So, it is difficult to prove the view that protection given to Indian companies has really harmed them.

Table 9.2

India-Russia Trade from 1993-94 to 2002-2003 (in US$ Million)

Year	*Exports*	*% Share of Total Indian Exports*	*Imports*	*% Share of of Total Indian Imports*	*Total Trade*	*% Share of Total Indian Trade*
1993-94	648.60	2.92	256.89	1.10	905.49	1.98
1994-95	807.38	3.07	504.54	1.76	1311.92	2.39
1995-96	1046.55	3.29	857.53	2.33	1904.09	2.78
1996-97	811.84	2.42	628.96	1.61	1440.80	1.98
1997-98	954.12	2.72	679.02	1.63	1633.14	2.13
1998-99	706.26	2.14	545.42	1.29	1254.68	1.66
1999-00	948.99	2.58	623.94	1.25	1572.93	1.82
2000-01	869.93	1.97	517.19	1.03	1387.12	1.47
2001-02	796.83	1.82	538.36	1.05	1332.19	1.41
2002-03	704.00	1.34	592.00	0.96	1296.00	1.14

Source: Centre for Monitoring Indian Economy.

It is evident that Indo-Russian trade has declined substantially in the last decade. There were some signs of an upward swing in the middle of 90s, but this trend was again reversed, partly by financial crisis in Russia. In recent years, bilateral trade with Russia is less than 1.5 per cent of total Indian trade. Less than 2 per cent of Indian exports enter Russia and only about 1 per cent imports come from Russia. Throughout the 90s, trade balance was in favour of India. These statistics, however, do not reveal the full story. Many imports from Russia, particularly metal, metal scrap, fertilisers, paper and paper products are sourced through international suppliers. So they do not reflect in these figures. Similarly, many Indian goods enter Russia *via* 'Shuttle trade' or through third countries.

The composition of official Indo-Russian trade is given in Tables 9.3 and 9.4. Main items of traditional export from India are tea, readymade garments, drugs and pharmaceuticals, coffee, tobacco, rice, leather goods, etc. Recently some non-traditional items like electronic goods, plastic and linoleum products, etc. have also shown some growth. But there has been some negative growth in tea, coffee and rice. The Confederation of Indian Industry (CII) however, expects Indian pharmaceutical exports to Russia to rise steeply by about 60 per cent in the next three to four years. Traditional imports from Russia include fertilisers, iron and steel, non-ferrous metals, newsprint, synthetic rubber, chemicals, etc. In 1999-2000, India also imported coal, coke and briquettes, worth 43 million US$ from Russia. Overall, imports of almost all products are on a decline from Russia.

State Linkages

Since 1992, 10 summit level meetings have taken place and about 100 agreements have been signed between the two countries. To improve economic relationship, an Indo-Russian Inter Governmental Commission on trade, economic, scientific, technological and cultural cooperation has been working towards promoting bilateral cooperation. The Commission covers 11 joint-working groups *viz.*, Trade and Economic Cooperation; Pharmaceutical; Petroleum; Coal Industry; Metallurgy; Science & Technology; Cultural Cooperation; Information Technology; Power and Energy; Environment and Natural Resources; and Cooperation with the Regions. Some infrastructural projects are being implemented with Russian participation. India and Russia have also cooperated in the oil and gas sector.

Table 9.3

Composition of Indian Imports from Russia 1995-96 to 2001-02 (US$ Million)

Commodities	*1995-1996*	*1996-1997*	*1997-1998*	*1998-1999*	*1999-2000*	*2000-2001*	*2001-2002*
All Commodities	857.53	628.96	679.02	545.42	623.94	517.19	538.36
Fertiliser Manufactured	168.33	29.52	77.17	149.44	200.96	86.31	134.63
Newsprint	85.38	74.13	82.26	60.93	53.01	64.04	63.54
Non-ferrous Metal	179.1	164.33	136.17	55.57	60.7	61.38	59.32
Iron & Steel	130.66	77.17	157.42	75.16	60.91	101.27	51.46
Synthetic & Reclaimed Rubber	4.42	4.83	8.1	12.41	17.1	16.76	30.83
Non-electrical Machinery	47.57	27.83	39.09	21.88	30.81	16.78	17.59
Other Crude Mineral	2.86	3.66	4.13	3.08	5.71	6.85	14.99
Coal, Coke & Briquettes	—	—	—	5.71	43.41	6.27	12.01
Printed Books, Newspaper, etc.	1.98	0.84	0.05	0.08	4.39	14.91	10.92
Gold	—	—	—	—	0.5	—	8.43
Organic Chemicals	45.72	29.19	34.73	19.19	15.33	5.09	6.87
Silver	—	—	—	—	8.38	1.12	6.83
Transport Equipment	12.9	37.58	16.82	5.9	7.44	30.28	6.32
Electronic Goods	2	1.52	1.51	1.34	6.51	11.06	5.88
Manufactures of Metals	2.49	1.4	1.56	2.36	3.04	3.17	5.34
Medicinal & Pharm. Products	2.57	5.22	5.78	5.56	5.08	5.01	5.09
Inorganic Chemicals	1.88	14.43	17.89	13.11	3.2	10.49	4.85
Metalliferous Ores & Metal Scrap	9.97	10.89	17.21	13.4	21.91	7.26	4.02
Primary Steel Pig Iron Based Items	28.68	8.51	10.46	4.15	23.42	13.99	3.65
Non-metallic Mineral Mnfs.	0.71	0.32	1.47	1.7	1.9	0.49	3.47
Project Goods	16.3	9.27	1.18	18.32	17.82	4.45	3.1
Professional inst. Optical Goods, etc.	1.29	1.64	1.09	0.94	2.14	1.27	2.57
Pulp & Waste Paper	23.23	6.44	10.73	0.7	0.96	1.08	2.39
Chemical Material & Products	1.08	0.15	0.1	0.24	0.13	0.83	2.3
Pulses	—	0.06	—	—	—	—	1.98
Artificial Resins, Plastic Materials, etc.	4.65	1.98	1.73	0.29	1.12	1.21	1.66
Electronic Machinery	0.86	0.47	1.36	1.27	2.7	0.51	1.02
Wood & Wood Products	0.03	0.55	0.73	0.09	0.05	0.08	0.91
Cotton Raw & Waste	5.36	—	—	1.51	15.35	9.45	0.8

Source: Centre for Monitoring Indian Economy.

Table 9.4

Composition of Indian Exports to Russia from 1995-96 to 2001-02 (US$ Million)

Commodities	*1995-1996*	*1996-1997*	*1997-1998*	*1998-1999*	*1999-2000*	*2000-2001*	*2001-2002*
All Commodities	1046.56	811.84	954.12	709.26	948.99	869.93	796.83
RMG of Cotton Incl. Accessories	39.66	30.47	52.92	93.13	152.37	208.23	215.95
Drug, Pharm. & Fine Chemicals	90.92	108.99	106.07	47.65	122.89	108.95	100.38
Tea	142.69	75.04	198.49	197.89	162.07	105.01	84.04
Coffee	102.1	85.78	93.97	59.17	56.77	63.19	67.02
RMG of Manmade Fibres	12.26	12.22	16.6	26.01	44.56	44.95	50.78
RMG Wool	33.23	33.52	25.76	15.74	38.14	33.12	40.99
Cotton Yarn Fab. Madeups, etc.	35.52	61.78	76.61	51.23	69.18	66.78	26.47
RMG of Other Textile Materials	8.07	5	6.59	3.58	10.61	23.1	22.06
Electronic Goods	18.2	4.75	20.1	5.84	33.63	15.16	18.64
Tobacco Unmanufactured	21.63	30.35	59.27	25.12	46.6	27.49	21.62
Machinery & Instrument	20.39	20.92	14.15	18.84	24.27	10.09	16.95
Plastic & Linoleum Products	27.94	32.82	30.8	12.64	25.48	21.35	16.35
Castor Oil	13.54	2.2	1.83	1.06	11.57	10.91	11.97
Cosmetics/Toiletries	34.88	19.09	20.26	7.86	8.12	6.73	9.06
Leather Goods	5.61	6.41	8.28	5.37	13.2	18.77	7.91
Transport Equipments	10.07	3.82	4.25	3.93	3.48	2.22	5.69
Non-*basmati* Rice	31.61	89.51	41.37	33.51	36.09	0.45	5.34
Finished Leather	13.95	2.61	3.55	1.72	1.19	2.58	5.06
Natural Silk Yarn Fab. Madeup	0.32	0.19	0.42	0.11	0.16	0.21	4.73
Manmade Yarn Fab. Madeups	6.77	6.72	5.02	2.65	5.72	6.22	3.72
Inorg./Org./Agro. Chemicals	15.11	4.3	6.97	5.88	1.41	4.14	3.53
Sesame Seeds	—	—	—	—	1.02	0.71	3.4
RMG of Silk	2.05	2.52	0.35	0.91	0.18	1.52	3.18
Manufactures of Metals	2.37	2.16	2.26	2.91	2.88	3.32	3.1
Glass/Glassware/ Ceramics/Cement	1.16	0.71	2.5	0.04	0.49	0.54	2.83
Rubber Manufactured Products	4.78	2.34	3.77	3.81	5.78	4	2.48
Dye, Intermediates	0.81	2.06	1.85	0.67	1.19	2.03	2.26
Marine Products	3.6	1.72	0.94	0.05	0.1	0.24	1.94
Spices	8.96	9.09	14.7	8.29	11.01	3.63	1.86

Source: Centre for Monitoring Indian Economy.

A major turning point in bilateral relationship was the signing of 'strategic partnership' between the two countries during the visit of Russian President Putin to India in October 2000. Broadly, this agreement means enhanced cooperation in the political, economic, defence and cultural fields. The agreement talks of, "Deepening and diversifying cooperation in sectors such as metallurgy, fuel and energy, information technology, communications and transport, including merchant shipping and civil aviation." To promote bilateral trade it also talks of, "Further development of cooperation in banking and finance, and improving credit and insurance facilities." There was also mention of simplifying rules and procedures for travel by entrepreneurs and businessmen of both countries. It was also agreed to jointly explore the possibilities of regional trading arrangements with third countries. Altogether 16 agreements were signed during the visit including an agreement on establishing an Inter-governmental Commission on Military-Technical Cooperation. It was also agreed that there will be an annual summit meeting between the two heads of states.

In 2001, during Indian Prime Minister Vajpayee's visit to Moscow, another 16 documents were signed including Moscow declaration on international terrorism; line of credit agreement between EXIM Bank of India and Vnesheconombank of Russia; and MoU between Confederation of Indian Industry (CII) and Russian Union of Industrialists and Entrepreneurs (Employers)(RUIE) for opening representative offices in Moscow and Delhi. Another 6 documents were signed during President Putin's visit to India in 2002. Further 10 documents were concluded during Indian Prime Minister's visit to Russia in October 2003.

The crux of all these summit meetings has been common positions on major global issues like international terrorism and desire for a multipolar world and bilateral relations. These summits have been a very useful platform for formulating common positions and responses to emerging global political and economic issues. However, in pure commercial terms very little has been achieved from Indian point of view despite very long nicely worded declarations.

Although, it can be argued that under new circumstances, business in both the countries is no more the business of the governments. Therefore, it is up to the private sector to take advantage of conditions created by these agreements. Despite this, these high level visits could have been used more effectively to promote Indian economic interests in Russia. Compared to India, Russians have done good business during these visits. Russia has comparative advantage in arms industry, and India has purchased arms worth billions of dollars during these visits. Four annual summit meetings in the last four years were good opportunities where some special bilateral economic relationship could have been created, even under entirely different circumstances.

Still Military-Industrial Complex/Public Sector Dominates

Despite economic policy changes in both the countries, Indo-Russian economic relationship is still dominated by the defence/public sector. Strong economic linkage is still in the military-industrial complex. In 1991, 70 per cent of army armaments, 80 per cent of air force armaments and 85 per cent of navy armaments were of Soviet origin. This is an established fact that India still relies heavily on Russia for its arms. During the Cold War years, the former USSR and India maintained very close defence ties. According to some estimates India has bought some $ 33 billion worth of weapons from Moscow since the 1960s and Russian weapons account for nearly three quarters of India's arsenal. Some other estimates suggest that India imports US$ 1.5 billion worth of military hardware every year. In the next few years India is going to purchase arms worth $ 10 billion. And a major portion of these imports will come from Russia. Russia's annual military sales to India and China are believed to amount to some 80 per cent of Moscow's overall arms exports, which reached $ 3.7 billion in 2000 and $ 4.5 billion in 2001.

According to the SIPRI arms transfer database, at 1990 constant prices, India imported weapons worth $ 9 billion in the period between 1993 and 2002. As the following table shows, about 75 per cent of these weapons came from Russia. There are estimates that about 800 Russian defence production facilities are kept in operation by Indian defence contracts.

As shown in the Table 9.6, the major purchases in the last 10 years from Russia have been about Su-30MK FGR aircrafts, T-72MI and T-90 battle tanks, Ka-31/helix helicopters and variety of other armaments. According to SIPRI data, major deals worth billions of

Table 9.5

Major Exporters of Weapons to India, 1993-2002

(Figures are Trend-Indicator Values Expressed in US $ Million at Constant 1990 Prices)

Exporting Country	*1993*	*1994*	*1995*	*1996*	*1997*	*1998*	*1999*	*2000*	*2001*	*2002*	*Total 1993-2002*	*% of Total*
Russia	311	251	574	628	1127	362	913	420	693	1529	6808	75
Netherlands	75	75	77	75	87	80	54	18	39		580	6
Germany	22	182	11	15	18	11	11	44	11	11	333	4
Slovakia			67	74	74				40	40	295	3
UK	14	14	86	22	51	15	12			9	223	3
France	31	31	30	26	20	1	19	19	19	15	211	2
Israel					22	38	8	27	68	18	188	2
Ukraine			9		55	17	26	26	17	17	167	2
Poland						1	8	17	67	27	121	1
Singapore	2				38	19					59	1
Kyrgyzstan			57								57	1
Italy								10	10	2	22	0
South Korea	4			4	4	4					16	0
South Africa							6		5		11	0
Total	**459**	**553**	**911**	**844**	**1498**	**549**	**1058**	**581**	**909**	**1009**	**9091**	**100**

Note: The SIPRI data on arms transfers refer to actual deliveries of major conventional weapons. To permit comparison between the data on such deliveries of different weapons and identification of general trends, SIPRI uses a trend-indicator value. The SIPRI values are therefore only an indicator of the volume of international arms transfers and not of the actual financial values of such transfers. Thus, they are not comparable to economic statistics such as gross domestic product or export/import figures.

Source: SIPRI Arms Transfer Database.

dollars are under serious consideration or already signed on variety of SAM and SAM systems.

Recently, after nearly a decade of negotiations, India has finally agreed to purchase aircraft carrier Admiral Gorshkov. The 45,570 tonne vessel was built in 1978 and was known as *Baku* until the Soviet collapse in 1991. The modernisation of the carrier will cost India around $ 700 million, and the remainder of the billion dollar deal will include up to 30 MiG-29K fighters and 6 Kamov-31 anti-submarine helicopters.

India also has a long tradition of collaboration in space with Soviet Union/Russia.

Thumba Equatorial Rocket Launching Station was set up with Soviet help. Many Indian experimental and remote sensing satellites were launched with the Soviet cooperation. In 1990, India had entered $ 350 million contract agreement with Russia to supply the cryogenic engines and technology for their manufacture within the country. Russia earlier agreed to provide India the technology but reversed the decision after it signed the Missile Technology Control Regime with the United States. The United States objected to giving India the technology because of its potential use for nuclear missiles. Later, commercial and political factors compelled Russia to sell the rocket engines while withholding the technology. Very soon, Indian scientists were able to develop Indian engines.

After more than a decade, when it was first conceived, India and Russia also signed a deal in 2001 for the construction of two large reactors for nuclear power station at Kudankulam in Tamil Nadu, expected to generate 2,000 MW of power. Under the deal, Russia will design the plant and supply 90 per cent of the equipment and materials. Kudankulam-1 is scheduled to go online in December 2007 while Kudankulam-2 is due to begin operating in 2008. Under the agreement, Russia will provide technical credit to India equivalent to 54 per cent of the total cost of the $ 2.6 billion project in the form of the equipment and services. Moscow will also supply nuclear fuel to Kudankulam for 40 years at the fixed cost of $ 157 million annually.

In the energy sector, Indian public sector company Oil and Natural Gas Corporation (ONGC) is active in Russia. Under an agreement signed on February 10, 2001, between Rosneft-Sakhalin (Rosneft-S)

Table 9.6

Transfers and Licenced Production of Major Russian Conventional Weapons to India, 1993-2002

Transfer Weapon Designation	*Weapon Description*	*No. Ordered*	*Year of Order/ Licence*	*Year(s) of Deliveries*	*No. Delivered or Produced*	*Comments*
Ka-31/Helix	AEW Helicopter	4	1999	2002	(2)	Deal worth $ 92 million; delivery 2002-2003.
Ka-31/Helix	AEW Helicopter	5	2001	—		Deal worth $ 108 million; delivery 2003.
Mi-17/Hip-H	Helicopter	40	2000	2000-2001	(40)	Deal worth $ 170 million; Mi-IV version; modified in India to combat helicopter.
MIG-21 PFM/Fishbed-F	Fighter Aircraft	(10)	1995	1995	10	Ex-Russian MIG-21 trainer version.
MIG-29/Fulcrum-C	Fighter Aircraft	2	1995	1996	2	MIG-29SE version.
MIG-29/Fulcrum-C	FGA Aircraft	8	1994	1996	8	MIG-29SE version.
Su-30MK/Flanker	FGA Aircraft	40	1996	1997-2000	(28)	Deal worth $ 1.55 to 1.8 billion; Su-30MKI version; ordered while still being developed and first 16 delivered as Su-30K version to be modified to Su-30MKI after delivery; delivery 1997-2003.
Su-30MK/Flanker	FGA Aircraft	10	1998			Su-30MKI version;ordered while still being developed; delivery 2003/2004.
Tu-22M3/Backfire C	Bomber Aircraft	(4)	(2002)		-	Ex-Russian; Lease; contract not yet signed.
140mm RL	Naval MRL	(4)	(1992)	1997	(2)	For 2 Magar Class landing Ships; designation uncertain.

Contd. ...

...Contd. ...

Transfer Weapon Designation	*Weapon Description*	*No. Ordered*	*Year of Order/ Licence*	*Year(s) of Deliveries*	*No. Delivered or Produced*	*Comments*
AK100	Naval guns	3	(1986)	1997-2001	(3)	For 3 Delhi Class (Project-15) destroyers produced in India; ordered from Soviet Union and delivered from Russia after breakup of Soviet Union.
BM-9A52 Smerch	MRL	(14)	(2002)			Deal worth Rs. 12 billon; contract not yet signed.
M-46	Towed gun	321	(1993)	1994-95	321	Ex-Russian.
2S6M Tunguska	AAV(G/M)	24	1996	1997-99	(24)	No. ordered could be up to 50.
2S6M Tunguska	AAV(G/M)	(14)	(2001)	2002	(14)	Deal worth Rs. 6 billion including SA-19 Missiles.
T-90s	Main Battle Tank	310	2001	2001-02	(124)	Deal worth $ 600-700 million (incl. 55% advance payment); ordered as reaction on Pakistani acquisition of 320 T-80UB tanks; incl. 186 assembled in India; delivery 2001-2004.
Bass Tilt	Fire Control radar	10	(1992)	1997-2002	10	For Delhi Class (Project-25A) corvettes.
Cross Dome	Air Surv. radar	4	(1992)	1998-2002	4	For 4 Kora Class (Project-25A) corvettes.
Front Dome	Fire control radar	18	(1986)	1997-2001	(18)	For 3 Delhi Class (Project-15) destroyers produced in India; for use with SA-N-7 SAM; ordered from Soviet Union and delivered from Russia after breakup of Soviet Union.

Contd. ...

...Contd. ...

Transfer Weapon Designation	*Weapon Description*	*No. Ordered*	*Year of Order/ Licence*	*Year(s) of Deliveries*	*No. Delivered or Produced*	*Comments*
Half Plate	Air/sca. sur. radar	3	(1983)	1997-2001	(3)	For 3 Delhi Class (Project-15) destroyers produced in India; ordered from Soviet Union and delivered from Russia after breakup of Soviet Union.
Kite Screech	Fire control radar	3	(1986)	1997-2001	(3)	For 3 Delhi Class (Project-15) destroyers produced in India; ordered from Soviet Union and delivered from Russia after breakup of Soviet Union.
Kopyo	Combat ac. radar	(125)	1996	2001-02	(28)	Part of deal worth $ 428-626 million for modernisation of up to 125 MiG-21bis fighter aircraft to MiG-21bis UPG (MiG-21I) version; option on 50 more; delivery 2001-2004/2005.
Plank Shave	Air surv. radar	7	(1993)	1997-2000	7	For 3 Delhi Class (Project-15) destroyers and 4 Kora Class (Project-25A) corvettes; for use with SS-N-25 missiles.
SA-12/S-300V	SAM system	(4)	(2002)			Deal worth $1.5 or $2.5 billion incl. 150 missiles; contract probably not yet signed.
Zmei/Sea Dragon	MP aircraft radar	(27)	(2000)	2002	(3)	For modernisation of 8 Tu-142 and ASW/MP aircraft to Tu-142J and some 14 Ka-28 ASW helicopters and 5 Il-38 ASW/MP aircraft.

Contd. ...

...Contd. ...

Transfer Weapon Designation	*Weapon Description*	*No. Ordered*	*Year of Order/ Licence*	*Year(s) of Deliveries*	*No. Delivered or Produced*	*Comments*
53-65K 533mm	AS torpedo	(36)	(1997)	1997-2000	(36)	For Kilo (Sindhughosh) Class submarines.
53-65K 533mm	AS torpedo	(15)	(1993)	1997-2000	(15)	For Delhi Class (Project-15) destroyers.
AA-10a/b Alamo/R-27	BVRAAM	(300)	(1995)	1995	(300)	For MiG-29 fighter aircraft.
AA-10c/d Alamo/R-27B	BVRAAM	1140	1996	1997-2002	(300)	For Su-30MK1 FGA aircraft.
AA-11 Archer/R-73	SRAAM	(180)	1995	1996	(180)	For MiG-29S fighter aircraft.
AA-11 Archer/r-73	SRAAM	(3900)	(1996)	1997-2000	(600)	For Su-30MK FGA and modernised MiG-21bis(MiG-21-93) fighter aircraft and possibly for MiG- 29 fighter and modernised MiG-27ML FGA aircraft.
AA-12 Adder/R-77	BVRAAM	(750)	(2000)			For Su-30MK FGA aircraft and MiG-21-93 (modernised MiG-21bis) fighter aircraft; possibly also for MiG-29 fighter and modernised MiG-27ML FGA aircraft.
AT-16/9M120	Anti-tank missile	(1440)	(2000)	(2002)	(480)	For Mi-17 helicopters.
AT-6 Spiral/9M114	Anti-tank missile	(800)	(1995)	1998-99	(800)	For Mi-24 (Mi-25 and Mi-35) helicopters.
SA-11 Gadfly/9M38M1	SAM	(216)	(1993)	1997-2001	(216)	SA-N-7/9M38M1 version for Delhi Class (Project-15) destroyers.
SA-11 Gadfly/9M38M1	SAM	(108)	(2000)			SA-N-7/9M38M1 version for Krivak-4 (Talwar)Class frigates.
SA-12b Giant/9M82	SAM	150	(2002)			Deal worth $ 1.5 or $ 2.5 billion incl. 4 SA-12 SAM systems; contract probably not yet signed.

Contd. ...

...Contd. ...

Transfer Weapon Designation	*Weapon Description*	*No. Ordered*	*Year of Order/ Licence*	*Year(s) of Deliveries*	*No. Delivered or Produced*	*Comments*
SA-14 Gremlin/Strela-3	Portable SAM	(500)	(1992)	1995-97	(350)	SA-N-8 naval version for use on Pauk Class patrol craft and Kilo Class submarines.
SA-18 Grouse/Igla	Portable SAM	(2500)	2001	2001-02	(1500)	Deal worth $ 32-50 million.
SA-19 Grisom/9M111	SAM	(384)	(1996)	1997-98	(384)	For 24 2S6 AAV(G/M)s.
SA-19 Grisom/9M111	SAM	(224)	(2001)	2002	(224)	Deal worth Rs. 6 billion incl. 14 AAV(G/M)s.
SA-19 Grisom/9M111	SAM	(360)	(2002)			SA-N-11/9M111 version for 6 Kashtan AD/ SAM systems on 1 Gorshkov Class aircraft carrier; contract not yet signed.
SA-19 Grisom/9M111	SAM	(360)	(1997)			SA-N-11/9M111 version for 6 Kashtan AD/ SAM systems on 3 Krivak-4 (Talwar) Class frigates.
SA-7 Grail/Strela-2	Portable SAM	(250)	(1981)	1992-94	(250)	Incl SA-N-5 naval version; probably ordered from Soviet Union and delivered from Russia after breakup of Soviet Union.
SA-8b Gecko/9M33M	SAM	80	1993	1994	80	For SA-8b SAM systems.
SET-65E 533mm	ASW torpedo	(15)	(1993)	1997-2001	(15)	For Delhi Class (Project-15) destroyers.
SS-N-25/Kh-35 Uran	Anti-ship missile	(416)	(1992)	1997-2002	(300)	For Delhi Class (Project-15) and modernised Kashin-2 (Rajput) Class destroyers, Brahmaputra Class(Poject-16A) frigates, Kora Class (Project-25A) corvettes and Tarantul-1 (Vibhuti) Class FAC.

Contd. ...

...Contd. ...

Transfer Weapon Designation	*Weapon Description*	*No. Ordered*	*Year of Order/ Licence*	*Year(s) of Deliveries*	*No. Delivered or Produced*	*Comments*
SS-N-27/3M54E1	Anti-ship missile	(96)	(1998)	2001-02	(38)	For Krivak-4 Class frigates and new and modernised Kilo Class submarines.
SS-N-2d Styx/P-21	Anti-ship missile	(40)	(1983)	1992-97	(40)	For Tarantul-1 (Vibuthi) Class FAC; probably ordered from Soviet Union and delivered from Russia after breakup of Soviet Union.
TEST-71 533mm	AS/ASW torpedo	(36)	(1997)	1997-2000	(36)	For Kilo (Sindhughosh) Class submarines.
Akula-2 Class	Nuclear submarine	2	(2002)			Possibly ex-Russian; lease; delivery 2004; contract not yet signed.
Fedko Class	Tanker	1	1995	1996	1	Indian designation Jyoti Class.
Gorshkov Class	Aircraft-carrier	1	(2003-04)			Ex-Russian; modernised and modified to conventional take off/landing (CTOL) carrier before delivery; modernisation will cost $ 700 million. Delivery by 2008.
Kilo Class/Type-877E	Submarine	2	1997	1997-2000	2	Incl. one originally built for Russia, but sold to India before completion; Indian designation Sindhughosh Class.
Krivak-4 Class	Frigate	3	1997			Deal worth Rs. 35.4 b ($ 0.82-1 billion); Indian designation Talwar Class; Russian designation Type-1135.6; ordered due to problems with Indian production of major warships; delivery delayed from 2001-2002.

Contd. ...

...Contd. ...

Transfer Weapon Designation	*Weapon Description*	*No. Ordered*	*Year of Order/ Licence*	*Year(s) of Deliveries*	*No. Delivered or Produced*	*Comments*
			Weapons Under Russian Licence			
MiG-27M/Flogger-J	FGA aircraft	(54)	1983	1992-97	(54)	Indian designation Bahadur; ordered from Soviet Union and produced under Russian licence after breakup of Soviet Union.
Su-30MK/Flanker	FGA aircraft	140	2000			Deal worth $ 3-4.2 billion; Su-30MKI version; for delivery 2005-2014 or 2005-2017/2018.
BMP-2	IFV	400	(1985)	1992-95	(400)	Ordered from Soviet Union and produced under Russian licence after breakup of Soviet Union; Indian designation Sarath.
T-72M1	Main battle tank	(350)	(1980)	1992-2000	(350)	Indian designation Ajeya; no. could be considerably higher; ordered from Soviet Union and produced under Russian licence after breakup of Soviet Union.
AT-4 Spigot/9M111	Anti-tank missile	(900)	1983	1992-2002	(900)	Ordered from Soviet Union and produced under Russian licence after breakup of Soviet Union.
AT-5 Spandrel/9M113	Anti-tank missile	—	(1988)	1992-2002	(4800)	For BMP-2 IFVs; ordered from Soviet Union and produced under Russian licence after breakup of Soviet Union.
Tarantul-1 Class	FAC(M)	7	1987	1992-2001	7	Indian designation Vibhuti Class; ordered from Soviet Union and produced under Russian licence after breakup of Soviet Union.

Note: Information concerning the year of order, year(s) of deliveries, and number delivered/produced figures are in brackets if the accuracy of the data is uncertain. This does not imply that there is any uncertainty over whether the deal exists, or whether deliveries have taken place.

Source: SIPRI Arms Transfer Database and newspaper reports.

and Sakhalinmorneftegaz-Shelf (SMNG-S), subsidiaries of Rosneft, the Russian oil company, and ONGC Videsh Limited (OVL), acquired a combined 20 per cent interest in the Sakhalin-1 project from Rosneft-S. The American Exxon Neftegaz Ltd. is an operator of the Sakhalin-1 international consortium and owns 30 per cent of its shares. Other participants are the Japanese Sodeco group of companies (30 per cent), The ONGC and the Russian Rosneft companies each holding 20 per cent stakes. ONGC Videsh's initial investment in the Sakhalin-1 project is expected to be about US $ 1.7 billion This project envisages the development of three deposits on the shelf of the Sakhalin island—Chivo, Odoptu, Artukun-dagi, and the construction of an oil pipeline along the floor of the Tatar Straight to the De kastri port, the Khabarovsk Region. It also envisages the construction of a gas pipeline linking Sakhalin and the Japanese island of Honshu *via* Northern Lapanese island. The construction of the pipeline is scheduled to start in 2003, oil supplies in 2005 and gas supplies in 2008.

Other public sector companies active in Russia are: State Bank of India, Canara Bank, India Trade Promotion Organisation (ITPO) and Tea Board of India. State Bank and Canara Banks have representative offices only and do not undertake full-fledged banking operations. However, both banks are in the process of opening a joint venture bank called the 'Commercial Bank of India' in Moscow. ONGC (Videsh) also has only representative office in Sakhalin to coordinate the Sakhalin-1 project with its joint venture partners.

It is clear from the above analysis that most of these initiatives are cooperations at the public sector level. Since the future of most of these units is uncertain in both the countries, the presence of some big Indian business houses in the Russian market is very important. Economic relationship based mainly on defence contracts will lose its meaning in the long run if this is not matched by other private commercial content. Indian industry has already identified areas of mutual interest *viz.*, information technology, pharmaceuticals, telecommunications, financial services, hydrocarbons, energy and power, oil and gas, food processing, financial consultancy, management services, textiles and diamond processing. The recent agreement on India-Russia transport corridor may also help in reducing transport costs. The present route, which passes through the

Suez Canal and enters into the Russian port of St. Petersburg *via* Kotka (Finland) and Rotterdam (Netherlands), is long and time consuming. The new route would comprise sea and land links across India, Iran and Russia and will shorten travel time by as much as 10 days. The new route will be Mumbai-Bandar Abbas (Iran)-Astrakhan (Russia).

In the last few years, the major Indian private company to invest in Russia has been 'Sun Group of Companies' in the areas of beverage and food processing. According to company sources, the cumulative amount of its direct and portfolio investments into various industrial units in Russia is about $ 500 million since 1991. In 2001 Indian electronics company Videocon Ltd. signed an MoU with Russian Voronjeh Electronic Tube factory to jointly manufacture colour TV tubes in Russia. The company plans to invest about $ 100 million.

Future Possibilities

In the 1990s, the relative economic position of India and Russia has dramatically changed. In many discussions, economically both the countries find themselves in the more or less similar economic weight category. Military-technical cooperation seems to be the only solid pillar of the 'strategic partnership'. A few academic studies have tried to analyse this new relationship. Some have argued that while the relationship at bilateral level has been critical so far, the global level has receded and continue to do so, while the regional aspects hold the key to future relations. Others have said that bilateral relationship which is based only on military-technical cooperation is 'unlikely to acquire alliance like dimentions.' A senior Indian strategic analyst has warned that military-technical relationship is a product of the broader strategic relationship rather than the reverse. While analysing the history of Indo-Russian military and nuclear cooperation, an American scholar concludes that earlier 'special relationship' between the countries was based upon Indian needs, American ambivalence, and Soviet opportunism. In the post-Cold War era this relationship has persisted due to continued American ambivalence, short term Indian military needs, and Russian economic needs. In the post-Cold War period, this relationship is shifting from Indian needs and Soviet opportunism to Russian economic needs and Indian military needs and opportunism. He argues that this bond, may be fractured by an eventual improvement in Indian military self-reliance or a deepening in Indo-American military cooperation.

Future bilateral economic relations will depend on Russia's importance to India's developmental needs and *vice versa*. In the past, USSR played an important role in India's industrialisation process. It had a comparative advantage in sectors like steel, which was central to its needs. India has to assess now, where Russia has a comparative advantage. So far, India is able to identify only defence production and oil and gas sector. Similarly, Indian companies could help Russian restructuring and modernisation through its expertise in information technology, management and financial services. In the immediate future, two factors will determine the future of Indo-Russian economic relations. Firstly, sustained growth of the Russian economy and secondly, competitiveness of Indian industry, commerce and services. The strong political will in both the countries to improve bilateral economic relations could have been converted into real economic gains if some imaginative initiatives were taken. The present Indo-Russian commercial relations are certainly not commensurate with the existing potential. To improve these relations, some bold policy initiatives are needed. If policy makers were serious and imaginative, they could have proposed some kind of a bilateral free trade agreement. Although, there would have been reservations from some industries in both the countries, this had the potential to give new direction to bilateral relations. This could have created a feeling of special economic relationship. The 'strategic partnership' document also says that both the countries will jointly explore the possibilities of regional trading arrangements with the third countries. So far, nothing has happened on this front. Some kind of regional economic initiative is possible in the CIS region, particularly in Central Asia. Russia and other CIS economies are picking up in the last few years. Indian economy is expected to grow about eight per cent this year. This is the right time to give a new direction to Indo-Russian economic relations.

References

Blarov, Sergei (2004). "Arming Asia: Russia's $5 Billion Forte", *Asia Times*, January 15.

———. (2002). "India, Russia: Friends in Arms", *Asia Times*, April 13.

Devraj, Ranjit (2001). "Russia Shrugs off Nuclear Ban to Seal Deal with India", *Asia Times*, November 10, *http://newsmen.net/indorussia.htm.*

Evgeny, Gavrilenkov (1999). "Permanent Crisis in Russia: Selected Problems of Macroeconomic Performance", *Hitotsubashi Journal of Economics*, Vol. 40,No. 1.

Igor, Khripunov and Anupam Srivastava (1999). "Russian–Indian Relationship: Alliance, or Partnership?", *Comparative Strategy*, Vol. 18, pp.153-171.

Isenberg, David (2003). "Bees Swarm Around India's Honeypot", *Asia Times*, March 11.

Jayashekar, (1983). "India's Trade with the Soviet Bloc: Growing Dependence and Commodity Inconvertibility", *Problems of Non-Alignment*, Vol. 1(2), pp.115-140.

Jerome, M. Conley (2000). "Indo-Russian Military and Nuclear Cooperation: Implications for U.S. Security Interests", USAF Institute for National Security Studies, *Occasional Paper* 31, February.

Kumar, Suresh (ed.) (1987). *Indo-CMEA Economic Relations*, New Delhi: Ashish Publishing House and Indian Council of Research on International Economic Relations, p.141.

Ministry of Finance (2003). *Economic Survey 2002-03*, Government of India, New Delhi.

Nayyar, Deepak (ed.) (1977). *Economic Relations between Socialist Countries and the Third World*, London etc.: Macmillan, p.xi.

Ollapally, Deepa (2003). "Indo-Russian Strategic Relations: New Choices and Constraints", in Sumit Ganguly (ed.), *India as an Emerging Power*, London, Portland: Frank Cass, pp.135-156.

Pant, N.K. (1999). "ISRO's Cryogenic Boost to Indian Space Commerce", *Free Press Journal*, January 15.

Sachdeva, Gulshan (2000). "Reviving Economic Interests", *Frontline*, Vol. 17 (21), October 14-27, *http://www.flonnet.com/fl1721/17210170.htm.*

Sen, Proneb (1990). "Rupee-Rouble Exchange Rate", *Economic and Political Weekly*, March 24.

———. (1999). "Hard Goods and Soft Currencies: A Note on Bilateral Payment Arrangements", *Working Paper* No. 2, Planning Commission, New Delhi.

Singh, Jasjit (2002). "Putin the Right Perspective", *Indian Express*, December 4.

UNDP (2003). *Human Development Report* (2003). New York: Oxford University Press.

Valkenier, Elizabeth Kridl (1986). *The Soviet Union and the Third World: An Economic Bind*, Allied Publishers, p. 142, New Delhi.

For details of these agreements see: *http://www.meadev.nic.in/foreign/newrussia.htm.*

For text of this agreement see *http://www.india.mid.ru/india/summits/04d_02.html.*

http://www.india.mid.ru/india/summits/03d_15.html.

http://www.india.mid.ru/india/summits/02d_03.html.

http://www.india.mid.ru/india/summits/01d_11.html.

ibid http://oasis.fortunecity.com/rio/444/ISRO.html.

http://oasis.fortunecity.com/rio/444/ISRO.html.

Part III

Restructuring and Strategies of Firms

10

Foreign Direct Investment in China's Automotive Industry

HUA WANG

Introduction

The Chinese automotive industry boomed in 1990s. Furthermore, it has recorded a significant development after the accession of China to the World Trade Organization by the end of 2001. The average annual growth rate since 1979 has been 15 per cent. Total production volume ranked 8th in the world in 2000 and jumped to 5th in 2002. Since vehicle import represents less than 4 per cent of the domestic production, various forms of foreign investment play an important role in the Chinese automotive industry during the process of its restructuring and modernisation.

What are the incentives for foreign firms to enter China's markets? What are their strategies? What is the impact of FDI on the restructuring of China automotive industry? After the outlook of China's automotive industry and its inflow of FDI, this chapter tries to explain the strategic choice on the form of FDI, the ownership-control relationship during the investment. While looking in detail, the interaction between world class giants and Chinese auto groups, we finally illustrate the impacts of FDI on the restructuring of Chinese automotive industry.

Brief Review

The Chinese automobile industry has been established since 1955 under a planned economy system. The industry could be seen as a big beneficiary of China's economic reform and opening up policy. It has recognised a dramatic development since the 1990s. Up to the end of 2002, the annual output has been over 3.2 million. More than 33 million employees work for the automotive and its directly related industries.[1] It is to say that one person out of every 22 Chinese employees is related to the automotive activities. There is no doubt that the automotive industry is one of the most important industry in terms of the significant market that it generates. Table 10.1 and 10.2 show the main indicators and output structure over a period of years.

Table 10.1

Main Indicators of China's Automobile Industry by the End of 2002

	Total	*Automobiles*	*Motocycles*	*Parts*
Number of Firms	2436	117	156	1540
Output Value (billion Euro)	68.8	38.9	8.0	14.4
Fixed Assets (billion Euro)	19.0	9.9	1.7	5.2
Pre-tax Profit (billion Euro)	7.5	4.8	0.4	1.8
Export (Million USD)	336	25	65	221

Note: 1,000 RMB = 100 Euro. Fixed assets here indicate the average balance of net value of fixed assets.

Source: China Automotive Industry Yearbook, 2003.

Table 10.2

Output Structure of China's Automotive Industry 1955-2002

Year	*Total*	*Car*	*Jeep*	*Bus*	*Truck*	*Others*	*Platform*
1955	61	0	0	0	61	0	0
1960	22574	98	1182	0	17148	4146	0
1965	40542	133	2308	0	26538	11563	4146
1970	87166	196	19621	0	47101	20248	14279
1975	139800	1819	30791	0	77606	29584	18585
1980	222288	5418	28034	0	135532	53304	27497
1985	443377	5207	25172	11897	236934	164167	114069
1990	509242	42409	44719	23148	269098	129868	90574
1995	1452697	325461	91766	247430	571751	216289	161808
2000	2069069	604677	NA	700387	764005	NA	252063
2002	3253655	1092762	NA	1068347	1092546	NA	425601

Note: Data for Jeep and Others since 2000 are consolidated into category of car and bus respectively.

Source: Related years of *China Automotive Industry Yearbook*.

---

1. Unless mentioned, the rest of data are from *China Automotive Industry Yearbook*, various issues.

If the statistics would seem to justify the optimism within the automotive industry in China, the following problems remain to be urgently resolved.

Market Concentration versus Sequential Entry of New Car makers

As indicated in Table 10.1, China has the largest number of automobile enterprises in the world. However, China's total output may reach less than any top five world class car maker. Therefore, the priority of automotive industrial policy promulgated in 1994 is to consolidate the industry and promote several national leaders. As a result, three large automobile groups have emerged and seen rapid growth. However, the extremely dispersed structure persisted. What is more, numerous domestic and foreign investors attempted to penetrate the market and joint what was already fierce competition. For example, in the passenger car sector, the number of car makers rose from 7 in 1990 to 24 in 2002.

Production Promotion versus Consumption Limitation

The industrial development is the ultimate objective of the government. Pursuit of the economies of scale and the quick expansion of production capacity are central to its success. Some of the car makers have built a capacity of 1,50,000 units per year. On the other hand, the government still hinders the private purchase of cars. At the national level, as many as 200 types of taxes and fees are payable from the process of manufacturing to the consuming for a China sedan. In Shanghai, it still needs to pay about 3000 Euros through auction to get the driving board (licence). This is the main reason for the high prices of cars in China. The result of these taxes and fees has been holding back the development of the industry and benefit to the consumers.

Infant Industry Protection versus Legitimate Market Competition

There is a long tradition of government intervention in the Chinese automotive industry as the industry is in its infancy. This protective regime has persisted despite the large volume of production. However, its protective measures are mainly served for those state owned enterprises (SOEs), whatever they are in low efficiency or not. Foreign and Chinese private investment received additional barriers to enter the industry. The difficulty for policy makers is, drawing the distinction between legitimate competition and crowding out of domestic car makers by foreign competitors. Making industry promotion and creating national leaders as the priority, will lessen the importance of competition in practice.

FDI in the Chinese Automobile Industry

Foreign direct investment in the Chinese automotive industry started with the creation of Beijing Jeep Co. Ltd. in 1983, a joint venture (JV)with Chrysler to assemble the Cherokee Jeep. In the 1980s, foreign investment was prudent as it was in the early stage of the Chinese economic reform. Up until the end of 1989, there were only around 20 automotive JVs. From 1992, there was a veritable flood of investment. The total number of JVs was 120 in 1993 and 381 in 1995. At the end of 2002, there were over 600 JVs in China's automotive industry including over 80 automobile producers. The accumulated real investment totalled US$ 24 billion till 2002. FDI mainly comes from over 20 countries, including the USA, Germany, France, Japan, Korea, etc. In fact, top 15 world automobile groups have all invested in China through various ways.

It is, however, difficult to forecast FDI in terms of investment volumes in the coming years because the volume of investment in the past fluctuated greatly, and depended more or less on the short term macroeconomic consideration. But one point is clear, Japanese, US and European car makers are locked in intense competition. There are at least two incentives for car makers to seek entry into China's automotive industry: the emergence of a new market and the strategy of globalisation.

China's automotive market is emerging as one of the largest in Asia. The open-door policy has facilitated a two-digit growth in GDP for almost two decades. Improved living standards and the trend towards privatisation are significant signs of a high demand for vehicles. In 1978, there were only 1.36 million vehicles, while in 2002 there were more than 20 million vehicles on the road. Besides these 'standard' vehicles and cars, there is another special type of vehicle tailored for Chinese peasants—the farm vehicle.[2] The demand for farm

2. Farm vehicles are those three-wheel and four-wheel vehicles of 0.5 and 1 tonne, but not tractors. They are historically not listed in the national automaker catalogue. Their outputs are not accounted for in the output of the automotive industry. In China, about 900 million (70 per cent) of the population are living in the rural area.

vehicles has been expanding and 2.6 million were made and sold in 2002. The population of this vehicle has reached 23 million. In total, over 43 million vehicles are in use by the end of 2002. The above data has revealed that there are two automotive industries in China due to the unbalanced economic development between rural and urban areas in China (Wang, 2003). It is to say that from one side, the market structure and product structure have its strong particularity, and on the other side, the size of actual auto market has already reached 43 million units by the end of 2002.

Figure 10.1

The Joint Ventures in Chinese Automotive Industry, 1981-2002

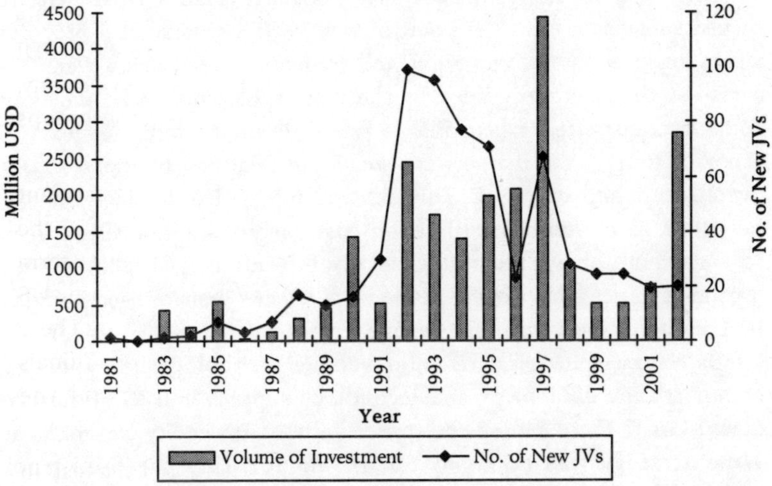

Source: Related years of *China Automotive Industry Yearbook*.

The strategy for 'wanna-be a world-class manufacturer' in the new era is—how to globalise, and finally to become worldwide producer and competitor. This issue becomes more complicated when the strategy is to be realised in a developing country such as China, generally characterised by weak financial and legal institutions, strong governmental intervention, and cultural differences. Furthermore, transaction costs are much higher in a less developed country (Wang, 2003). However, this trend of globalisation seems inevitable in the context of recomposition of the global economy and the political environment. Presently, all of the top 15 world-class car makers are represented in the Chinese market. Periphery car makers are striving to strengthen their competitive position in this market as well. What is more, many word-class spare part suppliers are following the MNCs into the Chinese market.[3] They have found it necessary to invest in upstream and/or downstream industries in order to supply complementary services.

Strategic Choice on the Form of FDI

A foreign company's primary decision is pattern of investments: external technology transfer (licensing) or internal technology transfer (JV or wholly owned subsidiary).

Generally speaking, licence is less secure than a JV or wholly owned subsidiary, from the point of view of IPR (intellectual property rights such as patent, copyright and trademark laws). However, this arms-length operation guided by the market has more advantages in some circumstances; where FDI is relatively unprofitable (at least in the short term), and markets are small and relatively unimportant for overall corporate strategies. This external mode of technology transfer may tend to minimise coordination costs, while still allowing a firm to earn rents on its technological assets (Dunning, 1988a). Those technologies tradable on the market are usually standardised and can be commercialised without serious problem with regard to IPR. In 1980s, Isuzu transfered its light vehicle technology by exporting manufacturing equipment and technology support and KD (knocked down) kits to four Chinese enterprises without any equity control.[4] The same strategy was taken by Suzuki in licensing the mini-truck manufacturing technology to four Chinese firms in different regions.[5] This pattern of foreign investment secures economies of scale on

3. For example, Delphi Automotive Systems, Bosch, Valeo, Siemens, Dana, Allied Signal, Lucas Varity, United Technologies, ITT, TRW, Rockwell, Tenneco, Cooper, etc.

4. They are Beijing Light Automobile Co. Ltd., Qingling Motors Co. Ltd., Jiangling Automobile Co. Ltd., and China Jiangnan Aerospace Industry Group Corp. Those four enterprises are located in north (Beijing), west (Chongqing), middle (Jiangxi province) and southwest (Guizhou province) respectively.

5. They are Faw Jilin Light Automobile Plant (Jilin province, north), Harbin Hafei Motor Co. Ltd. (Heilongjiang province, north), Shanxi Aircraft Manufacturing Corp. (Shanxi province, middle), Liuzhou Mini Auto Factory (Guangxi province, southwest), and Changan Automobile Co. Ltd. (Chongqing, middle west) respectively.

home-based production of CKD (completely knocked down) kits for Japanese firms. Chinese licencees receive the same technology and therefore encounter severe competition due to a lack of difference in product across this section of market.

The internal technology transfer (JVs or wholly owned subsidiaries) is a major channel of FDI. In China's automotive industry, JVs are the principle investment vehicle (Table 10.3). There are two reasons for this equity share structure. Foreign investment is subject to equity limit constrains. MNCs entering China's vehicle assembling and key component projects (motors, air bags, and ABS braking systems) have a restricted share stake no more than 50 per cent.[6] Foreign investors may, however, prefer JVs in the early stages of operation, finding that a JV setup is essential. Chinese partners are necessary to help in understanding the local market and business norms so as to accomplish goals in the Chinese system. Managing the cross-cultural aspects of relationships is difficult if foreign firms want to exploit the market independently. This pattern of investment can also reduce initial risks. The formation of Shanghai Volkswagen is a perfect illustration of such strategy (Jiang and Qiu, 1998).[7]

Ownership Arrangement

A firm possessing superior assets will opt for a strategy that enables it to retain tight control over foreign operations in order to protect the value of those assets (Teece, 1981). The different forms of foreign investment which reflect the ownership structure arrangement will influence the performance of foreign firms in the host country

6. In the component industry, on the contrary, foreign investors can have total equity control over subsidiaries.
7. VW chose Shanghai Automobile Industrial Co. (SAIC) as partner, which has a complete industrial network for the key components. To ensure the foreign currency payment, the Bank of China was invited to become shareholder of the joint venture. Since the SAIC is the automotive group under the jurisdiction of Shanghai municipality, VW thought the local support was not sufficient. To get more tangible and intangible support from the central government, the Chinese National Automobile Industry Co. (CNAIC) became the fourth partner in Shanghai VW. As it was the earliest passenger car project in China, started in the 1980s, it was risky to invest in a forward-integrated sales network by VW itself when the market demand was uncertain. Therefore, VW stated on the joint venture contract that the sales of assembled cars should be the responsibility of one subsidiary of SAIC. This became a risk-free solution for Volkswagen. Since 1990 the market has expanded quickly. Shanghai Volkswagen then developed its own sales network and put it under its control by setting up another vehicle sales joint venture with SAIC.

Table 10.3

Patterns of FDI in Different Auto Sectors

	Vehicle Assembling	*Component Sector*	*Motorcycle Industry*	*Rest*	*Total*
Till 1995 (381 FDI in Total)					
Joint Venture	96%	85.3%	82.1%	100%	85.0%
Cooperative JV	4%	11.7%	10.7%	0%	12.1%
Wholly Owned Affiliate	0%	3.0%	7.2%	0%	2.9%
Till 1998 (604 FDI in Total)					
Joint Venture	NA	284	NA	NA	87.7%
Cooperative JV	NA	31	NA	NA	6.8%
Wholly Owned Affiliate	NA	29	NA	NA	5.5%

Note: There is no systematic statistics on this issue in the *China Automotive Industry Yearbook*.

Source: Wang (1997: 178); SETCIPD (2001: 497).

(Gedajlovic, 1993). More precisely, the property rights that accrue at different levels of ownership (minor, equal or main control on equity share) have a different impact on performance outcomes (Chhibber and Majumdar, 1997).

Table 10.4 shows the quick evolution on forms of ownership arrangement. Before 1995, in terms of equity share, more than half of the JVs were under the control of Chinese partners (58.8 per cent over 381 JVs). This figure has dropped to 47 per cent in 1998. On the other side, the percentage of the JVs with over 50 per cent of foreign equities increased from 25.2 per cent to 34.4 per cent. In fact, it is the result of deregulation of FDI policy. The early Chinese automotive industrial policy has made more institutional constrains. The negative impact from the institutional factors has been investigated by several studies (Poznanski, 1986; Huang, 1997; Chhibber and Majumdar, 1997). The more regulations there were, the less foreign firms would implant in the host country. Therefore, deregulation becomes one important measure to attract FDI. The 50-50 equity is the smallest part of the property arrangement, that accounted only 16 per cent and 18.5 per cent of the total JVs in 1995 and 1998 respectively. The use of equal ownership has depreciated because this invariably leads to a deadlock in corporate decision-making.

Table 10.4

Equity Control by Foreign Firms in China Automotive Industry

Sector	*>50%*		*50%:50%*		*<50%*		*Total*	
	In %	*In Unit*	*In %*	*In Unit*	*In %*	*In Unit*	*In %*	*In Unit*
In 1995								
Total	**25.2**	**96**	**16.0**	**61**	**58.8**	**224**	**100**	**381**
Car	13.7	8	19.6	12	66.7	41	100	61
Component	28.4	74	15.2	40	56.4	147	100	260
Motorcycle	32.1	10	25.0	8	42.9	13	100	30
Others	15.0	4	5.0	1	80.0	23	100	29
In 1998								
Total	**34.4**	**208**	**18.5**	**112**	**47.0**	**284**	**100**	**604**

Source : Wang (1997: 179); SETCIPD (2001: 497).

Even when Chinese firms become majority shareholders, it does not mean the control of the company as showed by some other empirical results in developing countries (Beamish, 1988). Chinese firms sometimes are not able to enforce the decisions and put them into practice. For example, the annual production of Dongfeng Citroën is planned by the joint venture but gets approved by the State Administration of Machinery Industry (SAMI). However, the marketing and sales, the technology transfer are under the control of French partners. Citroën execute the efficient control on the joint venture with 25 per cent of the equity share (including Société Genérale 4 per cent and BNP 1 per cent), compared to the Chinese partner, Dongfeng Motor Company who possess 70 per cent of the equity share.

MNCs in the Passenger Car Sector

The most strategic sector of the Chinese automotive industry is the passenger car assembling. Sequentially, leading multinational car makers have set up joint ventures with Chinese auto groups (Figure 10.2). The industrial structure is taking a considerable reorganisation in the last two decades. Some of the car makers have quitted the market. However, the number of car makers is continuously increasing from only 3 in mid-1980s to 26 in 2002. It is now composed of 15 joint ventures and 11 Chinese enterprises. Therefore, the coming years will be a phase of fierce competition.

Figure 10.2

Evolution of the Number of Car Makers in the Passenger Car Sector, 1983-2002

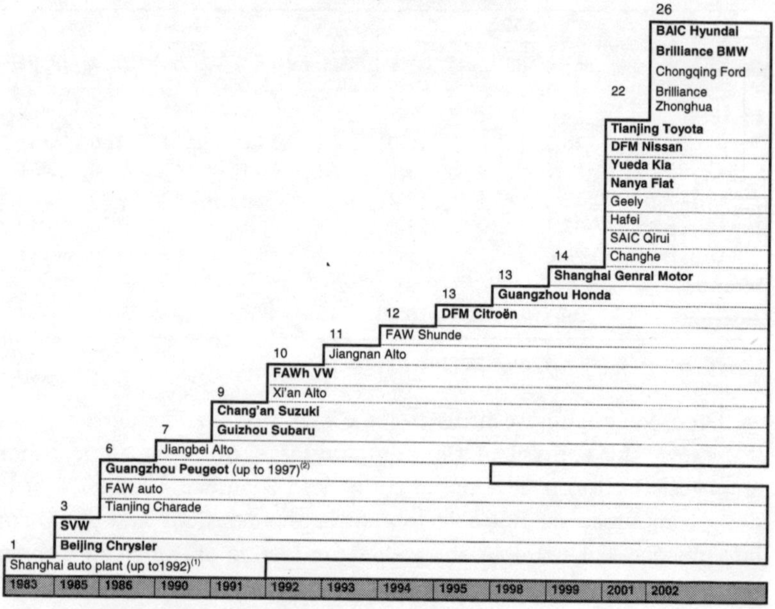

Note: Those companies in bold text are joint-ventures.

The entry year of each car maker is represented by its year of initial production (but not necessarily the year of creation)

(1) This plant stopped its production in 1992.

(2) Peugeot retreat the investment in the joint-venture in 1997.

Source: Related years of *China Automotive Industry Yearbook*.

Top 10 leading car makers (GM, Ford, Toyota, Renault-Nissan, Daimler-Chrysler, Volkswagen, Fiat, PSA, Honda and Hyundai) have all passenger car projects. Together with Chinese automobile groups, they are creating a very complex joint venture alliance (Figure 10.3). Chinese car makers are looking for several foreign partners so as to avoid locked-in situation during the cooperation. It is the case for First Auto Works (FAW), Dongfeng Motors (DFM), Shanghai Automobile Industrial Corporation (SAIC), and Beijing Automobile Industrial Corporation (BAIC). This configuration is not the stabilised situation. After BMW set up the joint venture in 2002, Daimler-Chrysler is planning to follow up and assemble Benz sedan in China in the coming two years. It is still uncertain that whether the injection of FDI in this sector will accelerate or postpone the consolidation of Chinese automotive industry due to the continuous increase of car makers.

Figure 10.3

The Configuration of Passenger Car Makers, 2002

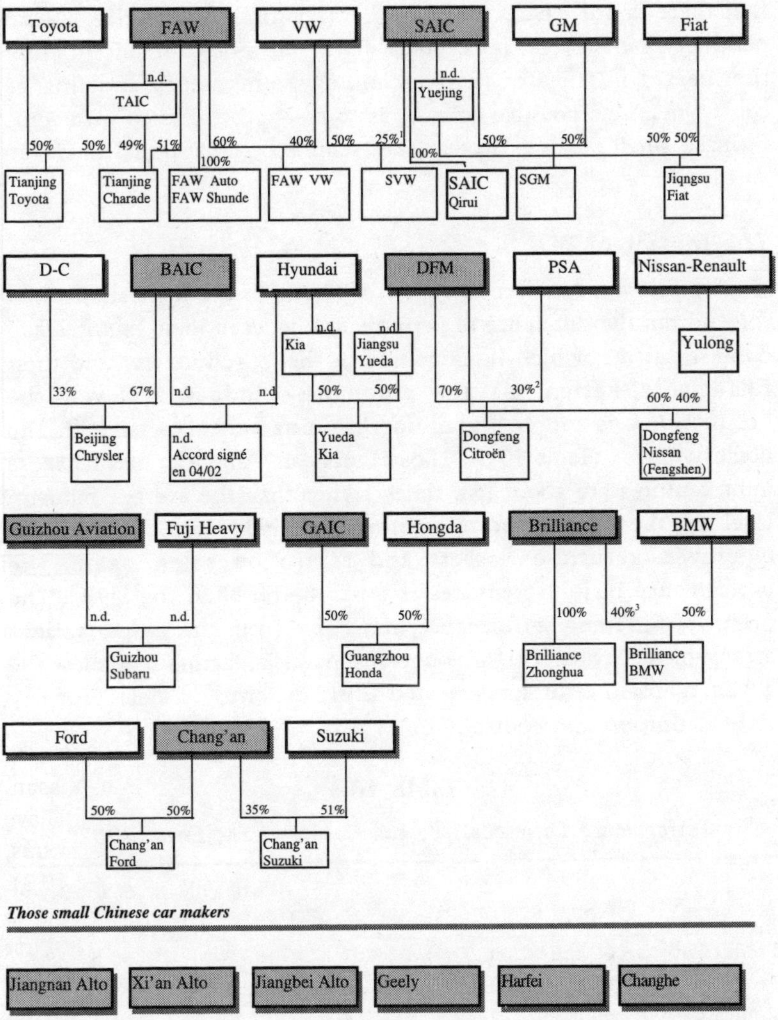

Note: For (1), (2) and (3), besides the investment from Chinese and foreign car makers, some other institutions have invested in the joint-venture. Quite often, they are financial institution like bank, or Chinese local government.

nd: not divulgated.

Source: Related years of *China Automotive Industry Yearbook*.

Historically, the theoretical entry barrier imposed by the automotive industrial policy is high. Meanwhile, the sequential coming of European, American and Japanese companies has showed that there is still space to set up joint ventures in practice. But to periphery car makers, it becomes more and more difficult to enter the market because of their technology competency and finance constraints. One possible solution is to create the alliance with some Chinese small size car makers to assemble certain special model in small volume.

The Impact of FDI

The first impact after the entry of MNCs in the domestic market comes from the difference of performance between joint ventures and domestic firms, which is embodied in their productivity and their financial situation. At the automotive industrial level, the productivity is much higher in the joint ventures than in the domestic firms (Table 10.5). Those European, American and Japanese joint ventures are about two times higher than the average industry level and the SOEs. Concerning other three indicators: the profit per employee, return on assets and return on sales, again, the performance of joint ventures is much better than the SOEs. The origin of different performance may come from the property right arrangement. Property right is one of the crucial factors that show the advantage of the foreign invested firms in terms of clear property right definition and control.

Table 10.5

Performance Differences by the Nature of the Firm, 2002

	JV	*JV with H.K. Macao, and Taiwan*	*SOE*	*Average*
Productivity (1,000 Euro/Employee)	90.7	50.3	36.6	39.6
Profit/Employee(1,000 Euro/Employee)	11.4	2.6	1.8	2.4
Return on Assets(%)	14	6	4	6
Return on Sales(%)	13	6	5	6

Note: Return on assets = the ratio of profit to the total equity for the year.
Return on sales = the ratio of profit to the total sales of the year.
1,000 RMB = 100 Euro.

Source: China Automotive Industry Yearbook, 2003, pp. 381-383.

The second impact is the 'spill-over effect' from the technology transfer viewpoint. Is many developing countries, the great part of the passenger car sector initiated its production with KD assembling. Under the restrain of 'Local Content Policy', the manufacturers are obliged to increase local component rate gradually within certain years. Searching for the qualified local component, suppliers become one of the most important missions for the car maker. It is a heavy investment for the car makers but the beneficial spill-over effects are demonstrated after decades of operation. In 1980s, it took around 5 years to reach 50 per cent, and 10 years to reach 90 per cent of the local content. Till the late 1990s, nearly all the new CBU (completely builtup) projects can locally procure 40 per cent of components in their first year of production (the case of Shanghai GM for example). A complete manufacturing system is building up in China after two decades of efforts jointly by the domestic and foreign component makers. At the present stage, the spill-over effect is limited to the absorption of imported technology, instead of the capability of independent R&D works for the new technology. For those foreign firms, they have different attitudes and approaches towards the technology transfer. The common point is that few of them have transferred updated technology, especially in the fuel efficiency field (Gallagher, 2002).

The emerging competition between the foreign companies is the third impact on China's automobile industry. In 1980s, China had carried out policies to restrict entries into the passenger car market and allocated car production to eight manufacturers with defined market segments. During that period, VW had captured around 60 per cent of the Chinese passenger car market. In the late 1990s, the industrial policy aimed at creating a competitive environment. By allowing more foreign car makers to enter the market, those first-movers begin to feel the pressure from those latecomers. The intensification of competition between MNCs has pushed them to modify their strategy of competition. Starting from assembling one or several models, those world-class car makers are trying to make the following measures in China:

- Expand the field of cooperation to the commercial vehicle sector.
- Set up local R&D centre for the modification and adaptation of localised model.

- Extend the sales network nationwide.
- Provide financial service as soon as getting the approval from the government.
- Gradually integrate component suppliers in China into its global purchasing system.

Last, but not the least, Chinese automotive industry is integrating into the world auto industrial system. The creation of large Chinese automobile groups like FAW, DFM and SAIC, and their close links with MNCs mainly in the form of joint venture, have helped them become part of the world automobile system. Chinese groups are becoming the centre of large volume production for certain kinds of vehicle (e.g. medium size truck). After two decades of cooperation with foreign car makers, some Chinese companies are intending to build their own cars so as to avoid the heavy technology transfer fees. Some large Chinese groups (like SAIC) have taken the strategy of international expansion by investing in foreign car makers (10 per cent share of Daewoo).

Conclusion

In this chapter, we have demonstrated a brief view of FDI in China's automobile industry. China with its large population and the booming of real needs of automobiles, has become the most important market in emerging countries. The sequential coming of foreign investment has had a positive impact on the Chinese automotive industry. It is the essential driver towards the profound industrial restructuring, the building up of assembler-supplier relationship, the construction of complete industrial organisation, and finally, the capacity of designing the vehicle, oriented for the domestic market. In the coming years, automobiles 'made in China' will not only satisfy the domestic market, but also orient towards exports.

Before China entered the WTO, most of the forecast held that the automobile industry will be the biggest victim. However, the unexpected growth rate (over 20 per cent) during year 2002 and 2003 has more or less shown certain level of maturity of Chinese automobile industry. It is not so vulnerable as some study had estimated. In fact, since the adoption of 'opening up' policy in early 1980s, Chinese automotive industry has gradually accumulated the experience on how to cooperate with foreign investment. It is a process of learning by doing. Even though there is still a lot of uncertainty on the future development trajectory, it is certain that the foreign direct investment has positively contributed to the integration of Chinese automotive industry into the world automotive system.

For those foreign firms, the road to success and profitability will still be full of obstacles. It demands the company to have more knowledge about the Chinese market, the correct choice on the pattern of investment, the profound understanding of the complex organisational structures, and the proper reaction in accommodating the Chinese institutional regulation. What is more, the directly imported vehicles will become more competitive starting from 2005, which is the end of the transition period of China's accession to the World Trade Organization. The competition will not only come from the price and costs of vehicle, but also the image building and sales network development. Surely, the fluctuation of foreign exchange rate and some other macroeconomic conditions will also be important external factors which will affect the competitiveness of foreign investment.

References

Beamish, P.W. (1988). *Multinational Joint Ventures in Developing Countries*, London and New York: Routledge.

Buckley, P.J. and M. Casson (1976). *The Future of the Multinational Enterprise*, London: Macmillan.

Chhibber, P.K. and S.K. Majumdar (1997). *Foreign Ownership and Profitability: Property Rights, Strategic Control and Cooperate Performance in Inland Industry*, the William Davidson Institute, University of Michigan Business School, *Working Paper* No. 64.

Davies, H. (1977). "Technology Transfer through Commercial Transactions", *Journal of Industrial Economics*, Vol. 26, pp.161-75.

Dunning, J.H. (1977). *U.S. Industry in Britain*, Boulder Co. Westview Press.

———. (1981). "Alternative Channels and Modes of International Resource Transmission", in T. Sagafi-nejad, R.W. Moxon and H.V. Perlmutter, (eds.), *Controlling International Technology Transfer*, New York: Pergamon Press, pp 3-26.

———. (1988a). "The Eclectic Paradigm of International Production: A Restatement and Some Possible Extensions", *Journal of International Business Studies*, 19(1), pp.1-31.

———. (1988b). *Explaining International Production*, London: Unwin Hyman.

Kelly Sims Gallagher (2003). "Foreign Technology in China's Automobile Industry: Implications for Energy, Economic Development, and Environment", *China Environment Series*, Issue 6.

Gedajlovic, E. (1993). "Ownership, Strategy and Performance: Is the Dichotomy Sufficient?" *Organisational Studies*, Vol. 14(5), pp.731-52.

Gallagher, K.S. (2002). "Foreign Technology in China's Automobile Industry: Implications for Energy, Economic Development, and Environment", *China Environment Series*, Issue 6, The Woodrow Wilson International Center for Scholars (wwics), *ttp://wwics.si.edu/topics/pubs/2-feature_1.pdf*

Huang, Y. (1997). "Between Two Coordination Failures: Automotive Industrial Policy in China with a Comparison to Korea", *Working Paper* No. 67, the William Davidson Institute, University of Michigan Business School.

Jiang, T. and L. Qiu (1998). "Open and Reform Shed Lights on Shanghai Automobile Industry", review on main questions during the construction of Shanghai VW', *Shanghai Automobile* (in Chinese), Vol. 12, pp.22-25.

Kojima, K. (1977). "Transfer of Technology to Developing Countries: Japanese Types versus American Type", *Hitotsubashi Journal of Economics*, Vol. 17, February, pp.1-14.

Lee, C., J. Chen and T. Fujimoto (1997). *Different Strategies of Localisation in the Chinese Auto Industry: the Case of Shanghai Volkswagen and Tianjin Daihatsu*, 97-F-2, Institute for the Japanese Economy Faculty of Economics, The University of Tokyo.

LU, M.H. (1994). "Evaluation and Comparison of Investment Environment in Regions of China", (in Chinese), *Economic Studies*, Vol. 2, Beijing, China.

———. (1997). "Foreign Direct Investment, Regional Distribution and China's Investment Environment", (in Chinese), *Economic Studies*, Vol. 12, Beijing China.

Ozawa, T. (1979). "Multinationalism, Japanese Style: the Political Economy of Outward Dependency", Princeton, N.J., Princeton University Press.

Porter, M.E. (1990). *The Competitive Advantage of Nations*, New York: The Free Press.

Poznanski, K. (1986). "Patterns of Technology Imports: Interregional Comparison", *World Development*, Vol. 14(6), pp.743-56.

SETCIPD (State Economic and Trade Committee, Industrial planning division) (2001). "Qiche gongye shiwu guihua yanjiu ziliao huibian" (Research for the 10th Five-Year Plan in the Automotive Industry), SETCIPD, China, June 20.

Teece, D.J. (1981). "The Multinational Enterprises: Market Failure and Market Power Considerations", *Sloan Management Review*, Vol. 22(3), pp.3-17.

Wang, L.L. (ed.), (1997). *Zhongguo waishang touzi baogao (Report on Foreign Direct Investment in China)*, Beijing: Jingji guanli chubanshe (Economic Management Press).

Wang, H. (2003). "The Coexistence of Two Automotive Systems in China: The Chinese Way of Industrialisation", International conference on the *Structural Reform and the Transformation of Organisations and Businesses*, Ashcroft International Business School (AIBS) & Athenian Policy Forum (APF), Homerton College, University of Cambridge, September 3rd–6th.

11

On the Role of Foreign Investment in the Development of a Market Economy in China

RIGAS ARVANITIS,
PIERRE MIÈGE and ZHAO WEI

In a speech to Chinese academics, Milton Friedman predicted that, "Anyone who can give a clear account of the reform process in China, will win the Nobel prize in economics." The main focus of all economic analyses is centred on the institutional changes, known as 'reform and opening' (*gaige kaifang*) promulgated by Deng Xiaoping from 1979 onwards. So, every discussion of the Chinese economy is concerned with trends in economic policy, and particularly with positing a contrast between the Chinese policy of gradual reforms[1] and the 'shock therapy' adopted by the Soviet Union.[2] But for all their very real interest, these perspectives remain at the macroeconomic level. There is a need to go further and examine the operations of the economic institutions and agencies responsible for wealth creation, such as the Chinese enterprises, public institutions, foreign investors, and organisations to promote technological development.[3] We propose

---

1. See Justin Yin Yifu, Cai Fang, and Li Zhou (2000). *Le miracle chinois, Stratégie de développement et réforme économique*, [The China Miracle], Paris: Economica.

2. Sachs, Jeffrey D., Wing Thye Woo and Xiaokai Yang (2000). "Economic Reforms and Constitutional Transition" (pp. 48). Harvard Business School, Center for International Development: *CID Working Paper* No. 43, April. Although not partisans of a shock therapy, Jeffrey Sachs and his team promote a highly aggressive modification of the constitution.

3. There is a large body of literature on Asian economic development. On Japan, see in particular Ian Inkster's excellent book, *Japanese Industrialisation 1603-2000: A Global and Analytical Approach*, London: Routledge, 2000; and on South Korea, A. Amsden's (1989) *Asia's Next Giant: South Korea and Late Industrialisation*, London, Oxford University Press. We have argued ourselves on the need to examine technological development as a centrepiece of economic development in a special issue of *Science, Technology & Society*. Rigas Arvanitis and Daniel Villavicencio (1998). "Comparative perspectives on Technological Learning: Introduction", *Science, Technology & Society*, Vol. 3, pp.1-9. Fieldwork was done under the projects of the Research Institute for Guangdong Development, Zhongshan University.

to take a new look at Chinese growth by examining more closely the operations of the systems of production, since these are the real producers of that growth. It is only on this basis that the veil of mystery surrounding the 'growth miracle' can be lifted, in China just like anywhere else.[4] We will take the example of Southern China, not because it is the most dynamic area in economic terms but because Guangdong contains a multiplicity of productive systems, thanks to its being the earliest to open up and therefore, the fastest to develop.[5]

China is a particularly interesting case for economic theory, and for a comparative approach to economic and socio-political analyses. It confronts us in a new way with questions over the role of government in economic development,[6] forcing a fundamental rethinking on the social bases of growth. Studies which restrict their analysis to the gradual transition of the socialist regime to the market economy, like those which focus narrowly upon 'privatisation', seem to overlook at least three relevant areas of investigation: the renewal of the oldest the systems of production, the role of the state as promoter and regulator of economic activity, and the degrees of efficiency achieved by the systems of production which appeared with the reforms. In this chapter we would like to offer a framework for thinking about these profound modifications that go, in our understanding, much beyond transition to a market economy. To this end, we will resituate the empirical studies of separate enterprises within a wider frame of reference, showing that Chinese economic expansion is largely due to its being investment driven, and that the economy itself is still quite away from being demand driven. This explains a considerable number of the practical difficulties encountered by all enterprises in China—

4. The view of this growth as miraculous arises from a macroeconomic perspective. See Robert E. Lucas' lecture, "Making a Miracle" in his collection *Lectures on Economic Growth*, Cambridge Mass.: Harvard University Press, 2002.

5. Ezra Vogel, *One Step Ahead: Guangdong Under Economic Reform*, Cambridge Mass., Cambridge University Press, 1989. Since the publication of this work, many others have also shown the persistence of certain economic and social structures. cf. Thierry Sanjuan, A l'Ombre de Hong Kong: le delta de la rivière des Perles, Paris, L'Harmattan, 1999. Examples are drawn from our own field research. A first immediate product of this research is our article: Rigas Arvanitis and Zhao Wei (2003). *Industrialization of South of China: Learning and Limits of a Succesfull Model*. In ALTEC (ed.), Proceedings of the "X Seminario Latino Iberoamericano de Gestión Tecnológica ALTEC 2003. Conocimiento, Innovación y Competitividad: Los Desafíos de la Globalización" (pp. 15). 22, 23 y 24 de octubre del 2003, Ciudad de México, D.F.

6. A critical overview of the role of politics in Asia is to be found in the collection by S. Rowen Henry (1998). *Behind East Asian Growth: the Political and Social Foundations of Prosperity*, London and New York: Routledge.

Chinese, joint ventures or foreign-owned, large or small. The main question is whether this new economy and its systems of production can sustain themselves. By 'systems of production' we mean the totality of plant and human resources contributing to a productive activity.[7] A system of production may include several enterprises; in fact, that is frequently the case in developing economies, where enterprises are subcontracted to those who place orders with them, and whose brand name appears on the finished product. To restrict discussion to the nature of the enterprises themselves would be to focus on the internal organisation of each one, and especially on the nature of its ownership, whereas all the evidence suggests that in China, the question of ownership is less important than how the links between the different units of production operate. Accordingly, our concept of a 'system of production' puts the emphasis on the arrangements made for the productive process and its development, as well as on the interrelationship between the sites of production and their users.

The Three Waves of Investment

The history of the rapid growth of the Chinese economy can be broken down into three successive waves of investment. These waves, and the resulting growth, were not the fruit of an overall strategy of the government and its economic and financial bodies. They were, rather, the outcome of an accidental conjuncture of some perfectly identifiable factors.

The first phase of the expansion was the result of the industrialisation of the countryside, for initially the reforms were aimed at that sector in particular. The ability to grow and sell products outside the state planning system led to a rapid rise in agricultural production. In the early 1980s, the profits from the sale of agricultural produce were massively invested in the rural enterprises, the so-called 'township and village enterprises' (*xiangzhen qiye*). This growth phase lasted six years, from 1983 to 1988. The investments from it were like *manna* from heaven for the local authorities and the most adept among the inhabitants of the rural areas. They found themselves in quite exceptional circumstances, given the absence of any competition

7. Definition used by Jean Ruffier, *L'efficience productive: comment marchent les usines*, Paris, Editions du CRNS, 1996.

and the existence of a large demand hitherto unsatisfied by the planned economy. This new economic opportunity allowed the development of an economy out of the plan.[8] There was considerable demand for foodstuffs, clothing, and domestic durables. This demand was initially directed at light consumer producers, but it was later redirected towards heavy industry. So, at that stage, agricultural resources provided the motor for growth, but the period of rapid expansion was followed, in time-honoured fashion, by a period of overheating characterised by overinvestment. By the late 1980s, the purchasing power of the peasantry began to diminish, and the rural market, which represented 75 per cent of the population, could not sustain the growth in demand. At the same time, all the city families had already satisfied their basic need for durable domestic items, and the upward curve in demand for agricultural products and clothing flattened out. In the early 1990s, therefore, this slowing consumer demand could no longer function as the engine for economic growth. The investment patterns of the previous decade had been directed towards light industry, which is characterised by short term production and rapid returns. The consequence was overcapacity in the durable consumer goods industry, which meant that the current economic model was no longer viable.

The early 1990s saw the arrival of another source of investment, the so-called 'foreign' investments, which mostly came from Taiwan, Hong Kong, and overseas Chinese. In 1994, foreign direct investment (FDI) represented 20 per cent of the overall investment. In 2001, foreign investment from Hong Kong, Macao, and Taiwan continued to represent 18 per cent of the total (158 billion Yuan) and 47.5 per cent of foreign investments in Guangdong province (55 billion Yuan).[9] The Chinese government, wishing to take advantage of this capital inflow, set up a great number of economic development zones in the coastal regions. Everywhere 'hotels for overseas Chinese' sprang up to accommodate the influx, and these provided the engine for growth in the first half of the 1990s.[10] Some of them, like Shenzhen, are still major poles of attraction for foreign investment. Investors were

8. cf. Barry Naughton (1995). *Growing Out of the Plan: Chinese Economic Reform 1978-1993*, Cambridge: Cambridge University Press.

9. *China Statistical Yearbook, 2000*.

10. These special economic zones were established in the early 1980s, but their major expansion occurred in the 1990s.

attracted by favourable policies, the nature of the labour force, and the Chinese market. In addition, the common language and cultural proximity, along with shared attitudes towards combining political connections with business, encouraged this source of investment. During this phase, two-thirds of the foreign investments were in the hands of small and medium-sized firms from Hong Kong and Taiwan. These made use of labour-intensive production to assemble imported parts and re-export them to supply the international market. This system received the blessing of local officials, since such *manna* from heaven also blessed them with great decision-making powers. The enterprises involved did not represent direct competition, either with the China-based township and village enterprises or with the private or state-owned ones. On the other hand, they contributed towards improving the trade balance and towards increasing employment and incomes. Moreover, the demand arising from this poorly paid labour force was directed towards the low quality products from the communal and the state-owned enterprises. These benefited from the growth in domestic demand, and still do. That is why all these enterprises survived throughout this period, despite producing goods which were in many ways outdated (Figure 11.1).

Figure 11.1

Evolution of Fixed Assets Investment (Million Yuans)

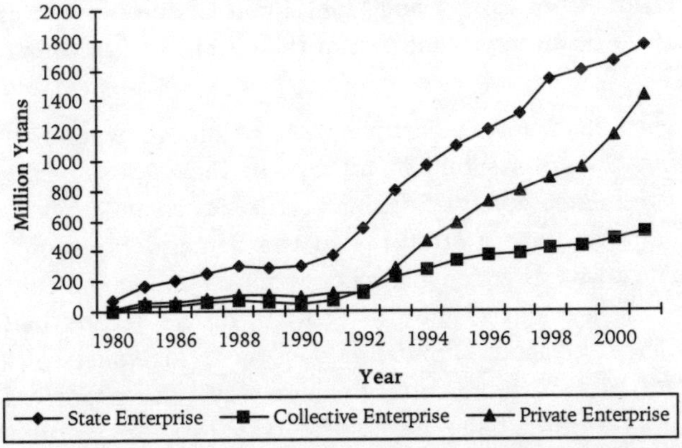

Note: The category « private » entreprises comprises of individual entreprises (*getihu*), entreprises by shares and mixed capital entreprises. This is probably an overestimation of the private sector, notably so for entreprises by shares; also there is an overestimation of the "collective" economic type since collective entreprises are run like private entreprises. See Guiheux, 2002, for a good analysis of these categories.

Source: Annuaire statistique de Chine, édition 2002. Tabl. 6-2, p.176.

This growth model, which depended upon FDI from Taiwan and Hong Kong, could have lasted for at least 20 years, by following the set pattern of integration with foreign manufacturers. But the Asian crisis of 1997 modified the underlying situation. The developed economies reduced their orders placed with Chinese enterprises, while the latter remained essentially geared to the supply of overseas markets. Simultaneously, the new exchange rates restored a degree of competitive advantage to the other Asian countries, by making their production costs attractive again. So, this second engine for growth no longer worked.

The third phase of development began at this juncture, with the arrival of FDI funds from industrialised countries like the United States, Japan, and Europe. The Chinese government reacted extremely fast, by adopting a whole range of measures to attract this foreign investment. The huge campaign in favour of entry into the WTO must be understood in this context. That is why WTO membership became the main objective of official policy. Since 1997, investment in real estate has greatly increased, and the big cities have become showcases for China's growth.[11] Forthcoming events like the Beijing Olympic Games in 2008, and the Shanghai Universal Exhibition in 2010, provide an additional seductive appeal to international investors. As a consequence of the spectacular take-off in international investment, capital inflow from Taiwan and Hong Kong has picked up again, and continues to be an important part of the overall FDI in China (Figure 11.2).

Between 1978 and 2002, the value of Chinese exports rose from 10 billion US dollars to 226 billion. In the 1980s, income from exports stimulated domestic demand for basic consumer goods. In the 1990s, exports gave a stimulus to the demand for sophisticated electronic consumer goods, particularly household equipment, making export trade a major engine for growth. In the second half of the 1990s, China set about stimulating demand in the sphere of tourism, real estate, and car production. In these ways, the reforms launched by Deng Xiaoping have paved the way for expansion in both consumption and production.

---

11. cf. the work of Guilhem Fabre, which shows nonetheless that the growth in real estate sales, encouraged by various means, has still been unable to efface the effects of the property bubble brought about by speculation in land values; Guilhem Fabre (2000). *Le miroir chinois de la transition: Genèse d'une crise 1989-2000*, Paris: L'Harmattan.

Figure 11.2

Evolution of Foreign Investments (Billion US Dollars)

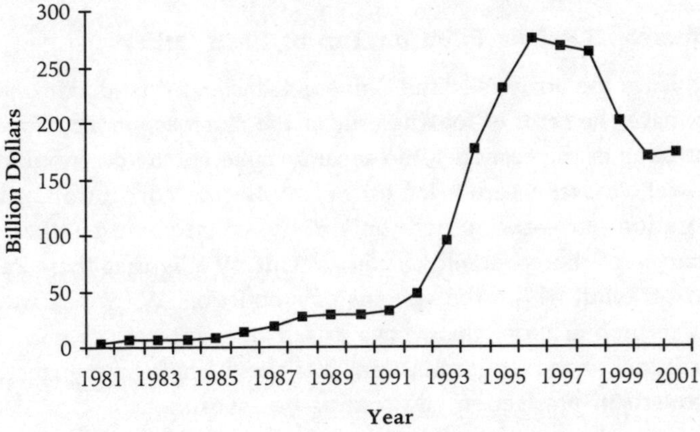

Source: Annuaire statistique de Chine, édition 2002. Tabl. 6-3 p. 177.

In a well-known article in *Foreign Affairs,* Paul Krugman defines the nature of the growth in East Asian countries as an effect of resource mobilisation, not of increasing productivity. He was commenting on a little known article by Alwyn Young[12] and his article concludes that Asia has achieved remarkable growth rates without any corresponding increase in productivity. In his view, these growth rates were more the outcome of mobilising available resources than of increasing efficiency. In short, it was a matter of "more perspiration than inspiration".[13] Essentially, China has been following this same model of accumulation, with some variants of her own.

Firstly, average individual income is low and the level of household savings is high. The rapid increase in China's GNP in the first stage of growth was accompanied by an increase in income disparities. Secondly, given the size of the Chinese economy and the importance of regional disparities, a single wave of investment is simply not enough. Thirdly, the Chinese state has a powerful capacity for mobilising resources, and has been able to make use of the structures

12. Young, Alwyn (1992). "A Tale of Two Cities: Factor Accumulation and Technical Change in Hong Kong and Singapore", *NBER Macroeconomics Annual,* MIT Press.

13. Krugman, Paul (2000). *The Return of Depression Economics,* London: The Penguin Press, p.32ff.

of production which were actually introduced to ensure social and political stability. This mode of economic organisation lies at the very heart of its current difficulties.

Productive Systems Piled on Top of Each Other

To leave the analysis of the Chinese miracle at this juncture would be to make the error of looking only at the macroeconomic data—like the breakup of the economy into separate spheres, the decentralisation of power, and the return of former evils like corruption, gangs, prostitution, etc.—taking note only of the consequences rather than the causes of the economic changes.[14] Our view is that these causes are to be found within the systems of production. With each wave of resource mobilisation, there have arisen new enterprises with their own distinct systems of production. It is these which have engendered the growth in production and returns on investment.

The Rural Enterprise Systems of Production

The first type of productive systems is the township and village enterprises. These enterprises grew up in the early 1980s, and they operate as private companies, but for reasons of ideological acceptability they are officially registered as collective enterprises.[15] They work on raw materials and employ low-cost labour, and they are concentrated in various sectors of production, which they quickly came to dominate.[16]

---

14. A good journalistic account of the various opinions on the economic and political future of China is to be found in Gordon G. Chang, *The Coming Collapse of China*, New York, Random House, 2001. A recent special issue of the *China Economic Review*, December 2002, Vol. 13(4), also addresses the issue. See in particular the catalogue of problems drawn up by Thomas Rawski in "Will Investment Behaviour Constrain China's Growth?", *ibid*. pp.361-372. There is a fiercely critical analysis of the economic reality in China by He Qinglian in "China's Listing Social Structure", *New Left Review*, No. 5, 2000, pp.69-99. When this was republished in China, in the review Shuwu (Changsha, March, 2000), it cost the author her professorial post.

15. Gilles Guiheux (2002). "The Incomplete Crystallisation of the Private Sector", *China Perspectives*, No. 42, pp.24-35. Strictly speaking, collective enterprises do not include private enterprises, but actually a good many collective enterprises are 'lent' to a private enterprise management team. Often the most important enterprises are to be found in this category.

16. In nine sectors the total output increased in value by 10-15 per cent per year; these were domestic electrical goods, hand tools, paper, domestic chemical products, organic chemicals, furniture, textiles, agricultural products and beverages, and coal and ferrous metals.

At the same time, the larger collective enterprises already in place started to operate as 'private' firms. A good example of this is the Yueqing enterprise in Shuikou (Guangdong province). Starting as a tap manufacturing plant, it modernised and became the origin of a myriad of small plumbing firms. Consequently, Shuikou township is now at the head of a whole industrial sector, and Yueqing is just one among many new enterprises. A large number of other enterprises have set themselves up along the same lines, both in Guangdong and in the rest of China. Well known brand names like Legend, TCL, Haier, Konka, and Galanz are similar enterprises which arose with the first phase of expansion, and they prospered mostly because their status as collective enterprises gave them access to public funds (Figure 11.3).

Figure 11.3

Industrial Production by Type of Enterprises, 2001—Comparison of China and Guangdong (Billions Yuans)

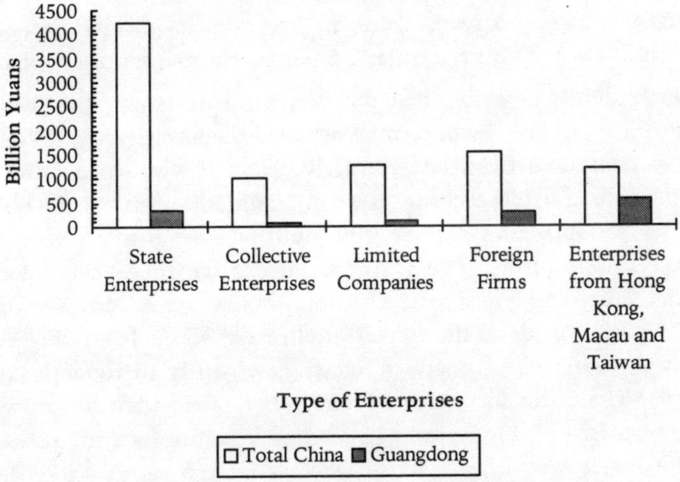

Source: Annuaire Statistique de la Chine, Edition 2002. Tabl. 13.3 p. 425.

These enterprises—mostly collective but also shareholder enterprises—were primarily suppliers to the domestic market, only turning later to production for export. Galanz in Shunde, a town close to Guangzhou, is typical. It started as an assembly plant for microwave cookers, whose step-up transformers and magnetron tubes were imported from Japan for US$ 20. The same components imported from Europe cost US$ 30. The leaders of the enterprise made a quick visit to the European manufacturers and offered to buy transformers at US$ 8 and become the own equipment manufacture (OEM) producer for the European firm. The Europeans made their own rapid calculations and accepted the offer. They transferred all their equipment and production lines to Shunde, including their assembly technology. The Japanese offered the same OEM arrangement, with a purchase price for the transformer at US$ 5. Today Galanz produces the transformer *in situ* for US$ 4, and the enterprise claims to control 30 per cent of the world market and 70-80 per cent of the domestic market. How has that been possible? In an interview, the owner explained that in Europe the production line runs for six hours a day, and five days a week, adding: "Because of strikes, they actually only work an average of four days, or between 24 to 30 hours a week. I took over their production techniques and set up a system of three eight-hour shifts, which works out at a 160-hour week. My productivity is six to seven times higher than in Europe, but each wage bill is between 3 per cent and 5 per cent of the European wage."

But it should be added that the success of these enterprises is to be explained not only by the match between the foreign clients' search for low costs and Chinese productive capacity, but also by their entering into a stable exchange system along OEM lines. The Galanz factories produce on behalf of 200 multinational firms from every quarter of the globe. The Chinese enterprise takes care of the manufacturing end while the technology, brand name, and marketing remain in the hands of the foreign multinationals. It is striking how quickly the enterprise has grown, which is why it is a frequently cited example. The quest for increased turnover is a constant factor, with the enterprises taking advantage of their low production costs. In addition, such enterprises actively seek out foreign partners to ensure access to technology and market outlets. What the Chinese enterprises are looking for is this technology transfer, both material (in the form of products, equipment, and processes) and organisational (quality control and management skills).

The Systems of Production Set Up by the Overseas Chinese Investment

A second type of production system appears in enterprises which were established by the second wave of investment from Taiwan and Hong Kong. Industries producing textiles and clothing, electronics and electrical household goods, were relocated to the Pearl River delta. These enterprises share some features with those of the first wave, but they also have some specifics of their own. Firstly, the investors not only established the enterprises, but brought with them their own networks of suppliers and customers. The Taiwanese and Hong Kong enterprises which set themselves up on the mainland to take advantage of low production costs, were backed by more than 30 years experience as suppliers to the multinationals. In addition, they have their own way of doing business, to which the entrepreneurs from Guangdong were quick to adapt. Secondly, they had more complex production techniques, even in the case of less sophisticated industries like shoes, clothing, and basic electrical goods. Thirdly, these overseas Chinese established strong ties with mainland officials and local government bodies. They involved the local power structures into the very operations of their own systems of production. More effectively still, in an increasing number of cases, the local authorities appealed to them to help strengthen technological development and to launch technical education initiatives (such as practical demonstrations, technical training, and apprenticeship schemes). In some cases, innovation centres were set up to promote technological innovation, aimed at providing technical know-how to enterprises in a particular sector of production (for example, shoes and underwear in Nanhai). In the industrialised world, such centres are usually organised by the chambers of commerce or public education bodies. In China, they are handled by the joint enterprises, to which a foreign partner brings both his expertise and his market.

In the Pearl River delta area, these enterprises owned by foreign capital employ 30 million workers from the most impoverished provinces of China. There are reckoned to be another 30 million potential migrants in the inland provinces, which guarantees continuing low labour costs. The foreign enterprises have easily been able to make use of this situation, turning the whole area into one huge factory, with intense local concentrations according to the type of products. Shunde is the main centre in China for the manufacture of electrical household goods, Ronggui is the largest centre in the world for producing air-conditioning units, Shaxi is the centre for leisure wear, Humen (Dongguan) for clothing, etc.[17]

Dongguan, which is close to the border with Hong Kong, provides a good example for examining the operation of the systems of production financed by FDI from Taiwan and Hong Kong. Dongguan is a relatively small town which serves as a centre of production for a great number of specialised products: coffee, computer mice and other computer components. Its systems of production are known by the expression *sanlai yibu*,[18] and are similar to the Mexican *maquiladoras*, in which products are manufactured from imported materials, and assembled according to models provided by the foreign client. The industrialisation of Dongguan began in the early 1980s, well ahead of the surge in the second wave of investment in the rest of the country, thanks to the relocation of industries from Hong Kong.[19] The driving force behind its growth has been the manufacture of OEM products for its clients. Since 1989, Dongguan has attracted numerous Taiwanese enterprises specialising in information technology and in shoes, and these have built up a network of local suppliers to reduce the time and costs expended in purchasing raw materials and parts, while meeting the standards set by the needs of international clients. The supply networks provide a link between local and foreign enterprises. They are all members of a single constituted system of production: customers, suppliers, and manufacturing units are all closely integrated, and the whole system benefits from the comparative advantage of cheap labour. The parameters are set by the global market, and contributions from the local authorities in terms of innovations or technical support are minimal. The key question confronting these systems of production is

17. See Qiu Haixiong (2001). *Establishing Nanhai as a Technology Model City*, Guangzhou, Research Institute for Guangdong Development, p.234.
18. Literally 'three resources and one obligation': *sanlai* or 'three resources'; these are the raw material, the parts, and the samples provided by the foreign investor. *Yibu* designates the repayment by the local enterprise to the foreign investor in the form of the finished products.
19. In Dongguan, as in the rest of the province, the impossibility of setting up private enterprises at the time led to the flow of local investment into joint enterprises, thus showering the Hong Kong investors with an additional layer of riches. See the work of Huang Yasheng on foreign investments in China during this period, *http://www.people.hbs.edu/yhuang*. Maybe, part of today's difficulties—such as large competition coming from other regions of China—in these kind of developing zones is due to this artificial type of investment flows. Nonetheless, firms are created, people work there and there is now an industrial base in Dongguan, as is shown in the case of computer manufacturing, cf. Wang Jici and Xin Tong (2002). "Global-local networking of PC manufacturing in Dongguan, China" in R. Hayter and H.L.R. (eds.), *Knowledge, Territory and Industrial Spaces*, Ashgate.

Table 11.1

Basic Indicators on Foreign Firms, Investments and Exports (Million US Dollars)

2001	*Number of Foreign Enterprises*	*In Per Cent*	*Total Investment Foreign Enterprises*	*In Per Cent*	*Exports from the Province*	*In Per Cent*	*Exports of Foreign Enterprises*	*In Per Cent*
China	202,306	100.0	875,011	100.0	266,155	100.0	133,235	100.0
Guangdong	47,102	23.3	221,823	25.4	95,828	36.0	54,374	40.8
Jiangsu	19,602	9.7	92,001	10.5	29,387	11.0	16,642	12.5
Shanghai	18,160	9.0	112,688	12.9	26,864	10.1	15,958	12.0
Fujian	15,403	7.6	51,259	5.9	13,926	5.2	8,288	6.2
Shandong	13,753	6.8	42,516	4.9	18,120	6.8	9,236	6.9
Liaoning	13,158	6.5	63,797	7.3	10,748	4.0	6,299	4.7
Zhejiang	11,194	5.5	34,064	3.9	24,261	9.1	7,099	5.3

Source: *Statistical Yearbook of China, 2002*. Total Exports: Table 17-10, p.626; Foreign Firms Exports: Table 17-12, p.628; Investments: Table 17-20, p.636.

how to move on from the stage of providing low cost assembly to foreign customers, to become complete OEM suppliers, or even achieve ODM (Own Design Manufacture) status.[20]

By the end of the 1990s this system had reached its limits.[21] Production costs were relatively high in comparison with other regions of China. Foreign enterprises were being set up in China with their own supplier networks, and some regions were becoming direct competitors. In Suzhou, which is close to Shanghai, a number of firms have taken advantage of the cheap local labour and the availability of direct links with the multinationals. Consequently, Suzhou is now

---

20. Under the Own Design Manufacture arrangement, the supplier designs his own production methods while still retaining the designation as supplier to a foreign customer. The most systematic study of the training delivered by this technological upgrading is provided by Gary Gereffi (1999). "International Trade and Industrial Upgrading in the Apparel Commodity Chain", *Journal of International Economics*, No. 48, pp.37-70.

21. This phenomenon can also be observed in the border regions of northern Mexico, here the *maquiladoras* developed from being simple low-cost assembly plants to become more complex systems of production, participating in the international flows of capital and commodities: the latter are in turn the source of investment capital for the factories located in Mexico or other foreign countries. Not only have the *maquiladoras* changed in form and function, but they have become part of a truly innovative economic and technological dynamism. Cf. Daniel Villavicencio (2003). "Le développement des maquiladoras du Nord Mexique et l'importance des réseaux binationaux d'innovation", a paper given to the IRD seminar, *Savoir et développement*, Paris, January 27th-28th.

about to overtake Dongguan as the world's largest producer of computer parts. The Shanghai and Zhejiang region has entered into direct competition with Guangdong.[22] The exhaustion of the model of production in Dongguan is due to the difficulty in upgrading the systems of production. This illustrates a key point in the theory of industrial development, namely that the creation of enterprises is a process quite distinct from their development (Figure 11.1).[23]

The Systems of Production Set Up by FDIs

The third wave of investment was provided by the industrialised countries. Currently, numerous 'third generation' systems of production are being piloted by foreign firms. The 400 largest of these have investments in China. The world's leading manufacturers of telecommunications and oil industry equipment, cars, and machine tools, have already set up their own production networks in China. These investments are often focused on the Shanghai region. Foreign firms begin by setting up a representative's office, and then establish their production sites. Foreign investors' objectives are no longer just to relocate the manufacturing process to cut costs and then re-export, but to develop a market in China itself (Figure 11.4).

These new systems of production are still at a preliminary stage, and the foreign firms involved are beginning to perceive the problems which any enterprise must encounter, in whichever country it first sets up operations.[24] Even those foreign firms which are already established are still finding it difficult to make any profit. For a foreign

22. It may well be that the current advantage enjoyed by Shanghai over Guangdong is due to the availability of skilled labour for managerial work. In Shanghai, foreign enterprises seem to occupy the more sophisticated sectors like pharmaceuticals. What we are witnessing in Shanghai is perhaps less the growth of a capacity for autonomous development in this region than the expansion of foreign direct investment in the technology-intensive sectors.

23. The more heavily industrialised areas bring about the dismantling of industries in the less advanced areas. This phenomenon, first noted in the case of 19th Century European industrialisation, is being repeated nowadays. Currently the 'winning' areas are those which have invested heavily in new technologies, even within the traditional industrial sectors. Cf. Georges Benko and Alain Lipietz (1992). *Les régions qui gagnent*, Paris: PUF.

24. This has again been verified by a recent enquiry on behalf of French firms, headed by the 'Mission Economique de Canton'; see the Report by Verillaud, "Les investissements étrangers en Chine", *Mission Economique*, Canton, April-May 2002. See also Xavier Richet, Wang Hua, and Wang Wei (2001). "Foreign Direct Investment in China's Automotive Industry", *China Perspectives*, No. 38, pp.36-42; and S.T. Walsh *et al.*, (1999). "Direct Foreign Manufacturing Investment Decisions for China", *Engineering Management Journal*, No. 11, pp.31-39.

firm everything is more expensive in China, from land purchase to building costs, installations, employee recruitment and training, communications with headquarters, relations with government offices handling labour and the environment, and commercial dealings with suppliers. It is more expensive to set up an integral system of production than to collaborate with a local supplier (Figure 11.5).

Figure 11.4

Schematic Presentation of the Piling Up of Productive Systems

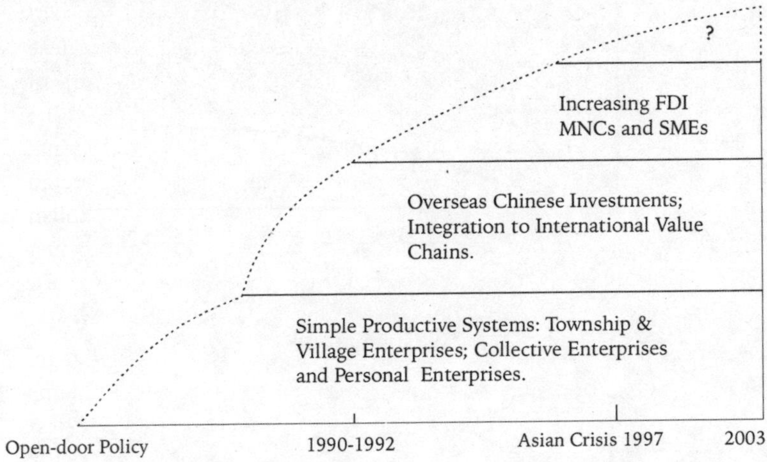

Unlike the systems of production established under the first two waves of investment, these firms have no difficulty in making use of efficient managerial techniques, and in setting up organisational structures geared towards their production goals and their market. Their difficulties arise solely from their relations with their social environment. The future legal and institutional setting within which they will operate, will be a decisive factor for these 'third generation' systems of production, and so the foreign investors who back them are relying on the complete opening of the Chinese economy in accordance with international agreements. It is still too early to make a full assessment of this third wave, and of the eventual outcome of the superimposition of these three different systems of production on top of each other.

Figure 11.5

Investment in Fixed Capital, China and Guangdong
(Billions Yuans)

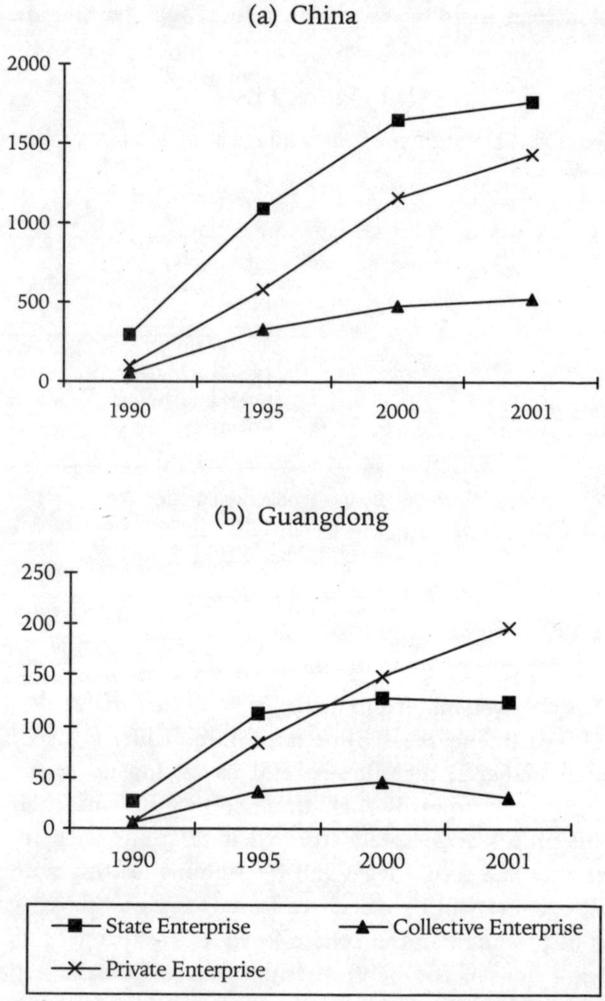

Source: *Annuaire Statistique de la Chine*, édition 2002, Tabl. 6-2, p. 176.

Do the State Enterprises Amount to a Distinct System of Production?

Discussions of the modernisation process in China tend to focus mainly on the emergent systems of production, namely on those which arose after the opening-up reforms. But there is another system of production which is easily overlooked because it is out of harmony with all the talking of the 'miracle'. This system of production, namely the state sector, plays a very important role in the economic ethos of the country.

Before the reforms, China was a socialist country whose economy was based on the state enterprises. The enterprises, the Party administration, the schools, and the hospitals were all single 'work units' (*danwei*), and were in turn all completely integrated into the structure of the planned economy of the single-party state. These "work units" were there not only to produce goods, or supply services and training; they were also charged with major administrative, political, and socio-economic functions (like health, education, housing, and ration coupon distribution), fulfilling the role of different areas of state administration. This system still remains the social and economic basis of the so-called 'socialist market-economy system'. The different newly emergent systems of production have established themselves on top of this underlying economic and political basis of society. For over 20 years now, the reforms have been seeking to improve the operations and achievements of the state enterprises, while also making their property rights and management powers more transparent, but without dismantling the enterprises themselves, along with the political and administrative apparatus of which they are a part. So, even though the planned economy may have disappeared, this economic and political system still remains. As the new millennium dawns, this system still includes government administrative offices and Party organs, both central and local, along with social organisations, and state monopolies like banking, radio and TV, and the other media.

The state enterprises are the very heart of this system. Although, they have lost many of their markets to the new systems of production, they still enjoy privileged access to the financial resources of the country. Between 1985 and 1992, the share of the state enterprises in the GNP fell by 6 per cent, but their financial resources only went down by 4.7 per cent. Since 1992, the share of the state enterprises in overall industrial production has continued to decline, but their investments have been increasing by 1.5 per cent. In the 1980s, the government transferred considerable resources to the state enterprises by reducing the taxes on their returns. Next, in order to continue its financial support to the state sector, in the early 1990s the government introduced the sale of public debt in the form of bond issues, and then, in the second half of the decade, it organised support through bank loans, making it easy for the state enterprises to obtain credit at preferential rates. More recently, the government has set up and supported the stock markets with the same goal of financing the state sector. In this way, the state enterprises benefit from public financial resources unavailable to the so-called 'private' firms, and at the same time they have greater ease of access to other types of resources like, for example, the publicly funded research centres and universities.[25] At the present time, the policy of supporting industrial giants (*zhuada fangxiao*), which is still far from successful, is centred on several very large-scale public enterprises.[26]

The state enterprises have not only used their privileged access to finance investment in production. Over the last two decades, a large part of their investments have gone into housing their employees, and into funding social security payments and pensions, that is to say, into the social benefits needed to maintain social stability.

With the coming of the reforms, the state enterprises underwent major transformations, but their basic nature has not changed. There is no question of entirely privatising the state sector, but rather selling off certain parts of it to procure new sources of finance. But the offers of shares for management buy-out did not deliver the promised results, and they have since then become the focus of intense debates over the chances for personal gain which they afford. A large proportion of these systems of production are in decline, and their future depends on the ability of the government to keep up the flow of investment towards them. The banks and the stock exchange seem only to exist to channel this flow in their direction. And despite

---

25. According to informants in January 2002 in Shuikou, a Guangdong industrial centre for the production of plumbing installations, and in December 2002 in Jiangmen, in a collective enterprise producing washing machines. The traditional clientele served by the major industrial research centres has always been the large state enterprises.
26. Jean-François Huchet (1999). "Concentration and the Emergence of Corporate Groups in Chinese Industry", *China Perspectives*, No. 23, pp.5-17.

everything, these public enterprises still enjoy easier access to other major resources, of a technological nature, than the other kinds of enterprise.[27] So, to a large extent, the challenge facing the state enterprises is to improve their ability to produce more and to innovate.

On the Role of Foreign Investment in Productive Systems

How long will these growth engines continue to perform? And how long can the present structure of the Chinese economy be sustained? Will foreign direct investment be an important component of the Chinese economy? These persistent questions dominate all the debates about China. To answer them, a fundamental reflection on the nature of the market economy is unavoidable. In a previous chapter, we proposed such a reflection in a way that does not focus exclusively on the question of property rights.[28] We could summarise our argument in the following way: Economic development requires trust, and the actual rules of the game in China seem not to encourage this trust. Everything indicates that a large amount of new enterprises will emerge in a rather more difficult business environment. As the new competitive pattern will be shaped, uncertainties about the behaviour of enterprises and other economic players will become conflictual points difficult to resolve. In the end, what will make the difference between enterprises is their ability to master larger and more sophisticated markets, by mastering more complex technologies.

The clearest indication, to our view, of this lack of trust is the fact that even in very small and well-structured industrial clusters in the coastal provinces of China, enterprises do not collaborate. Exchange of information between owners and managers of the firms is rather rare. Not only do enterprises look mostly for short-term profits, without bothering about long-term capital accumulation, but they also seek to avoid partnerships and external input, with the unique exception of partnerships with foreign enterprises. They focus on speed, rapid expansion, and competitive prices. Even when they know each other by name, which is often the case, the owners of enterprises

27. Here we have in mind the great number of research and technical development centres. cf. Gu Shulin (1999). *China's Industrial Technology*, Routledge.

28. Arvanitis, Rigas, Miège, Pierre and Zhao Wei (2003). "A New Look at the Development of a Market Economy in China", *China Perspectives*, Vol. 48.

producing the same items and in the same municipality never inform each other of their training needs or their labour problems. The large number of dinners which they attend, are merely intended to show that everything is alright, not to discuss together their technical, legal, or economic needs. A shared space for social intercourse is far from being established. As for the imposition of any official limitation, for whatever motive (including labour and environmental protection rights), this appears to such proprietors as an unacceptable state encroachment into private business, and an infraction of the mandate: "Enrich yourselves!". Finally, the interviews we have done in the Guangdong province have shown that the enterprises know their clients well enough, but they do not know the state of their market.[29] Only very few of the owners are able to say whether their market is rising or falling, and very few can give an indication of its size, whether at the national or regional level. This uncertainty is quite cearly at the heart of their behaviour.

Even the state enterprises are forced into this competitive pattern,[30] although it is in marked contrast to the known and respected rules which pertain in the political order. Both Chinese and foreign economists talk of an opposition between the market and the state. However, the crucial factor is not to be found in this opposition between the public and the 'private' sectors, but rather in the difficulty of even imagining the emergence of an economic sphere outside the political system, in which confidence in a shared respect for the rules would itself be the rule rather than the exception. At present, it even seems rather difficult to maintain that Chinese society is dominated by the market economy, because it lacks the essential ingredient of such an economy, namely respect for the rules which underpin mutual trust. In its place there is deep uncertainty, and this engenders opportunist behaviour, whatever the existing property laws or the kind of market in operation, private or public. That is why it seems vain to believe that the growth of the structures of production outside state control will eventually lead to the adoption of rules which will inspire trust in the proper workings of the market. All

---

29. See paper mentioned in footnote number 5.

30. And it seems this competition is the main source of their problems, not their budget constraints. See Dong Xiao-yuan and Louis Putterman (2000). "Investigating the Rise of Labour Redundancy in China's State Industry", *Working Paper* No. 9, Dept. of Economics, Brown University, June.

indications are that the rules based on the socialist system are still firmly in place. Such things as the laws restricting personal freedom of movement, budgetary rules, employment laws, purchase regulations in the public markets, and the lack of trustworthy statistics are all signs that there has been no change in the political system.

Now the role of foreign investments in these productive systems can be examined. For the enterprises set up by the first wave of investment, survival is achieved through meeting immediate demands, and this depends on extremely short-term calculations. Until now they mostly survive because of the very active support of the local authorities.[31] The very few enterprises which seem capable of reaching a higher level, in technical expertise and in relations with their suppliers and customers, are those which often just happen to have a joint agreement with a foreign partner, or those whose market conditions just happen to force them to make more dynamic choices, such as investing in research and development (R&D), or undertaking engineering improvements. But in any given town, such enterprises can be counted on the fingers of one hand, and in a whole region they amount to no more than a few dozen.

The enterprises belonging to the second wave of investment depend for their survival on their ability to offer their clients a range of OEM items, an ability which they have usually developed before setting themselves up in China. These are inside the globalised commercial world, have been set up mostly by Taiwanese and Hong Kong Chinese owners. This kind of foreign investment has been instrumental in creating some of the industrial clusters in China like Dongguan and Suzhou industrial park. A large part of the ability of the local industrial investors to enter in these kinds of industrial systems will depend precisely on the ability to make dynamic clusters.[32]

Finally, the Western, US and Japanese enterprises which have established operations in China have done so, precisely for long-term strategic goals, namely to be present as players on the Chinese

31. Peng Yusheng (2001). "Chinese Villages and Townships as Industrial Corporations: Ownership, Governance and Market Discipline", *American Journal of Sociology*, Vol. 106, pp.1338-1370.

32. Thompson, Edmund R. (2002). "Clustering of Foreign Direct Investment and Enhanced Technology Transfer: Evidence from Hong Kong Garment Firms in China", *World Development*, Vol. 30, pp.873-889.

market.[33] For these companies the improvement of the legal framework is of crucial importance.[34]

For its part, the state enterprise system of production is destined to continue. This is not because of any economic logic, but because of a decision to support them for political and social reasons. For these enterprises, modernisation is still on the agenda. Until now, the modernisation of the state sector enterprises has only been considered from the angle of the ownership of capital. It has been just a question of share sales, financial takeovers, and debt cancellations. But for the state enterprises themselves, as for the banks, productivity remains a key question. This involves improvements in management efficiency, the introduction of planning capabilities, the development of the engineering and R&D side, and the ability to actively adapt and improve products and procedures. All these aspects of innovation seem to us not merely useful but absolutely necessary. What is at stake is not the present sharing of the diminishing pile of goodies, but increasing these firms' capacity to produce real value.

Conclusion

For all these reasons we believe that the key to future growth in China is not merely the financial aspects or the legal and political framework but rather on the ability of Chinese firms to adopt, adapt and develop technologies bought, 'borrowed' or copied from their foreign partners. In the immediate future, the new systems of production will still need to feed the political structure and the state enterprises financially. But they are no longer capable of sustaining the national growth by themselves. To achieve this, a new wave of investments must be encouraged. If growth is to continue in the future, new systems of production will have to appear on the scene. Moreover, the different systems of production will find themselves increasingly engaged in collaborative activities.

---

33. Wang Pien, Kulwant Singh, and Tong Wenfeng (2001). "Determinants and Outcomes of Knowledge Transfer: A Study of MNCs in China", Singapore, Best Paper Proceedings, Academy of Management Conference.

34. The importance of the stakes here is reflected in Jefferson's hope that changes in the legal framework will be brought about by pressure from international agreements. See Jefferson, "China's Evolving (implicit) Economic Constitution", *op. cit.*

Foreign direct investment will be sooner or later caught in the strategies of national firms and cannot be developed only inside the strict walls of wholly owned foreign firms (which seems to be preferred by foreign investors as compared to the scheme of joint ventures). Sooner or later—and the economic literature tells us this is rather sooner than later—technologies and innovation would leak out of enterprises and get developed in companies other than the ones they were initially designed in. Maybe national and local authorities will take this as a new challenge and develop a solid support from the state to the new emerging productive systems, linked to a strategy for the various sectors, and to thorough-going training schemes, as the examples of Japan and South Korea amply demonstrate. Sustaining growth requires a strengthening of the systems of production currently in place.

We would like to thank Professors Cai He, Qiu Haixiong, Wu Nengquan, Xu Yong, Jean Ruffier, Gilles Guiheux, and Sophie Faure, in addition to two careful anonymous readers of this article, for their many helpful discussions and reflections on China's social and economic development. The research involved was conducted through joint collaboration between the IRD (Institut de Recherche pour le Développement) in France, the Guangdong Institute for Research and Development (ZURIGuD), and the Centre Franco-Chinois de Sociologie de l'Industrie et des Technologies (Zhongshan University, Université de Lyon-3, and the IRD). The opinions expressed are our own. A preliminary draft was a paper presented in the seminar on *Ethics and Productive Efficiency* at the University of Lyon 3, in January 2003. A first translation was done from the French original by Jonathan Hall. Parts of this research have been published in *China Perspectives*, number 48, July 2003, which we thank in giving permission to publish partially some parts of the article.

12

A Theory of Buy-outs in Joint Ventures

SUGATA MARJIT and PRABAL ROY CHOWDHURY

Introduction

In this chapter, we seek to develop a simple theory of joint venture buy-outs that is motivated by the Indian experience.

In the recent decades, the Indian market has witnessed a boom in joint venture activities. At the same time, however, many of the joint ventures have broken down within a few years of their formation (Bhandari, 1996-97; Ghosh, 1996). Both these trends reflect the international experience in the field of joint ventures.

In the last two decades, worldwide the rate of joint venture formation has accelerated dramatically. There has also been a change in the nature of industries where joint ventures are prevalent. Earlier, joint ventures were concentrated mainly in the extractive industries like mining, etc. Nowadays, joint ventures are much more widespread and occur in most industries including relatively new ones like telecommunications, biotechnology, etc. (see, among others, Hergert and Morris, 1988 and Pekar and Allio, 1994).

Studies that examine this phenomenon at a theoretical level include, among others, Al-Saadon and Das (1996), D'Aspremont and Jacquemin (1988), Bardhan (1982), Chan and Hoy (1991), Chao and Yu (1996), Choi (1993), Combs (1993), Das (1998), Katz (1986), Marjit (1990, 1991), Purakayasthya (1993), Roy Chowdhury (1995), Singh and Bardhan (1991) and Svejnar and Smith (1984).

At the same time however, there has been an increase in joint venture instability. Kogut (1988), finds that about half of the 92 joint ventures that he studied had broken up by the sixth year. Killing (1982) surveyed 37 international joint ventures and found that 36 per cent of them performed unsatisfactorily.

The average life span of a joint venture firm in Harrigan's (1988) study was only 3.5 years. The survey by Miller *et al.* (1996), covers 70 joint ventures in six developing countries and finds that at least 27 per cent of them were unlikely to survive. McKinsey did a worldwide survey of more than 200 alliances. The median time span of joint ventures was found to be seven years only (Bleake and Ernst, 1995). Thus, while the rate of joint venture formation is large, so is the rate of breakdown. This issue has also been studied by Beamish (1985) and Gomes-Casseres (1987).

During the mid-1990s many of the Indian joint ventures had serious problems. For example, the joint ventures between Daewoo and DCM, GE and Apar, Bausch and Lomb and Montori, GEC Alsthom and Triveni Engineering, Suzuki and TVS, all witnessed severe instabilities (Bhandari, 1996-97 and Ghosh, 1996).[1] A major area of dispute appears to be that of capacity expansion. While the multinational corporation (MNC from now on) partners were keen on capacity expansion, the domestic partners, who, for various reasons were fund constrained,[2] were unwilling to do so. As a result, the MNC partners insisted on either partial or complete buy-outs as a precondition for capacity expansion. Often, the threat of opening a fully owned subsidiary was also used.

We take the viewpoint that joint venture formation and breakdown are driven by the same forces. Thus, what is required is a theory of joint venture life-cycle, a framework that is capable of explaining both joint venture formation and breakdown. In this chapter, we use a formal model in the industrial organisation framework to establish that asymmetric access to capital and the level of demand can explain both joint venture formation, as well as their breakdown.

---

1. The joint venture between DCM and Daewoo was formed to manufacture light commercial vehicles i.e., the Cielo. Initially the project was a success, but then Daewoo decided to buy out DCM. Another well-known example involves the joint venture between Procter and Gamble and Godrej. The objective was to market Cinthol and other Godrej products, as well as the international products of Procter and Gamble. The joint venture, however, has broken up now. Other examples include the break up between Tata Sons and Unisys. Unisys has set up a wholly owned subsidiary in India and has sold off its 40 per cent holding to Tata Sons.

2. During this period, debt was very expensive with the Reserve Bank of India following a tight money policy. Moreover, during the early 1990s many Indian companies had invested in unprofitable ventures due to the easy financial conditions then prevalent. This also created a situation where liquid cash was not available.

Joint venture instability could have several manifestations. This could take the form of renegotiating the existing contract, and even complete buy-outs. Alternatively, this could be manifested in subsidiary formation by either one of the joint venture partners.[3] In this chapter, we study joint venture instability which takes the form of buy-outs, though the possibility of opening a subsidiary plays a critical role in the analysis.[4]

We model a situation where an MNC and a local firm from a less developed country (LDC from now on) decide on whether to form a joint venture. Thus, this chapter is also a contribution to the analysis of cross-border acquisitions.

The MNC has access to cheap capital, whereas the domestic firm has no access to capital and, thus, cannot open a subsidiary at all. Moreover, joint venture formation involves synergy. In joint ventures involving a foreign multinational and a domestic firm from an LDC, it has often been observed that the MNC provides the superior process and product technology, management know-how, international reputation, finance, etc., while the domestic firm provides a knowledge of local conditions (markets, legal systems and customs, local reputations, politics), access to distribution channels, etc. (Miller *et al.*, 1996). In the Indian joint venture between Hewlett and Packard (HP) and HCL in computers, HP hoped for a quick access to the Indian market, while HCL hoped to utilise HP's competence in business processes, production and quality maintenance (*Business India*, 1992). Thus, if a joint venture forms, it can produce much more efficiently compared to either one of the parent firms.

We find that whether a buy-out takes place or not is a function of the demand level. To begin with, suppose that the demand level is low so that subsidiary formation is not feasible, even for the MNC. Given the synergistic effect, however, the joint venture is more efficient compared to the MNC subsidiary, and may earn positive profits. Thus, for low levels of demand there is joint venture formation.

---

3. Franco (1971), studies different forms of joint venture breakdown. In a broader sense, instability also implies any unplanned changes in equity or profit shares, or a major reorganisation of the venture structure, including a shift of control.

4. In fact, in the study by McKinsey, in more than 80 per cent of the cases it ends up with one partner selling its share to the other (Bleake and Ernst, 1995).

We then consider a situation where there is an incumbent joint venture. Next, suppose that there is an increase in the demand level. Now the MNC has to re-evaluate its earlier decision. The options are threefold, either to remain with the joint venture, open a subsidiary, or buy out its joint venture partner. If the increase is large enough then, opening a subsidiary becomes more profitable compared to remaining with the joint venture. The intuition has to do with the asymmetric access to capital of the two firms. For a large enough demand, the MNC will obtain almost the whole of the market profits *via* the subsidiary while the joint venture obtains only a small proportion of the profits. Thus, the threat of subsidiary formation is credible whenever the demand is sufficiently large. In case of a buy-out, the MNC can use this threat to drive down the pay off of the domestic firm to its reservation level. Given that a buy-out avoids the inefficiencies associated with subsidiary formation, the aggregate pay off from a buy-out exceeds that from subsidiary formation, so that a buy-out is profitable for the MNC. Hence, for a large enough demand a buy-out takes place.

We then relate this chapter to the literature.

Roy Chowdhury and Roy Chowdhury (1999; 2000; 2001) attribute joint venture instability to organisational learning. In their framework, joint venture formation involves two benefits, synergy and avoiding the rent dissipation associated with competition. The costs of forming a joint venture could be exogenous (e.g. the costs of building a joint venture headquarters, adjusting to the different culture of the partner firm, etc.), or it could be endogenous (e.g. a moral hazard problem regarding the supply of inputs by the two firms). With time, however, there is organisational learning, so that the firms learn about each others' strengths. Thus, over time the value of the synergistic effect declines. Once the costs of joint venture formation exceeds its benefits, there is breakdown.

The present chapter, however, is driven by asymmetric access to capital, rather than organisational learning. Moreover, note that while in our model an increase in demand leads to instability, in Roy Chowdhury and Roy Chowdhury (1999; 2000; 2001) such an increase leads to greater stability. Clearly, however, the two approaches are complementary rather than competitive. We can think of our model as providing a theory of joint venture instability in situations where learning effects are weak or has already been exhausted.

We then discuss papers on joint venture breakdown by Kabiraj (1999), Kabiraj and Lee (2000) and Lin and Saggi (2000).

Kabiraj (1999), argues that a joint venture may break up because a third firm, not part of this joint venture, may become more efficient. This increases the competitive pressures in the industry, leading to breakdown. This chapter also determines the optimal timing of breakdown. Kabiraj and Lee (2000), on the other hand, studies the evolution of an industry with three firms, two domestic and one foreign. They show that depending on the synergic effects, various different industrial pattern may emerge. One interesting possibility is that though a joint venture forms, the composition of the joint venture changes over time. Another related paper is by Lin and Saggi (1998). They assume that after a joint venture forms the partners decide on the type of investment. If it is complementary then synergy increases and the joint venture is stable, whereas if it is competitive then synergy decreases and there is breakdown. However, they do not allow for either organisational learning, or moral hazard problems.

Among the other papers, Kabiraj and Roy Chowdhury (2003) develop a theory of joint venture breakdown, where the result is driven by the different time preferences of the partner firms regarding future pay offs. Such different time preferences among partner firms is an attempt at capturing an element of joint venture instability that is well accepted in the management literature, *viz.* cultural differences among an MNC and its LDC partner. They examine a situation where a new project becomes available to the joint venture. Because of different time preferences, however, the two parent firms value the project differently. The MNC partner, having the larger time preference, values the project more and is eager to adopt it, while the domestic partner is not willing to adopt it. In such a situation the only way to resolve this problem may be for the MNC firm to open a subsidiary, leading to joint venture breakdown.

Finally, there are a few papers dealing with sequential liberalisation and the consequent instability.

Mukherjee and Sengupta (2001), examine a scenario with sequential liberalisation whereby a less developed country allows foreign firms to open fully owned subsidiaries. In such a situation, the MNC may then bid to raise its stake in the joint venture, or failing that threaten to compete with them. They examine the incentive for opening a subsidiary *vis-à-vis* continuing with the joint venture. The analysis is carried out under different assumptions regarding the intensity of competition and the mode of control. They examine the cases both when investment is sunk, as well as the case when it is reversible.

Sinha (2001) also examines a model of sequential liberalisation. In the context of a developing country, Sinha (2001) examines a two period model with uncertainty about government policy, as well as the possibility of imitation. The joint venture forms in response to government restrictions on subsidiary formation. It is also argued that uncertainty about government policy is an important reason why a joint venture forms in the first place. He argues, uncertainty about government policy, as well as successful imitation by the domestic firm, are responsible for joint venture instability, where instability is interpreted as pay off renegotiations.

The Framework

In this section, we discuss the basic model somewhat heuristically. The formal model can be found in the Appendix A-12.1.

We model the interaction between an MNC and a domestic firm. We follow the neoclassical paradigm in assuming that all firms are profit maximisers.

The cost functions of both the firms are capacity constrained in the sense that production beyond the capacity level is not possible. If firms want to produce beyond the exiting capacity levels then they have to incur capacity costs. One central feature of our approach is motivated by reality, the fact that expanding the level of capacity is cheaper for the MNC. In fact, for simplicity we assume that capacity cost is too high for the domestic firm, so that only the MNC can invest in capacity.

Initially, the firms have the following two options. Either, the foreign firm can operate as a subsidiary, or it can form a joint venture with the domestic firm. Given the assumption on the capacity costs, the domestic firm cannot open a subsidiary.

Why should the MNC think of opening a joint venture, rather than a fully owned subsidiary? The benefit comes from the synergistic effect discussed in the introduction. Because of synergy, a joint venture can produce at a lower per unit cost compared to a subsidiary. The cost of opening a joint venture, on the other hand, comes from the fact that a fraction of the joint venture profits must go to the domestic firm. For simplicity, we assume that the fraction of joint venture profits going to the domestic firm is exogenously given, perhaps fixed by the government.

Thus, the MNC first calculates its maximal level of profits under the two options, joint venture or subsidiary. Note that under both options the MNC has to decide on the level of capacity, as well as production. Of course, in this framework production is always till capacity. Next, depending on the maximal profit levels under the two options, the MNC decides on whether to open a subsidiary, or opt for a joint venture.

We show that if the demand level is not too high then opening a subsidiary is not profitable, this is because the cost of operating a subsidiary is too high (after taking the costs of capacity expansion into account). Joint venture formation, however, may be possible since, because of the synergistic effect, opening a joint venture is less costly. Thus, for initial low levels of demand, there is joint venture formation.

We next consider the case where the demand increases to very high levels.

Now the MNC has three options, either to continue with the joint venture (with an increased capacity level), or open a subsidiary, or buy out its joint venture partner. Note that in case it decides to open a subsidiary then the subsidiary and the existing joint venture firm will compete among themselves. We assume that firms compete over quantities, and solve for the Cournot-Nash equilibrium of the subsequent game.

We first argue, that if the demand level is large enough, then opening a subsidiary always dominates the *status quo* option. The argument is simple. Recall that for the MNC the advantage of being in the joint venture lies in the synergistic effect, while the attraction of subsidiary formation lies in the fact that the MNC obtains the whole of the subsidiary profits. As demand becomes very large, however, the synergistic advantages become relatively less important. At the same time subsidiary formation becomes more attractive. Thus, if the demand is large, then the disadvantages of being in a joint venture outweigh the advantages. Hence, the result.

We then argue that for a large level of demand, a buy-out dominates subsidiary formation. If the increase in demand is large enough, then for the MNC, opening a subsidiary becomes more profitable than the *status quo* option, so that the threat of subsidiary formation is credible and the MNC can use this threat to drive down the pay off of the domestic firm in case of a buy-out. Hence, a buy-out is profitable for the MNC, provided that the aggregate pay off from a buy-out exceeds that under subsidiary formation. Since a buy-out avoids the inefficiencies associated with subsidiary formation, this is always true. Finally, since a buy-out dominates the opening of a subsidiary, and subsidiary formation dominates the *status quo*, a buy-out, in this sense dominates the *status quo* option as well. Thus, for a large level of demand the MNC buys out its domestic partner.

Conclusion

Empirical facts suggest that an asymmetric access to capital, plays a critical role in joint venture breakdown. In this chapter, we build a simple theoretical model capable of explaining these facts. *Inter alia*, we also show that joint venture breakdowns are more likely if the level of demand is high.

References

Al-Saadon, Y. and S.P. Das (1996). "Host Country Policy, Transfer Pricing and Ownership Distribution in International Joint Ventures: A Theoretical Analysis", *International Journal of Industrial Organization*, Vol. 14, pp.345-364.

D'Aspremont, C. and A. Jacquemin, (1988). "Cooperative and Non-cooperative R&D in Duopoly with Spill-overs", *American Economic Review*, Vol. 78, pp.1133-1137.

Bardhan, P.K. (1982). "Imports, Domestic Protection, and Transnational Vertical Integration: A Theoretical Note", *Journal of Political Economy*, Vol. 90, pp.1020-1034.

Beamish, P.W. (1985). "The Characteristics of Joint Ventures in Developed and Developing Countries", *Columbia Journal of World Business*, Vol. 20, pp.13-19.

Bhandari, B. (1996-97). "Losing Control", *Business World*, December 25, 1996-7th January, 1997, pp.34-39.

Bleake, J. and D. Ernst (1995). "Is Your Strategic Alliance Really a Sale?", *Harvard Business Review*, Vol. 73, pp.97-105.

Business India (1992). "A New Byte", November 23-December 6, pp.66-68.

Chan, R. and M. Hoy (1991). "East-West Joint Ventures and Buy-back Contracts", *Journal of International Economics*, Vol. 30, pp.330-343.

Chao, C. and E. Yu. (1996). "Are Wholly Foreign Owned Enterprizes Better Than Joint Ventures?", *Journal of International Economics*, Vol. 40, pp.225-237.

Choi, J.P. (1993). "Cooperative R&D with Product Market Competition", *International Journal of Industrial Organization*, 11, pp. 553-571.

Combs, K.L. (1993). "The Role of Information Sharing in Cooperative Research and Development", *International Journal of Industrial Organization*, Vol. 11, pp.553-571.

Das, S.P. (1998). "On the Choice of International Joint Ventures: The Role of Policy Moral Hazard", *The Journal of Policy Reform*, Vol. 2, pp.135-150.

Franko, L.G. (1971). "Joint Venture Survival in Multinational Corporations", New York: Praeger Publishers.

Ghosh, I. (1996). "Jinxed Ventures", *Business World*, July 24th-August 6th, pp.54-60.

Gomes-Casseres, B. (1987). "Joint Venture Instability: Is It a Problem?", *Columbia Journal of World Business*, Vol. 22, pp.97-102.

Harrigan, K.R. (1988). "Strategic Alliances and Partner Asymmetries", in F.J. Contractor and P. Lorange, eds., *Cooperative Strategies in International Business*, Lexington Books.

Hergert, M. and D. Morris (1988). "Trends in International Collaborative Business", in F.J. Contractor and P. Lorange (eds.), *Cooperative Strategies in International Business*, Lexington, Mass and Toronto: Heath, Lexington, pp 99-109.

Kabiraj, T. (1999). "A Simple Theory of Joint Venture Breakdown", *Keio Economic Studies*, Vol. 36, pp.87-98.

Kabiraj, T. and C.C. Lee (2000). "Synergy, Learning and the Changing Industrial Structure", *Mimeo*, The Chinese University of Hongkong.

Kabiraj, T. and P. Roy Chowdhury (2003). "Joint Venture and Adoption of New Technology: The Effect of Bargaining, Control and Demand Shift", *ERU Discussion Paper* No. 2003-9, Kolkata: ISI.

Katz, M.L. (1986). "An Analysis of Cooperative Research and Development", *Rand Journal of Economics*, Vol. 16, pp.527-543.

Killing, J.P. (1982). "How to Make a Global Joint Venture Work", *Harvard Business Review*, May June, pp.120-127.

Kogut, B. (1988). "A Study of the Life-cycle of Joint Ventures", in F.J. Contractor and P. Lorange (eds.), *Cooperative Strategies in International Business*, Lexington, Mass. and Toronto: Heath, Lexington, pp.169-185.

Lin, P. and K. Saggi (2000). "Complementarity, Investment Incentives and Evolution of Joint Ventures", *Mimeo*, Southern Methodist University.

Marjit, S. (1990). "Rationalising Public-private Joint Ventures in an Open Economy—A Strategic Approach", *Journal of Development Economics,* Vol. 33, pp.377-383.

———. (1991). "Incentives for Cooperative and Non-cooperative R&D in Duopoly", *Economics Letters,* Vol. 37, pp.187-191.

Marjit, S. and P. Roy Chowdhury. (2004). "Asymmetric Capacity Costs and Joint Venture Buy-outs", forthcoming, *Journal of Economic Behaviour.*

Miller, R.R.; J.D. Glenn; F.Z. Jaspersen and Y. Karmakolias (1996). "International Joint Ventures in Developing Countries: Happy Marriages?", *Discussion Paper* No. 29, Washington DC: International Finance Corporation, World Bank.

Mukherji, A. and S. Sengupta (2001). "Joint Ventures *versus* Fully Owned Subsidiaries: Multinational Strategies in Liberalising Economies", *Review of International Economics,* Vol. 9, pp.163-180.

Pekar, P. and R. Allio (1994). "Making Alliances Work-guideline for Success", *Long Range Planning,* Vol. 27, pp.54-65.

Purakayasthya, D. (1993). "Firm Specific Advantages, Multinational Joint Ventures and Host Country Tariff Policy", *Southern Economic Journal,* Vol. 60, pp.89-95.

Roy Chowdhury, I. and P. Roy Chowdhury (1999). "Learning, Liberalisation and Joint Ventures", *Keio Economic Studies,* Vol. 36, pp.33-52.

———. (2000). "A Learning-based Theory of Joint Venture Life-cycles", *Group Decision and Negotiation,* Vol. 9, pp.457-470.

———. (2001). "A theory of Joint Venture Life-cycles", *International Journal of Industrial Organization,* Vol. 19, pp.319-343.

Roy Chowdhury, P. (1995). "Technological Asymmetry and Joint Product Development", *International Journal of Industrial Organization,* Vol. 13, pp.23-39.

Singh, N. and P.K. Bardhan (1991). "Government Policy Towards Joint Ventures with Multinational Rivalry", *Mimeo,* Santa Cruz: University of California and v: University of Californi.

Sinha, U. (2001). "Imitative Innovation and International Joint Venture: A Dynamic Analysis", *International Journal of Industrial Organization,* Vol. 19, pp.1527-1562.

Svejnar, J. and S. Smith (1984). "The Economics of Joint Ventures in Developing Countries", *Quarterly Journal of Economics,* Vol. 119, pp.149-167.

Appendix A-12.1

The Model

In this appendix we briefly discuss the formal model underlying the analysis.[5]

Low Initial Demand

The market comprises of two firms, an MNC, denoted as firm 1 and a domestic firm, denoted as firm 2.

In this sub-section the market demand is taken to be:

$$q = a - p, \tag{1}$$

though, in the next sub-section we shall consider the case where the market demand increases to $q = A - p$, $A > a$.[6]

The cost function of the joint venture firm is:

$$C(q) = \begin{cases} cq, & \text{if } q \leq \tilde{k} \\ \infty, & \text{otherwise,} \end{cases} \tag{2}$$

and that of the MNC subsidiary is given by:

$$C_s(q) = \begin{cases} c'q, & \text{if } q \leq k_s \\ \infty, & \text{otherwise} \end{cases} \tag{3}$$

where $\tilde{k}$ and k_s denote the capacity level of the joint venture and the subsidiary, respectively. Joint venture formation involves a synergistic effect, in the sense that the production costs are lower under the joint venture, so that $c' > c$.

Access to capacity is asymmetric, so that the per unit cost of capacity formation is r for firm 1 and infinitely high for firm 2.[7] Thus, firm 2 cannot open a subsidiary.

Under a joint venture the capacity costs are borne by firm 1. The gross joint venture profit is divided in the ratio $(1-\alpha)$ to α among firms 1 and 2. For simplicity, we assume that the sharing rule α is exogenously fixed by the government.

5. The formal model draws heavily on Marjit and Roy Chowdhury (2004).
6. All our results generalise even if the demand function takes the more general form, $a - f(q)$.
7. This assumption is for simplicity alone, the results go through qualitatively as long as the costs of capacity expansion for the two firms are different enough.

The following assumption will be required subsequently.

Assumption 1. $c+\frac{r}{1-\alpha}<\alpha<c'+r.$

Note that initially firm 1's only option is to open a joint venture. This follows since, given that $c'+r>a$, subsidiary formation is not profitable for firm 1.

In case of joint venture formation the MNC decides, on how much capital to invest in the joint venture. The joint venture management then decides on the level of output that will maximise the gross joint venture profits. Finally, the gross joint venture profits are divided among the two firms according to the given sharing rule α.

If the capacity level in the joint venture is $\tilde{k}$ then firm 1's equilibrium profit level is:

$$\begin{cases}(1-\alpha)\frac{(\alpha-c)^2}{4}-r\tilde{k}, & \text{if } \tilde{k}\geq\frac{\alpha-c}{2},\\ (1-\alpha)\left(\alpha-c-\tilde{k}\right)\tilde{k}-r\tilde{k}, & \text{otherwise.}\end{cases} \quad (4)$$

Clearly, the optimal capacity level

(see Assumption 1).

Next, let $J_i(a)$ denote the equilibrium level of profit of firm 1. Then:

$$J_1(a)=[\,(1-\alpha)\,[\frac{(a-c)^2}{4}-\frac{r^2}{4(1-\alpha)^2}]-r[\frac{(a-c)(1-\alpha)-r}{2(1-\alpha)}] \quad (5)$$

$$J_2(a)=\alpha[\frac{(a-c)^2}{4}-\frac{r^2}{4(1-\alpha)^2}] \quad (6)$$

Thus, for low levels of demand a joint venture obtains. Moreover, the greater is α (the share of the domestic firm in joint venture profits), the lower is the capacity installed in the joint venture.

Demand Increase

Consider a situation where there is an incumbent joint venture with a capacity level of $\widetilde{K}$. Now suppose, that the demand function shifts up to $q = A - p$, where $A > a$. We argue, that if A is large enough, then there is always a buy-out.

We examine a one period, multi-stage game where, in stage 1, firm 1 decides to opt for any one of the three options: *Status quo* (i.e. stay with the joint venture), opening a subsidiary, or buy-out.

Status Quo: Firm 1 decides on how much to invest in the joint venture, followed by production till capacity.

Subsidiary Formation: The MNC decides on how much to invest in the joint venture firm and/or the subsidiary. In the next stage, there is Cournot competition among the original joint venture firm and the new subsidiary. We assume, that the management of the subsidiary firm maximises the profit of the subsidiary.[8]

Buy-out: The MNC makes a take it or leave it offer to firm 2 that specifies the price that firm 1 is willing to pay to firm 2 for buying up the company. If firm 2 rejects the offer, then firm 1 can either open a subsidiary, or opt for the *status quo*.

To begin with, we solve, the equilibrium under *status quo*. We first consider, the outcome under a joint venture. Clearly, for large A, the joint venture is going to be capacity constrained. The question is whether firm 1 would find it optimal to invest in the joint venture.

Let k ($\geq \widetilde{K}$) denote the capacity level of the joint venture firm. A straightforward-backwards induction argument shows that firm 1's profit level is:

$$\begin{cases} (1-\alpha)\dfrac{(A-c)^2}{4} - r(k-\widetilde{K}), & \text{if } k \geq \dfrac{A-c}{2}, \\ (1-\alpha)(A-c-k)\,k - r(k-\widetilde{K}), & \text{if } \widetilde{K} \leq k < \dfrac{A-c}{2} \end{cases} \tag{7}$$

Thus, in equilibrium the capacity choice of firm 1, K, involves

$\mathrm{K} = \dfrac{(A-c)(1-\alpha)-r}{2(1-\alpha)}$. Let $J_i(A)$ denote the equilibrium level of profit

8. The argument goes through qualitatively even if we assume that the management of the subsidiary firm maximises the aggregate MNC profit.

of firm 1 when the demand level is A. Then:

$$J_1(A) = (1-\alpha)\left[\frac{(A-c)^2}{4} - \frac{r^2}{4(1-\alpha)^2}\right] - r\left(\frac{(A-c)(1-\alpha)-r}{2(1-\alpha)}\right) - \widetilde{K} \tag{8}$$

$$J_2(A) = \alpha\left[\frac{(A-c)^2}{4} - \frac{r^2}{4(1-\alpha)^2}\right] \tag{9}$$

We then examine the equilibrium under subsidiary formation.

For simplicity, we assume that firm 1 only invests in the subsidiary and does not invest in the joint venture at all.[9]

We begin by solving for the optimal level of k_s. Note that whenever

$k_s \leq \frac{A-c'-\widetilde{K}}{2}$ the profit function of firm 1 is:

$$k_s(A-c'-k_s-\widetilde{K}) + (1-\alpha)\widetilde{K}(A-c-k_s-\widetilde{K}) - rk_s \tag{10}$$

This is because under Cournot competition the equilibrium output level of the subsidiary is k_s and that of the joint venture is $\widetilde{K}$. For A large, there is an interior solution where:

$$A-c'-2k_s-\widetilde{K} - (1-\alpha)\widetilde{K} - r = 0 \tag{11}$$

Thus, letting K_s denote the equilibrium value of k_s we have that

$$K_s = \frac{A-c'-r-\widetilde{K}(2-\alpha)}{2}$$ [10]

Let $S_i(A)$ denote the equilibrium profit level of the i-th firm when $k_s = K_s$ and the demand level is A. Thus:

$$S_1(A) = \frac{1}{4}(A-c'-r-\widetilde{K}(2-\alpha))(A-c'-r-\alpha\widetilde{K}) + \frac{(1-\alpha)\widetilde{K}}{2}(A-2c+c'+r-\alpha\widetilde{K}) \tag{12}$$

9. The argument goes through without too much alteration even if we relax this assumption (Marjit and Roy Chowdhury, 2004).

10. Note that whenever $k_s \leq \frac{A-c'-\widetilde{K}}{2}$ the profit function of firm 1 is $k_s(A-c'-k_s-\widetilde{K}) + (1-\alpha)\widetilde{K}(A-c-k_s-\widetilde{K}) - rk_s$. This is because under Cournot competition the equilibrium output level of the subsidiary is k_s and that of the joint venture is $\widetilde{K}$.

$$S_2(A) = \frac{\alpha\tilde{K}}{2}(A - 2c + c' + r - \alpha\tilde{K}) \tag{13}$$

We are now in a position to write down the main result of this chapter.

Theorem 1: For the MNC the profits from a buy-out are greater than that under subsidiary formation. Moreover, for A large, for the MNC the profits from a buy-out are greater than those under the *status quo* option.

Proof. We first argue that for the MNC, buy-out dominates subsidiary formation. Given that firm 2's reservation pay off is $S_2(A)$, firm 1's payoff from a buy-out is $\frac{(A-c-r)^2}{4} + r\tilde{K} - S_2(A)$. Hence, for firm 1 a buy-out dominates subsidiary formation if and only if:

$$\frac{(A-c-r)^2}{4} + r\tilde{K} - S_2(A) > S_1(A) \tag{14}$$

Since a buy-out avoids the inefficiencies associated with subsidiary formation, the aggregate profit of the two firms under a buy-out, $\frac{(A-c-r)^2}{4} + r\tilde{K}$, exceeds $S_1(A) + S_2(A)$, the aggregate profit of the two firms under subsidiary formation by firm 1. Hence, equation (14) necessarily holds.

We then argue that for A large, for the MNC, buy-out dominates the *status quo* option. To begin with, note that for A large $S_1(A) > J_1(A)$.[11] Next, using equation (14), and the fact that $S_1(A) > J_1(A)$, we have that:

$$\frac{(A-c-r)^2}{4} + r\tilde{K} - S_2(A) > S_1(A) > J_1(A) \tag{15}$$

Thus, if A is large enough, then there is always a buy-out.

11. This follows since, using l'Hospital's rule, it is straightforward to show that $A \to \infty \frac{S_1(A)}{J_{1(A)}} > 1.$

13

Asset Specificity, Partnerships and Global Strategies of Information Technology and Biotechnology Firms in India

JOËL RUET

Information technology (IT) firms have no doubt emerged in India, not only as major exporters, but also as a new model for private business and perhaps as a sector capable of contributing to the renewal of public development models. Biotechnology firms (BT), or at least those in the 'modern part of the biotechnology sector' wish to follow the same path ('modern biotechnologies' are defined as involving the understanding, mapping, manipulation or change of the genetic pool of a living organism (Maria, Ruet and Zérah, 2002).

This chapter describes the pioneering-cum-critical phase of the emergence and take off of these two sectors in India, their technological progress and their recent 'climb up the value chain' over the 1990s, precisely till 2002 (Section I)[1]. It then analyses the specificity of the assets they have built in order to explore two points of industrial organisation:

- Firstly, how asset specificities explain the various contractual arrangements observed in these sectors and the more or less deep levels of partnerships with other firms or laboratories (Section II).
- And secondly, since the globalisation of firms implies the 'formulation of global strategies for the worldwide integration and optimisation of technical and academic resources', how we can determine India's place in the strategies of western firms and determine to what extent Indian firms adopt global strategies (Section III).

---

1. We chose these years for they have exemplified the constitutive years of these sectors where, (i) business strategies got elaborated from technological capacities, (ii) integration in the world value chains took place, and (iii) then diverse strategies started showing signs of convergence.

SECTION I

What Do They Produce? Services, Products, and Markets

Let us look at the 'pure IT' sector (which includes telecommunication software but not telecommunication systems) and restrict our discussion on BT to 'modern' biotechnologies used in the pharmaceutical and clinical sectors, especially for manufacturing biogeneric products and drug discovery processes.

Stylising the Indian IT Sector

A study of the 'pure IT' sector shows that the Indian IT industry has grown between 40 per cent to 50 per cent per year since 1994. Its turnover was US$ 8.7 billion for the year ended March 2000 and reached US$ 13.5 billion in 2001-02, based on the export of services (60 per cent exported to the US and 24 per cent to Europe).[2] From the mid to late 1980s large numbers of Indian IT professionals migrated to the US, where deregulation and the technological revolution in the telecom sector had created a huge demand for software for switching, routing and multiplexing technologies. By the early 1990s, US as well as European companies had started developing 'off-shore platforms' in India (the first ones to do so were Lucent, Cisco, Sun, Microsoft, Siemens and Alcatel). They mostly addressed lower modular tasks such as debugging and transcoding, using the wage advantage (nearly one-tenth at that time) between India and the US.

In India, IT covers a large variety of products and services with a wide range of technical content in both these segments. Table 13.1 shows the evolution and breakdown of turnovers from 1994 to 2000. Software as also training and maintenance constitute the major part of the turnover amounting to 73 per cent of the total (also see Figure 13.1).

The sector currently (2001-02) represents 2.7 per cent of India's GDP. The year 2001-02, which witnessed a global crisis in the IT sector (in terms of the evaluation of assets as well as growth) and a recession in the United States (the market leader), reinforced the significance of India's comparative advantages. Indeed, growth

2. Unless specified differently, IT figures are from NASSCOM, various annual reports.

Table 13.1

Changes in the Breakdown of Turnovers from 1994 to 2000

(in Million US$)

	1994-95	*1995-96*	*1996-97*	*1997-98*	*1998-99*	*1999-2000*
Software						
Domestic	350	490	670	950	1250	1700
Exports	485	734	1,083	1,750	2,650	4,000
Total	835	1,224	1,753	2,700	3,900	5,700
Hardware						
Domestic	590	1,037	1,050	1,205	1,026	1,450
Exports	177	35	286	201	4	86
Total	767	1,072	1,336	1,406	1,030	1,536
Peripherals						
Domestic	148	196	181	229	329	435
Exports	6	6	14	19	18	27
Total	154	202	195	248	347	462
Training	107	145	183	263	302	400
Maintenance	142	172	182	221	236	263
Others	36	710	156	193	237	310
Grand Total	**2,041**	**2,886**	**3,805**	**5,031**	**6,052**	**8,671**

Source: NASSCOM.

Figure 13.1

Breakdown of Turnover (Domestic) in 1999-2000

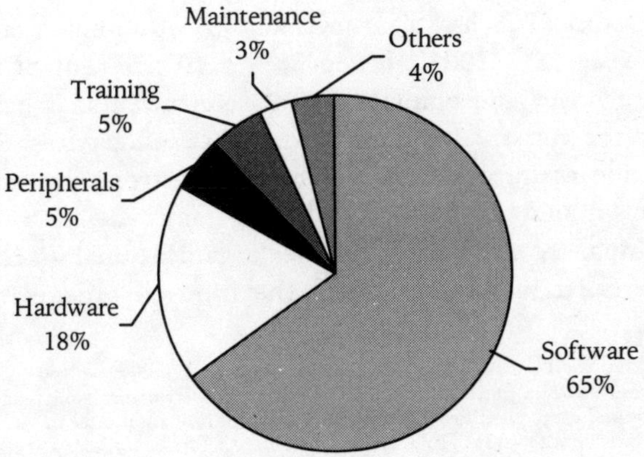

Source: NASSCOM.

remained positive at 10.6 per cent and earned US$ 13.5 billion in revenue. There is no doubt that growth slowed down considerably after the crisis (annual average growth between 1998-1999 and 2000-2001 had been 42 per cent). Nevertheless, this business model of development was firmly established. Thereafter, analyses forecasting the acceleration of outsourcing of American IT firms to India were reinforced by subcontracting.

Simultaneous to outsourcing, some Indian companies have built a strong industry not only capable of generating large cash flows, but also capable of gradually climbing up the value chain. In other words, of addressing and selling cutting-edge technologies with an integrated offer of services and, sometimes, products. In this chapter, we will focus on three groups of enterprises of this type (traditional conglomerates, large 'pure-IT players' and global niche start-ups) whose typology and strategy stabilised at the turn of the 2000s.

Traditional Conglomerates

Traditional companies, already in existence, partially migrated from their previous businesses to constitute strong IT poles. The most successful are Tata Consultancy Services (TCS), the leading exporter in the IT sector, and Wipro occupying the second position.[3] Their model still inspires other traditional companies (like Kanoria Enterprises dealing in cement who aim to enter the IT services and education sectors). They are now the main players in the Indian IT sector. These groups went into offshore IT services and built a new global strategy.

For instance, TCS had a turnover of US$ 700 million during the financial year (FY) 2001.[4] It represents 10 per cent of the Tata Group's turnover and employs 17,000 consultants. It has totally integrated the entire value chain of digitalisation services. Since the digitalisation of information systems has a strong impact on the client firm's monitoring systems, it has an immediate effect on power relationships. By optimising on the 'organisational slack' in the middle-term, it inevitably affects the internal organisation and

3. Ranking for FY 2001. The fact that rankings marginally evolved from 2002 to 2006 is not our concern here. The chapter focuses on the 'globalising moment' of the industry. Identified phenomenons have proven right later on and deepened. We look at the 'stabilising models' that then allowed today's trajectories.

4. The financial year is from April to March in India. So FY 2001 started on April 1 and ended on March 31, 2002.

favours organisational restructuring. Apart from software, the entire gamut of classical consultancy functions needs to be addressed sooner or later. TCS now provides the complete range of consultancy and services (consulting, architecture, design and testing) as well as the systems integration and management involved in these processes. This activity is mainly export-oriented and 55 per cent of the work is done for the US. TCS sets up Offshore Development Centres for its major contracts. It looks after all the staff redeployment and is certified SEI-CMM level 5.[5]

Similarly, Wipro (turnover of US$ 350 million in the IT sector during FY 2001) has gone beyond the body-shopping and development platform model to deal with software development consulting and even build its own brand and software products. It is the first company in the world to get the SEI-CMM level 5 certification. It has a tie-up with hardware vendors like IBM, i2e, etc.

Large 'Pure IT' Players

Companies like Infosys, NIIT, Satyam and HCL (respectively occupying the third to sixth place among exporters; NASSCOM) have emerged as significant IT players. They started as small companies but were supported by capital markets. Along with TCS and Wipro, they have all managed to move up the value chain. For instance, Infosys has succeeded by developing domain competencies in software development services and end-to-end facilities and Satyam, by developing an integrated competence in telecom and internet services and, at a later stage, in finance and insurance. Generally speaking, "To keep profit margins, the best solution is to sell licenced products for which competition is based on customer utility even as the firm gains from economies of scale and recurring revenues" (Bomsel and Ruet, 2001). Products must therefore be very innovative. Since they have a high entry cost and require strong branding, they demand a long-term strategy that requires a steady and constant investment. This is why companies that do not have Wipro's size consider it as a 'next step' strategy. Until 1998, most of the software licences and brands were owned outside India. The period between

5. This measures the number of errors after the first coding and hence the cost of internal checks. Levels go up to 6 which has been reached only by a dozen companies in the world. At level 5, checking and correcting initial errors represents roughly 30 per cent of the total costs.

1998 and 2000 witnessed a change of course with support from the US internet market; things have obviously changed since then (Bomsel and Ruet, 2001, based on the 'products and package' category of NASSCOM figures). However, the situation is gradually moving towards the licensing of products in the case of some Indian companies.

Global Niche Start-ups' and 'Product Start-ups

In global markets, some 'niches', that is opportunities for innovating products or more focused and specialised services, remain unoccupied. Some Indian companies are now trying to develop services and products related to these niches; their business models are generally well thought of and global in spirit and implementation is from day one of their incorporation. An (extreme) example is TechSpan, which focuses on e-commerce integration in the US market. It was founded towards the end of 1998 and already had a turnover of US$ 67 million in FY 2001! This is an extreme case since the company, founded by one of the co-founders of HCL, was incorporated in the US with two R&D centres in the US and one in India. Product companies often have to tie up with bigger companies if they need bank support. For instance, Trivium had to tie up with Infosys.

The Sector's Structure

The sector could actually be considered mature enough in terms of concentration as early as from FY 2000. Indeed, apart from the niche companies, its main activity is in fact concentrated in the hands of a few companies for they are the only ones capable of using their technological skills to foster real growth (Figure 13.2).

To sum up, the IT sector in India is now at a much more advanced stage of development than it was in the mid-1990s, in sharp technological contrast to what many outside observers usually underline (the mere outsourcing).

Stylising the 'Pharma-BT' Sector

A key feature of the BT sector is that it does not consist of firms with a common output like other industrial sectors or even, in some respect, the IT sector. On the contrary, it is defined more by the

Figure 13.2

Cumulative Revenue of IT Firms by FY 2000 (in US$ million)

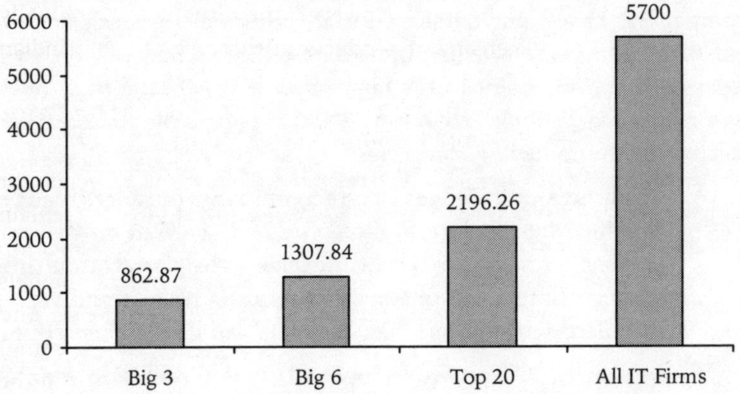

Source: NASSCOM.

common use of similar technologies, that is, common inputs (Maria, Ruet and Zérah, 2002). As regards outputs, let us restrict ourselves to the pharmaceutical sector. Since the BT sector is essentially structured by its inputs, the fragmented nature of its output will nevertheless have a radical and structural impact on the type of assets it can aspire to, as we will see in the next section.

The economic delimitation of 'modern' Biotechs offers scope for controversy, since it does not encompass the classical biotechnologies which cover the centuries old breweries. Additionally, its sectoral industrialists' association, the All India Biotech Association, created in 1994, does not wish to make this distinction. It is thus far more complex than for the Information Technology sector to provide aggregate figures and to retrace its evolutions. Since the definition of modern BT is unofficial, the number of modern BT firms can be estimated only on the basis of information available in the directories of BT companies. If we take into account the firms addressing the pharmaceutical sector and the bioinformatics companies, we find that there were about 120 to 130 companies in India in 2002 (Maria, Ruet, Zérah, 2002). The 'BT' turnover is simply impossible to evaluate, since most of these companies are not 'pure BT' companies, but only use these technologies in their production or research processes. There are however, a certain number of dedicated start-ups.

The Indian BT sector is still quite a new field for industrial economics and even more so since business models have not stabilised as yet. Here we mostly provide a stylisation of these companies, based on: (i) their intial industrial research activity, (ii) their business target, (iii) the business models they rely on, to go from their starting point to the target they have. On the basis of the writings of Maria, Ruet and Zérah (2002) it is possible to analyse the 'sector' in the following categories:

- Firms making biogeneric-recombinant products can be classified into four main categories and analysed on the basis of their former activity which explains their asset acquisition strategy (integrated pharmacy, diagnostic reagent and vaccine manufacturers, enzyme manufacturers and dedicated start-ups).
- In the field of drug development, it is possible to separate companies involved in genomics-proteomics, which includes the stage of drug discovery itself (where we have once again opportunity driven companies *versus* technology driven companies), from those involved in clinical trials, those involved in an integrated (discovery plus testing) process of BT-based drug development and finally those involved in bioinformatics, which can be a support function at all stages of the drug development process (Figure 13.3).

Figure 13.3

'Concept to Market': The Comprehensive Drug Development and Marketing Chain

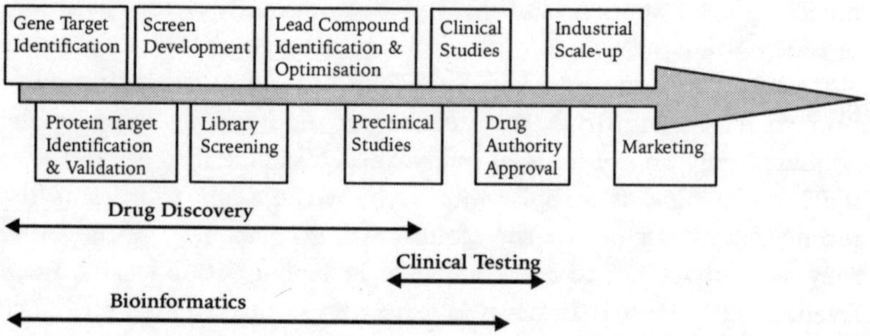

Source: Augustin Maria, in Maria, Ruet, Zérah, 2002.

Of course, a company may be involved in one or more of these activities at the same time as they can coexist with a more classical activity. Without going into too many details, let us focus on three kinds of firms: the industrial company wanting to enter the field of biogeneric-recombinants, the pharmaceutical company wishing to become a molecule discoverer through BT and the dedicated start-up (either in biogeneric-recombinants or bioinformatics).

Stylised Type 1: The Industrial Biogeneric-Recombinant Producer

The technological breakthrough in biogeneric-recombinant products will make it possible to identify BT-produced macromolecules, including their spatial configurations. This has been partially achieved in the case of a few molecules and enables some companies to produce BT-based biogeneric products. The first asset to be acquired in this field is a laboratory capable of carrying out all the tests that can prove the presence of the key characteristics of the initially targeted molecule in the BT-produced molecule. The next assets will be the acquisition of production capacities and engineering know-how to scale up production. In India, very few technology-based companies (and no laboratories) have this industrial capacity. They have to tie-up with industrialists, and ultimately it is reagent and enzyme manufacturers who have a key advantage in this field which retains a strong industrial dimension. This explains the success of Biocon or, at a lower level, of Bangalore Genei and Bharat Serums and Vaccines. Unlike Wipro or TCS in the IT sector, here the core activity of the group plays an important role in designing and providing the key assets needed right from the beginning. Also, unlike the IT sector, where support is essentially financial, the type of initial industrial activity matters a great deal.

Stylised Type 2: The Pharmaceutical Company

Classical pharmaceutical companies can target the emerging market for biogeneric-recombinants or even try to use BT technologies to reduce their costs in the drug development process or they can even move up the value chain by accessing an integrated level capacity in the drug development process. Indeed, the major cost increase occurs at the clinical testing stage, which can be considerably simplified through the use of bioinformatics for the analysis of clinical databases. On the other hand, the discovery process itself can be optimised through the biotechnological production of target molecules by using proteomics or bioinformatics. Most classical Indian pharmaceutical companies are moving in this direction. Their strategies are however very different. For instance, Ranbaxy focuses on in-house BT-based drug discovery, while Dr. Reddy's strategy is to simultaneously address recombinant product manufacture, drug development, both in-house and through Aurigene, a specific contracting firm it has set up for this purpose. As these examples reveal, the strategies and business models of integrated pharmaceutical firms have not yet stabilised as far as the integration of BT is concerned.

Stylised Type 3: The Dedicated Start-up

Some of the smaller dedicated start-ups are really technology-generated and were initially developed in public research laboratories. Shanta Biotechnics or Bharat Biotech are two such start-ups in the field of bio-genetics. They usually have a well-defined and well-focused strategy, very similar to the niche-seekers in the IT sector. However, they do not develop products on their own, but build competencies which can later be transferred to other fields. An interesting example of such mature start-ups is Avesthagene, which initially focused on plant genomics and is now also getting involved in medical applications. The key asset of such start-ups is a close partnership with a laboratory, which provides them for some time (sometimes several years) the equipment they need and also the academic network they require to build their databases.

This brief description of the sector gives an idea of its diversity. It is characterised by models still under construction at the firm level, which have not stabilised at the subsectoral level (as the market has not yet separated the 'good' models from the 'inefficient' ones). And given the predominance of technological assets in the sector, economic models may end up being a mere second parameter...after luck! Besides, the diversity of the sector (modern BT *versus* classical BT) makes the measuring of its activity no more than a 'guesstimate'. Let us, however, discuss the articulation between its various assets in the following subsection.

SECTION II

Asset Specificity and Partnerships

Let us now detail how the type of industrial activity and business strategies articulate to the construction of specific assets, and how these necessitate the building or fostering of certain types of partnerships. This will allow us to state out how Indian firms are placed in this partnership and asset-building tasks. Biotechnology firms are based on a close cooperation between research and industry and are a part of both Indian and international networks. They require considerable technological investment that is often comparable to what is needed in the information technology sector. However, we wish to point out in this section that the assets to be built are far more specific in the BT sector. Therefore the capital and intellectual investments in BT are much higher. Further, due to the fragmentation of BT into niche techniques and technologies, it is comparatively uneasy to build and stabilise market shares based upon brand-type assets only.

The Theory of Asset Specificity and Economic Integration

The concept of asset specificity (Williamson, 1985) is based on a contractual relation between supplier and client where the supplier produces a good or a service that is to be sold to the client in a context where the supplier has built an identifiable asset in order to do so. This asset is said to be specific when it is not standardised for use in the general market, but is intended only for this particular (specific) client. In such a case, the asset's value depends directly on supplier's ability to use it, that is, its ability to serve the client. If the supplier-client relationship stops, the asset's value is diminished and can even become nil, depending on the degree of specificity of the concerned asset. The concept also applies in case of partnerships where the use of the asset makes sense only through a common exploitation/operation, or further co-development of the asset. The degree of specificity can be explained as follows. If the asset can be used only by a particular client and cannot be transformed to serve another client, except at a prohibitive cost, then the specificity is complete. If it is client-specific but can be modified with a reasonable investment, then the asset is moderately specific (specific in the short run, but not in the long run). However, adapting it for other purposes entails some expense. If, on the contrary, the asset can easily be modified to serve an existing market, then its specificity is very low.

Whenever asset specificity is fairly strong, there must be a proper coordination between the supplier and the targeted client while building and operating the asset. From the supplier's point of view, the asset can be built only if there is a firm guarantee that the client will accept its products. And such a guarantee must be provided (if, as assumed here, the two firms are different) through a contractual agreement. It thus follows that the higher the specificity, the greater the need for a stronger long term guarantee which would ideally include a provision for a penalty to be paid to the supplier by the retracting client. It must also contain provisions to prevent the client from using his power opportunistically by threatening to renege on the contract. Conversely, the situation may be reversed when the supplier holds up the client by threatening to discontinue the supply. According to Williamson, and as empirically verified in several other studies, this kind of situation favours long-term relationships, and even vertical integration, since the writing and operation of such elaborate long-term contracts is costly in terms of transaction costs.

When we consider the specificity of assets involved in a supplier-client relationship, we find the trade-off is usually between the possibility of both sides allowing competition to take over and the desire to secure the supply (respectively the sales) at a reasonable contractual cost. Vertical integration and therefore hierarchical coordination, by comparison to a market (price coordination), is the ultimate way of securing such deals. Intermediate ways include long-terms contracts with lenient clauses due to the existence of previous long-term relationships. This way, relations between firms can develop over a period of time, moving from low-asset specificity relationships towards high-specificity coordination. This type of relationship will be more enduring if they can manage to maintain a symmetrical relationship of threat *versus* threat.

Since integration is not so noticeable in markets that are not fully mature or stabilised, we will not address the problem here. Further, we will also pass over the dynamic aspects of contractual provisions *versus* gradual intensification of relationships. To start with, we will consider only the main mechanisms, namely specificity of assets which calls for closer and more long-term contractual relationships.

We will limit ourselves to four kinds of asset specificity, following Shy (2001). Site specificity can occur when the result of the production or the construction of an asset cannot be geographically shifted and when this fact impacts its value or its transferability. Second, Physical specificity relates to situations where the product or the process has been designed or 'tailored' specifically in reference to a particular client. Third, the dedicated asset refers to a situation where the result of the production of this asset has no potential market other than the one for which the asset has been built. Lastly, temporal specificity occurs when production and consumption have to be adjusted in a synchronic manner or 'just on time' (for further details, refer to Glachant, 2002 or Brousseau & Glachant, 2002). These different kinds of asset specificity differ in nature, but not in terms of intensity. Any kind of specificity can be either strong or weak, depending on the market structure (number of clients, degree of segmentation, degree of differentiation across segments).

After More than 15 Years of Service, What are the Assets of the Indian IT Sector?

What are the assets of IT companies? The 'Big Six' (TCS, Wipro, Infosys, NIIT, Satyam and HCL) are already Fortune 500 companies. They are in a position to set up large teams for performing any kind of outsourcing work with high quality standards. Besides, "in Infosys and Wipro, the involvement in telecom equipment coding (modern switches, fibre optic terminals...) provides them with high-tech expertise and a quasi integration with their large customer network" (Bomsel and Ruet, 2001).

Their assets are of three kinds: (i) their clients' portfolios and networks, (ii) software modules that they can reuse, and (iii) the brand they are trying to build. The whole issue for them is to know how to capitalise on them for future gains. As far as the brand is concerned, in an 'economy of lemons' like IT where it is difficult to check the internal quality, a reputation and a brand harmoniously complement all the quality certifications one can think of. Since they are already centrally implanted in the structures of their clients through their platforms, they need not get amalgamated or diluted by further tie-ups with big multinational companies. Developing their own brand and their own visibility is crucial for them, if they want to sell their services and labelled products at a far higher price. This structure of assets calls for both high networking and communication with as large a number of firms as possible and more lenient contracts. Long term contracts, joint ventures and joint ownership of products are not only unnecessary for them in view of the physical and immaterial assets they already have in the form of clients' modules and portfolios, but even dangerous considering the importance given to the brand's immaterial assets. Similarly, product start-ups have the very same long term compulsion of acquiring a name and a brand. They do not, however, have either the module or the client's portfolio assets to bring them the much needed cash flow. Following the slowdown of venture capital and angel investors due to the slowdown in the US, they have to turn to the classical model of service through offshore platforms (like TechSpan, for instance).

Let us analyse the type of specificity of these assets in greater detail. Material assets are few and not essential in the IT industry (this is the reason why it is called the 'virtual economy'). Further, its products do not require transportation costs and Internet connectivity is the sole prerequisite for their 'physical' trade. Therefore, IT companies do not face the problem of site specificity. They do, however, face the problem of temporal specificity in the sense that they have to deliver most of their services 'on time'. Their main component is 'man-hours', which cannot be stored. Companies in outsourcing, performing more standardised tasks, definitely face the problem of temporal specificity. More elaborate and high value services and consulting allow a comparatively higher flexibility. Ultimately, such products can be stored and can retain their value for at least a few months. In view of this, top IT companies hardly face the problem of temporal specificity. It is naturally overcome thanks to strategies intended at 'climbing up the value chain', which allow a smoother allocation of resources. Therefore, the problem does not arise in the case of high-value products, while for low-value services the compulsion to integrate is equally low (because these can be more easily standardised or simply transferred to another outsourced company).

Lastly, physical specificity and dedicated assets are interrelated. They are those that matter in contracting and in the integration dynamics of IT firms. Indeed, high value Indian IT companies produce services that are fully tailored to their users. It is actually this tailoring and the ability to do so, that get them their clients. The main thing for them is to publicise the fact that they possess this know-how. However, in a business that requires confidentiality this poses certain problems. Ultimately, their brand value lies in the fact that they can boast of a portfolio of long-lasting relationships with reputed clients. Their biggest asset ultimately consists of developing and strengthening these ties and this gives rise to the phenomenon of quasi-integration with their biggest clients. At the same time, the steps taken jointly with these clients (like giving them access to crucial information together with the internal distribution of power and so on) make these IT companies indispensable. The relationship is based on mutual interest which also sustains it. The relationship does not mean total integration in the sense that it leaves the IT company free to work with other companies though, normally, not in the same sector. By dealing with a set of physically specific clients, IT companies can overcome the perils of building only dedicated assets. First, they must acquire know-how that can be transposed from one sector to another. Secondly, through internal organisation and special efforts to modularise their own activity, they can also build software modules as described earlier. Let us summarise the IT asset specificity in Table 13.2.

To conclude, the successful Big Six of Indian IT as well as the fast growing product start-ups are engaged in the crucial phase of moving

Table 13.2

Specificity of Assets in the IT Sector

Type of Specificity	*Its Presence in the IT Sector*
Site Specificity	None
Temporal Specificity	Very limited in the low-value segment but not structured enough to lead to integration; it can be eliminated by high value firms by climbing up the value chain.
Physical Specificity	It is inherent in nature of the IT market but can be overcome through quasi-integration and brand assets building.
Dedicated Asset	Problem can be overcome through modularisation.

up the value chain. They have started to establish their brands in a world market, that is already technologically mature, but where the product-differentiation can still make a difference. However, climbing up the value chain is closely related to long-term joint efforts to create a dedicated asset centred around the supplier-client contractual relationship.

The Nascent Indian BT Sector and the Assets to be Built

As we have seen, the production of biogeneric-recombinants requires a high level of industrial competence. More precisely, the assets include: (i) mastering R&D (in molecular biology, genetic and biochemical engineering), (ii) know-how in drug formulation, fermentation and purification, and (iii) legal and marketing capacities. These assets can be built only through:

- in-house R&D (which is costly and has comparatively fewer chances of success);
- collaboration with a public institute (but only when production has not yet reached an industrial scale);
- technology transfer (in which few transferring companies are interested in India); and
- joint ventures. As regards this last point, industrial capacity is still the key factor and the partner may be a reagent or enzyme manufacturer.

All these assets are costly in terms of both investment and time. BT firms have to follow a narrow path. Ultimately, it seems that the preferred model is the joint venture between an enzyme manufacturer, who has developed technological expertise, and either a pharmaceutical company or a dedicated start-up. This is the case, for instance, in the tie-up between Biocon and Shanta (a start-up) or Bangalore Genei who is now in talks with pharmaceutical companies. In such cases, the enzyme manufacturing company develops its technological assets before entering into talks in order to be on a par with the party to whom it is offering its industrial know-how.

Let us discuss the general features of the specificity of the assets of BT firms taken as a whole. Definitely, the BT sector is closer to the industrial sector than the 'virtual economy'. This is so because its material assets are not negligible and there may be site specificity (though limited). The clustering effect, in particular, has a stronger impact on companies that have established themselves as suppliers of pharmaceutical companies. Even though BT parks play a very limited role in technological interactions, classical supplier-client relationships are important for the specialisation of BT parks. Except for the products of the bioinformatics sector, the products/results of most BT companies have to be transported physically and, sometimes, even under specific conditions of temperature and pressure. This factor is certainly more important than for the IT sector. For most high value-added BT firms, the temporal frame is really long-term. As for low value-added firms, they are more like classical industrial groups that produce, store, market and sell. Temporal specificity does not occur in the BT sector.

Physical specificity, on the contrary, is extremely high for most non-integrated high value-added modern BT firms. They have to target a sequence of a few genes in order to address a particular disease or the special usage of a plant, and there are very few companies wanting these products in the 'classical' market. So they have to develop close links with these very few companies who constitute their only market (they are the opportunity driven companies; refer to Maria, Ruet, Zérah, 2002). Conversely, companies engaged in the development of a specific technology (technology driven companies) are a little less concerned about physical specificity, in the sense that they can use their technological knowledge to move from one product/market to another. However, this is a costly proposition and for each market taken separately, they will have to face the problem of physical specificity just like opportunity-driven companies. The physical specificity in this case is medium, but not negligible. And this really matters, given the low investment capacity characteristic of these nascent companies.

Dedicated assets emerge only when there is a clear segmentation of the market or there are long-term collaborations. As we have said earlier, most companies aim to build valuable and lasting assets in this manner. This will enable them to move up the value ladder and share intellectual property rights with the industrial companies they tie up with. However, the gradual process of quasi-integration observed in IT is still to emerge in the BT sector. Table 13.3 summarises these elements.

Table 13.3

Specificity of Assets in the BT Sector

Type of Specificity	*Its Presence in the BT sector*
Site Specificity	Limited but exists.
Temporal Specificity	None.
Physical Specificity	Very important for opportunity driven firms and important for technology driven firms.
Dedicated Assets	Still to be built by BT companies with their industrial partners.

In the field of drug discovery and development, it is too early to define the essential assets that these companies will have to develop. The pharmaceutical sector shows a contrasting picture. However, one particular 'integrated' approach is worth mentioning. The Biocon group has set up Syngene and Clinigene as subsidiaries in order to exercise control over the genetic engineering and clinical testing processes. These subsidiary companies can enter into contracts on their own, thereby creating a certain cash flow even as they provide an integrated drug-development capacity for the group. They actually try to develop internally assets that would otherwise be dedicated assets. This experiment (like the Aurigene business model) tries to emulate in the BT sector the service-based model that has contributed to the success of the IT sector, though on different asset grounds, as we shall now discuss.

Assets in BT versus Assets in IT

The main difference between the bulk of IT companies and the bulk of BT companies is that BT is more capital intensive. Physical equipment and building specifications are more structured and claim a higher share of the initial investment. Similarly, if BT is used in pharmaceuticals or genomics, the level of technical skills is much higher and, therefore, there is comparatively less scope of learning as one proceeds while moving up the value chain. As the example of biogeneric-recombinants shows, three kinds of assets (technological, industrial and functional) have to be assembled immediately. By definition and because the intellectual property has to be fully owned by one firm; no 'more advanced' company is willing to outsource any of its activities. So, unlike IT companies, there is no way BT companies can learn while outsourcing. At the same time, the return on investments is slower in the BT sector where the time between the starting of an enterprise and the point at which the product cycle starts creating adequate cash flows and reaches the breakeven point is much longer. Though some companies build their models on service derived revenues to sustain the product building phase, this strategy is comparatively less evident in BT companies than in IT companies. First of all, BT companies need a mixed strategy as they cannot take off if they start only with services without trying to build intellectual property. However, this is feasible in the IT sector. It is also less easy to find service outsourcing contracts since the level of specialisation and confidentiality is very important.

Some groups have tried to bypass this structural difference and attempted to set up services companies regardless. The idea is to have subsidiaries or 'independent' companies (Syngene and Clinigene in the case Biocon and Aurigene in the case of Dr. Reddy's) that have a separate commercial strategy offering services. These services may vary from the simple outsourcing of micro-arrays and constitution of gene and protein libraries to more elaborate partnerships in R&D. Aurigene plans to set up a business model with a 70:30 ratio between services and in-house research during its first years of operation. Still, the initial investment remains considerably higher than in the 'average IT company' (US$ 30 million for Aurigene).

Therefore, intellectual property assets are very important for BT companies whereas IT firms can rely only on body-shopping strategies for quite a long time. At the same time, BT companies have to master a specific technology while integrating numerous techniques externally (through partnerships, tie-ups and collaborations), when the bulk of IT firms can internally integrate different techniques and gain their specific advantages through a specific combination of these simpler techniques. Furthermore, as compared to the IT sector, the large number of Ph.D. level employees and the importance of scientific advisory committees are very striking in the BT sector.

In the BT sector, the technology is really not standardised, nor is it stabilised. As of now, BT is an input in other sectors which take precedence over the sector providing the input. This may be a little different in the case of drug development (where models have not yet stabilised). But, by and large, the BT sector cannot be autonomised in the evolving of its business strategies from its client industries, nor can its techniques be considered as standard enough for brands to emerge and allow the BT sector to move up the value chain independently. Business models are to be at a point or another, co-evolved. The IT model (where IT firms grow independently of the strategies of their clients) is less likely to succeed in the BT sector, where firms have to develop joint products or joint intellectual property without the same amount of financial support that the IT sector obtained from its service activity. Longer contracts are needed with more project-specific investment and longer-term implications, not only as far as the pay back period is concerned but also in terms of assured results. Let us compare this with the three assets of the IT sector:

- scientific discoveries and their applications are less 'modular' and transferable from one project to another than software modules;
- given the lesser modularity, relations to clients have to be closer and on a longer term; the contracting out and even the compulsion for quasi-integration is higher in BT; and
- again, the transferability of a BT application from one industrial sector to another is less; hence a BT firm is deemed to remain 'industrial sector-specific' for a long time as far as its clients are concerned; branding is, therefore, extremely difficult in the BT sector.

SECTION III

Global Strategies

Let us now discuss how the specificity of assets and the kind of assets to be built combine in favouring or impeding globalisation strategies of the IT and BT sectors in a comparative perspective.

Contractual Arrangements and Compulsion to Globalise

Site specificity impedes physical exchanges. In the IT sector, dedicated assets are actually a totally positive asset without the usual restrictions. The need to build assets such as services, know-how or products, while overcoming the risks connected to their physical specificity, compels enterprises to mitigate these very risks by diversifying their clients and tie-ups.

The possibility of greater modularity, relative standardisation and the smaller size of investments make the first strategy (diversification of clients) easier for IT firms. The absence of site specificity allows them to expand industrially through simple contracts over a wider area. In brief, this helps them to globalise faster and their globalisation is generally 'less contractualised but widespread'. As far as BT firms are concerned, relative site specificity combined with the absence of standardisation (high physical specificity) oblige them to go in for less widespread agreements. Finally, the necessity to build dedicated assets is explained by the need to 'develop a brand'. Similarly, this has to occur in BT (where the sector is less advanced in this respect). Biocon, because already a vertically integrated firm, may decide to do this in an already integrated manner, but other BT (or Bioinformatics) companies have to look for industrial partners. Again, all these factors favour the selection of partners who are culturally and geographically close. All other things being equal, less globalisation should be expected from the BT sector, at least in terms of relationships with industrial enterprises.

There are fewer theoretical limitations in the field of academic collaborations. Indeed, at the research level, experiments as well as theoretical models and interpretations are likely to be much more 'standard' than in the development phase. Researcher-to-researcher interactions going beyond social norms and the kind of opportunities provided by a cluster can be organised at various geographical levels, while physical encounters can be supplemented with modern communication technologies. Besides, scientific domains are well segmented and a few people meet regularly in seminars and conferences. Further, the recruitment of foreign members in scientific advisory committees (or sometimes even at operational levels) should help in the globalisation of BT firms and the establishment of relationships with academic institutions.

So much for the prediction the theory allows. What actually happens in practice?

Globalisation of Indian IT Firms

Let us first cite the example of the big IT companies. TCS aims at developing a worldwide geographical presence by targeting Europe, more specifically in terms of contracts and wishes to integrate management consulting in its activities. It is a direct competitor to the large US-based multinational consulting companies, though it does tie up with them in some instances.

Wipro managers feel that the competition will now emerge from developing countries due to the bridging of the technological gap and also due to the relative rise of wages in India. They have started thinking about relocation strategies. They too are in the process of developing a European strategy (the European market accounts for about 20 per cent of their sales at present and is expected to grow to 35 per cent, if they are successful). They have created Wipro Japan, recruited Japanese engineers, invested in learning the language (40 engineers a year), and tied up with several Japanese firms which have started working with Wipro (NEC, Fujitsu, Epson and Mitsui). They have even become the testing centre for Japanese versions of Microsoft software packages.

These companies, in the process of globalisation, have begun to think of redefining their location strategies. During interviews, Wipro managers mentioned the positive advantages of maintaining their Head Office in Bangalore because of the clustering effect of information sharing. They added that their competitors were mostly international, but they were keen on exploring other locations because of the low level of Indian infrastructure (power fluctuations, power cuts, high cost of captive generators and primary energy supply, problems caused by bad roads and poor customer service).

Satyam's globalisation strategy is the most exemplary strategy on the production side. The company has development centres in the US, UK, India, Japan and Singapore, especially for R&D. They believe that the Indian market has become sufficiently mature for them to conduct tests at home at a lower cost. This implies that their Indian activities are based in the subcontinent not for purely historical reasons or due to inertia, or even for reasons of cost, but really because of a carefully thought-out, well-integrated quality-cost ratio comparison.

However, this should not make us think that only the biggest companies are in a position to open branches abroad. For instance,

Figure 13.4

Evolution of Overseas Offices of Indian IT Software and Services Companies

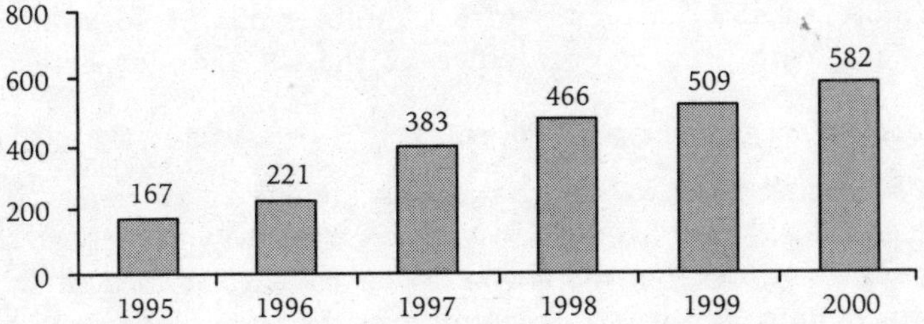

Source: NASSCOM.

Figure 13.5

Distribution of Overseas Offices of Indian IT Software and Services Companies

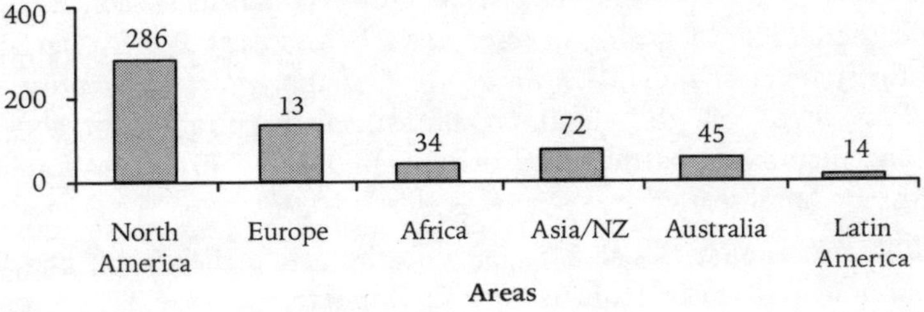

Source: NASSCOM.

IIS Infotech (now renamed Xansa India) is only the 24th Indian IT exporting company in terms of size, but it is involved in offshore development and has deputed its engineers to 15 countries. Geographical globalisation of activities is profitable for Indian companies and makes them self-sustaining. This is a general phenomenon, as shown in Figures 13.4 and 13.5.

As far as start-ups are concerned, the most active go global from day one and, as a matter of fact, they grow because they are global.

The case of TechSpan has already been discussed. Another company, MindTree Consulting, was started in 1999, at the same time in the US and in India, by 10 Indian founders who had lived in the US and brought with them contracts with US firms. By early 2001, they already had 450 consultants with a turnover of US$ 15 million for FY 2001 with plans to open offices in the UK and Singapore.

Globalisation of Indian BT Firms

BT firms have to simultaneously develop and invest in an integrated and complete set of assets. For this, they may rely on some strategic ventures, but the few examples we have studied show that partners must also have full control over the core technique in order to share the ultimate asset, namely the Intellectual Property Right. Hence these kinds of partnerships call for integrated long-term contracts, which are dynamically more tedious to conclude. Therefore, in a comparative scenario, though the compulsion to tie up is stronger in BT than in IT, it is also less easy since it is very important to enter into a successful tie-up (as a failure is extremely costly). As a result, globalising of production involves these types of contracts. Since the technology is far less standardised, contracting and, therefore, globalising is comparatively less easy. Due to the low maturity level of Indian BT firms, we find that there is, at present, a low level of globalisation measured through contractual arrangements and partnerships between Indian BT firms and foreign firms or laboratories.

BT firms must globalise to develop the assets they need, namely academic networks (this is not so important in the IT sector). However, in a survey of 54 leading modern BT firms based in India, Maria, Ruet, and Zérah (2002) found only 8 partnerships[6] with foreign laboratories (2 in the USA, 2 in France, 2 in Singapore, 1 in Japan, and 1 in the UK), and no partnerships with foreign companies. Though theoretically, academic relationships can be easily globalised, this low result shows a rather limited globalisation of these companies. It is interesting to note that the same set of companies by 2002 had 55 collaborations with Indian research institutions

6. Which had actually gone beyond the 'Memorandum of Understanding' stage.

(institutes or universities).[7] Of these 55 collaborations, 24 were with the top 5 research centres, 3 of which are based in Delhi. The modern BT sector, in terms of research and academic contracts and partnerships, already shows a strong concentration while remaining rather confined to itself. Even though the scientific councils of Indian BT firms include foreign scientific personnel, results in terms of globalisation are still unsatisfactory. The fact that the founders of these firms have obtained their Ph.D. abroad does not necessarily translate into joint ventures. We may, therefore, ask about the Indian BT sector the following question: Are there no 'Non-resident Indians' presently running BT firms in the US who are prepared to tie up with them in the future? This Human Resources model which has contributed to the success of some IT companies, could also benefit the BT sector.

Conclusion

The structural differences between an output driven sector (IT) and a technologically organised sector (BT) are very real. This translates into a far greater physical specificity of assets in the BT sector. This, combined with a relatively higher site specificity and larger material investments (added to slow returns on immaterial investments) in the BT sector, impedes its globalisation. Both sectors have to strategically build dedicated assets in collaboration with classical industrial firms in order to develop a 'brand'. It is true that the IT sector in India has a lead over the BT sector, but the latter is also faced with a stronger compulsion to tie up first with more local firms than the IT sector. The globalisation of the BT sector, we argue, is structurally less easy, a prediction confirmed by the ground reality.

However, it is surprising to see that the scientific interactions built by Indian BT companies, which are at the core of the future assets of the sector, are largely local and very rarely global. Considering the low investment they represent, this fact is all the more striking. The coming years will tell whether this is a dynamic factor in a young sector or something that will adversely affect the future structuring of Indian BT.

7. Besides, as seen in the discussion on the sharing of assets, there are very few Indian firm-to-Indian firm collaborations, while this model seems to be non-existent between Indian and foreign firms in the BT sector.

References

Bomsel, Olivier and Joël Ruet (2001). "Digital India 2001", *A Report on the IT Economy in India*, Paris: CERNA and New Delhi: CSH, p.170.

Brousseau, Eric and Jean-Michel Glachant (2002). *The Economics of Contracts: Theories and Applications*, Cambridge: Cambridge University Press.

Glachant, Jean-Michel (2002). "L'approche néo-institutionnelle de la réforme des industries de réseaux", *Revue Economique*, Vol. 53(3), May, Paris, pp.425-436.

Maria, Augustin, Joël Ruet and Marie-Hélène Zérah (2002). "Biotechnology in India", *Report to the French Embassy in India*, p. 247, CERNA & CSH.

Shy, O. (2001). *The Economics of Network Industries*, Cambridge: Cambridge University Press.

Williamson, Oliver (1985). *The Economic Institutions of Capitalism*, New York: The Free Press.

14

Emergence and Entry of Industrial Groups in Russia

The Case of the Car Industry

XAVIER RICHET

SECTION I

Introduction

Industrial restructuring in transition economies is probably one of the most difficult task. It has to be carried out by new entrepreneurs, the emerging financial sector, the government of these countries and possibly foreign investors attracted by potential growth of industry and services in the region. Restructuring, deals with many assets; organisation changes, change of output set, investments in new plants and machinery, as well as the development of new networks for supplying and marketing purposes. Even in mature market economies restructuring is not always a *sui generis* process. This is very obvious when looking at mergers and acquisitions, or brutal split of activities. These illustrate, how big groups (megalomanias purposes kept aside) concerned with the decline in their profitability, reallocate their capital by disbanding assets, aggregating others, rationalising production or other segments, in order to either attain an efficiency size, buy market shares or build up strategic positions (Batsch, 2000). In transforming economies, the process of industrial restructuring has been difficult to fulfil for different reasons. The three main reasons are; systemic heritage from the former Soviet industrial system, political and social barriers, and lack of capital and managerial know-how to be able to put these firms at the level of Western industrial standards.

1. All former socialist economies except CIS countries.

In most advanced transforming economies, of Central European Economies (CEEEs),[1] privatisations and opening up policies have created a new economic environment. In turn, this has facilitated the inflow of foreign direct investments, which have played a major role either in taking over existing firms, or in building up new greenfield investments (*The Russia Journal*, 2001, No. 3). The presence of foreign capital, added to the commitment of investors and their willingness to develop new businesses, have pushed local governments to set up attractive policies in order to retain investments. This was done by deepening legal procedures, establishing the rule of law and removing entry barriers. As a result, among countries that have followed this path, massive foreign investments have contributed to restructure their local businesses, develop new ones and generally, have created positive externalities (export increase, job creation in other sectors). On the opposite, domestic firms, especially the ones considered as strategic were taken over by foreign firms and integrated into their global or regional strategy.

The picture is quite different in CIS countries, most of all in Russia. Firstly, in spite of mass privatisation and the development of market relations, the enforcement of property right remains fuzzy. Secondly, strong barriers to restructuring have delayed the process of adjustment and kept away foreign investors. And thirdly, big financial-industrial groups have advocated and lobbied for conservative measures, and collusion of different interest groups has prevented the unbundling of assets. Considered in the framework of a 'virtual economy', in spite of noticeable progress, restructuring has made little progress, especially in the car industry.

In this chapter, we analyse the restructuring of a major industry in Russia, the car industry. For this, the involvement of a set of factors directly concerned with its modernisation will be studied:

- the owners of car companies,
- the government,
- foreign car makers eager to enter the market, and
- consumers (domestic and exports).

We will assume that, as in other post-socialist economies, the car industry cannot restructure itself without the cooperation of foreign companies bringing in capital and missing competencies allowing the upgrade of the industry (management, technology, suppliers, etc.). We will also assume that foreign companies, according to the level of risks and the property right regimes, either; absorb, turn around and integrate local companies in their world or regional strategy and networks; cooperate on some segments of production, setting joint ventures, without participating in the operation of the rest of domestic companies (GM-AvtoVAZ); or directly set up greenfield investments without cooperating with other domestic car plants (Ford, Renault-Avtoframos). In all cases, their involvement on this market doesn't contribute to the rapid creation of spin-offs and positive externalities, as is generally the case in CEEEs countries (De Sousa and Richet, 2000). This is mainly due to the high transaction costs involved in the setting up of suppliers and dealers networks, the increase of product delivery, or the quality control.

We will here define also a set of parameters. Firstly, that car company shareholders in Russia have moved from rent-seeking strategies (digging the hole) to value added strategies (expending the hole) in order to create more value launching both horizontal diversification and vertical integration strategies. Secondly, that the government has to fulfil different tasks: duties for protecting domestic car makers, some kind of horizontal and sectorial industrial policy to protect the main producers and allow them to rationalise their production by easing the access to R&D, credit, export facilities. And finally, that there is a direct link between economic growth, the growth of domestic purchasing power of Russian households and the demand for better cars. This, in a sector where demand plays a major role, even in the range of cars where Russian makers are still leaders.

The remainder of the chapter is divided in three parts. Section II analyses the causes of the institutional and administrative barriers attributable to the delay in restructuring Russian enterprises and the remaining of a soft budget constraint. Section III analyses the different entry modes of foreign companies and the trade-off between cooperation and competition. Section IV emphasises the difficulties encountered in the set up of cooperation between firms, and analyses the role of the State in the modernisation of the automobile industry.

SECTION II

The Roots of the Low Adjustment Process in Russia

Compared to CEEEs, the transformation of the industrial structure of the FSU economy has been more difficult to carry on, due to the long gap existing between the industrial organisation of the socialist economy and a fully-fledged market economy. Furthermore, this was made more difficult because of the entrenchment of the socialist system and the powerful administrative mechanisms that allowed this economy to fulfil its planned targets. The differences between the two regimes were ones of space, allocation of natural resources, economic objectives and also openness. Russia didn't have to trade a lot, except in order to buy the technology that the country was not able to produce and was missing to build up its military power. In spite of statistics produced under the former system, which aimed at over-emphasising the role of the manufacturing sector (through the distorted price system), Russia is still today an extractive economy even if industry and service sectors are growing at a rapid pace. Nearly 60 per cent of its exports revenues are still made from raw and energy goods.

Among the 10 first Russian companies, 8 produce gas and oil, 1 belongs to the heavy industry, another one to the car industry (AvtoVAZ). The underpricing of these natural goods on the domestic market and the opportunity to export them against high prices on market economies is the main source of income. It supports the existence of a soft budget constraint on companies and households and facilitates the concentration of assets in the Russian economy, especially among companies, which can rely on exportable goods in order to finance their acquisitions.

Russia and the Virtual Economy

Contrary to the other transition economies, in spite of the fact that almost all the production and services are done by private companies, Russia is far from having adjusted and carried out the transformation of its industrial structure. One explanation of this can be found firstly in the asset specificity of the former Soviet industrial organisation, and, secondly, in the bias created by the 'Dutch disease effect'. That is to say, relying on the abundance of oil and gas, which revenues can finance, the soft budget constraint and, in many areas, reduce incentives to restructure.

Gaddy and Ickes (2002), have coined the concept of 'virtual economy' to explain the functioning of the Russian economy and the behaviour of economic agents: households, companies and government.

'The virtual economy is the outcome of agents' adapting their behaviour to an environment that threatens their survival. It is characterised by a set of informal institutions that permits the production and exchange of goods that are value subtracting, that is, worth less than the value of the inputs used to produce them. Enterprises can continue such production because they have recipients who are willing to accept fictitious ('virtual') pricing of the goods at levels that mask their inprofitability. Buyers and sellers collude to hide the fictitious nature of the pricing (...). In the classic form of the virtual economy, they do so by avoiding money: they use barter and other forms of non-monetary exchange... Since value is being destroyed as the system operates, there also has to be a source of value infusion. The ultimate 'value pump' in Russia today is the fuel and energy sectors above all one single company, Gazprom—Russia's natural gas monopoly. In exchange for the rights to keep what it earns from exports, Gazprom pumps value into the system by supplying gas without being paid for it....Gazprom subsidies—which then lead to arrears to the government—are the primary ways in which unprofitable activity is supported today" (Gaddy and Ickes 2002: 5-6).

This system can survive as long as many economic agents feel that it meets their need. It can also evolve—see the cyclical retreat of barter relations—but is hard to eradicate. Whats more, many firms are still engaged in barter relations, making it difficult for companies relying on monetary relations to expand.[2] As a consequence, incentives for restructuring are weak and companies can easily delay the modernisation of their equipments and change their organisation.

---

2. In fact, many companies can develop market relations and use cash, depending on the nature of the technology, of their product and the size of their market. A company producing final good, selling to households in a limited market, can more easily use cash for its transaction, for instance in the food industry (interview with the director of the company Red October producing chocolate)

Privatisation and Conglomeratisation of the Russian Industry

The mode of privatisation favoured in Russia (Blasi *et al.*, 1996; Freeland 2000; Schleifer and Treisman, 2000; Hare and Murayev, 2002) has been radical, rapid, extensive and unprecedented in the world, creating two kinds of ownership. Ninety per cent of industrial output and 80 per cent of industrial enterprises went into private hands. This mode of privatisation, in almost one shot (in fact, two: in many firms the State has kept a minority control which has been sold later, often at a low price to shareholders who have been able to increase their power, often buying the share with the company's money) has not helped to restructure enterprises, although there is some evidence of progress both in terms of investment and productivity across firms in the same sector (Earle and Estrin, 2001).

Evolving in the virtual economy and benefitting from the soft budget constraint, most firms delay their restructuring. Rent seeking was the first aim (Aslund, Boone, Johnson, 2001) and it took some time to understand that asset stripping didn't create value in the long run. The rule of law has been more formal than real and new shareowners have developed internal coalitions to protect themselves from threats (bankruptcy, liquidation, hostile take-over), especially where insider control was dominant. Former relations between enterprises or the relational capital of managers, have contributed to develop the barter system even in sophisticated companies (aircraft industry). But, as Blasi *et al.* (1996), point out, in the mid-90s, according to the evaluation of the Russian National survey of corporations, no more than a quarter of Russian companies were clear winners (financially sound firms with well-established domestic or export markets). Among these firms, only a small number were able to finance their modernisation out of their profit. According to their study, three quarter of Russian corporations in 1996 were in need of radical and far-reaching restructuring. Furthermore, the nature of assets to be privatised as well as the distribution of ownership among insiders have made difficult a clear cut distinction between what should have been liquidated and what should have been recapitalised.

The possibility to sell or to exchange shares has led to a continuous concentration of property 'among the few' (Freeland, 2000) who were empowered with high relational capital, personal competencies, low adversity to risk and access to financing. Financial and industrial groups (FIG), also called Integrated business groups, which have been set up during the last decade, are a mix of the former industrial linkages among firms in the FSU, facilitated by strong relationships between politicians and industrialists (the 'relational capital', according to Gaddy and Ickes). This is an inevitable process, which has its origins in the Soviet era where enterprises where closely linked to strong bureaucratic structures. It is noticeable in the incapacity and unwillingness of managers of these big enterprises to adjust and split assets.[3]

This is also emphasised by the fact that financial capital and institutions have operated in fragmented and imperfect markets. Investing and restructuring, thus, could be achieved by combining financial and industrial capital (Popova, 1999). These big enterprises possess common features: within each integrated business group, there exists a core group of manufacturing and banking enterprises surrounded by a wide web of financial institutions, building companies, transport companies, mass media outlets and even health and recreation centres (Dynkin, 2002). They have come out of the former centralised system, and, now look up at similar big enterprises in emerging markets (Brazil, South Korea), or to what existed in the US at the turn of the 1900s. What is interesting to observe, at this stage of development, is that frontiers of these conglomerates are very resilient. For the main oligopolies, consolidation in some businesses can go parallel with diversification strategies by selling out equities at a good price to enter into new businesses with further growth prospects. Compartmentalisation of different businesses under one shareholding company is a recent trend in the diversification strategy, associating banks which have to raise external funds to finance the acquisition (Aris, 2000). But, as it can be understandable, merger of the new acquisition is often cut short or is not on the agenda as companies in Russia are used to work with overcapacities and that downsizing has not yet reached the business culture in this country.

3. For example, big car companies have to manage social assets (buildings for workers, health services) which are deterrent to the entry of foreign investors, not willing to control these assets. In depressed economic environment, these big enterprises are still considered as strongholds both by municipalities, provincial governors and have to perform social and public services. AvtoVAZ, for instance, still finances public services, that the municipality where the company is located is unable to perform, such as paying policemen.

At the present stage two interesting points have to be considered:

- an ever growing concentration of capital[4]
- a consolidation within and across industries

Concerning the first point, Boone and Rodionov (2002) point out that 8 major shareholder groups—Menatep, Interros, Millhouse/ Russian Aluminium, Sistema, LUKoil, Alfa, Surgutnefegaz and AvtoVAZ—had revenues of $ 62 billion in 2000, representing 50 per cent more than the federal budget. By comparison, the largest state controlled companies, Gazprom, Unified Energy Systems, Sberbank and Svyazinvest, had revenues of only $ 47 billion. Using their power and their political connections, these groups have absorbed the coal industry, steel, car manufacturing, aluminum and now timber and the yet untapped agro industrial sector. As a result, the 8 groups control 85 per cent of revenue from Russia's 64 biggest private companies.

Secondly, this process highlights a major change in the strategy of Russian firms. These have accumulated wealth and now face more difficulties to fly out their capital. Therefore, they now concentrate on the restructuring of businesses that they control. Not only do they bring in capital but also new management in order to turn around these companies. They can manage both the financial and industrial restructuring of their new acquisition. Furthermore, they have also increased their power to bargain with the government on crucial issues (budget, taxes, import duties, WTO accessions).

This doesn't mean that Russian enterprises will restructure faster, and will be able to fill the technological gap with their western

4. There have been four stages in the concentration of ownership in Russia:
    - 1st stage: mass privatisations of asset companies in 1992-1994: 50 per cent sold to workers, 9 per cent to managers, 41 per cent remained in the State's hands or were sold to outside shareholders.
    - 2nd stage: 'internal redistribution'—managers buy shares cheaply from workers, often with the company's fund.
    - 3rd stage: 'Loans for shares' deal, 1995-96—the Russian government allowed a small number of financiers—the oligarchs—to buy the state's biggest oil and mining companies at a small price. The aim was to create a business elite to support the re-election of President Yeltsin.
    - 4th stage: After Russia's default and the devaluation of August 1998, foreign investors and Russians banks sold their share in Russian companies. The oligarch who controlled export of oil and other natural resources had the cash to buy those assets at a very low price.

competitors, but these big vertically integrated groups will be one of the important feature of the economic development in Russia. As a consequence, as some government experts suggest (Mau, 2002), the government should develop macroeconomic and institutional policies to support and encourage investment by financial-industrial groups. At the same time, they will have to curb their monopolistic power and favour the development of capitalism 'from below' by favouring the emergence of a new class of private entrepreneurs and the development of SMEs, which today is certainly the weak point of industrial restructuring in this country.

SECTION III

Foreign Car makers in Transition Economies: Why Entry Mode Matters?

Big car makers from the Triade have followed different paths of investment in CEEEs economies, Russia and China (Richet and Bourassa, 2000; Richet, Wang, Wang, 2001). In CEEEs, car makers, either to serve local markets or to integrate local plants into their regional or world strategy, have followed acquisition strategies by taking over existing companies or/and building greenfields.

In China, most car makers have been obliged to set up joint ventures, with minority capital or just 50-50. Their operations concentrate on some limited segments of production with limited spin-offs in the local environment; the remaining part of the partner's assets being managed by local shareholders.

Russia falls slightly under the two cases. On the one hand, foreign companies will set up greenfields; on the other, they will create joint ventures to cooperate on some segments of production: jointly assembling cars, producing parts. In a way, Russia's case is closer to that of China, as there is no possibility for car makers to take the majority control of a Chinese company (Richet *et al.,* 2001).

Acquisition and Integrating Strategies in CEEEs: The Integration Model

With the opening up of former socialist economies, the landscape in the car industry in the region (Central and Eastern Europe) has deeply changed. In almost all countries of the region, existing manufacturers have been taken over by big European car makers (or by US based companies in Europe, such as GM). Western car makers have entered those markets through greenfield investment strategies, building new plants from scratch (Poland, Hungary) and acquisitions, turning around existing companies (brownfield investments) such as Skoda, Dacia, FSO. In both cases, this strategy meant, an integration into the network of these companies, which develop regional/continental strategies for designing, producing, outsourcing or marketing. This is particularly the case of first movers such as Volkswagen, GM/Opel, Renault in Europe (Table 14.1).

Table 14.1

Passenger Car Production by Leading Manufacturers, in CEEEs and Russia

(in Thousand)

	1998	*1999*	*2000*	*2001*	*2002*	*2003*	*2004*	*2005*
Volkswagen/ Audi/Skoda	569	482	584	650	694	736	750	750
AvtoVAZ	595	630	660	660	670	670	670	670
Fiat	334	350	360	360	360	360	360	360
Daewoo	198	215	245	250	260	260	330	350
GM/Opel	35	70	100	140	160	170	180	190
Renault	128	115	120	120	125	130	135	140
Dacia (Renault)	88	90	100	100	105	120	125	130
Total	**1947**	**1952**	**2169**	**2280**	**2374**	**2446**	**2550**	**2590**

Source: The Economist Intelligence Unit, 2000.

The acquisition of Skoda by VW has allowed the German car maker not only to get a monopoly position in the Czech market, to control the network of a well-known brand in the former socialist countries (Russia, Ukraine), but also to allow its further regional penetration in these new markets. It has also allowed VW to make both economies of scale (volumes) and scope (models) by integrating the Czech plant in its regional strategy. Skoda produces parts for other VW divisions while the Czech plant can rely on parts and components produced elsewhere by other partners of the group. The integration in these networks had another effect on suppliers networks and on outsourcing as well. In order to supply the new plants directly, many subsidiaries have accompanied the move of VW in the Czech Republic or in Hungary. Sometimes, this involved merging with local suppliers, who didn't have the technology or couldn't reach by themselves the minimal efficiency size. Renault in investing in Slovenia or in Romania is following a similar strategy. It chose to be present in the continent either to take advantage of low costs of factors or launch new products for new markets and new consumers.

It is slightly different for the second comers. These (Ford, PSA) are looking more for some cooperation with local manufacturers to produce volumes and to tap on local resources than to take advantage of local resources by integrating them in their regional networks. They also try to buy market shares (marketing, after-sales services) in order to build a stronghold in these countries.

Another factor that has to be taken into consideration is the level of country-risk for foreign investors. This is particularly true for the car industry. The industry relies on a high level of externalisation, that is, a big part of the production has to be undertaken outside the assembly plant.

This leads foreign investors to arbitrate between two entry modes in these countries (Figure 14.1), all of them choosing some kind of industrial cooperation which is more or less difficult to settle and is time consuming but allows the reduction of transaction costs and information asymmetry, to assess better the real commitments of partners in the deal. As far as transaction costs are high, property rights unclear, friendly local environment missing, foreign investors will favour direct export of cars or stay at a low level of industrial cooperation (representative office, agreement on the transfer of very limited technology), 'a wait and see' strategy. Long delays to reduce transaction costs have pushed several car makers to limit their entry, to postpone investments and to favour direct exports with limited added value in the host country (see, for instance, Renault in the first entry stage in Russia).

On the other hand, countries which have opened their markets to direct investment, reducing barrier to entry and shown a real commitment to develop industrial partnerships (such as Hungary, Czech Republic, Slovakia, Poland, Romania) have witnessed a rapid change of the industrial setting in this field. This meant, the development of both brownfield and greenfield investments leading to an integration model (Figure 14.2) into the regional/continental strategy of the Western car maker (Richet and Bourassa, 2000). Direct investments in Central Europe now account for 15 per cent of the total output of VW. Although, local markets are expanding, exports are crucial, representing 90 per cent for Hungarian and Slovakian output and 80 per cent for Skoda (*Financial Times*, 2002). This integration has led to a deep restructuring of existing plants, and an increase of productivity, almost to European levels (with labour costs only 25 per cent of those in Germany). But it has also forced Western suppliers from first even from second tiers, to invest in these countries forcing them to merge with local suppliers and, therefore, contributing to create a new industrial belt in the region by fuelling the integration process with Western European car makers.

Figure 14.1

Entry Mode, Country-Risk, and Commitment of Foreign Investors

Level of Country-Risk	*Entry Mode*	*Entry Coordination*
High	Product exports, Licences, Technical Assistance	Entry through commercial strategies
Medium	Joint venture often with a minority stake • Legal constraints • Wait and see strategy	↓
Weak	Acquisition: external growth of the firm Greenfield: internal growth of the firm	Entry through commitment and vertical integration

Restructuring the Russian Car Industry: A New Playground for Foreign Firms?

The renewal and future development of the Russian car industry is directly linked to several factors on both sides of the market. On the demand side, it relies on the growth of internal demand fuelled by the amelioration of the population's living standards, on the development of a sound credit system and also on the capacity of big Russian car

Figure 14.2
The Integration Model

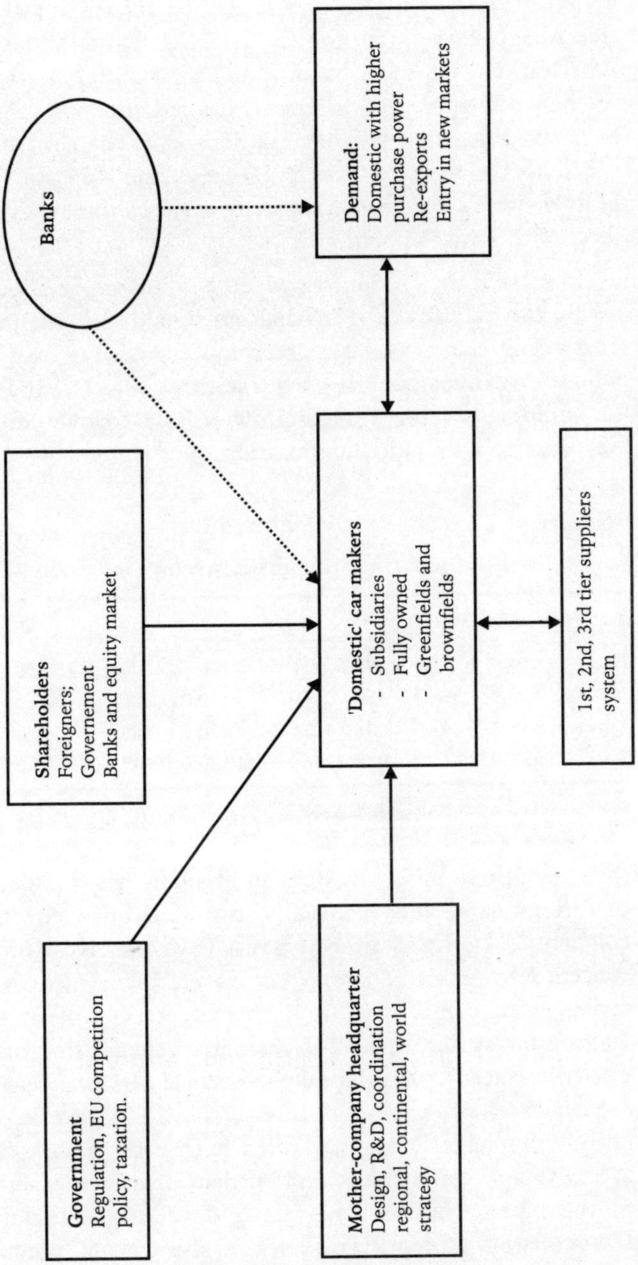

manufacturers to regain and to extend its market shares in their traditional markets (in the former FSU, India, Middle East, Latin America). On the other hand, Russian car makers have to cope with the new competitive environment: the presence of foreign car makers in the country, the lowering of tariffs and, in the near future, the new constraints coming from the WTO regulation—if Russia becomes one of its members and cannot negotiate exemption in order to reduce the level of foreign competition.

In spite of the 1998 crisis, which has strongly affected sales in this sector, the car market in the country should continue to grow (Table 14.2). The economic situation should push car manufacturers to adjust by investing in new facilities, R&D, and production technologies. This should allow Russia to overcome the main obstacles to its rapid modernisation.

Table 14.2

Vehicle Output Forecast in Russia (in Units, 1997-2005)

Year	*1992*	*1997*	*1998*	*1999*[1]	*2000*	*2001*	*2002*	*2003*	*2004*
Cars	963.0	981.9	841.5	475.5	1100.0	1200.0	1300.0	1400.0	1500
Trucks	562.2	148.6	143.0	82.1	180.0	200.0	220.0	240.0	270.0
Buses	48.1	43.4	42.7	26.8	50.0	55.0	60.0	65.0	75.0
Total	**1597.3**	**1173.9**	**1027.2**	**584.4**	**1330.0**	**1455.0**	**1580.0**	**1705.0**	**1845.0**

Note: [1]—Data as of January-June 1999.
Source: Carana Corporation.

The opening up of the Russian economy has favoured the import of foreign cars, and eventually, the used ones. Strong domestic competition is present even at a very low price. This is today a major concern for the main domestic car makers (AvtoVAZ, GAZ). They are facing strong competition from imported cars in the Russian market and are hit by the change of customer demand towards better and pricier imported or domestically assembled cars by foreign makers. In consequence, all major companies (Table 14.3) have looked to make deals with foreign investors in order to upgrade their production, have access to new technologies and efficient distribution networks. Most of them paid this greatly, facing dramatic financial situations (accumulation of debt, taxes, lack of investments, products with no future).

AvtoGAZ, is one of the largest and most advanced manufacturers, producing more than two-thirds of Russian cars. Hit by imports of foreign cars, their management has been unable to respond to the new challenges, and the company has lost market shares to imports as well as to more market oriented competitors (GAZ). The company still has a very low productivity level and needs to be reshaped with foreign investment, without the need to alter significantly the dominant ownership. The company has negotiated a project with GM and the EBRD to set up a joint venture to produce two kinds of cars: a revamped model of off-roads Lada Niva and Opel Astra. On the other hand, shareholders of the company are lobbying the Russian government to prevent the entry of imports of used cars. It is interesting to measure the technology and product quality gap by mentioning that six year old Western cars entering Russia are the main competitors of the low range products in which Russian car makers have their dominant market shares (they sell around the same price, between US $ 5000-6000).

Table 14.3

Original Plans for Foreign Investment

Brand	*Local Partner*	*US$ Million*	*Annual Capacity (in '000 Units)*
BMW	Avtotor	26	10
Chevrolet	EIAZ	50	50
Fiat	GAZ	500	150
Ford	Bankirski Dom	150	100
Lada/Opel	AvtoVAZ	2350	310
Opel	AvtoVAZ	200	150
Renault	City of Moscow	300	120
Skoda	Izhmash	250	80

Source: *www.just-auto.com* (2000).

GAZ, a more diversified producer, has also been faced with difficult financial issues. After the reception of a loan from the government, towards production line modernisation, the company started to focus on marketing and set up a dealer network. Two new products, Gazelle, a light commercial vehicle and more heavy truck Sobol have contributed to boost sales. At the same time, the production of the passenger car Volga has been upgraded and has contributed to keep its market share as the car remains at least twice less expensive than imported cars of this range. The company is considered as the best positioned Russian manufacturer today. This regards its restructuring, new investment, and development of new models and commitment of its management. Recently, the big aluminum financial and industrial group, Sibal (Siberian Aluminum) has taken strategic stakes in the company threatening a deal with Fiat. Fiat considered, an industrial cooperation with GAZ in order to launch a new generation of low cost platforms producing cars to be sold on emerging markets. Renault intends to develop the same strategy with its Dacia acquisitions in Romania and its further expansion in its Moscow joint venture, Avtoframos, launched in partnership with the Moscow municipality

The new owner of GAZ, Sibal has undertaken a deep restructuring of the top and medium management of the company. Sibal, as other big financial and industrial groups, is undertaking a strategic move. It takes stakes in downward industries and uses its output only after the company is willing to create more value and has lost the advantage of low prices of electricity charged by the federal monopoly, EUS, running electricity networks. It has also invested in other car companies (UAZ, in bus companies).

GAZ has been relatively successful in restructuring its scope of products and its organisation (although productivity falls far behind the levels of Western firms), its cooperation with Western manufacturers focuses on the supply of different kinds of components and parts with German, Austrian and US companies (diesel engines, fuel filters, fans, car design). For both, Russian and foreign companies working in the country, one of the main difficulties facing the up-grade of production, is the low level of quality of products delivered by suppliers.

Difficult Entry for Foreign Car Makers

Foreign companies investing in Russia face high transaction costs, entering in long discussions with their partners (domestic car makers, local and federal government and banks) is necessary in order to set up their cooperation. Being a strategic sector, the government is concerned that such direct deals are not enough to modernise the sector and that some kind of horizontal and sectoral industrial policies should be implemented. That is why the Russian government sets the rules, and to some extent expresses the wishes of the strong lobbies of the industry.

Main Russian car makers have been discussing with foreign car makers and part suppliers to encourage their investment in new joint ventures in Russia. The negotiations are about jointly producing new models or revamp and sell existing Russian models (Lada Niva). In other cases, joint venturing concerns supply of parts, engines and other components that are introduced in order to upgrade existing models (GAZ Volga for example) (Table 14.3). A few car makers consider, directly building foreign models from greenfield investment (generally without the collaboration of local makers), as Ford (Focus) and Renault (R19, Mégane), which have turned down a strategic alliance with AZLK Moskvich (Table 14.4).

With high transaction costs and high barriers to entry, four entry modes are possible for foreign car makers. All four are alternative but also sequential:

1. Importing cars to sell in the Russian market (buying market shares): Mercedes, Peugeot and Toyota.
2. Importing cars and/or parts to be assembled in Russia with the prospect to develop further investments to attain 3 and 4: Renault. Foreign car makers follow two strategies for assembling cars. First, a complete knock down (CKD) and second, a semi-knock down (SKD) assembly lines with limited capacity, importing almost 100 per cent of components (BMW in Kaliningrad, GM in Yelaguba and Renault in Moscow).
3. Negotiating cooperation deals with local makers, on some segments, without going further in the cooperation (no equities in the main business): GM and AvtoVAZ.
4. Creating a joint venture or greenfield investments (Ford, Renault), using local assembly lines utilising at least 50 per cent of domestic content (Ford) to produce foreign brands in Russia.

Generally, in all cases, there have been long discussions, initial projects revised, discussions with local government bodies which are time consuming. Renault had to have more than 236 authorisations to start importing and assembling cars in its Moscow site and has supported no less than four official inspections of its facilities. Other investors mention endemic corruption of some administrations, the difficulty to set network of dealers, upgrading quality of parts delivered by Russian suppliers.

Table 14.4

Investment Plans of Foreign Car Makers in Russia

Foreign Makers	*Fiat*	*Ford*	*GM*	*Renault*	*Skoda*
Name of Venture	ZAO Nizhzgorod Motors	Ford Vsevolozhsh	Undecided	OA0 Avtoframos	Skoda Auto Udmurtia.
Location	Nizhny Novgorod	Vsevolozhsk (near St. Petersburg)	Togliatti 1000 km southeast Moscow	Moscow	Izhevsk 1350 km east of Moscow.
Local Partner	GAZ	Bankirski Dom	AvtoVAZ		Izhmash
Ownership	40% Fiat, 40% GAZ, 20% EBRD	Undisclosed	43%AvtoVAZ 43%GM 14% EBRD	50%Renault, 50% city of Moscow	75% Skoda 25% Izhmash
Investment Plan	Originally $850 million, now $300 million	$150m	$500-$600m	Initially $420m Currently $300m	$250m
Start of Production	Originally Mid 2000, now 2002	Mid-2001	Q4 2002	Initially 1999 Postponed	4000 in 2000 100000 in 2005.
Products	Palio, Palio Weekend, Sienna	Focus	Lada Niva 2113, maybe Opel Astra T3000 (badged Chevrolet, model names may change)	Megane Classic R 19	Felicia, Fabia in 2002.
Annual Capacity/ Production Target	Originally 150000, now 75000 in 2 shifts	25000 in 2002	75000-90000 units /year in 2 shifts (target 2005)	Initially: 120000 Currently: 100000	Initially: 80000 Currently: 100000

Source:- www.just-auto.com

As a result, there are long delays and an important gap between initial projects and their development.

The launch of a joint venture between GM and AvtoGAZ in Tolyatti, illustrates the difficulty to negotiate and to strike a deal. It is significant in that it shows the means that have to be put together (facilities, equipment and know-how from the Russian side, cash and some equipment from GM side, finding an extra investor, the EBRD), the taxation of imports according to the degree of 'russification' of parts, the quality control of parts (which in the case of the new model assembled can reach more than 50 per cent arriving defective) as well as the stages necessary to increase the volume of production on the new line (which will represent 10 per cent) of the total of AvtoVAZ total output.

For suppliers, entry is easier for there are lower barriers to entry. Very few Russian automobile components are able to compete with western companies due to ineffective management, outdated technologies and equipments, and lack of financing for modernisation. Big suppliers are already present in the Russian markets such as Bosch, ZF, VDO/Kienzle, Steyr. Other main players are considering entering the market, among them are: Breed, Delphi Automotive, GKN, Johnson Controls, Magneti Marelli and Valeo.

With the growth prospect of vehicle production in Russia—Russia is considered as one of the six most promising emerging world markets for auto vehicles and as one of the greatest growth market for the next 10 to 20 years—pressures to reduce costs and to maximise local content will be higher bringing suppliers to invest more heavily in the country.

One outcome of this cooperation is that the cooperation model (Figure 14.3) departs from the integration model (Figure 14.2) which has resulted from the strong presence of car makers in CEEEs. In the cooperation model, car assemblers and suppliers are still strongly connected, and this is reinforced by the vertical integration strategy followed by shareowners. Competition is weaker because of an ambiguous strategy of the Russian State; trying at the same time to promote the entry of foreign investors and to protect domestic makers by rising import taxes.

Can an Industrial Policy Fill the Technological and Organisational Gap with Western Car Makers?

The Russian government has issued, in 2001, a memorandum on "The Main Directions of the State Policy for Development of the Automobile Industry in Russia until 2005." This memorandum

Figure 14.3

The Cooperation Model

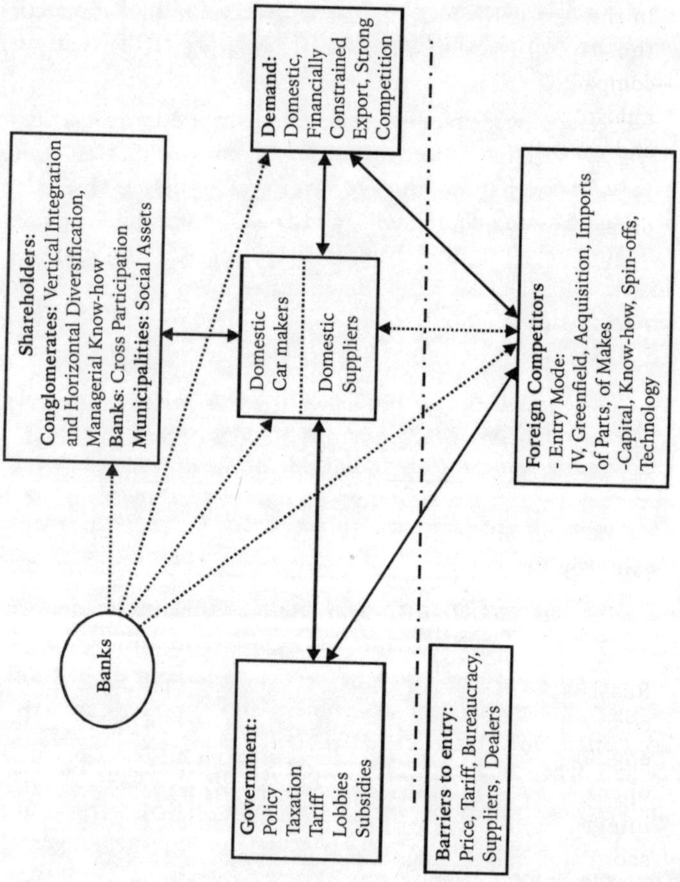

assessed the importance of this sector in the economic growth, its impact on the whole industry with upward and downward effects on other industries from raw material to more sophisticated industries such as electronics (50 per cent of the cost of a car is spent on materials and components) not to speak of other services directly related (finance, insurance, after-market services—dealers, repairing). In the first part of the 90s, most car companies were unable to raise the capital needed in order to modernise their facilities, few companies have been able to overcome the main weaknesses of car industry: heavy fuel consumption, non-conformity to modern ecology and safety standards, high dead weight and lower degree of safety.

According to this report, a positive policy should aim at reaching different objectives:

- To break down and externalise the big car complexes by concentrating on core businesses as in Western companies (engine, body production, electronic devices, assembling) and relying on outsourcing for the supply of other components which can be produced at lower prices by external and independent business units.
- To facilitate the transfer of technology in order to upgrade existing facilities, create new assembly lines, and produce new vehicles of domestic concept and vehicles under licence meeting international standards with the objective to progressively increase the Russian content of parts.

Another dimension of the programme points out the necessity for Russian car makers to concentrate on R&D, to produce up-to-date components in high value added sectors of the business such as engine, gearboxes, drive axle, components and systems for brake operation, or modern suspension systems. This would help to integrate production, design and technological improvements by shortening delays, upgrading final products and supplying cars able to support competition from imported makers. This project shows that industrial cooperation with foreign car manufacturers is an important means through which Russian car makers will be able to fill the gap and boost the growth of the sector. Up till now, incentive measures to promote the restructuring of Russian car companies and the development of domestic production have been taken negotiating on debt arrears with the government, on the one hand, and the adoption of different measures concerning imports of foreign cars and components on the other. The lowering of duties, from 30-33 per cent to 10 per cent, will allow Russian car makers and foreign makers in the country to feel the competition from abroad.

This may appear quite contradictory with the former policy, which intended to promote the 'russification' of the content of parts and components that had to be produced in the country. However, this measure can be interpreted as a move towards the WTO requirements. This also means that, the tycoons at the head of the main companies see their competitive advantage diminished. The range of price on which they could maintain their market share, between US $ 5000 and 7000, is regularly competed by second hand Western cars. The growth of the purchasing power of Russian consumers allows them to reach the upper ladder and move into the next range, where imported cars less than three years and even foreign cars assembled in Russia become more attractive. This explains the long bureaucratic delays in the negotiations with ministries to clear away entry barriers limiting imports of parts and SKD components to be assembled in Russia. This question of tariff duties on imported cars and parts is among the crucial points discussed in the WTO negotiation, especially due to the new competitive environment with a strong increase of domestic demand for second-hand cars (an increase of more than 30 per cent in 2002) and periodical closing down of factories (AvtoVAZ, GAZ) for a couple of weeks, in order to reduce the piling of unsold cars.

Conclusion

The Russian car industry is the most developed and the most important amongst CEE and CIS economies. Its prospects of growth in the near future are high. But, the industry is slowly recovering, in spite of the continuous decrease of its production levels in the first half of the 90s. Although privatised the 'Russian way', few companies have been able to adjust and to restructure. Most of them continue to manage overcapacities, have high debts ad tax arrears. With the exception of GAZ, no one has been able to change their product mix, or develop new models.

Restructuring in this sector means changing the industrial organisation by focusing on core businesses in which car makers have their competitive advantage. It also requires externalisation of business organisation by building up new networks of suppliers and distributors, as well as upgrading production, developing new models and integrating new technologies in order to fill the gap with Western makers in terms of quality, standards and efficiency.

Contrary to what has happened in CEE economies, where acquisition and development of new facilities have been the entry mode privileged by Western car makers, in Russia the entry mode follows another path. Due to country risk, and State regulation, but also owing to firms' strategy set up by new owners, industrial cooperation through licensing, export of cars and setting up of joint-ventures. Main Russian car makers have developed cooperation on some segments of production by cooperating in the construction of new cars with local maker, by assembling cars or, even, by building up new facilities with the support of local banks or institutions.

In all cases, the setting up of the cooperation has been due to high transaction costs, macroeconomic shocks and other uncertainties generally leading to postpone projects or reduce the scope of the initially planned project.

Foreign direct investment of Western parts and components makers should increase very stiffly in the near future as modernisation of facilities, development of new models (Western, Russian makes) will need to rely on important domestic outsourcing.

Certain factors should have a positive impact on cooperation with Western companies such as: changes in the institutional and macroeconomic environment, better growth prospects of the Russian economy, the commitment of the Federal government, regions, municipalities and firms to restructure firms. These should increase the presence of western companies in this market in the future by deepening their relations with their Russian counterparts. But the recovery has a strong price: domestic car makers will have to cooperate more narrowly with their foreign counterpart, open up their capital, come up with the clearing of imperfect privatisation by unbundling redundant assets, give away social assets and concentrate on core business. Nonetheless, it remains to be added that in Russia, as in other emerging market economies (China), the big transnational corporations in this industry will keep the lead and will leave few rooms for the development of domestic companies which will be facing for a long time an important technological gap.

References

Aris, B. (2000). "Picking Up and Passing on the Piece of Privatization", *The Moscow Times,* November 25.

Ashrafian, V.; P. Isaeva and P. Oppenheimer (2002). "The Prospects of the Russian Automotive Industry", *Working Paper,* RECEP, *mimeo,* p.32.

Ashrafian, V. and X. Richet (2001). "Industrial Cooperation in the Russian Car Industry", *Russian Economic Trend,* pp.3-4.

Aslund, A.; P. Boone and S. Johnson (2001). "Escaping the Under-Reform Trap", *IMF Staff Papers,* Vol. 48, Special Issue.

Batsch, L. (2002). Le capital financier, La Découverte: Paris.

Blasi, J.; M. Kroumova and D. Kruse (1996). *Kremlin Capitalism—Privatizing the Russian Economy,* Cornell University Press.

Boone, P. and D. Rodionov (2002). "Rent Seeking in Russia and the CIS", *Brunswick UBS Warburg,* Moscow.

De Sousa, J. and X. Richet (2000). "The Impact of Foreign Capital on Local Supply Companies: The Case of Hungary", *Economic System,* Vol. 24(4).

DREE Revue Elargissement (2001). Spécial IDE, December.

———. (2002). Spécial Automobile, September.

Dynkin, A. (2002). "Russia's Big Conglomerates and the Country's Modernization", Carnegie.

Earle, J. and S. Estrin (2001). "Privatization and Structure of Enterprise Ownership", in B. Granville and Peter Oppenheimer (eds.), *Russia's Post-Communist Economy,* UK: Oxford University Press.

Endowment for International Peace, Washington, D.C., April 17.

Financial Times (2002). "Russia's Rising Tycoons", August 6.

———. (2002). "Car Makers Up Sticks for Eastern Europe", Oct. 10.

———. (2002). "VW Brings Skoda up to Speed", Sept. 3.

Freeland, C. (2000). "Sale of the Century", Russias Wild Ride from Communism to Capitalism, Crown Business, New York.

Gaddy, C. and B. Ickes (2002). *Russia's Virtual Economy,* Washington DC: Brookings Institution Press.

Granville, B. and Peter Oppenheimer (eds.) (2001). *Russia's Post-Communist Economy,* UK: Oxford University Press.

Hare, P. and A. Murayev (2002). "Privatization in Russia", *Research Paper Series,* RECEP, *mimeo,* p.27.

Kansky, Alexander (2000). *BISNIS,* Moscow.

Mau, V. (2002). "Economic and Political Results for 2001 and Prospects for Strengthening Economic Growth", *Working Paper,* Institute for the Economy in Transition, *mimeo,* p.28.

Nash, R. (2002). "Russia-From Macro to Micro: Which Growth Path Now?", *Annual Equity Conference Russia: Reforming and Re-rating,* Renaissance Capital, Moscow, June 24-26.

National Auto Component Association (2000). *The Main Directions of the State Policy for Development of the Automobile Industry in Russia Until 2005.*

———. (2001). "Corporate Consolidation: Russia's Latest Lurch towards Capitalism", in P. Westin (ed.).

Pavlinek, P. (2002). "Restructuring the Central and Eastern European Automobile Industry: Legacies, Trend and Effects of Foreign Direct Investment", *Post-Soviet Geography and Economics*, No. 1.

Popova, T. (1999). "Curse or Blessing?—Financial-Industrial Groups in Russia", *Transition Newsletter*, July-August.

Richet, X. and F. Bourassa (2000). "The Reemergence of the Automotive Industry in Eastern Europe", (avec F. Bourassa) in Ch. von Hirschhausen & Jurgen Bitzer (eds.), *The Globalization of Industry and Innovation in Eastern Europe: From Post-socialist Restructuring to International Competitiveness*, Cheltenham, UK, and Northampton, MA: Edward Elgar.

Richet, X. (2002). "Transforming Economies, Technology Transfer and Multinational Corporations Strategies", *Working Paper*, RECEP, *mimeo*, p.23.

Richet, X.; H. Wang and W. Wang (2001)."Foreign Direct Investment in China's Automotive Industry", *Chinese Perspectives*, No.38, November-December.

Rinaco Plus Research: *Russian Industry Analysis.*

Russia Journal (2001). "Who Owns Russia: Inside Russia's Automobile Industry", December 7-13, *Transnational Corporations*, Special Issue: Privatization and Greenfield FDI in Central and Estern Europe: Does the Mode of Entry Matters?, Vol. 10(3), December.

Schleifer, A. and D. Treisman (2000). "Without a Map. Political Tactics and Economic Reform in Russia", Cambridge, Mass: The MIT Press, The Economist Intelligence Unit.

Sintserov, L. (2003). "New Trends in Russia", *Lettre du GERPISA*, No. 169, May-June.

von Hirschhausen Ch. and Bitzer J. (eds.) (2000). *The Globalization of Industry and Innovation in Eastern Europe: From Post-socialist Restructuring to International Competitiveness*, Cheltenham, UK, and Northampton, MA: Edward Elgar.

www.just-auto.com

Index

A

B

C

F

G

H

I

P

W

X